D1738383

*The Union Inspiration in
American Politics*

In the series
Labor and Social Change
edited by Paula Rayman and Carmen Sirianni

The Union Inspiration in American Politics

The Autoworkers and the Making of a Liberal Industrial Order

Stephen Amberg

Temple University Press —— Philadelphia

Temple University Press, Philadelphia 19122
Copyright © 1994 by Temple University
All rights reserved
Published 1994
Printed in the United States of America
The paper used in this publication meets the minimum requirements of
American National Standard for Information Sciences—Permanence of
Paper for Printed Library Materials,
ANSI Z39.48-1984 ∞

LIBRARY OF CONGRESS CATALOGING-IN-PUBLICATION DATA

Amberg, Stephen, 1953–
    The union inspiration in American politics: the autoworkers and the
    making of a liberal industrial order/by Stephen Amberg.
        p.   cm.   —(Labor and social change)
    Includes bibliographical references and index.
    ISBN 1-56639-189-X
    1. International Union, United Automobile, Aerospace, and Agricul-
tural Implement Workers of America—History. 2. Trade unions—Automobile industry workers—United States—History. 3. Industrial
relations—United States—History. 4. United States—Politics and government—20th century. I. Title. II. Series.
HD6515.A82I57 1994
322'.2'0973 dc20 93-43362

Contents

Preface

This book began as a quest for the strategic premises and goals of the New Deal liberal democracy that shaped the political world in which I grew up but seemed to be overwhelmed by the war in Asia and the virulent conservatism that emerged in the Republican party. I believed that young liberals were at a loss to defend themselves because many did not know what the New Deal had accomplished or why. Initially I personalized the gap in generational knowledge: I imagined that my father's father, Julius, knew the generative scheme of the New Deal—he was one of the pack of Harvard lawyers (class of 1915) brought to Washington by Felix Frankfurter and served as special assistant to the secretary of war during the Second World War—and had passed it on to his son, David (Harvard Law, 1948). My father was a liberal Democrat active in the civil-rights mainstream of the Urban League. His liberalism was individualistic, pragmatic, optimistically ahistorical. Also influencing the initial shape of the question in my mind was the geographic limit of the New Deal and the sense that the New Deal was unfulfilled; it was certainly true that Grand Rapids, Michigan, was a kind of rotten borough for the Republican party and, thus, did not reflect the spirit of New Deal Democracy. My congressman, Gerald Ford, became an advocate for the "impeach Earl Warren" groups. The primary liberal concerns were to maintain a space of free thought and ward off conservative encroachments. I was lucky, too, to be exposed to a wider range of ideas about human life—in the visual arts, drama, religion, and comparative literature, as well as in political history—that reinforced the notion that the ability of individuals to make something of the circumstances in which they find themselves means that political formations are tied to variations in the real world. The very principles of democracy that I had absorbed implied that the political world not only could be, but normally is, remade as individuals decide to remake it; in fact, they had already remade it through the New Deal and seemed about to do so again in the 1960s and early 1970s. But the liberal march of progress suffered serious reversals instead, especially intense racial conflict and imperialist adventures, one characteristic of which was the blocking of new democratic forces in the labor movement and Democratic party and the emergence of the new right movement that took over the Republican party. The experience shattered my complacency about progress and prompted me to join those Americans who had taken a radical approach to the state. Today the 1960s, let alone the New Deal, is unknown territory to most Americans. When recalled at all, often it is to explain what must have been or to halt debate about the present by caricaturing it. This book attempts to contribute to the democratic possibilities that lie at the heart of the vocation of politics.

This book germinated from my individual biography and matured with the help of invaluable teachers and friends. Foremost among teachers are Walter Dean Burnham and Charles Sabel who guided me at MIT in the early 1980s as I prepared my dissertation, which forms the core of this book: my intellectual debts to them are enormous. Nelson Lichtenstein has been a generous critic-reader without whose support this book would not have appeared. Playwright and novelist Ernest Ellis's passion for a humanistic politics was an early inspiration. Gerald Berk has been an irreplaceable interlocutor who made contributions to the development of the argument through many conversations and by conscientious readings of parts of this book. Many other individuals made significant contributions, sometimes without being aware of it: Thomas Ferguson, Joshua Cohen, Harley Shaiken, Michael Piore, Harry Katz, Rudy Yatsik, David Olson, John Powell, Margaret Weir, Steve Lewis, Serenella Sferza, Ted Perlmutter, Peter Bruce, Victoria Hattam, Suzanne Marilley, Mark O'Brien, Gary Herrigel, Chris Allen, Robert Zieger, John Hess, Charlie Gamble, Bill Guild, Ellie Walsh, Rudy Perkins, and Martin Blatt. Generously helping me carry out the project were James and Rosemary Dickerson, who conveniently moved from Detroit to Washington and back to Detroit just as my research needs dictated. The many people who were willing to be interviewed, especially those who discussed historical events with me, include Walter Dorosh, Leonard Woodcock, Douglas Fraser, Irving Bluestone, Victor Reuther, Irving Richter, Ronald Haughton, Malcolm Denise, Rick Karas, Chuck Dewey, Pete Kelly, Bob King, and Dwight Hansen. Also thanks to Thomas Klug, Joel Cutcher-Gershenfeld, Louis Ferman, the staff at the Walter P. Reuther Library, especially Warner Pflug, Carrolyn Davis, Tom Featherstone, and William Gulley; Dennis Bilger and Erwin Mueller at the Harry S. Truman Library; Will Johnson and Michael Desmond at the John F. Kennedy Library; Jerry Hess and Terry Matchette at the National Archives; David Crippen at the Henry Ford Museum; Julie Bennett at the Studebaker Museum; the American Society of Employers; Anthony Zito at the Department of Archives of the Catholic University of America; Jim Jacobs; Bob Deweuke; Edward Allard; Dan Luria; Mike Schippani; Seth Wigderson; and Jack Clark. Research can be a marathon and luckily I was favored with crucial material aid from Carl Kaysen at the MIT Science, Technology and Society program; Chuck Sabel; the MIT political science department; the Henry Kaiser Family Foundation; the Truman Library Institute; the John F. Kennedy Library Foundation; the University of Texas at San Antonio; and my parents, David and Barbara Amberg. Incalculably valuable support and patience were given by Anne Sullivan and Nora Amberg.

Parts of the book previously appeared as "Triumph of Industrial Orthodoxy: The Collapse of Studebaker-Packard" in *On the Line: Essays in the History of Auto Work,* ed. Nelson Lichtenstein and Stephen Meyer (Urbana: University of Illinois Press, 1989); "Democratic Producerism: Enlisting American Politics for Workplace Flexibility," *Economy and Society* 20, no. 1 (February 1991); and "Institutional Frameworks and Production Systems: The Contribution of Skilled Workers to the Flexibility of the American Automobile Industry," *International Contributions to Labour Studies* 3 (1993).

List of Abbreviations

ACW	Amalgamated Clothing Workers Union
ADA	Americans for Democratic Action
AFL	American Federation of Labor
AFSCME	American Federation of State, County, and Municipal Employees
AIF	Annual Improvement Factor
ARA	Area Redevelopment Administration and Area Redevelopment Act
ATDMA	Automotive Tool and Die Manufacturers Association now, Detroit Tooling Association
BLS	Bureau of Labor Statistics
CCAP	Citizens' Crusade Against Poverty
CDM	Coalition for a Democratic Majority
CEA	Council of Economic Advisors
CED	Committee for Economic Development
CETA	Comprehensive Employment and Training Act
CFL	Chicago Federation of Labor
CIO	Congress of Industrial Organizations
CIO FEC	Full Employment Committee of the CIO
COLA	Cost-of-Living Adjustment, as calculated by the U.S. Bureau of Labor Statistics
COPE	Committee on Political Education
CORE	Congress for Racial Equality
CTF	Chicago Teachers' Federation
CWA	Communications Workers of America

CUL	Civic Uplift League
DNC	Democratic National Committee
EAD	Employer's Association of Detroit
ERP	European Recovery Program
FAA	Foreman's Association of America
FE	Farm Equipment Workers Union
FEPC	Fair Employment Practices Commission
FTC	Federated Trades Council (of Milwaukee)
GAW	Guaranteed Annual Wage
GMAD	General Motors Assembly Division
IAM	International Association of Machinists
IBEW	International Brotherhood of Electrical Workers
IC	Industrial Commission (of Wisconsin)
ICCASP	Independent Citizens Committee of the Arts, Sciences, and Professions
IEB	International Executive Board (of the UAW)
ILGWU	International Ladies Garment Workers' Union
ISFL	Illinois State Federation of Labor
ISST	International Society of Skilled Trades
IUD	Industrial Union Department (of the AFL–CIO)
LMAC	Labor-Management Advisory Committee
LNPL	Labor's Non-Partisan League
MDTA	Manpower Development and Training Act
MESA	Mechanics Educational Society of America
MFDP	Mississippi Freedom Democratic Party
NAM	National Association of Manufacturers
NIRA	National Industrial Recovery Act
NLB	National Labor Board
NLRA	National Labor Relations Act
NMTA	National Metal Trades Association
NRA	National Recovery Administration
NSPIE	National Society for the Promotion of Industrial Education

NWLB	National War Labor Board
OCAW	Oil, Chemical, and Atomic Workers Union
OEO	Office of Economic Opportunity
PAC	Political Action Committee
PCA	Progressive Citizens of America
QWL	Quality of Work Life
RUM	Revolutionary Union Movement
SNCC	Student Nonviolent Coordinating Committee
S–P	Studebaker–Packard
SUB	Supplemental Unemployment Benefits
TULC	Trade Union Leadership Conference
UAW	United Auto Workers, officially the International Union, United Automobile, Aerospace and Agricultural Implement Workers of America
UDA	Union for Democratic Action
UE	United Electrical Workers
UMW	United Mine Workers Union
UNC	United National Caucus
USW	United Steel Workers of America
VISTA	Volunteers in Service to America
WMC	War Manpower Commission
WPB	War Production Board
WSB	Wage Stabilization Board

Liberal Democracy and Industrial Order

The stunning collapse of New Deal politics has had an equally stunning sequel in the post-New Deal politics that has taken its place. In the 1970s the New Deal Democratic party coalition of unions, reform organizations, liberal businessmen, professionals, and party officials and the institutions to which they were linked were no longer able to deliver the goods of economic growth and mass political consensus. Democrats were unable to win electoral support for their continued leadership in the White House and in economic policy. But the "free market" solutions vaunted by the Republicans who took their place have their own failures: international competitive pressures have yet to be turned back by free initiatives of entrepreneurs, managers, and investors; tax cutting and military spending have created gigantic budget deficits; the movement to deregulate has lost its appeal in the wake of the savings and loan debacle and the continuing crises of the air transportation industry; cutting back the welfare state incurs revulsion at homelessness and a rediscovery of an underclass; and popular support for continuing on the new path barely attracted 25 percent of the voting-age public in the last two presidential elections.

Despite general agreement on the collapse of New Deal politics, there is wide disagreement about exactly what failed and precisely why the New Deal coalition broke down. Indeed, the dominant explanation of the New Deal during its heyday was that it would not break down, that American liberal democracy was the culmination of a historical development of a modernized society, and that the New Deal's solutions to conflicts that arose from the economy were optimal. Virtually all of the existing accounts of the breakdown of the New Deal are fragmentary or overly generalized, and they discount the influence of politics on economic performance. Mostly they root the breakdown of the old system either in the peculiarities of American pluralism or in the general operation of a capitalist economy. Thus, some have argued that the high value that American culture places on individualism led to a hyperpluralism in which special interest group demands disrupted political order and prevented any stable reaggregation of interests, an outcome encouraged by the Constitutional weaknesses that encourage political entrepreneurs to go into business for themselves. Others have pointed to structured incompatibility between democratic politics and free market economies: political conflicts became expressed in inflation and uncontrolled government spending, which undermined the resource base of the welfare state.

These and other explanations are partly correct. Despite their disagreements, most share a common theme, namely the centrality of labor and industrial order to both the New Deal reforms and the chronic problems of economic justice and competitiveness that emerged in the 1960s. A major innovation of the New Deal was making organized labor a primary Democratic party coalition partner in national politics and a major prop of the national economy. The AFL-CIO (American Federation of Labor-Congress of Industrial Organizations) was able to influence the outcome of presidential elections and was powerful enough to command broad attention in the Congress. For twenty-five years unions negotiated with employers for steady increases in wages and benefits. But the world that labor inhabited is now clearly in ruins.

The public image of organized labor is that it is unresponsive to the interests of society as personified by employers who want to redeploy employees and other factors of production to make the economy more productive and competitive. The job structures and wage rules that frame the organization of work in unionized enterprises are especially under attack from managers as standing in the way of industrial change. Job structures define the tasks and responsibilities associated with specific jobs and the relationship of one job to the next, both in the flow of work through a factory or office and the career path of individual workers. Job descriptions and work rules are written into local and national collective bargaining agreements and represent a defensible code of conduct for employers and employees alike. They prevent arbitrary actions by supervisors that might discriminate against individuals or otherwise deny benefits and opportunities to workers. Individual employees can use the contract as prima facie evidence in grievance hearings that management has violated the rights of the worker. Wage rules are tightly linked to job structures. Wage rules guarantee organized workers equal pay for equal work. They also guarantee that income is protected from devaluation by inflation and that workers directly share in productivity gains that result from new technologies. But now critics consider these structures and rules to be reflections of bureaucracy and rigidity, not of fairness and equality. Collective bargaining now is considered the expression of distrust and selfish resistance to cooperation with management, not the fruition of rational adjustment. This new public image reinforces labor's loss of influence in Democratic party politics. The changing position of the United States in the world pressed American government leaders to adjust political and economic policies. The AFL-CIO has found it increasingly difficult to establish working relationships with the White House, even when occupied by a Democrat, and with Democratic majorities in Congress.

Most explanations of this turnabout in the public image of labor are rooted in either the logics of market and industrial shifts or political culture, and they rarely connect the two or consider the specific contexts of industrial decision making. Yet, the most revealing challenge to the New Deal achievement is the persistently successful competition from nations that have government policies and forms of industrial order that differ from ours in the quality of industrial governance and the capability of industrial organization. Japanese factories that are transplanted to the United States and run according to Japanese principles with American employees outperform American-based companies. This competition suggests that there are various ways to organize the relations between economy and society, and it casts doubt on the older understandings that the New Deal was the uniquely rational response to problems of a modernizing society.

The explanation of the rise and decline of the New Deal Democratic reform coalition proposed here is that the forms of settlement of historical conflicts over American industrial organization were successful because of the unusually stable background conditions that emerged from World War II, namely American hegemony and commitment to maintenance of that hegemony. The forms of settlement did not end conflicts in the factories and offices and, once the background conditions changed significantly in the 1960s, resurgent conflicts presented a new challenge to Democratic coalition leaders. The Democracy, however, was unable to innovate because it lacked flexibility of organization and ideology. The old forms of settlement had created incentives for rigidity in employee-manager and industry-society relationships. The old solutions to conflict appeared as an orthodoxy that blocked new competitive strategies to sustain the gains to income and rights that the working classes had won. This failure set the stage for a return of free-market ideologies and political leaders who espoused a conservative doctrine that held government and labor as the causes of crisis. And there was some truth to this. But the flaw in the criticism was the claim that reform based on managerial self-interest was the only alternative. The argument here is that the eventual inflexibility of New Deal politics was rooted in the narrow definition of employees' rights to collaborate at work; what was once a victory became an insufficient basis for further reform.

The following chapters present a case study of industrial relations in the automobile industry. The object is two-fold: first, to look clearly at what labor's role really was in the New Deal system of politics and to close the gap between near unanimity about labor's centrality to politics from the 1930s to the 1980s and the disagreement about labor's place in its breakdown; and second, through examination of one core element within the system, to illuminate the transformations of the broader system of politics.

I focus on the automobile industry because it has been central to the political and economic life of the United States for virtually the entire twentieth century. Mass production automobile manufacturing was once the paradigm of modern economic efficiency and served as the model for other industries both in America and abroad. The industry became the single largest generator of wealth and jobs. The New Deal's economic policy was based on perceived needs of a mass production economy. The successful unionization of the auto industry by the United Auto Workers' Union (UAW) was a major accomplishment of the early New Deal. The UAW became the largest union in the CIO and was a champion of a labor-based social-democratic welfare state. In the 1950s and 1960s the union was a leading force behind the Democratic party. Auto industrial relations were considered the epitome of mature, liberal democratic labor-management relations.

But by the late 1970s the automobile industry entered a period of crisis from which it has yet to emerge. The industry came to be seen as rigid, and both the union and the companies stood revealed as lumbering bureaucracies seemingly incapable of responding to the changed political and international economic conditions by restructuring their contractual relations and collaborating to beat the competition. Since 1978 the UAW has lost a third of its peak 1.5 million members while the major U.S. automakers have given up nearly 30 percent of the domestic automobile market to foreign-based firms. Some believe that automobile manufacturing, like steel, rubber, machinery, and garments, is an industrial dinosaur whose days in the new high technology and service economy are numbered. This study rejects this image. The auto industry's problems were not inevitable; the current crisis had a long prologue. Japan and Germany continue to have highly successful "mature" automobile industries. Their difference from America is that their politics foster an industrial order that masters change.

If the United States expects to continue to compete successfully in manufacturing, then the automobile industry must continue to be a leading employer, source of productivity, and market for new technologies. And it is in the automobile industry that some of the most concerted efforts at work reform are occurring. But these reforms need public support to prevent them from succumbing to managerial preoccupations with control and short-term profit and to defensive union tactics. The Democratic party has failed to develop a programmatic consensus on the microeconomic issues that are the heart of governing the economy today. The party regained the presidency in unusual electoral circumstances committed to a more aggressive trade policy and a fiscal stimulation program, but it was unprepared to establish a new framework for enhanced democracy that will enable it to serve its historical labor constituency as it seeks to improve American industrial performance.

CHAPTER I

The New Deal as System and Project

When the United States is compared with other advanced capitalist democracies, it is usually placed at the far end of a continuum with nations that have a low capacity to regulate economic change. This group of nations is defined by its reliance on market-driven choices; high-capacity countries, in contrast, employ policies by which government choices are focused on the strategic issues that affect the competitiveness of industrial sectors. But the image of American low capacity must be understood contextually, because the New Deal was both capable and accomplished. Capacity is not inherent to a country, but rather reflects historic political forces that are able to direct government policy to their ends. The concept captures what is meant by government powers and by the ideas and abilities that enable both leaders and citizens to change in the face of new conditions. Liberal Democrats, in fact, did achieve much of what they set out to do for social peace and a productive economy. In the New Deal era (1932–1968), the Democratic party had capacities to pursue certain goals and settle certain conflicts but not others.

The patterns of governance that emerged from the economic depression of the 1930s created a virtuous circle of stable labor-management relations; increasing wages, productivity, and profits; expanding markets; and steady expansion of the rights and liberties of citizens. The preexisting industrial order was democratized in several ways—workers were guaranteed the right to choose their own representatives without management interference; collective bargaining and grievance arbitration became the standard for settling union-company disputes: contracts established a constitution of rights and powers; wages and benefits were negotiated at the firm level but spread by patterning norms throughout the economy; and federal judges and national labor board officials maintained supervision over the private parties. Although the New Deal only partly democratized work while the achievement of civil rights was slow and only partly realized in the arenas of social and economic equality, New Deal governance seemed to ensure steady progress for a generation. But now it is more common to point to the shortcomings, such as the halving of the rate of unionization since 1955 and that collective bargaining no longer works to resolve disputes. The shortcomings as well as the accomplishments need to be accounted for.

THERE ARE FOUR major types of explanation for the patterns of New Deal governance, each of which is partly correct but all wrong. Modernization theorists argue, as I will discuss in more detail below, that the New Deal and its labor allies rose and fell with the maturation of the mass production economy—liberal Democrats applied government policy to ensure that mass consumer income matched the productive capacity of mass production industries like automobiles, which boosted union membership and Democratic voting. The supersession of mass production industries in the economy simply reversed the political process. Similar to modernization explanations are *marxisant* explanations based on analysis of class relations in the development of the mode of production. The New Deal was a coalition of investors in capital-intensive and multinational enterprises who coalesced with mass production unions under the Democratic party banner to sustain government policies for domestic expansion and free trade. The contradiction between domestic expansion and successful international competition eventually pushed Democratic businessmen into the Republican camp. Another type of explanation is cultural. What is significant about the New Deal is that a consensus on liberal democracy and capitalism characterized the views of all the major political forces during the depression, leading to broad support for the Democrats' pragmatic policies to solve problems. Once the collective problems of the economic depression were dealt with, other subcultural identities and group interests came to the fore and, over time, divided New Deal constituencies. In contrast, institutionalist explanations claim an autonomous influence for politics, especially the debilitating constitutional structure of government and historical administrative authority of the federal bureaucracy. The New Deal state was empowered—to the extent it was empowered—by historical contingencies, namely the unusually strong motives of economic collapse and world war. The New Deal's governing authority slowly dissipated as the reformist coalition was unable to use federal power to broaden its base.

My own explanation draws on elements of each of these others. It conceives the New Deal as a political network that encompasses both social and economic organizations and government institutions, that drove a reform cycle, that, in turn, structured these organizations and institutions. The New Deal represented a coalition of forces united by general agreement on governing formulas, the very successful operation of which depended on the structured participation of the members of the coalition. The collapse of the New Deal began when conditions for governance changed. The coalition needed to adjust or transform its formulas, but the Democratic Party was unable to concert participation in ways that established a new agreement.

Modernization

The explanatory ambition of modernization theory is far broader than the New Deal, but the dominant academic understandings of American politics during the era were strongly influenced by its conception of the underlying logic of historical development.[1] A modernizing society's development is driven by economic activity that has been freed from political and ecclesiastic control. Social interactions become based on individual rational economic calculation and contract, and politics is characterized by the competition of groups organized to press the material interests of specific segments of society. Political institutions become specialized and differentiated to successfully manage and respond to conflicts and insecurities that are no longer contained by traditional authority structures. Liberal democracies develop political parties to aggregate interests and present platforms, during elections, for public approval; legislatures pass the laws; government bureaucracies administer the law; and courts adjudicate disputes over the application of the law in specific cases. A basic characteristic of a modernized society is its rationality and flexibility: of individual belief, social interaction, economic organization and governing process.

According to this general conception, the New Deal represented a jump ahead on the path to modernity because the federal government acquired new authority to respond to problems associated with socioeconomic change. The New Deal ushered in an era of increased administrative capacity to manage interest group and partisan competition over the distribution of goods and services. Apparently irrational motives, rooted in race, ethnicity, ideology and religion, had given way to pragmatic deal making within a consensual system of rules for pursuing interests and resolving conflicts. Any problems with this style of politics had to do with matters internal to the framework, such as special interest groups pressing positional advantages to gain unfair shares or veto collective goods and the lack of democratic process within groups.[2]

This compellingly optimistic big theory ran into two types of criticism that are useful here. One was criticism from within the theory by political scientists who argued that the reality of increasing political capacity did not look the way the theory predicted it would. Cultural consensus typically was invoked to cover the lagging development of conflict resolution functions. A second type of criticism was over the structure-functionalism (and sometimes complacent) tone of modernization theory. Politics cannot be functional for the socioeconomy unless one assumes uniformity of societal development (i.e., that there is an inherent logic of compatible "good" outcomes and unilateral translation of socioeconomic interests into politics, and both of these assumptions looked increasingly untenable.)

In the late 1960s some scholars noted that the United States "lagged" or was exceptional in its governing institutions when compared with European countries or even the Soviet Union or, one would add today, Japan. In a widely read study, Samuel Huntington argued that social and economic modernization could take place without the requisite establishment of increased governmental capacity. A historical legacy to the twentieth century United States of divided and overlapping government authority inhibited the establishment of a bureaucracy capable of societal management, even after the New Deal reforms. Huntington broke with the socioeconomic determinism of the model to argue that economic change did not necessarily result in political development, let alone democracy. To a large degree his argument was directed at foreign policy efforts of the 1950s and 1960s aimed at the "developing world," but in a later essay on the United States Huntington argued that even in the most modern of societies political author- ities had not developed adequate capabilities to deal with the demands and inevitable social conflicts arising from a dynamic socioeconomy. In the first study Huntington argued that what saved the United States from political crisis was cultural consensus; in the later study he was not so sure, and he worried that the failure of government officials to control interest groups was undermining political order.[3]

A similar line of criticism also appeared in analyses of public law by Theodore Lowi and of political parties by Walter Dean Burnham.[4] Lowi and Burnham agreed with Huntington that there was what became called in the 1970s a "governability crisis," but Burnham rooted this crisis in the declining ability of political parties to aggregate interests and organize mass participation in ways that secured support for government policy. A striking feature of American politics as compared to other modernizing societies was the absence of a labor-oriented political party. Unlike other developed nations in which trade unions and laborist or socialist parties constituted the labor movement, in the United States this differentiation had not occurred. Instead, working-class interests were available to be aggregated by either major party or by none; the evidence from voting statistics was that "none" was the prac- tice. More specifically, historical evidence showed that the working classes and young people were excluded from substantial participa- tion in the American electoral process after the 1890s. The Demo- cratic party's landslide election victories of 1932 and 1936 are explained by the mobilization of the working classes to vote and their conversion to liberal democracy.

The new electoral alignment of the Republicans and Demo- crats still did not transform the Democratic party into a labor- based organization. It was true that the Democrats gained consistent voting majorities from working class precincts from the 1930s until recently, but labor organizations and leaders never gained a dom-

inant voice in party deliberations, and the party never committed
itself to building a popular organization. The only major study of
postwar labor politics found that there was at best a "partial
equivalence" between the AFL-CIO relationship with the Democrats
and European labor parties.[5] This fact helped explain why, once
the critical period of the realignment of partisan identities had past
and policy solutions to the problems arising from the economy had
been adopted, both political parties harvested votes based on their
past records instead of planting the seeds of future electoral bounty.
At the same time, according to Burnham, party leaders felt continuing exposure to ongoing socioeconomic forces and interest
group pressures from which they sought to insulate themselves. By
the late 1960s the parties had become a tenuous link between the
voters and the government, which was reflected in the decline of
voter turnout and party identification, electoral "disaggregation,"
growing issue differences between party leaders and voters, declining confidence in government, and a great increase in political
action committee (PAC) activity. The time was ripe for a new
electoral realignment that would readjust government to society
and enable modernization to proceed. The Republicans began a
long string of presidential election successes in 1968, but voter
turnout and social and economic standards have stagnated. No
new consensus has emerged.[6]

   This study suggests that one reason that realignment has not
played its historical role is that labor's problems could not be
brought to political market for resolution because the political
incorporation of labor was side-tracked into industrial relations.
Worker-citizens could vote for one of the political parties, but their
problems as workers were governed by the specialized agencies of
labor law. Most employees were unorganized and, therefore, had
few of the workplace rights recognized in law; on the contrary,
property law gave managers virtually dictatorial powers. Workers
were at the mercy of labor force demand in the economic marketplace. Those workers who were unionized were enmeshed in an
industrial relations "system" where problems were processed through
contract negotiation and administration, mediation, arbitration,
and court hearings. A consequence of depoliticizing labor problems in this way was to rob the Democratic party, and society more
broadly, of the capacity to steer labor-management relations toward

new public goals as conditions changed. Why was such a system established? Lowi suggests, generally, that New Deal leaders' "public philosophy" of interest group liberalism led the federal government to delegate public authority to unions and managements in the name of a process- but not goal-oriented democracy. This study suggests that the New Deal's industrial order encompassed substantive goals, but the incomplete establishment of employee rights to participate in workplace decision making entailed an increasingly cumbersome administration to process microeconomic conflicts. One of the causes of this was a strategy to keep industrial relations out of the partisan arena, for reasons explained more fully in later chapters.

A second problem is that the functionalism of both modernization theory and these first-order dysfunctionalist critics leaves the theory open to criticism for consequentialism. It washes-out the specificity and heterodoxy of historical situations that real individuals face and that lead them to form interests and interest-group organizations in the first place. The style of argument is to relate the functions that a society must perform—such as generating an economic surplus and assuring the legitimacy of political authority—to current practices (or values of the variables) and to explain how the latter fulfill the requirements or constraints of the former. Thus, partisan realignments adjust politics to the apparent needs of society. But the functions are forever in danger of overwhelming the practices. The observed outcomes serve precisely the purposes that theory conceives they must; and since they serve this purpose they must have been created to have these consequences. For example, despite all the great sophistication of voting analysis, as Burnham rightly points out, the causal explanation still must be supplied.[7] In modernization theory, politics often is conceived as a reflection of a logic of economic interests, but what were the substantive alternatives from which individuals believed they had to choose?

Consider more closely the model of societal change and the empirical claims about politics in modernization theory. The key to explaining political change is the logic of economic development based on expanding markets and economies of scale. Entrepreneurs specialize in a single product to sell in the market, and they break the production process into component parts to gain increased productivity. Capitalist-employers and wage-workers both concentrate on a narrower range of tasks and more readily perfect them. Moreover, machines can be designed to perform them. Specialization and mechanization raise total costs but lower unit costs of producing goods. Lower unit costs make available a greater array of goods to lower-income consumers and expand the market. This process is rational and autonomous: broader markets in turn encourage both greater production and further specialization and mechanization which further reduce costs and expand the market. On this economic-technological path large corporate enterprise arose, labor unions were organized, and "modern" pluralist forms of politics emerged.

The preeminence of giant enterprise in the United States, the argument goes, was a necessary outcome of a need to organize and finance the large investments to achieve production economies of scale and to reach geographically far-flung markets.[8] The late nineteenth century revolutions in production techniques made great volume production possible at unit costs generally lower than those of craft producers, dooming the latter to marginality. Yet the new technologies also resulted in cycles of overproduction, profit-less price competition, and depressions. An early step toward "modern" industrial order was made at the turn of the century when industrial magnates and investment bankers organized a wave of business mergers to reduce price competition and guarantee high rates of capacity utilization and stable profits. The newly consolidated corporations integrated forward into marketing, credit, and consumer service and backward into components and raw materials. The internal organization of industrial firms was patterned to best take advantage of markets and mass production technology. The new large, diversified, and integrated firms adopted forms of bureaucratic hierarchy that separated the functions of planning and strategy, administration and production. The first was localized in the general office, housing the top corporate leaders; administration was lodged in separate product divisions with support staff; while production was the task of the blue-collar workers who acted as the privates in the industrial army.

The rise of national trade unions is presented as the story of accommodation to large-scale corporate enterprise.[9] Once mass production and a corporation-dominated economy won out at the turn of the twentieth century, the argument goes, conditions had been created in which both labor and capital could prosper. Mass markets and standardized production initially had undermined workers' skills and the influence of the craft-based AFL, but the expansion of markets eventually sustained employment, national organizations of labor, and high wages. The new division of labor was the basis of industrial unionism of the CIO—all workers in an industry, now overwhelmingly semiskilled, would belong to one single union—as well as of stable relations among unions and employers. The union organizations that survived the historical transition to modern manufacturing based themselves on workers' income interests and on administering wage contracts and coordinating labor within a given production system. Mutual respect between labor and capital for the legitimacy of their respective interests—industrial pluralism—led to negotiations and industrial peace.

In theory the Democratic party in the 1930s was the vehicle for those elite groups who wanted to use government authority to adjust relationships in the economy and society to get the United States out of the depression while still maintaining liberal democratic capitalism.[10] There were two main problems that elites faced: technical issues concerning the most efficient way to organize the economy, and a social integration problem rooted in conflicts that arose from economic change that threaten political order. Political parties enabled elites to gain the political authority to regulate conflicts of interest that had deflated the legitimacy of certain institutions, like the stock exchanges, and had undermined the functioning of the corporation-dominated production system, in particular the distribution of surplus between wage earners and owner-managers. The new regulation was reflected in part by two pieces of legislation: the Social Security Act of 1935, which began such programs as unemployment insurance and old age pensions, and the National Labor Relations Act (NLRA) of 1935, which not only wrote into American politics legal guarantees for unionism, but proposed that unions would be a primary means to raise mass consumption. The proof that this "solution" to the economic and political crises facing the United States was the uniquely rational one was provided ex post facto: it worked. The economy grew, and the voters periodically reaffirmed their support for the New Deal's liberal Keynesianism and industrial pluralism over three decades. That the New Deal solution was obviously of superior efficiency compared to the "normalcy" of the 1920s was recognized even by Republicans who perpetuated major features of it after they regained control of the White House in 1952 and again in 1968.

But this is not what happened. Between the turn of the century consolidation of the political position of corporate capital, no later than the Federal Trade Commission Act of 1914, and the New Deal's National Labor Relations Act of 1935 an entire generation grew up in a political economy notably top-heavy. Not everyone appreciated the superior rationality of large-scale corporate organization; even those who were its champions disagreed fundamentally over the extent and nature of business obligations to employees, the broader consuming public, and government that went further than traditional notions of labor contract, market pricing, and tax paying. Historical research has made clear that there were several alternative industrial models seeking public favor during these years that seem to fulfill orthodox notions of rationality, including forms of regional flexible specialization, practiced in such sectors as textiles, garments, and machine tools, and industrial democracy in large-scale enterprise advocated by the Taylor Society and several leading unionists.[11] A functional alignment of economy and politics had to wait a long generation. But even then, the politics of the New Deal cannot plausibly be explained in the functionalist mode.

There is much evidence about what people wanted and tried to accomplish that leads one to suspect that the outcomes were less modus operandi than opus operatum. The New Deal solutions were solutions which developed from previous experience and, eventually, many years hence, worked, from a variety of causes not linked to solving the theoretical problems of society-government adjustment. Voters, for example, did not "choose" the New Deal in 1932 because it was not presented to them. The NIRA (National Industrial Recovery Act) was the Roosevelt administration's first answer to the depression crisis; it did respond to problems of growth and integration, but failed nonetheless. Social Security and the National Labor Relations Act were not clearly functional: the former paid out meager benefits until the 1950s, the latter was not found constitutional until 1937 and continued to be a highly contested

law thereafter, undergoing major judicial and administrative rein-
terpretations and legislative amendments. Which version of labor
law was the "right one"? Only, it is reasonable to argue, once the
act was implemented and many further policy pieces added over
the next fifteen years—as argued in this book—and their benefits
for coalition members could be enjoyed could they stabilize the
new style of politics. Some other policies may just as well have
served the purposes of ensuring economic growth and political
stability; they did in other democratic capitalist countries like
France, Sweden, and Great Britain, among others. In fact, as
discussed in this book, major "interest groups," like organized
labor, advocated several distinctly different government programs
at the same time. Top leaders of the CIO advocated "industry
councils" and national planning right into the 1950s. Also, the
halting adoption of Keynesian economic policy by the Roosevelt
and Truman administrations can hardly be called the unique choice
of the proper response to national economic problems. Finally, the
long-run functionalism of the industrial relations system is con-
founded by the decline of union organization, which has led some
critics to claim that that outcome is the true purpose of New Deal
labor policy; how could a functionalist deny it? Just why certain
policies were part of the New Deal must be explained by something
else.

Groups

Orthodox liberalism and pluralism are two types of theory that
explain New Deal-era politics and government performance by
reference to groups rather than to the needs of society and elites
with privileged knowledge of precisely what to do. However, the
orthodox view is closer to the inside critics of modernization in
concluding that forms of politics are responsible for declining
performance while the pluralists implicitly (and sometimes explicitly) interpret recent political behavior as functional for society.
Both have rigid notions of interests and virtually ignore the influence of politics on group formation.

Mancur Olson has argued that government intervention in the
economy was the cause of declining national performance since
1970.[12] Americans are lucky, he claims, that their government does

not have as much capacity to intervene as do foreign governments although we, too, are succumbing to temptation. Like a good neoclassical economist, Olson assume that capitalist economies are naturally efficient and productive. But, he goes on, they become encumbered with entitlements and government regulations in response to selfish groups with favorable political positions. By compelling the allocation of resources to less competitive sectors, interest groups and the state override price signals and inhibit the sectors of the economy that really would be competitive. These forces eventually take their toll in market imperfections and lost comparative advantage. Although the allocation of resources in 1950 was efficient, recent declining American industrial competitiveness is a consequence of employees and managers organized to prevent the redeployment of capital and labor to more productive industries in order to protect current employment and income. Similarly, welfare state expenditures sap resources from productive enterprise to marketplace losers. These conclusions, however, seem to fly in the face of the experiences of America's competitors, especially Japan and Germany, where conditions of labor and government regulation are even more demanding of corporate social responsibility.[13]

The pluralist variation on the orthodox theme that special interest groups compete to advance sectional gains, in particular by engaging in lobbying and electioneering, is that group competition is largely benign.[14] Given a modern polity with civil liberties and voting rights, any group of citizens could form an organization to promote the interests of the groups' members; also, given that modern individuals are self-interested, they would, in fact, do so. With many groups competing to advance their own interests, there are inevitable clashes over members and resources and government influence. To settle conflicts, rational actors will compromise and make deals: everyone will get something of what they want. And that sustains the legitimacy of the political system. Even if unions go into decline, that is certainly because they no longer serve the interests of individuals anymore. And if the political parties attract fewer strong adherents, functional equivalents have emerged, such as the mass media.

Both theories are strongly bounded; indeed, they take the "private sector" for granted, assuming its organization, and dynamics. For example, Olson assumes fixed endowments of and relations between labor and capital that are somehow prior to politics. But labor and capital are not fixed. The rights of employees and investors, the productiveness of labor, technological innovation, forms of industrial organization and the distribution of consumer income are and always have been influenced by government policies. The competitiveness of industry is linked not only to market exchanges, but to the political conditions that established those markets. The orthodox analysis of comparative advantage turns on allocating resources among industries of a national economy, but much of the current economic challenge is about competing with foreign producers. Orthodox assumptions tell us nothing about "competitive advantage."[15] Rather than assume that employers will do the "right thing," industrial managers who try to implement lowest-cost assumptions are just as likely to provoke labor opposition; fail to achieve productivity gains; cut training programs; forgo research and development; drive down wages; demand tax cuts, tax subsidies, and the dismantling of social provisions; and/or invest in other countries.

More deeply, why does anyone do anything? Olson says the only motive is calculation of economic benefits. Orthodox liberalism is based on a conception of microeconomic relations between employee and employer that is both more authoritarian and less realistic than the industrial pluralism of the modernization theory. In industrial pluralism, labor-management relations are ultimately governed by technology and market conditions, but these are mediated by collective bargaining in which unionists and personnel specialists come to agree on what those conditions will allow. In contrast, in Olson's orthodox conception, such cooperative behavior is highly unlikely and, even if achieved, too costly. On the one hand, cooperative behavior by self-interested individuals can arise only in small, communal group contexts where personal incentives and sanctions can be applied to recalcitrant members. In contrast, large organizations like unions and firms must operate in a context of extended constituencies that compel spokespersons to act as delegates of market self-interest rather than as fiduciaries. The internal order of unions and companies is hierarchical and coercive.

On the other hand, Olson allows, unions and firms may cooperate in the sense that they collude against the public (consumer) interest in low prices by agreeing to higher wages and to the use of the firm's oligopoly market position to pass on the increased costs to customers. Union federations and management associations may be able to act for the public interest, but the costs of such "encompassing" organization is so high as to make them less efficient than no organization at all (the condition that is assumed to be efficient). But this is a less realistic conception than the industrial pluralists'. Communal identities are not simply natural, arising from primordial associations, but can be created at work: for example individuals can learn to cooperate and be given incentives to cooperate. During the union drives of the 1930s and 1940s, ethnic and class identities were mobilized to win union organization. And, I will argue, collectively bargained rules were rational compromises under conditions of uncertainty. The real problem is creating a political framework that provides incentives for individuals and groups to act for what is determined to be the public good.[16]

One manifestation of alleged group interference with the market that goes to the heart of the New Deal are union demands for higher wages and greater mass consumer purchasing power. But the latter was supposed to be *the* solution to the crisis of corporate capitalism. Yet, in the orthodox conception, higher wages lead to lower profit or inflation if productivity slows. Indeed there is evidence that real wages for unionized workers increased significantly in the 1960s and even in 1970s while productivity and profits slowed.[17] But are they related? Since 1979 real wage growth has slowed and even become negative, and, ironically, union wages dropped the most. But at the same time, productivity growth continued to lag. Maybe the wage/profit distribution is not the source of the crisis. Instead, there is evidence that the problem is the productivity of investment, namely that employers increasingly sought technological fixes during the last twenty years, which raised the costs of production, and reduced the contribution of labor. The productivity problem, in short, may be in the organization of work and the distribution of authority to managers who are trying to escape the risks of collaboration.

Like orthodox economists, pluralists conceive the interests of groups as given and economistic. They concede that there are also primordial identities, such as ethnicity, race, religion, and gender, but these are being transformed by individual experiences in the modernizing marketplace. Rational interest-maximizing behavior takes place within a carefully delimited institutional context, which is taken for granted. Everything happens within the boundaries of a modernized society; no serious challenge is made to the distribution of authority and entitlements and group competition is compatible with capitalism. This means that pluralists do not (and cannot) explain significant changes other than voting outcomes that accompanied the failures of the Democrats in presidential elections. Thus, the New Deal Democratic party, the argument goes, was preeminently an electoral coalition that reflected the demands of the various groups that made up the coalition and that marked it sharply from the coalition of groups assembled behind the Republican party banner. What defined the power and policies of the Roosevelt and subsequent Democratic administrations was the durable partisanship of Protestant white southerners, union members, northern urban ethnics, Catholics, and lower-income and less-educated individuals. During the political realignment in the 1930s that led to the Democrats becoming the majority party, all of these groups supported Democratic candidates by impressive percentages and received from the federal government social and economic policy benefits. Later, once individual Democratic partisanship weakened, old interests were satisfied and new interests were manifested, the New Deal coalition began to disintegrate.[18] Most analyses leave these developments unexplained and assume that the political changes were functionally appropriate for industrial and "postindustrial" stages of development.

What most describe is that in the decades after World War II, Democratic groups increasingly came into conflict with one another over "cultural" issues, such as racial integration of schools and neighborhoods, abortion, patriotism, drug use, women's rights, sexual behavior, the public practice of religion, welfare dependency, and so on. Then the New Deal Democratic party (and the Republicans, as well) no longer represented a clear political image with which individuals could identify and use to express their beliefs on these issues. Instead, single issue interest groups and the media helped to determine political identities, further undermining the old basis of politics. Once the Republican party self-consciously began to run election campaigns that appealed to these cultural concerns, they found great success at the presidential level.[19] Although extensive studies of election statistics and opinion research readily lent themselves to various theories about why

THE NEW DEAL — 21

certain statistically-created composite voters voted Democratic or Republican, we are still left with important questions: why did this historic shift in individual preferences occur? why did economic issues recede and cultural issues become prominent? how did individuals and groups develop new partisan identities? and what relationship, if any, did this have to what elites were doing? Some studies were remarkable for avoiding explanations.[20]

When an explanation is given, the most common one is "postindustrialism," a form of the modernization theory according to which the New Deal succeeded so well in solving problems of social and economic management that an era of affluence emerged by the 1960s in which "postmaterialist" values increasingly were expressed by the well-off and even the not-so-well-off.[21] The new middle classes (including unionized workers' college-educated children) lost interest in New Deal issues of economic security and instead became preoccupied with life style issues. Most members of the new classes were historically Democrats, but their concerns brought them into conflict with cultural traditionalists and other groups that had never accepted the New Deal. The Democratic party's nomination of George McGovern for president in 1972 illustrates the capture of the party by the new forces and, the argument goes, began the alienation of the party's historical blue-collar supporters, including the AFL-CIO, which pointedly did not endorse the Democratic nominee that year, for the first time in decades. Voters started to realign with the opposition Republican party, a process that was as inevitable as the evolution of the economy toward tertiary service and "knowledge-intensive" occupations.

But how does economic change cause this particular electoral outcome? One clash between organized labor and the Democratic presidential nominee in 1972 is not a trend. Not only was the 1972 clash mostly based on the Vietnam War (McGovern had a virtually perfect labor voting record in the Senate), but in every election since then the AFL-CIO has endorsed the Democrat. And if it does seem odd that the so-called traditionalist blue-collar workers who are still very concerned about economic security would become securely aligned with the Republican party, which stands for unleashed managerial modernization, the reason is that it is not true. Union-member households still consistently support the Democratic ticket, in 1988 and 1992 by wide margins. Even nonunion blue-collar workers voted Democratic. The larger trend is that fewer blue-collar workers vote, not that the electorate no longer is mostly working class. Related to this false claim about blue-collar realignment is the presumption that economic problems have all been resolved, establishing a firm basis for shifting politics up the hierarchy of need to "self-actualization."[22] On the contrary, economic change is not clearly on a path to better, more interesting, more rewarding jobs available for everyone; ongoing industrial reorganization has been changing many roles and arguably creating as many worse jobs as better ones. Taken literally, the postindustrial thesis is nonsense: the great majority of American adults are wage and salary earners while individuals in "service" occupations are among the worst paid and most insecure; the proportion of the labor force in manufacturing declined only very slightly up to at least 1980. The notion that, in the 1990s, the working classes and even the middle classes no longer have worries about material conditions of life seems obviously absurd.

One observation is true: union membership as a proportion of the labor force has dropped by about one-half since 1960. But what explains this? A shift to postindustrial occupations that are somehow naturally less prone to unionization? The best evidence available after thorough research of many versions of this claim finds no evidence that this is so.[23] Moreover, in other countries also undergoing advanced economic development the rate of unionization increased during the same period, such as in Canada and the western part of Germany. Like the orthodox liberalism, pluralist theories accept the sharp distinction between economy and politics: they have no analysis of the economy. Is there something in the nature of different nations' industrial orders that might make a political difference? Why do interests become organized precisely in the ways that they do?

Mode of Production

Some researchers who became critical of pluralist explanations of politics began to reread what had been accomplished by the New Deal in light of Marxist theory.[24] The general argument is that the domination of politics by the bourgeoisie explains the limited new powers that the state acquired during the 1930s as well as the

Democrats' declining interest in aggregating the interests of working-class citizens. This argument is a welcome entry in debates over government capacity, suggesting as it does why not all interests are equal and have equal access to government authority. But Marxist theory does not get us much further than modernization theory on the question of group formation and government policy. There are several varieties of *marxisant* analysis of American politics, but to merit the name they all have in common the theory that political change is driven by developments in the forces of production that come into conflict with the social relations of production and, thereby, periodically touch-off intense political class struggles that lead to a recomposition of social relations, which ensures the next stage of development of the mode of production. Theoretical debates among Marxist social scientists have revolved around a problem that also characterized modernization theories, namely that the explanatory status of the framework tends to overwhelm consideration of historically specific sequences of political and policy change. In what way does the crisis of the forces of production lead to a recomposition of social relations?

This issue was brought out in the debate between instrumentalists and structuralists. The instrumental or "corporate liberal" theory conceives the New Deal reforms as demands by far-sighted capitalists that the federal government reestablish conditions for profitability and tame the newly unruly labor force. That is, the New Deal, far from being a prolabor or radical departure from American political norms, was devoted to serving the interests of employers—especially the big capitalist-managers and their integrated firms—and stifling radicalism with appeasing reforms. In this way the New Deal can be assimilated into the framework of successive modes of production that was brought about by developments in the forces of production the conflicts over which are mediated by a class-dominated government that acts to restructure social relations in ways that ensure continued capital accumulation. One of the most concrete versions of the story analyzes dynamics within the ruling classes that lead to divisions over government policy.[25] The establishment of large bureaucratic capital-intensive businesses—understood largely as described by mainstream business historians and modernization theorists—began a split between those capitalists clinging to market forms of regulation and those whose firms' productive potentials outstripped market demand for their products and who, therefore, were much more concerned to expand the market and realize scale economies, through some mildly reformist labor and social policies and/or through expansion of foreign trade. These big business leaders were the corporate liberals, and they, in the 1930s, were able to form a political coalition with noncapitalists who wanted policy reforms for other reasons. This historic bloc included labor union leaders, as junior partners but partners nonetheless, in restructuring, and hence preserving, the status quo.

Much very useful history has emerged from this perspective about differences among industrialists and bankers, about personnel policy and forms of efficiency. The problem is that history does not work out as predicted. Neither the NLRA nor the Social Security Act fit the picture of employers directly prescribing the law: mass production firms bitterly opposed virtually all labor and social reforms. That big employers eventually accommodated themselves to both unemployment insurance and industrial unions should not be read back into history as evidence that they were initiated by employers as the means of solving problems that arose from their production systems.

Critics of instrumentalism within the Marxist tradition have argued that because capitalists are not a unified class, they do not directly control the state, that the ruling class is split between capitalist-managers and state managers, and that the latter have relative autonomy in their positions in the state apparatus from the former. This autonomy allows them to craft responses to economic crisis that serve the long-run interests of the class.[26] Yet, like the instrumental theory, this structuralist theory still presumes that what state managers in fact do is serve the needs of the mode of production. What are these needs? Presumably to reestablish profitability, but how? Should the state guarantee union organization to prevent violence and radicalization, or should it suppress unions? Should the state enact universal social entitlements and broad-based taxes, or should it target benefits and narrow-base taxes? Should it seek free trade or protection? If there is more than one answer to these questions—and historical and comparative evidence suggests there is—then what determines which specific policies are adopted? It does not answer the question to point to the policies eventually adopted and "in practice" since ex post facto arguments throw the explanation into a consequentialist mode.

Similarly, when explaining the breakdown of the New Deal, structuralists argue that the New Deal "Keynesian welfare state" represented a compromise position between free-market capital accumulation and the majority rule principle of electoral democracy.[27] However, the argument goes, this is a compromise that is not sustainable. By the 1970s, western democratic capitalist states were experiencing fiscal crises and slow growth as welfare programs undermined the labor market and investment incentives and dragged down the economy. The solution to this crisis—cut back the welfare state and abandon Keynesianism—revealed the limits of reform under capitalism and the dominance of the deep logic of the mode of production. Interestingly, this scenario shares some features with orthodox liberalism. However, not only is the Keynesian welfare state image not universal, even in the core capitalist countries of the postwar era—such as Germany, let alone in the United States with its comparatively cheap and fragmented welfare state—the theory leaves no possibility for political learning and increased capacity by reformist coalitions of the sort going on in some of these countries. Instead, it starts with the assumption that historical actors are indeed working out problems of capitalism as conceived by Karl Marx one hundred years ago.

Two attempts to get around this issue are a renewed focus on class struggle and *regulation*. The renewed emphasis on the balance of class forces is meant to show how government institutions and the policy-making process are constrained by class struggle as well as by the apparent need to reestablish profitable production. Rhonda Levine argues that "the state is located within the contradictions of capitalism" and approvingly quotes Nicos Poulantzas to the effect that the state is not an independent historical subject across which class struggle plays, but leaves no mark. Undoubtedly so; but the conception that each conjuncture is like the last and reconfirms "the" class character of the state tends to hollow-out the alleged attentiveness to the historical materials and to throw the analysis back into the hands of the "economic structures" that are developing according to their own laws.[28] Thus, the argument goes, the u.s. labor system established weaker unions than did Sweden's system because organized labor was divided, and the u.s. welfare state was less comprehensive than Britain's because American unions did not form a independent political party.[29] But why? The theorist is supposed to be able to focus on the specific historical conflicts that characterize the class struggle; the array of classes is now expanded a bit beyond proletarians and capitalists to include class fractions of these two basic groups. Yet this is only a spurious historicism because the historical actors still are acting out a script written for them by theorists about what demands of the mode of production they are responding to, however detailed the theorist chooses to get in telling the story.

Regulation theorists focus on the coordination between the production system and the system of consumption, including wage labor and social spending, with the object of understanding the principles of the "schema of reproduction." They claim to allow an indeterminate and multiclass struggle to establish the terms of reproduction. The allocation of resources between production and consumption constitutes a "regime of accumulation," which is formed of "norms, habits, laws and regulating networks which ensure the unity of the process and which guarantee that its agents conform more or less to the schema of reproduction in their day-to-day behavior and struggles. . . ."[30] Actors' internalization of the rules and norms is called the mode of regulation. Therefore, regulation theory maintains a theory of the frameworks of society (regimes of accumulation), but one that explicitly conceives them as under-determining and compatible with some range of alternative modes of regulation that are only provisionally stable. When regulation theorists descend from the abstract, they are likely to sound like either the class struggle or structural Marxists. Either they analyze specific political conflicts in terms of "labor" and "capital" or they presume that what the conflicts are about is resolution of the internal problems of the capitalist mode of production.

Regulation theorists identify the modern era with the emergence of Fordism, a system based on Henry Ford's mass-production system of dedicated technology, unskilled labor, standardized products, and expanding consumer markets. This image of "intensive accumulation," associated with machine-paced work and Taylorist forms of personnel management in the 1920s, has been challenged as overly stylized. The extent of Taylorism was far narrower than claimed.[31] The New Deal reforms of the intensive regime during the 1930s and 1940s are conceived by Samuel Bowles and Herbert Gintis as a "class accord" that settled the terms of coordination between production and consumption.[32] The evidence for this are the collective bargaining contracts of 1948 and 1950 in the automobile industry that became a pattern for other sectors. But as they acknowledge, the class accord is a structural feature of the political economy and has no causal power—"labor" and "capital" did not, in fact, negotiate a social treaty. The collective bargaining contracts were negotiated for other purposes, which will be discussed in later chapters. Finally, in recent years, the argument goes on, the Fordist system has been challenged by the stagnation of mass markets and the emergence of global competition in which "third world" firms have mastered mass production with much lower labor costs, putting a premium on high value-added products. The "old deal" that included real wage raises and Keynesian demand stimulation has to be restructured to ensure continued productivity and profits. Theorists now search for evidence of struggles to reestablish a new mode of regulation and find it in neoliberal attacks on the welfare state, in the new industrial relations ("management by stress") that seeks to gain employee identification with the goals of the firm, and in the new world order. Undoubtedly these are phenomena to investigate; but rather than stay true to their intentions and investigate how interests are being transformed and new forms of collaboration being tested, regulation theorists force the multiform innovations into a Procrustean Bed.[33]

Institutions

Some of those who accept the importance of the problem of determinism have pushed the structuralist argument into a "new institutionalism." What these theorists argue is that, contrary to claims that government policy is determined by the balance of class forces and in particular by the strength of labor or capital, the specific solutions that government officials adopt are determined by the historic qualities of the state administration and policy practice and by contingent factors, such as war or sequential timing of initiatives.[34] Moreover, policies and procedures adopted have "feedbacks" on the formation of groups and coalitions. This is a very useful, open way to proceed.

Thus, economic crisis in the 1930s was the basic problem facing state managers and elected officials, but the solution to the crisis is neither, thereby, determined by the purported needs of capitalism nor by the class struggles between labor and capital in society. The historical and institutional features of the state—its electoral traditions and coalitions (which extend beyond the two-class model), its administrative capacity—constrain the types of response political leaders can make. Thus, for example, the NIRA failed to resolve the crisis in part because the federal government did not have in its repertoire the ability to authoritatively administer a program of industrial coordination. The kinds of solutions that were eventually implemented successfully were those that state officials were able to fashion out of the repertoire of constitutional procedure, divided and decentralized authority, and partisan politics. The comparatively skimpy American welfare state programs arise from such specific historic features of u.s. development as the one-party agrarian southern states, whose congressional representatives helped constitute an antiwelfare state bloc and who were able to prevent the unionization of southern industry.[35]

Institutionalist analysis begins to look remarkably like the "exceptionalism" of the modernization theorists as it highlights the special American political structures that determine policy capabilities. But it suffers from a similar problem, namely it assumes too much about how economic change effects individual identities and group interests. By trying to avoid economic determinism, neoinstitutionalists have been driven to separate the state from interest group struggles which leads them implicitly to accept as given the organization and dynamics of the economy. In turn, this leads to taking for granted what various coalitions of interests want and to the flabby argument that policy battles are between an indeterminate reformist coalition and a more determinant "conservative" coalition of business.[36]

The Method and Argument of This Book

Most theories of American politics do not account very well for the rise and fall of the New Deal because such theories conceptualize politics in a dualist and determinist way. We need to investigate the constitution of the industrial order—how it was developed and how it operated as a form of representation—not just voting patterns in the electoral arena; the decisions of private actors about

the organization of work, not just public officials and policy debates; and group formation, not just interest aggregation and
expression. There is a need for a new conceptualization that keeps
the notion of a structure in order to maintain the reality of alternative forms of politics in democratic capitalist nations, but which
stops before the framework overwhelms historical specificity.

In line with this objective I am going to analyze ideal types of
labor systems while focusing on the exemplary case of the automobile industry. To make this investigation, I set up ideal types of
industrial orders rooted in or built up from American history and
ask why, in several historical sequences of events and possible
behaviors, certain alternatives were chosen. The ideal types define
the possibilities for collaboration and reform in a democracy. They
are producerism and managerialism.[37]

The producerist ideal is an industrial order in which all participants take part in both conception and execution of tasks, where
skills are broadly distributed and individual capacities are con-
stantly upgraded, where work relations depend on the substance of
the job to be done, and where a community of firms and unions
collaborate to spread risk across a sector and region.

The managerialist ideal is an industrial order characterized by
a chain of command in which all strategic decisions are made by
owner-managers and executed down the line, where employees
know only what their immediate task requires them to know, where
work relations are based on contract, and where firms seek to
externalize risks.

What I will suggest now, and explain throughout the book, is
the theme of flexibility and rigidity: individuals and organizations
must change (develop new capacities) with change (as new problems arise) to maintain their authority in the social division of
labor. Different industrial orders have consequences for the capacities of individuals to contribute to the continued success of democracy, defined as a self-governing polity. Variations in labor relations
or the terms under which social collaboration occurs, including
who has authority to do what, are a major cause of variations in
political freedom; and, conversely, the political institutions—especially the parties and electoral system—have the ability either to
help or to disorganize and rob individuals of their chance to gain
new capacities for self-government. The Democratic coalition held

executive power for thirty-two of forty-eight years from 1932 to 1980, it could rely on fairly consistent legislative support on core issues, and it staffed the federal judiciary. But New Deal hegemony was both less and more than control of these institutional redoubts. It was less because the reach of national governmental institutions depends on interinstitutional coordination among the branches and with state and local governments. Long historical practices blunted national standards and central administration. It was more because the New Deal Democratic party, while hardly a cadre organization, encompassed a broad network of private citizens, unionists, economists, corporation leaders, teachers, industrial relations experts, ministers, publishers and writers, and others who shared a general commitment to, and helped to devise, the governing formulas that Democratic officials propounded and applied to specific policy problems. These shared formulas and understandings were invoked repeatedly and elaborated in countless meetings and conferences and other forums, including national collective bargaining sessions, where Democrats and the broader network met. Adherence to the formulas made the Democratic party representative and constituted its fund of ideology when officials made appeals for support on legislation and in elections. The governing formulas were interest group liberalism, industrial pluralism, and commercial Keynesianism.[38]

The case is set up as a comparison of historical sequences and as a comparison within each sequence between the auto industry and other political formations in order to draw inferences about causal processes that shape the emergence of dominant forms of labor politics. Note that the American labor movement in the standard history of modernization adopted its Gompersian style in the era of 1900-1920, just when the auto industry was born. This is compared with the early New Deal period during the 1930s and 1940s, with the 1960s and 1970s when new problems were identified with labor-management relations in an internationalizing economy, and with the situation since then in which the terms of international competition have permanently changed but the domestic arrangements are still being established. My analysis distinguishes between what Arthur Stinchcombe calls the "cumulation ideal type" and the "virtual ideal type":[39] between the theorist's concept that defines an outcome—producerism and managerialism—and the actual range of alternatives from which individuals had to make intentional choices, although the alternatives are positions along a variable of capacity-enhancing industrial democracy.

The cumulation ideal types are analogous in that they allow or block collaboration. First, I am looking for analogies between distinct industrial orders, whose characteristics include unions, parties, managements, class fractions, sectors, sections, government officials of various types including members of Congress and school administrators, laws, ideologies, markets and technologies. The questions are what did they have in common or how did they differ—for example, in the ways that members and leaders were linked—how coherent were their programs, what were members and leaders willing to sacrifice to reach their goals, what did members and outsiders want. Then, secondly, I want to note how the auto industrial order developed. I accomplish this by analyzing the series of characteristics that specify one "set" (e.g., welfare capitalism) and by showing how they changed into another (e.g., industrial pluralism) through choices from alternatives that real historical individuals faced. Thirdly, I am making an argument about New Deal institutionalization (or what Stinchcombe calls institutional disposition), namely, that a certain kind of imperfectly institutionalized orthodoxy of New Deal politics reigned and "caused" things to happen during the late New Deal era from 1950 to 1980. I want to explain how the New Deal system was created and stabilized, and I am making an evaluative argument (based on the notion that the "institutional disposition" is not perfectly determinative) that what really made the New Deal Democratic formation incapable (as it turned out) of internal transformation (or innovation) was the managerialism of the industrial order that it helped to establish and manage. The elitism of the Democratic party limits capacity-enhancing political responses to industrial problems.

Historic forms of politics significantly influenced the changes in the specific characteristics that make up the industrial order, but that is not the only influence, by any means. Therefore, to underline an important quality of the argument, I am pursuing a different type of causal explanation, one in which historical particularity is used to point out that the frameworks associated with functional or structural theories do not determine everything and are always liable to be overturned by disputes of various types and that the ability of humans to go beyond the "rules" or "limits" is what ensures the success of a project for "enhanced liberty."[40] However, the indeterminacy of the structures does not mean that they lack staying power. The second half of the book is really about rigidity—the containment of disputes over entitlements at work (e.g., that rigid hierarchy blunted attempts at collaboration; and virtual monopoly of high government positions by business and professional people made negotiation over reform very difficult)—rather than the theme of flexibility and change.

The book discusses the rise of the New Deal labor system, some consequences of its stabilization for the internal politics of the auto industrial relations system, and the attempt to manage industrial order in the face of changing international economic conditions. Chapters two, three, and four focus on the creation of the labor system. It is explained in part by the ideologies of unionists and managers which organized perceptions of the problems of collaboration at work and the possibilities of political action. The UAW and CIO, in the 1930s in particular, articulated a broad plan for the reorganization of production and the relationship of industry and society. The pieces of the system that emerged in the postwar 1940s were a refraction of this vision through political struggles and historical forms of political mobilization, especially party alignments, elections and policy making. One characteristic of the new system was that it established a macropolitical role for labor unions while leaving their micro role at work politically undefined.

Next, the book discusses the restructuring of the UAW's politics after the postwar settlements by focusing on the changing interests of skilled autoworkers (chapter five) and the union's response to the crisis of a small firm, Studebaker Corporation (chapter six). In brief, the postwar settlements created institutional incentives for union and company managements to cooperate in national collective bargaining while leaving the organization of work to be shaped by both managerial designs for rationalization of production and workers' defensive strategies that relied on contractual restrictions on management and pressure tactics. A consequence of this new politics of work was to transform skilled workers from articulate advocates of flexible work organization into militant defenders of existing job designs. In the case of Studebaker, a more flexible model of work had already taken root before the postwar settlement. But in the 1950s, when a financial crisis struck the company, political incentives led company and workers alike to a major clash over work organization and eventually to Studebaker's closing.

The last two chapters investigate attempts to make the system continue to work as international economic conditions begin to change. Chapter seven focuses on UAW and AFL-CIO actions to prosecute their macro role in collective bargaining and the Democratic party even as they acquiesce in Kennedy-Johnson macrosteering of the economy. The UAW was central to these developments. The failure to successfully concert a reformed national strategy is explained by the difficulties of overcoming the continuing incentives of the New Deal system at work and in politics. Chapter eight discusses the implications of this legacy for responses to rapid and qualitative changes in international conditions in the 1970s and early 1980s. Then neither micro nor macro practices lent themselves to capacity-enhancing restructuring to meet competitive challenges. A concluding theme is that the question of whether or not there are still opportunities to reshape the incentives of labor politics is bound to the lessons learned during the previous decades.

CHAPTER 2

Creating a Low-Capacity Industrial Order

So long as we manufacture for our own people and are not seeking our markets very largely abroad, this sort of thing may go on indefinitely. . . . By and by the great markets will not be so much within ourselves and we shall have to look abroad . . . and if we are going to compete we must have our foundations well laid.

—H. W. Hoyt, 1911

The industrial restructuring that characterizes our era has parallels with the transformations associated with the emergence of the integrated corporation at the turn of the century. Now, the internationalization of economic competition is widely claimed to demand particular kinds of responses from companies, unions, workers, and government. One rendition of what the competitive challenge demands is that American firms must reduce costs by eliminating social overhead (welfare and environmental obligations), getting more effort from current employees rather than hiring new workers, holding back wages and benefits, and shedding peripheral corporate units, such as supply operations, in favor of low-cost sourcing here and abroad. That might be called the orthodox managerialist rendition. What might be called the liberal producerist rendition is that firms should decentralize authority and empower the people on the "front lines" to improve products and processes and thereby increase productivity, which would enable America to maintain employment and its superior standard of living. Workers and union leaders in particular are called upon to cooperate with corporate managers' competitive plans. They are urged to invest themselves on behalf of the firm with a faith that managers will reciprocate by investing in new capacity-enhancing technologies and new products that will produce jobs and income.[1] But exhortation to cooperate in a context of managerial authority has the form of a confidence game and is subject to the degenerative dynamics of disenchantment and distrust, which vitiate gains from cooperation and lead to outcomes that are worse than the initial adversarial relationships. Cooperative forms of industrial government depend on trust that is established by a symmetry of power among the participants.[2]

What the language of games makes evident is the importance of the rules that are the foundation of competition. Different rules in different regions of the world enable workers, unions, and firms to play different competitive games. That is, the very constitution of competition depends on governing arrangements based on a distribution of rights to decide questions of investment, industry organization, work design and product market strategy. Setting up and maintaining such forms of decision making may involve conflict and the ability to apply sanctions on recalcitrant players.

Then, at the turn-of-the-century, the transformation of the economy was accompanied by wide-ranging debates about the nature of the new competition and how work should be linked to the broader society. Various stripes of liberals, conservatives, and socialists agreed that many choices and decisions had to be made by many people in order that "our foundations (shall be) well laid." Should the United States forsake its historic protectionism for free trade? What should be the basis of American competitive advantage? How should labor be regulated? How should corporations be regulated? What value should attach to the production knowledge of craft workers and entrepreneurs? What are appropriate goals for public agencies? Which aspects of labor market organization should the government be involved in and which aspects should be left to the discretion of private organizations and to local governments?

By the 1920s a new industrial order had been established based on substantial self-regulation by the leaders of integrated manufacturing corporations within a protected domestic market. But rather than ascribe this outcome as a necessary response to technological change or economic incentives grounded in economies of scale, as in standard histories, this chapter takes turn-of-the-century heterodoxy seriously and reconceives the new corporate order as an outcome of political conflicts among groups with diverse visions of work and authority. The new industrial order was constituted by the settlement of a variety of conflicts through the enforcement of existing rules and creation of new rules that distributed authority to specific groups, which empowered them to try to put their visions of work into practice.

One critical piece of the industrial order that was transformed was the labor market, which was broadly conceived to include "industrial relations," "personnel management," education and training, immigration and citizenship. At the end of the nineteenth century, the allocation of labor was haphazard among cities, industries, and occupations; most commonly, employers tracked the labor force by supposed ethnic and racial qualities.[3] The organization of production, in contrast, was through "cooperation" between industrial capitalists and craft workers, in ways more fully discussed below. But at the same time, widespread interest emerged in the systematic organization of work and hence in the regulation of labor allocation among firms and within them. Over the course of twenty years, the working classes became part of a new regimen of unskilled labor, mechanical control of work, and corporate hierarchy. In the managerialist rendition of history, mass production technologies caused the demobilization of skilled workers.[4] The great corporations' huge investments in the new technologies required new bureaucratic forms of business organization and techniques of market control. Mass production entailed a high degree of division of labor. Jobs were minutely divided into simple tasks and intensely studied according to scientific management techniques to squeeze out wasted motions and seconds and to enable machines to substitute for human labor. Jobs were linked mechanically and planning tasks were removed to new professional staffs.

And yet, the evidence about the specific transformations of the labor market presents a picture of the extension and recomposition of the division of labor, not its wholesale split between conception and execution, and regional and industry variations on the relationship between firms and society.[5] In fact, even the large firms were surrounded by a sea of competitive economic organizations that provided critical supports to the integrated companies. Moreover, after a short time (before the World War I) during which traditional craft methods were destroyed, the number of skilled workers in manufacturing steadily increased; even the proportion of skilled workers inched up in the 1920s. Few employers adopted the new doctrines of scientific management until the 1920s, and then it was the very largest employers who did so. The evidence suggests that the new control over work that factory managers gained was shaped by political struggles for the right to decide what competitive game to play.

Another producerist world of possibility coexisted in those years, associated historically with a very diverse range of individuals, unions, and firms. In this alternative ideal, traditional methods of production are transformed, and yet workers and managers remain collaborators at work. And, though workers and managers continue to have conflicts, industry-wide collective bargaining and public mediation/arbitration are the preferred means to settle them. Unions in the alternative industrial order also are the representatives of shop-floor interests and agents of local problem-solving and consent. Scientific management is a tool used to gain efficiencies through the analysis of operations and the prevention of error rather than discretion. Firms focus attention on product quality and process technologies as the means of competition.

Now, the outcome in the 1920s was closer to the first managerialist world—though in fact a mixed picture—but in the 1930s it was closer to the second. What needs explaining is: what structured the situations in which individuals were making decisions about what to do as well as what they thought and did, that led the industrial order from an approximation of one into an approximation of the other. The rest of the chapter focuses on the transformation of the labor market in Detroit with comparisons to two other industrial regions centered in Chicago and Milwaukee. Detroit, Chicago, and Milwaukee provide critical evidence for an explanation that emphasizes not technology and culture, but politics and ideology, of the outcomes that emerged by the 1920s. All three were boom towns of the industrializing era. But Detroit became a progressive Republican showcase and a bastion of the open shop and nonpartisan government, while Chicago remained a partisan and union city, and Milwaukee developed a Socialist-trade union coalition that experimented with public regulation.

Structuring the Labor Market

The capitalist economy was multiform, but not everything was possible. At least part of the pattern of industrial order that emerged was structured precisely by productive and commercial technique, constitutional forms, electoral rules of the game, and traditions of political organization; and yet these are all undergoing change in this era. Another part of the pattern is that the specific outcomes were determined by contingent factors of the ideas that were employed and by the diverse political conditions in which individuals and groups competed for the authority to shape work.

The structures are a useful place to start. One of the defining qualities of turn-of-the-century American life was the combination of several processes of change: economic growth, industrial transformation, urbanization, and political realignment. After Reconstruction, the United States and, especially, the northern states underwent rapid industrial growth, led by metalworking manufacturing. By the turn-of-the-century, a metropole had been knit together into a huge national marketplace, spanning from the north Atlantic coast, west to the Mississippi, and north of the Ohio River, and bound by ties of commerce and politics. Milwaukee, Chicago, and Detroit each were powerhouses of metropolitan development. The population of Milwaukee grew from 115,587 in 1880, to 373,857 in 1910. In 1880, the city was 40 percent foreign born; in 1910, the city was 78.6 percent foreign stock, mostly German and Polish, but with significant Italian and central European nationalities, as well. The city's economy was transformed during these decades from the largest flour milling center in the country to a major food processor, iron and steel maker, and machinery producer, its largest industry in 1900 in value of products. The largest employer, Allis-Chalmers, was a home grown success story of a metalworking producer that competed nationwide. Its engines powered the New York City subway system. In other respects, Milwaukee industry was closely tied to New York and Chicago business interests. U.S. Steel was formed in part from Milwaukee companies; U.S. Steel's Judge Gary was on the board of Allis-Chalmers; Milwaukee Harvester became part of International Harvester; the Morgan bank was the syndicate leader for financing some of the city's major industrial firms; ownership of the city's street railways and utilities was consolidated in 1894 by a single

New York based investment trust. Half of Milwaukee workers were employed in manufacturing in 1910.[6]

Chicago experienced even more explosive growth in population, expanding from 503,298 people in 1880, to 2.4 million in 1915. Like Milwaukee, Chicago was 40 percent foreign born in 1880 and 77.5 percent first- and second-generation American in 1910, with large German, Polish, and Irish communities. A bigger economy than Milwaukee, Chicago, nonetheless, was dominated by manufacturing. Chicago was a formidably unionized city at the turn-of-the-century, challenging London for the title of union capital.[7] Detroit more than tripled in size in 30 years from 116,340 in 1880, to 375,000 people in 1910 and then doubled in ten years to 793,000 in 1920. The city was 74 percent first- and second generation American in 1920. Also, there was a sizable southern American population, including over 40,000 black residents. Even before the automobile, Detroit was a major metalworking and machinery center; while its population was increasing 2.5 times from 1880 to 1900, the number of workers in manufacturing increased 10 times. As the automobile market expanded, over 130,000 new jobs were created in the auto plants alone between 1900 and 1920. The city was intensely working class: 71.3 percent of the city's labor force was nonsupervisory wage workers in 1917.[8]

Crucially important is that industrial growth was accompanied by industrial transformation and political change. The craft-based system of manufacturing that was predominant in the mid-nineteenth century went into crisis at the end of the century as interregional markets were created for consumer products and producer goods, which increased competition among firms. The responses of firm owners and skilled machinists and other manufacturing craft workers were diverse but, from hindsight, the pattern that became dominant was based on managerial strategies to consolidate production in new large corporations, standardize and specialize products and to reorganize the labor process to accomplish these goals. Such managerial initiative not only disrupted traditional forms of work, but challenged traditional ideas about the appropriate roles of skilled workers and managers in the factory and society.[9]

Metalworking firms typically had been small and produced short runs of products, changing products or product designs to fit specific customer needs. Custom work placed the firm in close association with customers and helped ensure markets. Custom work also made employers dependent on their skilled workers whose broad knowledge could adapt experience to new products. Even the companies that produced high volumes of consumer products relied on craftsmen to fit and finish goods. Many producer-goods firms practiced inside contracting whereby employers would contract with a skilled workman or craft organization, letting the craftsmen determine the methods and organization of work and even the hiring and pay policies for the less skilled. In turn, skilled machinists were highly mobile among businesses, a practice that they saw as crucial to ensuring the broad training that could not be had in one firm alone and to gaining wage increases. The machinist was the organizer and innovator in the labor process and machinists' pride of workmanship grounded an ideology of republican producerism that characterized the AFL: participation and self-determination at work was a critical complement to republican government.[10] However, these conditions began rapidly to change. As manufacturers perceived the opportunities of expanded, nation-wide consumer goods markets for sewing machines, clocks and watches, and bicycles, and for agricultural machinery and producer goods, they standardized machine designs to enable large scale production.[11] Use of dedicated equipment and standardization of products, though costly, could be made feasible by expanded sales and by economies gained from further divisions of labor. Employers could employ unskilled labor to operate machines that produced parts and substitute managerial control of the labor process for inside contracting.

The tremendous growth of the automobile companies in the second decade of the century presented the clearest case of work innovation. The Ford Motor Company became the model example. Beginning in 1908 with the Model T, it produced just one product, and its machine tools were highly dedicated to particular tasks, "making a single cut on a single part and capable of doing nothing else."[12] Still, in 1910 some three-quarters of all auto employees were "skilled." But the development of mass production technologies in 1913 eliminated craft workers from the assembly of automobiles by building precision into parts production. Skilled workers were still critical; it was their job to keep the highly mechanical process going and to maintain its precision. As automobile production and sales rapidly multiplied, Ford and other employers had a continuing need for highly skilled craftsmen who were able to work on nonstandard problems. At the same time, more extensive markets brought greater instability for individual firms who were heavily invested in particular products and dedicated production technologies. Thus, most auto companies still focused on product design and assembly and subcontracted substantial portions of parts production to the metalworking supplier firms that clustered around them. Machine tool and machinery companies and specialty tool and die firms and their manufacturing craft employees provided crucial flexibility for the larger companies.[13] They also began to take great interest in gaining public policy supports for their new organizations.

Craftsmen increasingly perceived the new work organization as a loss of control and sought to negotiate their way through the changes. They began to unionize in greater numbers at the turn-of-the-century and such craft unions as the Iron Molders, Boilermakers, Patternmakers, Metal Polishers, Typographers, and the International Association of Machinists (IAM) challenged manufacturers across a broad range of issues. Some craft unions began to broaden their conception of the jobs and skills that members should have and to include the less skilled machine operators and others who worked in the new workplaces. AFL leaders began to negotiate national "trade agreements" with employers' associations as some business and political leaders came to believe that peaceful adjustments were the prudent course to take. Thus, President Roosevelt personally intervened in the 1902 anthracite coal strike to convince employers to settle with the United Mine Workers' union (UMW).[14] The United States was rapidly becoming a wealthy country, but if American firms were going to compete successfully abroad with high-quality European products, they were going to have give more systematic attention to labor management.

In metalworking, IAM strikes in Detroit, Chicago, Milwaukee, and other midwest industrial centers in 1900 led to the national Murray Hill trade agreement between the IAM and representatives of the National Metal Trades Association (NMTA), a new organization of metalworking employers that was brought to the negotiations by the National Civic Federation, an association of business leaders from the nation's largest firms who hoped to gain labor's consent to the new workplace.[15] Craft workers sought to gain the closed shop, a shorter work day, to slow down the introduction of new machinery that deskilled labor, and to control the use of unskilled "handymen," gain seniority for layoffs, revive apprenticeship traditions, end piece work, and raise wages. The NMTA agreed to a nine-hour day, no discrimination against union members in hiring (though it rejected the closed shop), and national arbitration of wages, apprenticeship rules, seniority, and other grievances in exchange for IAM commitments to scrupulously adhere to contracts, disavow sympathy strikes, and agree not to interfere with management plans to increase production. The national agreement broke down the very next year after little was accomplished through arbitration. Local unionists and employers began to take direct action, spawning bitter conflicts virtually everywhere in manufacturing for the next twenty years.

In many of these industrial conflicts, workers and managers (and other groups outside of manufacturing, such as retailers, publishers, women's associations, churches, and reform clubs) directly sought the intervention of public officials to support their claims for rights in, and authority to, decide about the labor market. The American constitutional framework presented serious hurdles for those who desired concerted federal government action on emerging issues of national scope, such as monopoly power, working conditions, and corporate finance.[16] The governmental system was designed to frustrate easy majority control of public power by the separation and division of powers. The institutional structure was conducive to "parochial" vetoes and to extensive bargaining and localist deals to implement national policy. State and city officials had influence over the labor market in many ways, and they had already moved to establish authority to inspect factories for safety, health, and other conditions of work, including hours of work and the age and gender of the work force; to provide "relief" for the unemployed as well as job-search services through public employment bureaus; they controlled the police and local courts, which could have a decisive influence on the course of strikes; to expand the school population and extend the curriculum; and to adopt personnel policies for their own employees. However, the existence of state governments with local regulatory authority, but increasingly porous economic boundaries, was conducive to "lowest common denominator" standards. Moreover, the court systems provided an avenue for aggrieved parties to press traditional rights against any policy alliance that might be established. In fact, state and federal judges persistently decided that voluntary agreements by firms and unions to establish conditions of competition were unenforceable and illegal.

The two major American political parties had grown up with this structure: both were highly localistic in organization and oriented toward the integration of cultural subcommunities.[17] State and local party leaders kept control of nominations, managed campaigns, and turned out the vote. The fruit of electoral success was rarely "regulative" policy, but more often patronage and protection of local interests which, significantly, included the traditions of the ethnoreligious communities that constituted the electoral coalitions at the state and national levels. "Horizontal" class interests were swept into, and broken up on, the shoals of the "vertical" social composition of the two major parties. The salience of the ethnoreligious communities contributed to the intensity and extensiveness of electoral campaigns and the parties' success at mobilizing a high percentage of the electorate to turn out and vote.

Thus, industrial cities such as Detroit, Chicago, and Milwaukee were competitive between the Republican and Democratic parties after Reconstruction, though each more often than not found itself a Democratic bastion, locally at odds with a rural- and Republican-controlled state government that insisted on limiting urban home rule. The local Democratic parties were unexceptionally ethnocultural and patronage oriented. In Milwaukee, the Democratic and Republican parties vied to fashion ethnically competitive local election lists, to appeal to the "swing" Polish vote, and support local determination of the language in public schools; and otherwise pursued a minimalist program of public services and fiscal retrenchment. The Democratic mayoral victor in 1898 was notably successful after attacking civil service and engaging in patronage-style politics with the police and fire departments and with road paving and traction companies.[18] Similarly, Chicago politics in the 1880s and 1890s was patronage oriented and periodically rocked by scandalous revelations of sweetheart deals between utility companies and city hall. "Chicago politics was a bipartisan jungle of rival bosses and factions." The Democratic Party followed a policy of retrenchment in the 1890s, but held onto city hall through ethnic appeals, personalistic followings of ward leaders and saloonkeeper-politicians, and through "decidedly broad-minded views on gambling, liquor and prostitution."[19] Detroit was a Democratic city. In contrast to the "out-state" voters, Detroit had voted against every Republican presidential candidate except two between 1868 and the 1890s and had voted for every Democratic gubernatorial candidate except one since 1854. Democratic leaders constructed victories on the bedrock of antitemperance and on an ethnically crafted slate of candidates that appealed to the large foreign-born population. Germans and the Irish competed to control the spoils of office while saloonkeepers and liquor dealers financed the organization.[20]

Despite the institutional structure, changes in work and society were the occasion for political change. The 1896 national critical electoral realignment decisively turned momentum toward the transformation of historical partisan coalitions and linkages and opened new possibilities for policy alliances. One of the consequences of the 1896 national election between Republican William McKinley and Democrat-Populist fusion candidate William Jennings Bryan was a Republican swath cut across northern electoral districts; the Democratic party practically ceased to exist in presidential elections throughout much of the metropole industrial northeast and north-central states. In 1896, all three cities became "aligned" with the Republican party at the national level. Except that Detroit and Chicago voted for Theodore Roosevelt on the Progressive ticket in 1912 and Milwaukee for Wilson in 1916, the cities became reliably Republican. The breakup of the "vertical" or "island community" based electoral coalitions by national economic integration was, by most accounts, followed by coalition formation based on functional economic lines (still with an important sectional quality to it). But that only meant a new set of alternatives from which real people had to choose. Nation, occupation, class, industry, and/or interest group all are categories consistent with the general trend. The choices that people made were part of the process of creating a new industrial order.

Work and Politics in Detroit

It is in Detroit that changes in the technical organization of work appear to drive political change. Yet the defeat of craft unionism at work that is so closely associated with the introduction of mass-production technologies occurred in the wake of their political demobilization in the city. Detroit stands out from the other cases for the thoroughness with which this double demobilization was accomplished. The specific connections between what is going on in the labor market and the electoral market are mediated by employer and labor strategies and local political conditions. By the 1920s, Detroit's employers established virtually complete control over the city, but they created an industrial order that proved wholly unstable a short decade later.

In the wake of the collapse of the Murray Hill agreement, the employers' drive to gain the authority to reorganize work led to an open-shop campaign whose goals were to defeat striking craft unionists and rid their plants of union organizations. The campaign was spearheaded by the Detroit Metal Trades' Association, the Detroit Founders' Association, and the Detroit Brass Manufacturers' Association, which joined together in 1902 to form the Employers' Association of Detroit (EAD). The cofounder of the EAD was one of the strongest personalities among Detroit industrialists, Henry Leland, a successful machine tool builder and founder of the Cadillac Motor Company. By 1905–1906, the EAD had largely tamed the AFL unions by blacklisting unionists and gaining the assistance of local police and judges to break strikes.[21] But employers then began to turn the EAD's sights on new aspects of the labor problem. Indeed, the apparent victory of the open-shop drive was in some respects more than they bargained for. The employers now were in control of the workplace which they were in the process of transforming. But three problems were associated with this. First was discipline: workers did not like the intensified pace and supervision of the new factory. There was enormous turnover for years; at Ford in 1913, 52,445 men were hired to maintain a work force of 13,632.[22] Employers believed that this problem extended beyond the factory to the kind of society that Detroit was becoming. Immigrants and working-class radicals were recalcitrant. Second was wages: the great increase in automobile industry demand for labor meant that a worker could quit a job with one employer and easily get a new one somewhere else. Unless employers collaborated to establish a new mechanism of wage setting, the free labor market was leading to upward pressure on wage rates. This circumstance also made it more difficult to maintain discipline. Third was the fact that employers had a continuing and increasing need for skilled labor but no ready source of supply. Thus, even after the craft unions had been routed, EAD leaders continued concerted efforts to manage the labor market. They established a Labor Bureau, a Trade School, and a political action association known as the Civic Uplift League.

The EAD's Labor Bureau quickly established itself as a prime regulator of labor allocation among member firms, including maintaining the blacklist, the stabilizer of wage rates, and the recruiter of labor to Detroit. The bureau accumulated referrals on some 585,551 workers from 1902 to 1925. The bureau's success at wage stabilization can be gauged by Henry Ford's January 1914 decision to pay qualified employees $5 a day, more than double the going rate. Ford had already broken with the EAD over labor allocation, and, thus, his wage policy further shocked local employers, but Ford judged that wages were too low to gain employee consent and stabilize working-class families. Few employers followed his example.[23]

To replace union-based sources of skilled labor, the EAD set up a Trade School in cooperation with the Detroit Builders' Association. Initially, the school was part of the open-shop strategy developed by the National Association of Manufacturers (NAM). But in 1909, when the EAD gave up direction of the school to the YMCA (Young Men's Christian Association), a role played by the YMCA nationwide, EAD leaders had wanted to expand training because they really needed some mechanism to replace the craft workers who historically had served a double role as experts in production and teachers of the next generation. The activist companies, however, had decided to cutback their plans to build and equip a new school because most employers were simply "poaching" skilled labor from each other. The EAD warned Detroit employers of the "menace impending" if firms did not train skilled workers and it urged members to show "esprit de corps." The EAD went beyond exhortation in 1910 and established an Automobile and Accessories Division of more than sixty members, led by Leland, Emil Moessner (Briscoe Manufacturing), Howard Coffin (Hudson Motors), and Hugh Chalmers (Chalmers Motor Company), that directed businessmen in over a year of discussions on apprenticeship and training.[24]

All employers not only had an obligation to concern themselves with their particular businesses, believed Leland and R. B. Weaver (Timken-Detroit Axle Company and the chair of the Automobile and Accessories Division in 1911), but a responsibility to help create the new industrial society being formed. The Division's first meeting was devoted to the training and discipline of machine tool operatives, the new social unit of the factory system. At this meeting, Weaver declared that "[t]he very first thing we have to consider is what constitutes a machine operator."[25] Weaver proposed that the operator's job should include, not only the ability to produce a high volume of high quality parts, but knowledge of the construction of the machine, machine maintenance, and understanding of the principles of the technology to the extent that the operator would know the machine's capacity. Despite the name of the occupation, then, the machine tool operator's job was conceived as considerably broader than the popular image of mass production allows.

Leland urged members to broaden the scope of their vision to the creation of the next generation of labor. Apprenticeship "would be an ideal system" for raising the moral and skill levels of young people; he had served a machinist apprenticeship himself in Massachusetts at a textile machinery maker and worked as a young man at the Springfield Armory and at Brown and Sharpe. His company had an apprentice program. Already, division leaders had investigated the German school system, and many were convinced that it was a critical element of Germany's competitive challenge. H. W. Hoyt of Great Lakes Engineering argued that "we shall be shut out of the markets in the foreign countries unless we make the master workman. . . . If we are going to compete we must have our foundations well laid." To accomplish this, said Leland, the employers had to be organized on the industrial front to defeat unions and radicals preaching "class hatred" and in politics to change "the vicious legislation in our city, state and national government" that blocked their path. Specifically, the EAD proposed that all employers agree to train apprentices and that the public schools recruit students and use tax revenue to subsidize the classroom part of the training.[26]

Leland already was the chief financial backer, with Joseph L. Hudson (Hudson Department stores) and Richard H. Fyfe (a shoe manufacturer), of the Detroit Municipal League, founded in 1902, and he now promoted its successor organization, the Civic Uplift League.[27] The Detroit Municipal League collapsed in 1912 over the issue of municipal ownership of the street railways, with some members opposing it (such as Leland and Hudson) and others in favor (such as James E. Scripps, owner of the Scripps Motor Company and the *Detroit News*). But Leland provided the financial support for the Civic Uplift League (CUL), established the same year. The CUL was organized through existing evangelical Protestant churches and men's clubs in the city. It shared the evangelical movements' attraction to the social gospel of Walter Rauschenbusch, and it led local campaigns against saloons and dance halls. Although its exclusively pietist Protestant membership seemed destined to limit the CUL's appeal to the German Lutheran and, increasingly, Catholic population of Detroit, partly for that reason Detroit's political struggles continued to have a cultural cast to them. Of course, CUL members already had social and economic position to push their agenda. It numbered among its active leadership some of the most prominent employers in town, including Joseph Boyer (president of Burroughs Adding Machine Company), S.S. Kresge (president of Kresge Department Stores and an activist in the Anti-Saloon League), James Vernor (president of Vernor's, a leading soft-drink maker and an ardent "dry"), Frederick Gilbert, and C. W. Dickerson (both of Timken-Detroit Axle Company), and it gained support of some thirty-five other manufacturers, including executives at Ford, Studebaker, and Packard. The CUL and EAD went on to wage successful campaigns for trade education in the public schools and "businesslike" city government.

Employers sought to clear their path and gain new "rights of way" to keep it clear. Education and training were critical to the new labor market they were creating, touching as they did on the skills that individuals acquired and hence their economic autonomy, the age at which children left the schoolhouse for a lifetime of work, the responsiveness of a public institution to all citizens, and the role of schools in fostering good citizenship. Thus, Michigan's mandatory age of schooling had been raised to sixteen; apprenticeships, historically, began as early as age twelve, and employers did indeed want to start workers before the legal age of school leaving. The EAD was successful at gaining revision of state law to allow under-age boys and girls to leave school for apprenticeships with the permission of the Detroit school superintendent. In fact, to make apprenticeships more appealing, employers advocated further raising the mandatory school age, so that only by entering an apprenticeship could young people get out of school.[28]

But there were still other problems. There were legal risks for employers who made apprentice agreements with boys (and sometimes girls) under the age of legal adulthood, as Cadillac and other companies quickly discovered. An apprentice agreement had the standing of a contract between employer and employee (and his or her parents or guardian) and, according to Michigan law, its supervision was the province of the local probate court. In particular, the court had the final say on whether employers could fire apprentices. When Cadillac tried to dismiss some young workers, the apprentices and their parents sued the company for damages. This led Cadillac to switch to making only verbal agreements with its apprentices, whom it began to call "employees in the Instruction Department." The EAD's Apprentice Committee prepared a model apprentice agreement for other employers to help them avoid Cadillac's legal entanglements. Yet another problem was Michigan's workman's compensation law, one part of which prohibited boys under eighteen from working in hazardous occupations. Employers were held liable when young workers were injured. The EAD joined the Michigan Manufacturers' Association to win revision of the law to specifically remove the machinist trade from the list of hazardous occupations.[29]

After winning changes in state laws to entitle employers to direct apprentice training, Detroit manufacturers then sought to enlist the school board and city government. This proved more difficult than dealing with the Republican-dominated state legislature. By this time, many people apart from employers were actively involved in various local and national movements for social reform, and the employers' vision seemed to many wholly self-serving. The schools were under increasing pressures to expand their services and to provide education efficiently. A higher age of mandatory schooling plus the great increase in urban populations required a huge expansion of school construction and personnel as well as the taxes to pay for them. The employers and their representatives, including the National Association of Manufacturers and its allied organization, the National Society for the Promotion of Industrial Education (NSPIE), entered the national debates about schools to advocate, not only support for trade education, but for a low-cost, discipline-oriented program for the children of immigrants who would fill manufacturers' needs for unskilled labor. Traditional liberal arts programs were still alright for the middle-class, but any expectation that more than a few could aspire to occupations that afforded opportunities for self-direction, they argued, were bound to create social conflict when young people discovered how work was now being conducted. In contrast, many middle class reformers and educators, including John Dewey, supported adding vocational curricula to the traditional liberal arts in the public high schools with the goal of extending the years of schooling and broadening the scope of citizenship for everyone. Nationally, the Congress passed the Smith-Hughes Act in 1917, which extended federal technical and financial aid to local communities for vocational education programs that would be controlled by local school authorities. A few communities had local groups prepared to take advantage of the program, but in most places vocational education programs suffered from being disconnected from workplaces.[30] By 1917, Detroit employers and educators already had agreed to include industrial education programs and to create "technical high schools." The real weakness of the employer-sponsored policy in Detroit was that employer participation was voluntary and, calculating rationally under these conditions, most did not participate. This, in turn, became a further condition of competition: a low-skill industrial order that was not prepared to compete with European producers.[31]

The opposition to the employers' two-pronged campaign was fragmented and, as it turned out, not very effective in Detroit. AFL leaders were clear about the connection between the emerging workplace and the broader society: "We want the education in our schools not to be over-specialized. We want the knowledge to be broad enough to develop leadership. We believe that the problem is not only one for the school. We find that industry likewise needs to be regulated and that the industries must be shaped to meet the requirements of the youth and of the man."[32] But the open-shop drive in Detroit had seriously weakened the craft unions at work. In addition, they had little political leverage to resist the employers' use of government authority or to create a role for themselves in the new programs because they had no political party base. In the 1890s, the Detroit AFL and the Knights of Labor had united against their erstwhile Democratic allies to endorse a reform Republican, Hazen Pingree, for mayor. Indeed, Pingree was a maverick political leader. Drafted for the mayoralty from his successful shoe manufacturing business by local Republican leaders in 1889, Pingree ran an unusual campaign that appealed to immigrants and openly courted organized labor. Soon his mayoral administration alienated his upper-class cohorts, but Pingree deftly consolidated his organizational base and gained the joint nominations for reelection from the Republicans, Populists, and Socialist Labor party. During his terms in office (1890–1897), Pingree developed a national reputation as a champion of the eight-hour-day, municipal unionism, school board accountability to parents, city ownership of utilities, an urban version of the Populists' subtreasury plan, and opposition to the national Republican party's imperialism. He refused employer requests to call in the state militia and to use local police to break strikes. He was an advocate of arbitration of industrial disputes and called on employers to maintain full employment. Pingree went on to become governor of Michigan, but died in 1901.[33]

An immediate political consequence of the end of Pingreeism was that it left the labor movement politically bereft. Even before his death, the Republican party virtually repudiated its standard bearer and, in fact, gained state legislative prohibition against fusion tickets to prevent Populists and Socialists from jointly nominating him. Local party leaders were glad to be rid of him when he became governor, although they had to bring court proceedings against Pingree to force him to relinquish the mayoralty after he was elected to the state executive. With Pingree gone, the major parties split into factions devoted to patronage and cultural warfare. The Democratic party was devoted to patronage and the defense of Lutheran and Catholic ethnic subcommunities against pietistic social reform backed by Protestant employers and Republican factions. It had no objection to antiunionism; in fact, one the leading Democratic law firms managed the EAD's open-shop drive. On the other hand, local Democrats opposed reforms that would undermine their control of public resources, which led them not only to manipulate popular issues like municipal ownership of the street railways, but to oppose many employer-backed reforms, such as expansion of night school.[34]

Rather than find a new partisan base to sustain broad working-class unity, Detroit craft unionists began to fight among themselves to protect historical occupational turf. The IAM and eight other unions challenged the legitimacy of an old affiliate of the Knights of Labor, the International Union of Carriage and Wagon Workers, which had since joined the AFL and changed its name to the Union of Carriage, Wagon and Automobile Workers, reflecting its intention to organize broadly on an industrial basis. Its leadership supported the new Socialist party, and its membership numbered several thousand just before World War I. But because it drew members from the constituencies of the craft unions, the unions sought sanctions against it from the national AFL. Finally, after many years of conflict, in 1918 the AFL ousted the Auto Workers Union; the union collapsed when, after the war, the Wilson administration refused to continue its policy of requiring employers to bargain with workers' representatives.[35]

In the meantime, the largest companies became impatient with continuing policy conflicts and began to act unilaterally. Ford's introduction of the moving assembly line as part of the innovation of mass production removed the need for skilled workers in assembly operations, but Ford still conceived mass production as requiring very precise mechanical operations. The company established an elaborate training system at its Highland Park and Dearborn plants in suburban Detroit. Ford created the Henry Ford Trade School to provide practical training in the classroom and shop for boys aged twelve to eighteen—originally the boys selected were orphans—and the company established an apprenticeship school in 1915.[36] Leland, at Cadillac, and then at his new company, Lincoln, was famous for demanding high precision work. Cadillac, General Motors, Burroughs, Packard, and other companies also established their own schools. But now companies increasingly began to adjust to the new conditions. Thus, after Ford bought Lincoln at the end of the war, to compete with Cadillac, now owned by General Motors (GM), he insisted that Leland should be less demanding of precision. At GM Alfred P. Sloan explained later that the company drove to simplify jobs because there was a dearth of skilled workers.

There were still problems with unskilled work. At first it had seemed that the technical reorganization of work associated with the moving assembly line would solve the discipline problem through machine pacing and, thus, ensure high productivity. But this was not so; at Ford, productivity did not greatly increase. Workers rebelled against the new factory regimen, reflected in huge rates of turnover. In addition, the cultural and language heterogeneity of the work force—some 71 percent of which was foreign born at Ford in 1914—quickly loomed as a major problem for the highly specialized and integrated new system of production that required precise coordination of the human beings still doing the work. Ford pioneered the introduction of "welfare services" for employees through its Sociology Department and Ford's premium wages were paid only to those workers whose homelives, upon inspection by company social workers, proved they were sober, thrifty, and Christian. But few other employers followed Ford's lead. Instead, Detroit employers launched new campaigns to control public affairs and instill factory workers with their obligations to employers.[37]

To gain control over local public policy, CUL organized to decisively defeat the remaining partisan forces. It turned its attention to structural reform of city government: to make elections nonpartisan and abolish the precinct electoral districts, to reduce the number of alderman and have them elected at-large, to increase the power of the mayor, and to separate the dates of local elections from state and federal elections. A City Charter proposal in 1914 included all the suggestions of the league, but voters decisively rejected it. Then the league turned its sights on the precinct organizations and called in the friendly state government to investigate vote fraud, the outcome of which was to crush them in advance of the next charter referendum in 1917. Then employers such as Ford, Packard, Studebaker, and Cadillac mobilized their own "machines" by urging employees to vote for the charter proposal. Standing against the new charter was the greatly weakened AFL; the Democratic party split. In a light turnout (about 36.9%), the new charter was approved.[38]

The final element of the new industrial order was the enlistment of the public schools to teach children and adult employees the English language and dutiful behavior ("I hear the whistle; I must hurry" one English lesson went). Americanization was anoth-

er means of closing the door against new threats from the demobi-
lized mass parties and divided labor movement. Educators were
won over to the employers' goals once labor discipline was rede-
fined as patriotism. Beginning in 1915, public school authorities
collaborated with the EAD, the Detroit Board of Commerce, Ford,
and leaders of the Civic League to aggressively promote language
training and obedience to create a united American citizenry.[39]

Americanization became part of what was touted as the American Plan for industrial relations and it was clearly identified with
the Detroit experience.[40] The public role in regulating the labor
market was reoriented to the "external" labor market while employers gained new control over work in the "internal" labor
market in their factories, an apparently typical pattern of the
managerialist 1920s. Ethnoreligious conflicts remained the basis of
electoral organization, worker and voter participation were low,
and the government was in safe hands. But these outcomes were
more contingent than part of a logic of industrial development, as
comparison with Chicago and Milwaukee makes evident.

Chicago

In Chicago, political developments took a different turn. The
city government was not "reformed"; the party machines retained
control of the government and continued to turn out voters. The
open-shop movement was blunted, except at some of the largest
factories, in part because of popular support for unions and labor's
loose alliance with social workers, the women's movement, and
educators. Moreover, the concerted attempt by the Illinois Manufacturers' Association to introduce a state-wide vocational-education system was defeated by an alliance of teachers and craft
unionists and a Democratic governor. Ultimately, however, neither
political party supported organized labor's movement to unionize
the city's mass production industries while union leaders, themselves, were divided about the wisdom of launching their own
electoral organization.

The collapse of the Murray Hill agreement in 1901 was followed, in Chicago, by widespread sympathy strikes among the
city's enormous union population. Unlike Detroit, where the craft

unions struggled separately, in Chicago strong shop committees of rank and file workers united the crafts and gained the strategic support of the unskilled teamsters. They even won shorter hours and the union shop in large scale firms in meatpacking and at International Harvester and Pullman. Although the latter companies were lost to the unions in a coordinated employer counterattack organized by the local chapter of the National Metal Trades Association in 1904, Chicago unions still had contracts with more than four hundred companies in 1905. The comparative success of labor in fending-off the first open-shop campaign is partly a consequence of the position of local public officials who were prolabor, another contrast with Detroit. Strikers received protection from local police and courts, which generally refused to run interference for employers on issues of "trespass, traffic obstruction, disorderly conduct and riot."[41] Moreover, organized labor found allies among the various women's clubs and associations, in part because of the notoriously poor working conditions for female employees at major companies, including International Harvester.[42]

Chicago Democrats were Bryanites, yet another contrast with Detroit. Still operating in machine style on the basis of the city's ward organization of government, the Democratic party, nonetheless, included within it a wide range of 1890s reformers, such as former Governor Altgeld (who, however, lost a bid for the mayoral nomination in 1901) and Populist fusionists. Though the city gave Republican William McKinley 57 percent of the two-party vote in 1896, voters supported his reelection with just 50 percent of the total vote in 1900. Also, the Socialist party began to rapidly gain supporters, almost tripling its vote totals for mayor between 1901 and 1903 and doubling again in 1905. The party's 1904 presidential vote also swelled, multiplying eight times over 1900, to 11.8 percent of the vote, an outcome that shocked The *Chicago Daily Tribune*.[43] With pressure from the socialist left, the Democratic-Populist fusionists were able, with AFL support, to win the 1905 mayoral nomination for their candidate, the prominent radical Edward Dunne, on a platform of municipal ownership of the traction (street railway) system and education reform. In the final election, Dunne made a "class appeal" and gained the endorsement of the Chicago Federation of Labor (CFL).[44] His opponent was the "progressive" Republican John Harlan, endorsed by "corporate liberals" in groups such as the Civic Federation and the Municipal Voters League (MVL). Some twenty-five thousand more votes were cast in 1905 than in 1903, a tribute to Dunne's close relationship with the traditional ward leaders of the Democratic party.

Yet, once in office, Dunne made a series of tactical mistakes that made it impossible to consolidate the reformers' position in the Democratic party and gave the Republicans another opening. First, most of Dunne's appointments came from the ranks of the Municipal Ownership League and fusionist radicals, which attracted not only the partisan wrath of employers and the Republican party, but cooled Democratic party regulars. For example, to the City Corporation Counsel office, Dunne appointed Clarence Darrow and Glenn E. Plumb, closely associated with the AFL; and to the Public Works Department he appointed Joseph Medill Patterson, an upper-class reformer who insisted on enforcing civil service regulations and limiting patronage. Mayor Dunne also vacillated on municipal ownership and mishandled the prohibition issue. Elected by "wet" voters, Dunne, nonetheless, agreed to enforce the Sunday closing law (urged by the Sunday Closing League, among others) and to raise license fees for new saloons. Yet his actions not only alienated the antisaloon groups as too mild, but it created an opportunity for ward leaders to reassert the ethnoreligious themes with which they historically appealed to voters. One ambitious Democratic ward leader was Anton Cermak, who formed the United Societies for Local Self-Government, a very large multiethnic organization dedicated to protecting the right to drink and financed by the Liquor Dealers Association. This organization was instrumental in Dunne's defeat, in a reelection attempt in 1907, to Fred Busse, a life-long Republican politician and businessman, who had been appointed postmaster of Chicago in 1902 by President Roosevelt.[45]

The 1907 election was not the end of partisan competition in the city, although the radicals were increasingly marginalized. Mayor Busse, a Republican Party reformer, also was unable to navigate the shifting waters of city politics. He endorsed the Municipal League's city charter reform, which was hotly opposed by the Chicago Federation of Labor, the Teachers' Federation, the United Societies, and some middle-class groups, because it would not democratize control of the schools; ruled out municipal ownership of the traction system; reduced the size of the city council by half; and increased terms of office to four years. The charter proposal went down in a landslide defeat in a September 1907 referendum and stymied further structural reform until 1920.[46]

Also, Busse reunited labor and the Democratic party by immediately ousting twelve school board members appointed by Dunne, including "middle class reformers" Jane Addams, Louis Post, Raymond Robins, Cornelia Debey, and members of the CFL (John Sonsteby and John Harding) and the Chicago Teachers Federation. Together with the radicals, the labor members had begun a highly visible campaign to ensure that "labor and middle class people are better able to determine what is good for their children than the merchants club." One element of the campaign was to collect the full amount of corporation taxes owed the city in order to raise teachers' salaries. The new school policy brought on a crusade against the board from the *Tribune*. The dismissal of the board members was hailed by the *Tribune* as designed to "give control of the city school system into the hands of a board dominated by a practical and capable business element." The CFL saw it differently: Busse wanted to make the schools "a cog in the capitalistic machine, so that the children may reach manhood's estate content in a condition of abject servitude."[47] Greatly unpopular, Busse bowed out of the race in 1911 and reformer par excellence Charles Merriam carried the Republican label. On the Democratic side, Edward Dunne sought the nomination, but lost a very close primary to another former mayor, Carter Harrison, who then went on to defeat Merriam in the final. This was Harrison's last hurrah. First elected in 1897, he was an old-style "gentle reformer," (i.e., the consensus candidate who could hold the party together but not accomplish anything). In 1915, he lost the nomination of the party to Robert Sweitzer, the City Clerk, who then lost to the Republican insurgent William Thompson. Thompson was a complete opportunist, appealing to Progressive reformers and patronage politicians and to the antiwar sentiment of central European ethnics and to Irish nationalist anti-British feelings. He dominated Chicago politics for two decades as mayor 1915–1923 and 1927–1931.[48]

Thompson was consistently hostile to organized labor. He reactivated the police against strikers; refused to meet with Sidney Hillman, leader of the Amalgamated Clothing Workers Union,

whose support for rationalization of the Chicago clothing industry
and for industrial arbitration was already making him the champion of "new model unionism" in the United States; and joined the
business members of the board of education to wage a campaign
against the Chicago Teachers Federation and to begin an Americanization program.[49] Under the banner of making the public
schools more efficient, the Chicago Association of Commerce and
the Chicago Commercial Club sponsored a plan to make over first
the Chicago schools and then the entire state's system. Chicago's
employers had two needs, explained their spokesman Edwin G.
Cooley. First, the demands of expanding industry for unskilled
labor meant that the schools, which were experiencing great growth
in student populations as a result of immigration, should emphasize obedience, punctuality, and the "moral value" of hard work in
its curriculum. The traditional liberal arts high-school curriculum
could still be used for college-bound students of the middle class,
but a manual or vocational curriculum should be introduced for
those who "choose" to enter the labor force after age fourteen.
Second, because most employers needed skilled labor, the public
schools should lay the foundation for trade programs. These reforms (and related administrative changes) would not only make
the schools more socially efficient users of resources, but would
make citizens "individually efficient" by raising their earning power.[50]

Opposition to the employers' vocational education plan was
broad, persistent and successful. It was based on a republican
perception of how changes at work challenged historical concep-
tions of the role of education in American society. Although the AFL
initially opposed vocational education as all of a piece with the
deskilling of work, education reformers who disliked the employers' version successfully allied with organized labor to prevent the
subordination of education to the immediate needs of capitalists.
Matthew Woll, president of the Allied Printing Trades, one of the
strongest craft unions in Chicago, argued: "We believe that the
vocational studies ought to be part of our school system. While we
are in favor of that, yet we apprehend some degree of danger that
the studies in the school room may become too narrow or may
become over specialized as we find the industry itself."[51] The
Illinois State Federation of Labor (ISFL) commented after the defeat
of the vocational training bill in the state legislature in 1915: "It is

hoped that this will put a stop to the vicious attempt which has been made to destroy the democracy of the public schools, and that commercial interests and others who are trying to split the schools, create class distinctions and prevent proper education of children of working people will realize schools are held too sacred by working people to prevent misuse."[52]

This republican vision of the school was seconded by the Chicago Teachers' Federation (CTF), by leading educators such as John Dewey, and by prominent civic associations such as the City Club, which supported vocational training, but wanted educators to keep control over it, and which joined the CFL in calling for raising the age of mandatory education to sixteen. At the same time, the AFL supported tying vocational education to union-controlled apprenticeship programs by giving credit for public vocational-education courses.[53]

Despite the defeat of the separate vocational system, the state legislature, in 1917, approved another piece of the employers' and middle-class reformers' school agenda, namely centralized policy authority in the hands of the school superintendent. The Chicago Teachers Federation opposed this, favoring an elected school board (which voters had endorsed in two referenda years before, in 1902 and 1904). But because it was under additional legal pressure from Mayor Thompson, the business leaders, and the legislature to disband, it supported the reform in exchange for only the requirement that the CTF leave the AFL. The Chicago Federation of Labor and the Illinois federation became disenchanted with their new middle-class allies because they failed to protect the teachers' union and they stood on the sidelines during the ensuing struggle between Mayor Thompson and the reformers over the mayor's patronage-oriented approach to education. In the spring 1917 city council elections, Thompson waged a campaign against the middle-class reformers running for the council, including Merriam, and tied them to organized labor and the teachers' union.[54] However, this fight was not in fact organized labor's fight; turnout was very low and the reform councillors lost.

The Chicago labor movement was increasingly alienated from the two major parties at all levels of government. Yet, they believed that the Socialist party had reached the peak of its appeal to rank and file workers; the workers simply were put off by the socialist label. On the one hand, the Chicago Federation of Labor was frustrated by Chicago and Illinois political leaders who turned aside labor's legislative agenda. The state's courts continued to suppress strike actions, and implicitly support employers, and the u.s. Congress had passed the Lever Act to suppress the strike of the coalminers, an important group in the Illinois federation. They did not support Attorney General Palmer's repression of unionists and immigrants. On the other hand, the AFL had given strong support to Woodrow Wilson in 1916 and seemed to be gaining new respect in the larger political system as wartime rates of unionization mounted and the loyalty of unions was proved. The CFL had reorganized the city's "mass production" meatpacking industry under wartime conditions and had gained crucial support from Wilson's Mediation Commission in December 1917 in order to do so.[55] They decided to organize for more, both politically and industrially.

In 1918 the CFL requested that the Illinois Federation start an Independent Labor party in the state, modeled on the British experience but "adapted to American conditions." Some prominent Chicago labor leaders, such as Matthew Woll, however, were completely opposed to independent political action. Woll was part of the faction that controlled the national AFL executive council and that was adapting the AFL to new national political conditions in which the federation was playing the role of corporate representative of workers' interests. As such, the AFL leaders began to forsake their old republican producerist ideology. But the traditional view remained strong in Illinois, and the ISFL adopted a far-reaching "socialistic" program that included provisions on workers' rights, access to schools and nationalization of natural resources. At first the results were encouraging. In Chicago in the 1919 local elections, the Labor candidate received 54,467 votes, more than enough to claim the balance of power between the Democrats and Republicans, whose candidate, Thompson, won with a plurality of 17,600. The real comedown for the Labor party came just two years later, after industrial and political conditions had drastically changed in the city.[56]

At the same time that the ISFL had started the Labor Party, the CFL (with AFL support) launched one of the most ambitious unionizing campaigns in AFL history, the organization of the steel industry with its large ethnically polyglot, unskilled work force. They also began movements to unionize other big employers, including International Harvester. This was a test of whether old forms of unionism could be adapted to the emerging industrial order. The answer seemed to be yes: the Chicago unions formed a multiunion organizing committee that enrolled some quarter million steelworkers in Chicago and other steel centers. The steelmasters were adamantly opposed to recognizing the collective bargaining status of the steel union. Top AFL leaders appealed to the president's industrial relations conference, which was meeting to discuss postwar labor-management policies, to use the steel conflict to establish peaceful means to settle basic issues. But neither the conference nor the enfeebled president gave any clear indication of what should be agreed upon. The subsequent strikes in steel and at International Harvester were crushed in waves of Americanism and anti-red propaganda that changed the climate of public support for unions in Chicago. Whereas during a 1916 strike at International Harvester, the company had felt compelled to make concessions to the workers and to avoid militant tactics of strikebreaking, in 1919, the company joined its partners in steel to remake public opinion and break the strikes. The defeat of the steel strike undermined the basis for Labor party politics and for class (industrial) unionism until the 1930s. The workers' defeat was followed by U.S. Steel's adoption of Detroit-style personnel policies. International Harvester already was well into the new personnel management style, including establishing education classes "to win the loyalty of employees." Yet, unlike virtually the entire auto industry, Chicago firms established forms of employee representation which, while company dominated, modified management claims for dictatorial control and were sometimes able to gain improvements in working conditions.[57]

Milwaukee

Milwaukee politics presents several contrasts to Detroit and Chicago and some similarities. Though it was as ethnically diverse, an unusually committed and capable cadre of unionists and Socialists was able to knit together a union-party alliance early in the national realignment sequence. With the benefit of good timing and luck, the Milwaukee Socialists directed urban reform in the city in ways that prevented employers from successfully claiming sole authority to make economic decisions and that pioneered policies later adopted by the New Deal. At the same time, the Socialists were in some ways similar to reformers in other cities. They were committed to a "conservative" type of socialism that favored the technocratic management of public affairs in the public interest, but that did not deliver the government into the people's hands. Thus, although Milwaukee voters elected a Socialist mayor from 1916 to 1940, the working class generally was not directly empowered to participate at work or in society. The achievement was to raise labor standards and establish the authority of organized, skilled workers in manufacturing.

Voters in Milwaukee voted Republican at the presidential level. They had done so before 1896, but competition between the two parties had become keener as Blaine won with 49 percent of the vote in 1884, Harrison with 49 percent in 1888, and the Democrat Cleveland with 48 percent in 1892.[58] The balance had been held respectively by the Greenback, Union Labor, and People's parties, none of which, however, had been able to sustain a significant challenge to the major parties. However, Bryanism did not appeal to the city's voters: the Democrats gained just 41 percent of the vote in 1896 and 38 percent in 1900. On the other hand, the resolutely "metropolitan" Democratic presidential candidate in 1904 received just 26 percent. The collapse of the Democrats at the presidential level was not matched at the local level by Republican ascendancy, as in Detroit, nor by the rejuvenation of ethnoreligious-patronage party politics, as in Chicago. Instead, in a few short years just after the turn-of-the-century, Milwaukee developed thoroughly "modern" political parties that decisively cleaved the local electorate in ways that prevented the old conflicts from reemerging.

Industrial conditions in the city were similar to those in other metropolitan centers. The labor market was largely unregulated, although employers still stereotyped workers by their national origin, as they did elsewhere. In the late nineteenth century, manufacturers in such industries as iron and steel, meatpacking and brewing had beaten back craft unionists in the first wave of reorganization of the labor process. As Gerd Korman put it, "by the 1890s capital and labor had fought their battle and capital had won."[59] And when the Machinists countered with their campaign that led to the Murray Hill Agreement and the subsequent strikes, machinery firms formed the Milwaukee Metal Trades Association and established a private employment agency, the Milwaukee Metal Trades and Founders Bureau, to defeat them.[60] But this defeat was just the beginning of a continuing labor struggle to reassert some control over industry the outcome of which depended on the capacity of workers to organize themselves and the political conditions under which they struggled.

The Milwaukee labor movement in the 1890s was divided between German (e.g., the Brewery Workers Union) and non-German unions (the Amalgamated Association of Iron and Steel Workers and the Meatcutters) and between industrial (Brewery Workers) and craft organizations (Machinists and building-trades unions). However, the German-based unions and in particular the Brewery Workers were not organized on an exclusive basis; they supported the unionization of everyone, German and non-German (including blacks), skilled and unskilled. The Milwaukee Federated Trades Council (FTC), the local AFL affiliate, was a militant defender of workers' rights in the emerging industrial order and championed the eight-hour movement in the 1890s, opposed religion-based politics, and favored civil service. Moreover, the influential Brewery Workers were tightly organized nationally to operate as the "economic" arm in a broader struggle for the emancipation of the working class that would be led by a socialist political party. The union, at first, urged its members to vote for Daniel DeLeon's Socialist Labor party, but DeLeon's "dual unionism" eventually was too quixotic for them. But they were highly critical of populism and the Democratic-People's party fusion, criticizing it as another capitalist-controlled party. Instead, they turned to the Social Democratic party when it was organized in 1897. In Milwaukee in 1898, they spurned the "Popocrat" mayoral candidate in favor of the Social Democratic candidate, machinist Robert Meister. Finally, the Brewery Workers were able to win the FTC endorsement for the Social Democratic party candidate for mayor of Milwaukee in 1900.[61] Thence began a fruitful alliance that gave Milwaukee politics its special character. The unions had a vision of industrial development in which rationalization was a good (and inevitable) process, but one that should not be left in the hands of capitalists. The unions were a force in politics for the socialization of authority to decide how the labor market would be reformed. In this, they outflanked the employers and joined hands with middle-class reformers in the Progressive wing of the state Republican party to establish the "Wisconsin Idea" of government-guided industrial change.

In Milwaukee the labor-Socialist coalition benefitted from able political leadership and blunders by its opponents. The first alternative to the old parties was the Democrat-Populist fusion, whose candidate for mayor in 1898, David Rose, was elected. But afterward Rose attacked civil service and its chief sponsor, the Milwaukee Municipal League, and repudiated municipal ownership of utilities. Instead he proposed a new franchise for the traction company and reduced fares during rush-hours. The Populists promptly broke with Rose and joined the Municipal League to nominate their own candidate for mayor in 1900 who, however, did miserably. Rose gained the Democratic nomination in 1900 and was reelected with 49.7 percent of the vote over the Republican's perennial German-American candidate. Rose campaigned strongly among Polish voters and gained the support of the liquor industry. The new FTC-backed Social Democratic candidate carried 5.1 percent and held the balance of power.[62]

In the 1902 mayoral election, the Republican party split between groups that were pro– and anti–Robert LaFollette, the Progressive who had been elected governor in 1900. Interestingly enough, the pro-LaFollette wing tried to make a deal with Rose in his reelection effort, which came back to haunt them. The Social Democratic candidate again held the balance of power, while more than tripling the party's vote. The Social Democrats, as the "out" party, then benefitted from a major corruption scandal involving both Democratic and Republican members of the city and county governments. An anticorruption voters league was organized by businessmen to clean house and gave some support to the Social Democrats. The Social Democrats approached the 1904 city election as an untainted reform party and reaped wide benefits. Although Rose was reelected once again, partly as a result of his old tactics of splitting the Republican vote and appealing to Polish feelings that Germans dominated urban life, the Social Democratic mayoral candidate won 27.2 percent of the vote and the party elected nine candidates to the city council.[63]

The success of LaFollette state-wide and the prospect of Socialism locally spurred some Democrats and Republicans to sponsor "reform" candidates in the following several elections, splitting their parties. Finally, in 1910, the Social Democrats broke through with a major election victory. Under the generalship of Victor Berger, the Milwaukee party outmaneuvered its opponents through massive use of party-controlled media and a union organizing drive among Polish workers, whose Catholicism and subordinate social status had previously been a key to Democratic and Republican victories. The Social Democratic candidate, Emil Seidel, was elected mayor, and the party won a majority of the city council seats.[64]

The Socialist administration embarked on a thorough "reform" of the city government, establishing a permanent Bureau of Economy and Efficiency headed by John R. Commons from the University of Wisconsin, who performed a similar function for the Wisconsin Industrial Commission when it was established in 1911. Among the reforms were the establishment of a public labor bureau (free from employer control); the establishment of cooperation between the schools and trade unions to create apprentice programs in which students could earn academic credit; breaking the "asphalt ring" by creating an expert public works commission; the strict regulation of street railways; the establishment of new land, housing, and harbor commissions; union wages for public employees; the establishment of a tripartite unemployment committee; the expansion of school programs and use of schools as community centers; and nonpartisan administration of voter registration lists and poll watching. On the other hand, as the Socialists predicted, the state legislature would not allow the city government to municipalize utilities or establish city-owned housing, plumbing services, ice-houses, or slaughter-houses.[65]

Despite a record of accomplishment unmatched in city government, opponents of the Socialists now complained that the party's city council members were too partisan and simply supported whatever the party organization dictated. Good government groups like the Westminster Civic League and the City Club promoted charter reform to switch the city to nonpartisan elections. The idea

was endorsed by the *Milwaukee Journal* and by the two old political
parties. Indeed, the two parties "fused" in the 1912 mayoral election against Seidel and regained control of city hall. After the
election, they sought to lock in their victory and won legislative
support for a law removing party designations from the primary
ballot and making the final election a contest between the two
candidates receiving the most votes in the primary. This tended to
encourage the merger of all anti-Socialist forces. The Socialists,
however, were a resilient force, a political party with well established roots in the community and strongly organized in the union
movement.[66] The non-partisans won again in 1914, but in 1916 the
Socialists regained control of the mayor's office behind the candidacy of the popular city attorney, Daniel Hoan. The party, however, did not win a majority on the council. Hoan was reelected in
1918 and every other year thereafter until 1940.

The Socialist influence in Milwaukee, combined with the Progressive control of the governorship, was a major influence on the
subsequent course of labor-market conditions. Employers in the
city were no more amenable to unions than elsewhere—in fact,
they were, as noted earlier, interlocked with recalcitrant capitalists
in Chicago and New York, and they had organized to resist craft
unionism—but persistent popular support for public officials who
pursued a "cooperative," but nonetheless intrusive, industrial policy compelled them to moderate their labor strategies. Unlike
Detroit and Chicago, organized labor and educators designed and
implemented vocational education in Wisconsin, including the
reconstitution of apprentice training in industry.

The Milwaukee Socialist delegation to the state legislature
provided crucial support for the Progressive proposal for a state
industrial commission in 1911.[67] The state Industrial Commission
became the agency that implemented the state's protective labor
and social policies, including workmen's compensation, child- and
female-labor laws, apprentice training programs, regulation of
private employment bureaus, wage and hours laws, factory safety,
regulation of certain specific industries, plus many other detailed
laws. The commission was empowered not only to administer these
laws, but to investigate every place of employment, prescribe specific standards of practice, and enforce laws and regulations.[68]

The state created a new type of public school, the continuation (later "vocational") school, with its own tax base. The resulting dual system of public schools was consciously modelled on the German experience. The Wisconsin legislature established the right and obligation of all working children to attend school part time and of employers to let them off work a half day until the age of twenty-one. Continuation students were, initially, taught a wide range of subjects. Moreover, the Wisconsin legislature established a new apprentice program that bound participating apprentices and employers to include classroom training in the apprenticeship; this classroom work would take place in the continuation school and function, in part, as a practical demonstration to the continuation students of the aspirations that they should have.[69] The classroom work of the apprentice, too, would not be limited to technical subjects, but would include history, literature, and the like.

The Industrial Commission (IC) established a separate Apprenticeship Division with a supervisor to administer the apprentice law, and it created a State-Wide General Policy Advisory Committee to help the commission develop apprenticeship regulations. This committee was composed of three representatives of organized labor and three of employers, chosen from a pool of candidates recommended by these groups; the members of the Committee were representatives of their respective groups only in the sense of social representativeness—they were not elected and were not meant to be strictly accountable.[70] This approach was consistent with the Wisconsin Idea. The state agency consulted with private groups but was not their agent because the state's authority was more broadly based, in that it had to be responsive to the voters and elected government officials. This was reflected further in the fact that the IC adopted a very general definition of apprenticeable trades, and it, not the unions or the employers, determined the ratio of apprentices to skilled journeymen. State officials believed that these two groups each had their own interest in limiting the number of new tradesmen; there were about six hundred apprentices state-wide in 1914 whereas the state believed there should have been over twelve thousand.[71] The Industrial Commission also formed trade advisory committees for each trade for which apprenticeships were found to be needed. Similarly, the Apprenticeship Division consulted with local advisory boards composed of employers, unionists, and vocational educators to develop definite work and classroom instruction schedules, pay scales, and the like. Again, however, ultimately the state had the final say. The division wrote a standard apprentice agreement establishing the obligations of apprentices and the employer or employers to which the apprentice was indentured.

The classroom part of the training took place in a central public continuation (vocational) education facility; the state disallowed companies from operating so-called "vestibule schools" in their shops. The vocational education facilities were supported by a special tax authorized by the legislature and administered by a State Board of Vocational Education. When the federal Smith-Hughes Act was passed, the state of Wisconsin turned down federal aid because the price of accepting the money was to comply with federal guidelines, which they considered to overemphasize academic study; the federal Board of Vocational Education backed off and prevailed on Wisconsin to take the money. The Wisconsin State Vocational Education Board paid for the facilities, hired the staff, and arranged staff training, but (after 1915) it did not determine the content of classroom instruction. The responsibility for monitoring the progress of individual apprentices, to ensure that they were properly trained, resided with the state. The IC delegated the monitoring task to the local vocational school director, who normally hired a coordinator to organize relationships among the school, employer, and apprentice. Disputes between any of the parties to apprenticeship were mediated by the Industrial Commission.[72]

In fact, the administrative strategy of the commission was to "lay off" its considerable powers of enforcement in favor of an active campaign to win voluntary cooperation from the potential apprentices, educators, unionists, and employers. The IC acted as a kind of "industrial extension service" whose administrative procedures were left to the administrators themselves. The IC used advisory committees and public hearings to carry out the intent of the law, which was to aid industry in achieving the "public good" that employers and employees might all want, but could not attain by individualistic market action.[73] For several years after the initial law of passed in 1911, employers were reluctant to accept the tutelage of state officials. To break the resistance, the first state apprenticeship supervisor courted some of the big Milwaukee employers (first International Harvester) and flattered them that their own, good apprentice programs could serve as a model for the others.[74] Also, in 1915 and again in 1919, the apprentice law was amended to make the program more flexible mostly by removing required classroom subjects, the necessary role of local advisory boards of industrial education, and the part-time school requirement to age twenty-one, which was lowered to age eighteen. These policy revisions, in combination with the cooperative administrative practice of the IC, helped establish employers' confidence that the program would indeed serve their interests. By the early 1920s, the Milwaukee Metal Trades and Founders Association was deeply involved in the apprentice program and helped direct the most highly productive program—in terms of the numbers of apprentices becoming bona fide journeymen—of its kind anywhere.

With the encouragement of the state, several large Milwaukee employers established what they called a "district system," which gained the participation of many smaller companies who, otherwise, would have ridden free on the larger firms' efforts.[75] The big companies like Allis-Chalmers and the Kearney and Trecker machine-tool company agreed to be the home base for hundreds of apprentices. These companies shouldered the largest share of the supervisory costs, but the costs were spread as the employers' associations' apprenticeship committee hired a district apprenticeship supervisor who worked to group companies together in units to facilitate training. The actual training of the apprentices was shared by the larger and smaller, more specialized employers. The large companies would farm out apprentices to smaller shops who had the appropriate work and, thereby, somewhat like the construction industry, workers would rotate among many employers to learn all facets of the trade. The exchange of apprentices among firms also could be done by a unit of smaller companies. The employers' Apprenticeship Committee pursued an extensive public relations program to encourage applications and relied on close cooperation from the Milwaukee Vocational School (with its 15,000 students in 1926). In November 1919, seventy-four companies in Milwaukee were participating, the large majority of which were in the metalworking industry. In October 1926, the Milwaukee Metal Trades Association reported that 59 percent of its member firms were participating.[76]

State-wide, apprentices in the metal trades far outnumbered students in all other trades until the late 1930s. In 1919, there were 237 newly indentured metalworking apprentices; in 1922, there were 398 new indentures; in 1926, 461; and in 1929, 480. Including other trades and apprentices on course, there were 1,250 total apprentices in 1922 at 325 employers in Wisconsin, compared to 400 at 54 firms in Detroit; in 1926, there were 2,545 apprentices at 746 employers. By 1929, there were 3,317 apprentices at 1,002 participating firms. From 1915 to 1929, the program had graduated 2,391 journeymen and -women. No other state or industrial district could match this performance.[77]

For organized labor, Socialist and Progressive government significantly changed the terms of debate about vocational education. The stumbling block for labor in Milwaukee, and in other cities and states across the country, was that the government was in hostile hands. But in Wisconsin, the leaders of the state government simply did not appear to be captives of employers. On the contrary, the state never claimed to be neutral toward industrial organization: they wanted to improve it according to their own lights. Leading nonlabor reformers conceived that a modern industrial society should be a high capacity democracy rooted in the virtues of "good" work. Progressives were very critical of the trend in industry to expand low-skill work and to employ teenagers for these tasks. This was creating a polarized society, they argued, in which a large working class was being deprived of the knowledge and capabilities necessary to sustain a democratic community. On this point, they agreed with the Illinois AFL critics of employers' designs on skill training. But Wisconsin Progressives, like Charles McCarthy, the head of the Legislative Reference Library and one of the most influential reformers, argued that the alternative was not a classless republic either to be returned to in the mythical American past, or to be ushered in by revolution. The plain fact was that America was divided by class. The real objective of reform should be to provide, for working class children and adults, those requirements of training and education that they needed in order to maintain their place in a changing industrial world. Employers would have to agree to employ a higher percentage of skilled workers than they currently wanted; the state would promote creation of apprentice opportunities all across industry. McCarthy argued that the existing public education system was grossly unfair because the working class, whose children left school early to help families make a living, paid for the schools attended by the middle class. It was only fair to create new schools and new education requirements more appropriate to the reality of working-class life.[78]

These were winning arguments with Socialist labor leaders who, in any case, had a "producerist" outlook more akin to their German cousins than to the "republican" ideology of Popocrat unionists in Chicago and Detroit. Moreover, state officials were able to demonstrate to the Machinists' union in a strike in Milwaukee in 1916, that they would act to protect union rights by preventing employers from using apprentices as strike breakers. The state insisted that employers make this pledge and agree to state inspections of struck plants to ensure that apprentices were not training strike-breakers and that no penalties be assessed against apprentices who honored picket lines; moreover, the state refused to approve any new indentures and work permits at struck plants. From the unions, the state won agreement that apprentices would not be compelled to violate their indenture contracts by going on strike themselves.[79]

In short, Progressive and Socialist-labor influence combined to establish the political conditions in which training reforms developed in Wisconsin. There was some real balance among the major groups involved in industry in the years 1910–1920. This meant that not only did unionists support industrial education, but employers had no choice but to cooperate with the public officials who were able to sustain popular support for an interventionist industrial policy. Also, whereas the world war was taken as a great opportunity by Detroit and Chicago employers to campaign against allegedly subversive doctrines of unionism and socialism in order to consolidate control over their employees and government policy, in Milwaukee, the Americanization movement hardly made an impact. Manufacturers in the city were highly impressed with the Detroit and Chicago experiences in 1918, but the close links between the AFL and city and state government led officials to suspect the real motives of the employers and to oppose this manipulation of public programs for private use.[80] There was organized political repression of employees, unionists, and Socialists in Milwaukee as there was elsewhere, but the mayor, the Socialist party, the Federated Trades Council, and many ethnic organizations were lukewarm at best to the war and held firm against militant Americanizers.

The Political Constitution of Labor Markets

Several variations in capitalist labor markets were created in the wake of the 1896 realignment. The explanation of these patterns can be found in the structuring of the menu of governing formulas by the 1896 election and the local conditions facing working-class voters, employers, and party organizers. The structure allowed forms of voluntary interfirm and labor-management cooperation, but gave strong incentives for strategies of industrial consolidation and managerial self-regulation. What did these groups want; what were their opportunities to get what they wanted? Employers everywhere seemed to want the same thing from their employees—cooperation with their plans—but what this meant differed depending on the firms' production and market strategies. Some were willing to compromise if they had to, at least in the short run, even in Detroit in the midst of the open-shop drives, but few were willing to recognize the legitimacy of workers' authority to shape the workplace. Workers, themselves, were divided and were more or less ably led in each city. Moreover, each city had its own local political conditions.

In Detroit, a crucial factor was that the AFL unions were slow to adjust to the new organization of work and blocked the autoworkers efforts to get organized. Another crucial comparative factor was that the unions lacked political power to insist that their interests be taken into account in the restructuring of the labor market. The Republican party had been social reform's partisan base in the 1890s. Once Pingreeism collapsed, both of the main parties factionalized, and an aggressive employer movement mobilized to block unionism and further social cooperation. The AFL unions had no local party allies to fend off the open-shop drive and collapsed as a significant organized force in manufacturing. Manufacturers in the city not only campaigned to oust the unions from a position within their plants from which they could directly influence the labor process, and drew upon courts, friendly political leaders, and policy to do so, but they organized across industries to control labor mobility, education, and access to local government. The EAD was the chief vehicle in the industrial struggle; the Detroit Civic League was the driving organization in the electoral field. On the other hand, the employers did not get everything that they desired. The scope and scale of the training system that was established was far narrower than they had wanted it to be; moreover, it was voluntary. This forced the biggest companies to create corporation schools and effectively to subsidize the smaller firms.

In Chicago, the unions were initially more resilient, in part because of the more extensive reform element in the city, and together unions and women's groups attempted to engage the Democratic party in a reform alliance. The alliance blunted the open shop, blocked demobilizing structural reform of city government, and halted the vocationalization of the public schools. However, the Democratic and Republican parties remained patronage-oriented and would not press forward the labor-educator program. By 1920 leaders of both the Democratic and Republican parties had forsaken the union movement, but by then the reform alliance was badly split. The Illinois Manufacturers' Association and its allies within the middle class crushed unionism in the mass production industries.

In contrast, in Milwaukee, there was no Americanization of the labor force. The union movement allied directly with a political party in 1900, the Social Democrats. By the time that employers gave up on the Republican party and adopted nonpartisanship, the Socialists already were leaders in local politics. They benefitted from good timing—they were able to reap the gains when corruption scandals turned voters from the two major parties—and from capable electoral leadership. The Socialists locally, and the Progressives at the state level, were able to counter the employer-controlled recomposition of the labor process with a public-interest version of the economy that established high standards for industry. This alternative version turned out to be something that many manufacturers were willing to accommodate, and it helped sustain both the idea and practice of high-skill production into the 1930s.[81]

The Progressive Era Legacy

The automobile industry is rightly associated with labor relations consistent with large-scale mass production, but the Progressive legacy for labor-management relations comprises multifaceted political struggles over the uses of private and public authority, new management and labor ideologies, and heterodox shop-floor practices across industry. The background conditions for managerialism were created in the 1896 political realignment and subsequent policies that privileged the vision of industry modernizers. National Democrats and Republicans alike proved fairly disastrous allies for union efforts to establish independent worker representation on the job. National Democrats won AFL favor in opposition to the hostility of Republican judges and the Wilson administration sought the support of conservative labor leaders during World War I. But at the end of the war, the Wilson administration tilted sharply toward managerialism and corporate self-government and would not endorse collective bargaining. The few steps toward free trade were halted at the end of war, and both tariffs and immigration restrictions emerged as alternatives. Corporate liberals were resolutely opposed to cooperation with organized labor in the workplace. They created systems of job hierarchy and strict supervision and, in some of the biggest firms, they sought to gain the loyalty of employees by engaging them in extramural social programs.

Leaders of the AFL already had retreated during the war to a narrower, voluntarist version of their republican philosophy. Once the Wilson administration failed to support the AFL and postwar collective bargaining, top AFL leaders fell back to something like their stance of twenty-five years earlier that spurned political action in favor of direct dealing with employers. Indeed, the AFL presented itself as ready to cooperate with employers' work designs and help root out labor radicals. Yet, the stance of Samuel Gompers and his successor, William Green, was not the only expression of union aspirations. Within the labor federation, United Mine Workers activists continued to advocate industrial unionism and coal industry nationalization, a proposal that was defeated only in 1926 with the emergence of John L. Lewis, who preferred to cooperate with employers and Secretary of Commerce Hoover in the shrinkage of the industry. The broader reform network kept alive the vision of industrial democracy developed by Wisconsin labor experts and applied by such non-AFL unions as the Amalgamated Clothing Workers. The independent railroad brotherhoods sought to maintain government control of the railroads after the war. Also, they supported LaFollette's 1924 presidential election campaign and gained congressional support for the 1926 Railway Labor Act (though it included provisions for more government supervision of collective bargaining than they wanted).[82]

In the 1920s in autos, among other nonunionized industries, work became more routinized, onerous, and authoritarian—indeed, notoriously brutal at Ford. As the companies gained supremacy over the organization of work in mass production firms, they gained only the grudging cooperation of their blue-collar employees. The employment relationship was based on an implicit labor contract: so much labor time bought for so much price per piece. During the workday, companies like Packard asserted, workers should unquestioningly obey supervisors.[83] Yet, employees were not satisfied with the relatively high wages paid by the auto firms. That is, they did enjoy an increasing standard of living during the years 1922 to 1928, but the trade-off of wages for onerous work was conditional.

Throughout the decade a workplace culture of distrust emerged in which managers sought to further specialize jobs and specify exact work routines to remove discretion from the operators, assemblers, and skilled tradesmen, while autoworkers developed forms of solidarity and collective action. Though few production workers joined the industrial union that continued to try to organize the plants around Detroit, autoworkers engaged in many forms of resistance and sometimes accepted the direction of union organizers. Resistance to worklife took the form of persistent high turnover, quits and absenteeism; indifference to the job; restriction of output; sabotage; work-rule breaking; and countless short work stoppages. Moreover, some ethnic communities, including the large Polish Catholic population, resisted Americanization while seeking to preserve their own traditions, and others, notably the black community, found itself increasingly segregated in the melting pot.[84] Also, the communities of skilled workers were fortified in several ways. Certain highly specialized craft unions survived in the auto industry, such as die sinkers, and the number of skilled workers steadily increased with the expansion of the industry. Moreover, because most Detroit industrialists did not train employees, they continued to rely on immigrant tradesmen from Europe, who brought their union traditions with them and began to establish the social networks that later became the kernel of auto union leadership in the 1930s.[85]

CHAPTER 3

The Strategic Vision of Unionism

The ability of trade unions in the 1930s and 1940s to lay the basis for thirty years of substantial improvements in workers' incomes and a formal system of labor-management dispute resolution led industrial relations experts to reconceive collective bargaining routines as inevitable and uniquely rational accommodations by labor and managers to modern industrial conditions. The next two chapters show that the labor system that emerged in the 1940s was more a response to the balance of power and modes of state intervention and to ideological traditions of management and labor than a rational search for efficient solutions to problems of work.

CIO leaders such as Philip Murray, Sidney Hillman, and Walter Reuther of the United Auto Workers Union drew upon American reform traditions and their own experiences to argue for explicit political negotiations to ensure full employment, a union role in industrial decision making, and labor-management cooperation in the shops. This social democratic producerism was one version of a broader agreement during the 1930s among members of the Roosevelt administration and its close allies that the industrial order had to be newly regulated by the federal government to ensure that its full potential for employment and income was reached. The National Industrial Recovery Act and the Wagner National Labor Relations Act embodied the federal government's commitment to change in industrial authority. Yet, after several years of experimentation, the newly won rights of unionists, which promised an equal role for labor in industry, remained unfulfilled. Indeed, by 1937 a new antireform bloc emerged and gathered strength through the war years among manufacturing executives who sought legislative and judicial controls on labor participation in order to reassert managerial prerogatives. The clash of policy programs for dealing with America's new industrial order culminated in dramatic political contests during the postwar years 1945–1950 and led top CIO union leaders to shift gears to stave off reabsorption in management's sphere. Under broad pressures from manufacturing managements and the Truman administration and with prodding from labor experts and judges, CIO leaders adapted their vision of industrial democracy. These labor leaders still advocated democratic control of basic economic decisions such as pricing and investment and a full-blown welfare state, but they focused on strategies to protect their organizations and devised collective bargaining formulas that would guarantee worker income and contribute to national economic growth by concentrating on distributive issues.

To a significant degree labor leaders were successful. The UAW used collective bargaining to win agreements from corporate leaders that recognized the permanent rights of workers and unions in resolving disputes on the job and established wage rules in 1948 and 1950 that tied worker income to increases in the national cost of living and the national rate of productivity. Shop-level productivity was explicitly defined in terms of new technologies and managerial efficiency, not worker effort and cooperation. Moreover, the unions won "welfare" programs directly from employers to supplement public provision of health and hospitalization benefits, pensions, and unemployment insurance. These agreements included provisions that gave incentives to corporations to behave "more responsibly" according to the unions.

Yet, in following this strategy union leaders accommodated themselves to a large degree to the institutional incentives of political power rooted in historic American patterns of elections, political party support, and government decision making and, in the process, adopted a more rigid form of unionism. Although political action was crucial for the stabilization of unions as organizations, as well as basic to the conception that CIO leaders had of the need to democratize industry, labor's broad vision of reform became tied to these particular political and industrial-relations institutions. In this, labor leaders were encouraged by managerial preferences for bureaucratic styles of production and by federal officials who preferred to assimilate labor management to contractual norms. The seeds were sown in the 1940s for union preoccupation with administering collective bargaining contracts and on supporting Democrats who favored labor's organizational interests. Labor leaders came to pay less attention to reform goals, but this undermined their strategic flexibility and exposed the unions to new difficulties when it appeared that neither corporations nor government leaders would perform according to union expectations.

The industrial relations associated with the New Deal have been widely characterized as a rigid, rule-bound system in which work roles became tightly circumscribed and tasks were elaborately described, there was little room for worker participation in production decision making, all aspects of work organization was the prerogative of the management, unions collaborated with employers to settle the terms of pay and conditions of work under which their members would labor, and the micro relations of industry and shop were tenuously tied to the federal government's macroeconomic strategy. Why would anyone choose such a system? Or was it chosen at all? What decisions did lead to its establishment? Why did unions and managers and government officials not create a flexible system of joint production committees, industry councils, and government supervision? why did they not re-create the authoritarian labor system of the 1920s in which there were no unions and managements had virtually complete control over all aspects of the employment relationship? The qualities of the new industrial order that began to emerge during the early New Deal were responses to the regulatory strategy of government officials as they sought to revive the economy under specific political conditions, including the capacities of fractious industry and union groups, which, sometimes, were able to push policy in new directions.

The 1930s was a decade in which patterns of economic behavior were disrupted and government policy revolved around the problems of economic dislocation and reconstruction and, eventually, war. Reform of the industrial order should be conceived as a project rather than a transparent unfolding of industrial logic. Although union leaders necessarily focused on the details of workplace organizing for much of the time during the 1930s and later, no one ignored the economy-wide context of the crisis nor the realignment of national politics. The election of Roosevelt in 1932 opened possibilities for reform simply by making change seem practicable. Even critics of the administration who wanted the government to go further appreciated the favorable conditions that

Roosevelt created for continued debate, and conflict, over reform. At the same time, although rank and file enthusiasm for industrial battle was an important element of union effectiveness, it was not solely determinative of either union aspirations for the labor system or government policy toward industry. Political and economic background conditions also continued to figure prominently throughout the decade, during economic recovery, Roosevelt recession, and war boom, and during the unionizing surge, intense polarization during the 1936 national elections, and reemergence of a "conservative coalition" in 1937. But more important is what people made of these changing conditions and what individuals thought they should do in their consequence. Rather than a single episode of innovation, the creation of a new labor system went through several phases, during which unionists, government officials, managers, and other political forces rethought the purposes they sought to achieve, the alliances they made, their tactics and the requirements for pushing ahead.

This chapter does two things. First it looks closely at how the unionization of the automobile industry was affected by, and influenced, the policy debates about how to solve the economic crisis. Many economists considered the automobile industry the key case of what ailed the entire economy. The failure of the Roosevelt administration's initial strategy in autos, the NIRA, led to another major innovation, the NLRA, and eventually to the unionization of the major auto companies. The successful autoworkers' union was the project of the new CIO and both the UAW and CIO leaders engaged in the policy debate. In particular they proposed that the solution to the depression lay in the direction of structural transformation of industrial authority, which I call social-democratic producerism. Their proposals linked labor participation in workplace decision making to industrial efficiency and democracy in the broader society. Their proposals differed from those of many others in the orbit of the Roosevelt administration by their attention to the microeconomic relations in the firm. The new union movement did accept important aspects of the technical division of labor, but auto labor did not accede to the division of authority at work or elite management of the economy. CIO unions did not perceive themselves only as economic interest groups bargaining over the distribution of the productive surplus of firm or society—

which was drastically shrunk in any case—but as part of a broader popular tradition that critiqued the corporate organization of the economy on grounds that oligopoly firms, which were freed of many market constraints, usurped the government's role of setting the terms of the market and undermined attempts to regulate the economy in ways that expanded consumption and investment and ensured justice.

Second, it shows that this social-democratic aspiration was not overtaken by the actual policy decisions of the Roosevelt administration. On the contrary, the existence of the new unions was an asset in the government's policy portfolio; the new unions were part of that era's state building. Roosevelt and his advisors continued to consider such techniques for economic recovery as government economic planning and restructuring industrial organization in the late 1930s; they kept their options open and even added a new option, a kind of proto-Keynesian fiscal stimulation, at the end of the decade. The role of unions in redistributing income and checking corporate authority was widely appreciated. Moreover, during the war, a period that sometimes has been interpreted as the key formative experience for the New Deal industrial order, most of what was accomplished had a highly tentative quality to it, as labor leaders and employers planned and waited expectantly for postwar conditions to emerge. In 1945 UAW vice-president Walter Reuther reignited the debate over a partnership of unions and government in regulating the industrial economy.

Crisis and Opportunity

On the eve of the October 1929 stock market crash, a fairly stable system of labor management was in operation in auto manufacturing. Under conditions that few workers or managers believed could, or would, be changed much, worklife had become routine and acceptable in this specific sense. Although turnover of the blue-collar work force remained high compared to other industries, the rate had dropped dramatically from that of a dozen years before. Also, although real earnings were stagnant after 1927, workers preferred working in the auto plants at comparatively high wages to not doing so. Where and when working conditions and pay fell below expectations, autoworkers preferred wildcat strikes and quicky stoppages in the shop and absenteeism and restriction of output to more broadly concerted action to formally regulate the workplace with the real penalties (unemployment and blacklisting) that went with the attempt. Autoworkers also preferred fraternal, ethnic and religious associations to union membership and participation in political party affairs, including elections.[1]

The auto companies' labor, financial, and market strategies seemed rational and successful. There was no need to change. In particular, General Motors became the new industry leader in sales in 1927, a position it has never yet relinquished, through what later became called Sloanism. Like Ford, General Motors adopted mass-production technologies, radically divided responsibilities for conception and execution of production, greatly simplified production tasks, and integrated operations. Unlike Ford, General Motors elaborated its managerial hierarchy, deemphasized technical innovation and it differentiated products around a few standard platforms to create a new kind of consumer market based on status distinctions. The competitive success of GM compelled Ford and other firms to follow suit. Several other qualities of the strategy were that consumers were to be convinced to take what was offered; the companies had to be able to lay off and recall employees as needed and compel auto dealers to bear the costs of unsold products; and product market demand above that planned for by the major producers would be left for the smaller companies. General Motors called its policy "standard volume-normal profit."[2]

Both workers' and managers' chosen strategies were contingent on economic and political background conditions, a fact that is clear in retrospect. Workers were not socialized as factory drones whose lives were consumed by repetitive, unthinking behavior. Autoworkers' acquiescence on the job clearly was tentative and conditional. As long as income was high enough to maintain family life and there were no viable alternatives to this industrial discipline, it was prudent not to commit oneself too heavily to the job nor to one's fellow workers. Similarly, the financial success of the auto industry depended on product market stability. There had to be a consistently high demand for its products to justify the heavy capital investment in volume production, to bring down unit costs and pay investors a steady dividend. In turn, the aggregate market depended on real disposable income and the cost of credit. The involvement of the federal government in firms' labor and product strategies was minimal and focused on negative judicial constraints on unions, despite the proddings of Herbert Hoover, first as commerce secretary and then president, that firms could improve standards through voluntary cooperation. Nevertheless, government authority was considered critical in another respect, namely, virtually all firms in all industries coalesced to preserve high tariff barriers to foreign competition.[3]

After the stock market crash, market conditions rapidly changed and individuals and firms began to reevaluate their preferences and strategies. But they did so neither immediately nor with specific outcomes clearly in mind. The old industrial order persisted. Most employers maintained wage rates and eventually experimented with short hours to spread employment. The smaller firms and dealers absorbed the biggest percentage losses of sales and profits. Average car prices fell 14.2 percent while sales dropped 75 percent, from 5,337,087 in 1929 to 1,331,860 in 1932. Employment in the motor vehicle industry fell from 447,448 in 1929 to 243,614 in 1933.[4] Most autoworkers remained quiescent, excepting those unionists and radicals who had been active even during the 1920s, largely until election day in November 1932 when blue-collar workers entered the electoral arena in large numbers to help elect Franklin Roosevelt. The smashing rejection of the sitting president, and the capture of the White House by the Democrats, plus the election of an overwhelming Democratic majority in the Congress made an enormous impression on the entire country. Individual citizens collectively chose a new direction. Dramatic change could happen and a relationship of expectation, between voters and government officials, that much more was yet to come was established.

As many historians of the depression have pointed out, among the first groups to take direct action to relieve their personal crises of income and employment that led to new union organizations were skilled tool and die makers, machinists and other craft workers.[5] At the same time, much of this literature rightly focuses on the interference of AFL leaders with the aspirations of rank and file workers, in mass-production industries, for effective unions.[6] Yet the AFL craft leaders' preference for dividing workers into separate organizations should not be taken as reflecting the sentiment of skilled workers themselves. In Detroit, skilled workers formed the Mechanics Educational Society of America (MESA) in early 1933 and soon became one of the spearheads of a broad movement to organize the entire automobile industry.[7]

The formation of MESA seemed unprecedented, an outgrowth of economic crisis, but it had roots in craft culture. Even though Detroit employers and government leaders had collaborated to make the city a bastion of the open shop, in the area of tooling skilled workers had continued to enjoy a comparatively high degree of self-determination on the job, increasing demand for their services, and premium wages. In autos, the number of tool and die makers more than quadrupled in the 1920s and their proportion in the work force almost doubled.[8] Immigrant skilled tradesmen who came to Detroit from England and Ireland in the 1920s at first kept a low profile at work, trying to find their appropriate place in the new country, although they maintained the craft community outside work in many cultural and fraternal organizations. The economic depression upset these arrangements. Workers were laid off in large numbers and those who continued to work saw their hours, incomes, and working conditions deteriorate. Auto subcontractors reverted to a form of inside contracting based on individual bidding for work that led to longer hours and lower pay. Toolmakers began to organize to protect their wages and working conditions and the ensuing conflicts between skilled workers and employers led to employer recognition of the legitimacy of the workers' unions and to a new era of labor participation. Yet the outcomes were not simply the result of a bilateral test of strength. The conflicts transformed the ideology of the skilled toolmakers from immigrant craft-consciousness to industrial unionism. The outcomes also were influenced by factional conflict within the union movement, by changing partisan conditions, and by developing federal labor policies.

The workers in MESA rapidly developed a conception of what they wanted. From their experiences in Great Britain, they created a union organization based on local autonomy, shop steward representation and rank and file governance. The British experience was less clear as to who should be included in the union, but MESA adopted the form of a multi-industry metalworkers' union, based in part on British readings of American ideas going back to the

Knights of Labor and on German union practice, to which all types of workers in the industries would belong.⁹ MESA's first direct action, in the fall of 1933, was a militant strike against both auto supplier firms and mass producers in which strong alliances were made between toolmakers and production workers. The new union struck GM's tool rooms in Flint and were quickly joined by strikes in Pontiac and Detroit, affecting fifty-seven tool and die job shops of the Automotive Tool Die Manufacturers Association (ATDMA), sixty independent shops and "every major auto plant except Ford and Graham-Paige."¹⁰ The strike put an end to the inside contracting system, won union recognition and wage increases, and made MESA a union for both skilled and production workers. The MESA strike also was significant because it was won against the economic recovery policy that the Roosevelt administration was following, and it contributed to the independence of workers' action from the AFL as well as to a shift in the government's labor relations policy.

The Roosevelt administration's major policy response to the depression was the National Industrial Recovery Act. Passed by the Congress in June 1933, the NIRA created the National Recovery Administration (NRA) and provided for the establishment of industry associations throughout the economy with authority to coordinate company policies on prices, wages, and market shares. NIRA reflected a common perception that the depression was caused fundamentally by unbalanced relationships in the corporate economy, including the maldistribution of income in which the lower classes had not enough to spend to purchase the products that the mass producers were capable of sending to market. In fact, this under consumptionist analysis of the depression had been made before 1929 as a prediction by certain economists and social theorists of the consequences of the emergence of the large-scale corporate economy, but it took the crisis and a change in government control to bring the views to power.¹¹ The cause of the maldistribution of income was oligopoly power; that is, the power of large corporations that dominated their product markets to set prices to ensure a predetermined profit goal at any volume—much as Sloan did at General Motors—led to too much income directed to already well-off individuals, while high prices and reduced employment undermined the mass market. As the market shrunk, companies cutback production rather than reduce prices, creating more unemploy-

ment, worsening the distribution of income and further undermining the market. The NIRA was intended to halt the downward spiral
of market demand and production cutbacks by allowing individual
firms to formulate codes to coordinate wage rate policies—raise
them—and prices—moderate them. The law was a means of forestalling individually rational firm behavior that was collectively
disastrous by bringing the managers together. At the same time,
though the NRA would supervise the industry code authorities, each
industry would freely set its own standards.

The analysis came in several versions, some of which were
managerialist and others producerist. The managerialist version
was a bloodless analysis of the functional need of a modern economy to coordinate mass production and mass consumption. The
big corporations had developed the most efficient forms of production and the society had to adjust to the new economic organization by, for example, loosening antitrust regulations. Adjustment
was compatible with the welfare capitalism of the 1920s and with
Hoover's plea to employers voluntarily to maintain wages and
employment after the crash. The producerist version argued that
oligopolies could not make the proper adjustments themselves, but
would always favor their investors and owner-managers. The government should reassert its authority to set fair market conditions,
including prices and modes of competition. Proponents of the
latter view were disappointed with the voluntarist cast of the NIRA.
Letting industrial firms set their own standards was unlikely to
succeed in achieving economic recovery. When the NRA failed, one
of the main causes was that the federal government lacked effective
means of preventing the code authorities from raising prices faster
than wages (if they did so at all, which they did not in autos) and
thereby short-circuiting any gain to mass purchasing power.[12]

Another aspect of the policy followed less from the technical
analysis than from legislative politics. When the Congress considered the bill, it added a provision on union rights which forced the
Roosevelt administration to deal with the authority relations in
industry. This provision became perhaps the most highly contentious aspect of the policy and eventually destroyed the NRA. Before
the Congress considered the administration's recovery proposal,
Senator Hugo Black (D., Alabama) had introduced what was called
the Thirty Hours bill, a law to establish the thirty-hour work week

as a means of spreading employment. In order to head off this bill, the Roosevelt administration agreed to insert section 7(a) into the NIRA, which provided that workers could choose their own representatives to negotiate with employers about labor standards. Employers were more favorable to Black's bill than to section 7(a). GM's Alfred Sloan testified that hours reduction made sense as long as wages were not cut, but he and other auto executives flatly opposed the right of employees to their own representatives.[13]

The Roosevelt administration's application of the NIRA to autos led to two regulatory structures, one for the mass producers (although Ford refused to participate at all) and one for the parts suppliers and machine job shops.[14] The AFL was enthusiastic about the apparent endorsement of unions in the NIRA. Partially organized industries, like garments and bituminous coal, were rapidly unionized, and AFL organizers were sent to campaign in formerly ignored industries such as rubber, autos, steel, and electrical machinery. But organizers who arrived in Detroit in June to organize the auto industry under section 7(a) were frozen out of the administration's auto recovery policy. The automobile manufacturers' NRA Code Authority excluded labor representatives and left labor standards entirely to the discretion of employers. General Motors and other companies insisted that the act did not require them to negotiate with the AFL and officials at the NRA agreed. Instead, auto employers established company-dominated employee associations during the summer of 1933 to deal with the less pressing workplace issues (e.g., sanitation, but not wages and hours) to preempt independent unions. At the suppliers, the NRA was the occasion for the organization of firms into an association, the largest segment of which was the ATDMA which was closely tied to the production needs of the big auto companies. When the auto parts Code Authority refused to deal with the AFL and MESA, the auto companies bucked them up to reject negotiations. MESA then launched the strike referred to earlier, in September 1933, while the AFL sought federal government help in dealing with the Code Authorities. The Roosevelt administration responded by ordering a study of how to stabilize automobile employment, which did not commit the companies to any action.[15]

All across the economy, the situation was similar. Employers cooperated with each other, but rejected the idea that they should coordinate policies with their employees. Strikes and lockouts were the outcome. In August, President Roosevelt created the National Labor Board (NLB) to mediate disputes over the implementation of the section 7(a). But the auto companies refused to accept government mediation of the MESA strike offered by the National Labor Board chairman, Senator Robert Wagner (D., New York). Even so, the NLB, including its AFL members, followed GE's Gerard Swope's argument that the NLB could only direct individual companies to bargain, not entire industries. Ultimately, the strikers had little use for the NLB's temporizing. MESA organizer Mat Smith proclaimed that MESA intended to be part of the new public regulation of the economy. MESA's "immediate task is to temper wage slavery; its ultimate goal is to function in a planned society as a national instrument of production, cooperating with a recast distributive system."[16] During the fall and winter, MESA's direct action tactics won it a multiemployer regional contract with the ATDMA and vaulted union membership to over twenty-one thousand in spring 1934, making it far larger than the AFL's Auto Workers Union.

The MESA strike helped convince labor relations experts and federal officials such as William Leiserson, Wagner's secretary at the NLB, that federal mediation that relied on the voluntary cooperation of employers would not secure workers' rights. "By way of example I need only to mention the Philadelphia Bakers' case, the Tool and Die Makers strike in Detroit and Flint, and the Jamestown Art Metal Company's case. In each of these, mediators have failed because employers insisted they would not recognize unions of employees or strikers' committees."[17] The problem was that the NLB had no authority to direct employers to negotiate or to impose concessions on either party. After the MESA strike, Roosevelt authorized the NLB to conduct employee representation elections based on majority rule, which would lead to the defeat of the company unions, but only in cases where companies accepted mediation. Employer spokesmen Walter Teagle (Standard Oil) and Pierre Du Pont (Du Pont, General Motors and a member of the NLB) and the NRA, which retained final authority in NLB activities, interpreted this to mean that employers could participate in the elections and promote company-dominated representation organizations and that, even if the company "union" lost, proportional representation would allow "negotiations" between it and the company. Roosevelt countermanded the NRA's interpretation of his order but, after sharp protests from automobile industry employers that they would not allow the NLB to carry on a representation election between their company unions and the AFL Auto Workers Union, the president reversed himself and endorsed proportional representation.[18] That decision ended the effectiveness of the NLB.

The president's automobile labor policy never had a chance to institutionalize new labor management practices because of the continuing union upheaval. Auto workers simply bypassed the NLB and the other government agencies with a hand in labor policy, such as the NRA, Labor Department, and Justice Department, and persisted in organizing themselves. During 1934 and 1935, they put increasing strike pressure on the companies to negotiate with workers' representatives, raise wages, handle grievances, control overtime assignments, and adjust production standards. Their struggle to raise labor standards against company opposition and to achieve some measure of justice at work belied the opinion of federal judges, such as John Nields, whose opinion in the Weirton steel case, in February 1935 declared section 7(a) unconstitutional and simply denied that employees could have legitimate interests that would not be met voluntarily by employers.[19] Besides the federal government, autoworkers also had to contend with the incompetence and obstruction of the organizers sent by the AFL. They badgered the AFL to allow them to select their own national leaders and clearly endorse industrial unionism. In 1935, delegates to the Auto Workers Union convention in South Bend, Indiana, wrested control of their union from the AFL-imposed leadership. Then, when the AFL did not endorse the industrial union plan of Sidney Hillman (whose ACW [Amalgamated Clothing Workers union] had joined the federation) and John L. Lewis (Mine Workers), the UAW seceded and joined the new Hillman- and Lewis-created CIO.[20]

The merger in 1936 of most of MESA with the Auto Workers' Union-CIO reveals the new logic of solidarity. The principal instigators of the move to merger were Communist party members, who saw a "categorical imperative" for working-class solidarity. But only a year earlier, these same Communist toolmakers had been suspended from MESA for severely criticizing the organization for failing to ally itself with the production workers. Now, with the production workers gathering momentum, solidaristic arguments made more sense. And it was a calculation. Not all of MESA merged. A rump group, which included Mat Smith, maintained their independence. Smith, who by all accounts could have become one of the top leaders of the UAW if he had chosen to join, argued that merger with a nascent industrial union was still too uncertain a move. As it turned out, he was prescient in the sense that the specific interests of skilled workers at the big companies were mostly unmet for many years. Other autoworker unions also merged with the UAW–CIO, including the Automotive Industrial Workers Association, which had been formed out the Chrysler company union after NLB elections but which had never been able to negotiate satisfactorily with the company. The UAW then had about twenty-five thousand members.[21]

As NLB authority was collapsing in 1934, Senator Wagner had begun work on a new labor law, which eventually became the National Labor Relations Act in 1935, that included the majority rule principle and prohibited employer interference in worker representation elections. The Wagner NLRA was important in another respect as well. The justification for the Act was indicative of how worker rights and union status were an important element of the New Deal strategy for economic management. The NLRA preamble states the legislative finding that the denial of workers' rights to form unions maintains an inequality in bargaining power and leads to industrial conflict and disruption of the economy.

> The inequality of bargaining power between employees . . . and employers . . . tends to aggravate recurrent business depressions, by depressing wage rates and the purchasing power of wage earners. . . . It is hereby declared to be the policy of the United States to eliminate the causes . . . by encouraging the practice and procedure of collective bargaining and by protecting the exercise by workers of full freedom of association . . . for the purpose of negotiating the terms and conditions of their employment or other mutual aid or protection.

The purposes of the act are to secure workers' rights of association and create the policy means (i.e., unions) by which mass consumer markets could be secured.[22]

The Roosevelt administration had serious reservations about the new authority that the Wagner proposal would give to unions and about the independent administrative structure that would be set up. But administration officials had reasons to endorse the bill in the end. Even as disputes over section 7(a) were generating intense industrial conflict in auto centers and in textile towns, on the docks and truck loading bays, it was widely expected that the NRA was imminently going to be declared unconstitutional by the Supreme Court, which the court did eventually do in May 1935. Therefore, administration officials, such as Leon Henderson, argued that the government needed a new economic recovery plan.

The new federal policy pivoted, in fact, on two pieces of legislation, Wagner's National Labor Relations Act and the Social Security Act, both passed by Congress in 1935. President Roosevelt endorsed them after they were sure to pass. And, though leaders among employers were actively involved in drafting the bills, they almost uniformly rejected the legislation as passed. The NLRA created a new administrative apparatus independent of the Labor Department, the National Labor Relations Board, with real authority to carry out the goals of the act. The Social Security Act provided compensation for those without income from work: unemployment insurance, old-age pensions, aid to families with dependent children, disability and blindness benefits, and general relief. The pension policy was an echo of the demands of the Townsend Movement, which advocated government-provided pensions to encourage older workers to retire and open jobs to younger people and to redistribute income through progressive taxes.[23]

Big employers, in turn, went into hard opposition to the New Deal. Until 1934 and the industrial conflicts over section 7(a), employers had had little complaint with the Roosevelt administration, but now they blamed the administration for encouraging unionization, and they turned against the president. Sloan and William Knudsen from GM, Ernest Weir, Sewell Avery of Montgomery Ward, Howard Pew of Sun Oil, Edward F. Hutton and Colby Chester of General Foods, Al Smith, John J. Raskob, Pierre Du Pont, and others formed the American Liberty League, a militantly anti-Roosevelt organization. Its Lawyers Committee challenged the constitutionality of the NLRA, preventing its implementation until the spring of 1937, and the league worked strenuously for the victory of Republican Alf Landon in the 1936 presidential election. But by this time, labor was "on the march," contributing to a highly polarized political environment.[24]

The new CIO was well-financed by the Mine Workers' treasury, replenished by the successful union drives under NIRA, and Lewis placed an army of organizers in the field to unionize the mass production industries. Cio membership rapidly grew. The cio also was the single largest source of campaign financing for Roosevelt, who adopted rhetoric appropriate to the moment, castigating the "economic royalists" who would block America's recovery. The new economic and mass electoral forces, and a steadily expanding economy, secured for Roosevelt another landslide victory and renewed legitimacy for New Deal reforms. Moreover, election victory added momentum to the unionizing drive in autos. That winter, autoworkers sat down inside GM's plants in Flint and, with the critical help of Frank Murphy, the Democratic governor of Michigan, who refused to use state violence against the strikers, plus John L. Lewis and federal Labor Department officials, brought GM to the table in 1937 and compelled the company to sign its first labor contract.[25]

The Double Dynamic of Industrial Democracy

The signing of the largest automobile employer left a great deal still to be settled. The chief achievement was getting GM to make an agreement. Fulfilling the Wagner Act's goals was a long way off and the terms of the agreement were far from what workers wanted. The newly independent UAW was now a strongly membership-based organization most of whose elected leaders came out of local plant conflicts where militants were highly committed to workers' control on the shop floor and social-democratic government. Yet, a two-sided dynamic now emerged that sometimes led to bitter recriminations among unionists and that has been perceived by some later scholars, incorrectly, in my view, as the inevitable bureaucratization of the unions.

Union advocates of social-democratic producerism sought to establish representative democracy in industry with full civil liberties for employees; management by functional knowledge rather than authority; and a federal government planning process in which workers' representatives would participate and that would develop policies for social insurance and industrial modernization.[26] To convince the other social partners, especially corporate managements and government officials, that unionists should be included in the broad management of the industrial order, union leaders had to demonstrate their abilities to solve problems and fulfill agreements. On one side, UAW leaders faced rank and file union members whose penchant for direct action ran counter to steady production and stable relations. Provocative actions by plant managers contributed to the difficulty of the task of weaning members away from workers' control to a more bureaucratized system of representative rights. On the other side, union leaders sought to demonstrate to Democratic officials that organized labor was willing to employ collective bargaining in specific industries in the service of the national interest by, for example, wage moderation or acquiescence in technological unemployment, so long as government recognized its responsibilities for full employment and social justice. These dynamic relationships placed union leaders in the middle of conflicts that spanned economy and polity and led to charges that social-democrats were willing to sacrifice rank and file rights for cooperation from employers and favors from government. The more managers resisted collaboration with unions and government officials failed to ensure a policy framework for collective bargaining responsibility, the more compelling were militant tactics and concern for particular industries and companies. An academic view was that the new CIO unions were simply succumbing to the iron law of oligarchy, but this makes sense only if the union bureaucracy was not representative and if employers and Democratic officials can be said to have no influence on the character of union development.

Although the UAW was not firmly organized in all GM's plants in 1937, what they won from the company was not even close to what existed on the factory floor de facto. The kernel of the UAW as an organization was its shop steward system: each twenty, or so, workers elected a steward who acted as organizer of collective action, dues collector, representative to foremen and supervisors, handler of individual grievances, and coordinator of union-wide policy. The steward system had effectively undermined the authority of the company's front-line managers to dictate work rules and production standards. GM refused to recognize the steward system as the representative structure of the union. The company's negotiators, led by Charles Wilson, conceded the UAW's legal status as sole collective bargaining agent and gave ground on wages and hours. But under pressure from their factory managers, they insisted on a grievance-committeeman structure of local dispute settlement in which every two hundred fifty to four hundred employees would have a committeeman who would participate in a step-wise grievance procedure that took complaints from local to national levels of company and union authority. The union would have no role in running the plant. After three months of talks, during which stewards continued to lead walkouts and the company campaigned in public about the unreliability of the CIO, the UAW negotiators, who were two Communist party members, Wyndham Mortimer and Ed Hall, plus John Brophy as the agent of John L. Lewis and Sidney Hillman, agreed to ban the stewards.[27]

Apparently UAW leaders believed that the actual balance of shop-floor power would continue. The union's General Motors Conference approved the contract and shop stewards continued to directly solve conflicts. UAW members continued to endorse the steward system and GM continued to contest the union's shop-floor power. On the other hand, as the top UAW leaders soon fell into factional conflict, it became very difficult for the union to prevent plant- or even shop-level syndicalism from undermining the movement to establish industry standards and to formalize employee rights.[28]

This historical situation, in which individual autoworkers acted solidaristically without any authoritative leadership being established, lent a special (though not unique) character to the UAW. All bureaucracies, by definition, establish internal divisions of labor and standard operating procedures; indeed, the top leaders can manipulate internal communications and rules to maintain their dominance. The price such organizations pay is rigidity and loss of *elan* among the members actually doing the organizing work and who, in turn, can try to use the leaders' needs for support to advance their own specific interests. But in the UAW in the 1930s, the organizational dynamic was fueled by a strong self-organization capacity among the rank and file that persisted for years and that made the UAW one of few unions to maintain internal political pluralism and programmatic innovation.[29]

Beside the employers' resistance, another background condition was the continuing economic crisis. The economy fell back into depression in late 1937 and 1938, causing renewed hardship for millions, severe cutbacks of CIO and UAW staffs and new doubts about the administration's recovery strategy. One of the effects of the Roosevelt recession was that the new UAW began to disintegrate, losing members and confidence and breaking into CIO and AFL factions. The UAW–CIO leadership was dominated by a coalition of Communists and Socialists which, under CIO pressure, picked a neutral, nonpartisan president, R. J. Thomas, from the former Chrysler company union. The AFL faction was headed by Homer Martin, a Baptist preacher from a suburban Kansas City GM plant who had been picked first president of the UAW–CIO on the strength of his opposition to the AFL. Since then Martin had shifted back into the AFL orbit and sought to oust the leftists and establish stronger national union control over industrial action. Some companies, like GM, suspended negotiations with either union while others, like Ford, sought "sweetheart" deals.[30]

An important part of the AFL–UAW strategy was to appeal to craftsmen's job-control traditions.[31] Indeed, skilled workers had many grievances: some they shared with production workers, such as job security and wages, while some they did not. One important skilled-trades issue was how to deal with increasing specialization of labor. In the tool rooms of the major employers, assignments were so specialized that workers were not only deployed on specific types of machines, but on particular brand names of machine types. Also, skilled workers wanted agreements on apprentice standards and rates, and toolmakers wanted a new organizing effort at small job shops, which always sprang up during boom times, but which undermine wages and working conditions when the economy slid. The AFL–UAW promised to address these issues for skilled workers if only they would abandon the CIO.

The toolmakers stood firm against the AFL and used their City-Wide Tool and Die Council, in Detroit, to fight a battle against what seemingly were their own particular interests. Nevertheless, even after the AFL was vanquished in early 1939, the UAW–CIO continued to lose ground as a bargaining agent and the union had to reorganize General Motors, which it did through what was called a "strategy strike" of toolmakers. But the 1939 tool and die strike left unaddressed most issues that both the skilled trades and production workers had been raising; it was a union recognition strike. The difficulty of getting to collective bargaining overshadowed the substantive interests in work that autoworkers wanted protected.[32]

In this context of continuing labor-management strife and flux in 1937 and 1938, the unions began to lose Roosevelt's support. Though GM, US Steel, Chrysler and other large employers were in the process of unionization and the CIO looked like a king-maker in politics after the 1936 election, the workers movement still was largely a potential and the unions still needed the government's political support, especially the support of the Democratic party officials. But, in 1937, the momentum shifted; now the CIO was a supplicant and the Roosevelt administration began to exercise more discriminating support for various unions and union leaders.

The first chink in the CIO's armor appeared in the organizing strike of the so-called Little Steel firms, including Republic, Bethlehem, Youngstown Sheet and Tube, Jones and Laughlin, Inland, and Wheeling. Led by Republic's Tom Girdler, the companies fiercely resisted unionization and employed spies, local police, newspaper editors, clergy, and violence to break the strike. On Memorial Day 1937 in South Chicago, some two thousand strikers and their families peacefully picnicked and marched before the Republic Steel works. Chicago police, however, fired upon the marchers, killing ten and wounding thirty. The response to the massacre by elected leaders in cities and states where Little Steel firms operated was almost uniformly to call out forces of order to protect property and disperse pickets, thus helping the companies break the strike. President Roosevelt, when asked about the Little Steel strike, responded that most Americans, and by implication himself, wished a "plague on both your houses" to the CIO and steel employers. The president effectively sided with the companies.[33]

The president tried to stay aloof from the conflict between the AFL and the CIO, whose leaders bitterly disliked each other, but he was eventually drawn in, and his administration shifted key personnel at the NLRB to satisfy the AFL. The administration's labor policy officials at the NLRB were struggling to establish some industrial order. Yet they quickly found they had to contend with the AFL, which sought to block the new Labor Board's determination to decide the scope of bargaining units. The board's initial strategy was to promote what it believed were the most effective forms of unionism under contemporary industrial conditions, namely broad-based, industrial union–type organizations. The AFL gained the ideological support of the old Wisconsin labor experts, who argued that the Board's administrative directives were antithetical to workers' self-organization, and AFL leaders engaged in an increasingly opportunist coalition with antilabor members of Congress to reign in the NLRB. The board majority eventually lost its argument, in 1940, with Congress and the president. Roosevelt replaced them with appointees more to the AFL's liking. The new NLRB shifted determination of basic issues of labor relations to the power of the contending organizations and to the existing obligations of union organizations as contracting agents, not on the rights that workers might have to determine who should represent them. These shifts quieted the dispute over the board, in part because, by then, the CIO had recovered its membership strength and was handily winning representation elections. Labor law doctrine and administration were still permissive of union power: workers had the right to unionize and there were few limits on what aspects of work over which employees could demand to negotiate.[34]

Also, there were incentives for administration officials and the president himself to maintain good relations with organized labor. The recession led to another reevaluation by the administration of its economic recovery strategy. CIO leaders were part of the debate and among the strongest supporters of the direction the administration did take. There is still debate over the reasons why the economic recovery, which had been going on for several years, stalled, in late 1937. But the interpretation of prominent New Dealers, such as Leon Henderson, Gardiner Means, Mordecai Ezekiel, Harold Ickes, Henry Wallace, Hugh Johnson, and Marriner Eccles, continued to turn on the power of the integrated oligopoly firms to force the market to meet their price. Even if the government stimulated consumer spending through its fiscal policy, the gains could be nullified by corporate policy. For example, when conditions improved in 1935 and 1936, GM increased employment, made more money, and paid out its standard dividend. GM reacted by deepening its business strategy: more differentiation of models and renewed investment in more capacity and labor-saving process technology. It also teamed with Standard Oil of California and Firestone Tire to buy up and close down competing interurban rail transportation. In the renewed depression in late 1937 and 1938, GM promptly laid off workers, but did not cut prices.[35]

As the administration came under harsh criticism for what the Republicans now portrayed as Roosevelt's depression, activists in the New Deal network debated policy responses. Two twists on the income distribution and under-consumption analysis emerged that emphasized market competition and economic growth. Few New Dealers believed that oligopoly power was rooted in ownership; following Adolph A. Berle and Gardiner Means, the wisdom was that control over corporate decision making was lodged with the managers. Therefore, the government did not need to take over uncooperative corporations, but only control their decisions. Leon Henderson and Thurman Arnold, soon to be head of the Justice Department's Anti-Trust Division, argued that restoring competition could eliminate administered pricing. Of course, there was no guarantee that competition would not also lead to competitive wage reductions. On the other hand, another view, outlined by Ezekiel and Max Lerner, was that if the object was to control decisions that affected the distribution of income, some of the same aggregate benefits might be attained through increasing productivity rather than by direct redistribution of existing income (and at lower political costs), especially if this was encouraged within an appropriate framework of public controls and competition. What this framework would be was unclear.[36]

Social-Democratic Producerism

The direction toward productivity and growth was more appealing to organized labor than antitrust because of the potential for wages to increase. Philip Murray, the head of the CIO's Steel Workers Organizing Committee, claimed that the union recognized "mutual interests" with steel companies in more efficient production. Sidney Hillman explained that

> enlightened union leaders believe that the attitude of organized labor must be one of cooperation with the employer in their mutual interest—increased prosperity for all. . . . Greater production, guided by efficient management, means lower cost per unit. Lower costs tend

towards lower prices. This enables our people to buy and use more goods. This, in turn, makes possible putting our unemployed back to work. With little or no unemployment, the bargaining power of labor is increased, resulting in higher wages. Higher wages, coupled with lower prices, mean a high standard of living.[37]

Crucial to this vision of collaborative production and industrial expansion was the establishment of secure unions that could protect employees from exploitation. But worker protection could not be the only goal for unions. The union argument was that industrial democracy and the perfection of large-scale production went together. The worker's role was not so much in the specific job, but in helping manage the factory and industry. What that implied was a major change in the relationships of industry and polity. Morris Cooke, Murray, Hillman, Clint Golden, and Harold Ruttenberg, among others, addressed the connection between workplace organization and the broader society. The CIO proposed a social-democratic version of producerist themes such as public supervision of manufacturing, humanization of work through participation by workers in organizing production, continuous training and experimentation with new methods, technology transfers among industries, improving product quality, flexible deployment of skilled labor, and equalization of income.[38]

The basic idea was that labor participation in work would increase productivity by engaging workers' knowledge and initiative. Managers had come to define productivity almost solely in terms of reducing labor costs and had adopted several means to this end: specialization of task and standardization of methods, mechanization and detailed supervision of workers by foremen. Union leaders charged that such managerial habits robbed workers of their skills, turned them into enemies of work, and led to unequal distribution of the gains from productivity. Union recognition was prerequisite for constructive labor-management relations. This was necessary to shore up the imbalance of power between individual employees and corporations and to make real cooperation based on equality in production possible. Once workers had the protection of a secure union organization behind them, they could begin to consider the ways of improving the production process free of suspicion of managerial motives. Yet, unlike earlier versions, now

government would guarantee equality of bargaining power between workers and employers by sanctioning collective labor action and by taking responsibility for industrial modernization.

The new union power in mass-production industry at a basic
level got the supervisor off the worker's back as well as protected
workers' earnings. But unions sought an even more substantive role
and demanded changes in managerial practices that bound together the whole authority structure at work and the relationship of
work to society. The wage scale is critical to the quality of work life.
For example, before the unions, workers in industries like autos,
steel, and rubber were paid by their individual output—a price per
piece or tonnage, or piece rate—which routinely varied, even
among those doing the same work, according to whatever the
foreman or plant superintendent decided. There were over forty-
five thousand wage rates in the steel industry in 1945, a virtually
unending source of worker complaints about inequity, that steelworkers demanded be changed. Moreover, individual rates encouraged compulsive work, which was aggravated when managers lowered
the piece price once employees had demonstrated they could reach
a higher level of output. The UAW demanded the abolition of piece
rates in the auto industry and the substitution of a "day rate,"
according to which all workers would receive pay based on hours
worked. And the UAW sought to flatten the wage structure by
negotiating equal increases for all job categories. These demands
reflected egalitarian desires as well as a reckoning that the integrated organization of production made individualized pay an anach-
ronism.[39]

Moreover, the UAW and CIO wanted guaranteed annual wages
(GAW) for industrial workers. The GAW was critical to flexible work
organization was in two senses. One sense of work reorganization
in the automobile industry was to smooth out seasonal swings in
the industry's demand for workers by changing the schedules for
model changes and new tooling. A second sense of work reorganization was assigning workers to more than one job. If employers
were required to guarantee income to current employees, then they
wanted to be able to move workers around as the flow of work
declined in some production areas and increased in others.[40]

Closely related to the method of payment was that workers
sought to control standards of production that determined the

sheer individual effort required to hold on to a job and earn a living as well as influence total employment. Management hierarchy and norms of efficiency had equally major effects on workers' livelihoods and on labor involvement in work. An official of the International Ladies Garment Workers' Union (ILGWU) wrote to the UAW's Walter Reuther to point out that union influence in production-standard setting was the "key to participation in every level of management by the union."[41] Ford Motor Company, for example, had become notorious among autoworkers as the "speedup king."[42] In Ford's brutal plant regime, workers were "driven" to keep up with the pace of automatic machinery by threats and physical intimidation. The authority of plant management extended to the power to hire and fire and to determine who should be laid off, recalled to work, and promoted. A primary demand of UAW members was job security based upon workers' rights to help determine production standards (which they succeeded in winning in several auto plants); that job rights be based upon seniority (and not management-determined "merit" qualifications), thus transforming a device under craft conditions that protected the most highly experienced worker into one that protected older workers with less stamina; and that local plant managers negotiate directly with workers to resolve conflicts.[43]

The UAW insisted that the auto companies replan the production process to stabilize employment; completely change their payment systems; curb supervisor power; and change their price and product policies. Perhaps the key demand was that competition among companies in the industry should not include wages and direct labor costs and should instead focus on products and methods. The guarantee for this was industry-wide bargaining between a secure national union and the various firms.

Autoworkers and union leaders perceived that solutions to all problems of standards, pay, and job assignments could not be found through negotiations in the shop or even the company. Workers and unions were well aware of the integrated character of their industries and realized that production standards disputes and workplace authority had major ramifications for industrial performance. Moreover, while labor could help the corporation become more productive, the managers still controlled price policy. The government needed to develop the means of preventing corporations from hording all the productive gains for themselves at the expense of society.

The solution that the Roosevelt administration shifted toward in 1938 had three parts. The first was deliberate fiscal pump priming. The second was to break the apparent stranglehold that "monopoly" businesses had on consumer purchasing power through investigation of oligopoly pricing and new federal wage and hour legislation. And the third was to launch an investigation of "industrial concentration," by the Temporary National Economic Committee which was made up of members of Congress and the administration, one of whose imputed purposes was to lay the groundwork for planned economic restructuring.[44]

Democrats and the Politics of War

The combination of recession, the president's response to the Little Steel strike, the frustrations of the struggle with the Congress over the NLRA, and the continuing problems of workers in the mass-production industries contributed to the alienation of union activists from the Democratic party, many of whom began to urge the creation of a labor-based party. Of course, many activists were not Democrats at all; some traditionally were Republicans, including John L. Lewis, and many UAW officials were Socialists and Communists. But beyond the partisan segment, there was a large part of the CIO that had not had much commitment to any party and to whom switching allegiances may not have been a troubling matter. Some 21 percent of the American population said they would support a new party,[45] and the CIO had already created a means of channeling union support in the 1936 election—Labor's Non-Partisan League (LNPL). Also, the CIO (and increasingly the AFL, too) recognized that it did need political power. Its member unions had the muscle to tie up major industries to gain influence over individual employers, but this circumstance falsely magnified labor's power; the power was negative, and it did not translate well into the electoral and policy arenas. Moreover, mass-production union members, most of whom were less able to fend for themselves in the labor market than craft workers, because they only possessed company-specific skills, depended on broader economic conditions for employment. They needed a link to a political party in government that was willing to implement a full-employment policy.

But there were several factors that made independent political action a nonstarter. In consequence of debates over what the CIO should do, the bulk of the federation cleaved more closely to the Democrats. First, the union movement—both CIO and AFL—was regionalized in the late 1930s; it simply did not have much of a membership base outside the manufacturing belt of the northeastern and north central states. CIO unions launched organizing drives in southern textile, coal, and rubber areas, but the battles were fierce and success was hardly a foregone conclusion. Therefore, given the territorial basis of representation in the Congress on which the two parties were built—and no one proposed changing this structural feature of American politics—proponents of an independent labor party had to find an argument justifying years in the wilderness, while the unions did build a base in the southern states. As for the possibility that labor could multiply its strength through alliance with other movements, most of them had already made their peace with the reformist Democrats, including the Farmer-Labor and Progressive parties of the upper midwest and the Townsend Movement, while the leading farmer organization, the American Farm Bureau Federation, shifted to the ideological right. Also, "unchurched" voters had little reason to retract the vote decisions that contributed to the landslides of 1932 and 1936, although enough voter changes in the following years contributed to a slight resurgence of Republican and conservative Democrats. The UAW had an object lesson close to home. Prominent CIO leaders, including Walter Reuther, joined a slate for city council of Detroit in 1937, but not one of its candidates was elected. Moreover, in the 1938 Michigan gubernatorial election, Frank Murphy was defeated. Finally, the labor movement was then hopelessly split into CIO and AFL wings and the factionalism of the leadership, though widely criticized by lower-level union staffers on both sides, led directly to the collapse of labor's congressional electoral effort in 1938. In short, from the electoral perspective, the CIO needed the Democrats even though the party was not firmly prolabor.

At the same time, the Democrats—or at least the liberal reformers among them—needed the unions. The president's failed attempt to purge the party during the 1938 congressional elections reinforced the bipartisan "conservative coalition" in the Congress that had emerged in 1937 after the GM sit-down strike. Led by southern Democrats, it balked at fully continuing Roosevelt's proto-Keynesian policy and opposed Roosevelt's first executive reorganization plan, preserving the fragmentation of regulatory agencies and congressional autonomy from the executive. The Congress structured the unemployment compensation and employment service programs to preserve the states' powers and, not incidentally, to prevent establishment of national standards and the administrative capacity to implement them. Internal fragmentation was lessened a bit by the 1939 Executive Reorganization Act, but major regulatory agencies were exempted, including the NLRB.[46]

The congressional conservatives also teamed up with employers and the AFL to try to amend the NLRA in 1939, as already mentioned. Despite the apparently clear enunciation of a new national industrial policy in the Wagner Act, there were many outstanding questions of interpretation concerning government's involvement in determining the substance of collectively bargained contracts and the primary goals of national economic policy. For example, the act had created the board to implement the act's injunction that management desist from disrupting workers' associations and bargain with unions, but it was not clear what issues companies had to bargain over, and whether the government would go further than the Fair Labor Standards Act of 1938, which established substantive terms of minimum wages and maximum hours, to mandate specific agreements. Moreover, it was unclear whether workers had the right to participate in management—in what sense were they made "equal" according to the NLRA—or simply had the right to be represented by unions in negotiations with company officials over the terms of labor market exchange. Congressional conservatives were the mouthpiece of employer hostility to the law.

Paradoxically, it was the shift in President Roosevelt's attention away from domestic problems after the 1938 elections that created a new opportunity for the CIO for a closer alliance with the Democratic party. His attention, in 1939, was increasingly focused on German threats to peace and to America's role in world politics. He began a campaign to engage the United States in helping Britain, at first by amending the neutrality laws, which earned some strong opposition from auto and steel executives who argued that peace and supplying the belligerents was making business very good again.[47] If union leaders were willing, this was labor's opportunity to show that it was his most reliable ally. But this strategy was not without cost; indeed it led to a shift in the internal alliances that characterized the CIO. Thus, John L. Lewis was not willing to support the president in the 1940 elections. Although Lewis supported amending the neutrality laws, he demanded that the CIO repudiate Roosevelt's bid for a third term. But this position was so unpopular that he was compelled to resign the CIO presidency. Moreover, the Communist party unionists, who had figured prominently in the actual organizing of the mass production industries and who had gained leadership positions in confidence of their abilities, came out against Roosevelt after the signing of the nonaggression pact between the Soviet Union and Germany. In the UAW, where leadership factionalism persisted, Socialists and others roundly tasked Communists for their obeisance to Soviet needs. The remaining CIO union leaders rallied to Roosevelt's reelection and to the president's policy of involving the United States in the European war. In the summer of 1940, Roosevelt named Sidney Hillman the co-chair, with GM's William Knudsen, of the overall federal war preparedness agency, the National Defense Advisory Commission.[48]

The CIO unions in the auto, steel, electrical, and oil industries in 1940 prepared plans for industrial conversion to war based on reformed industry governance that gave equal participation to managers, employees, and the public. The plans foresaw a tremendous enhancement of the role of unions in the work process and in broad planning of industry. They called for extensive worker participation through joint labor-management committees in the shop, industry councils, and a national planning board.[49] Although the CIO plans were rejected by the Roosevelt administration—one administration official commented that the plans were good, but came from the wrong source—it would be wrong to underestimate the significance of the war industry proposals.

First of all, they further established the labor movement as a constituency of the executive branch. As in the First World War, CIO leaders intended to reap the gains of wartime social collaboration. By the end of the war, the CIO had a full international agenda similar to Roosevelt's. They argued that industry should be responsive to foreign policy goals based on international cooperation and the reconstruction of Europe, including international labor cooperation to raise work standards, support for the creation of the International Monetary Fund, World Bank, and the United Nations; transfer of capital to Europe; and, in the short term, an imbalance of exports, especially of manufactured goods, which would rebuild Europe and boost American employment.[50] But, while some important Roosevelt administration advisors stressed export market expansion and using government regulatory powers to ensure competition among industrial sectors as prerequisite for full employment in the United States, organized labor focused on government intervention in the financial and industrial structures of the economy and emphasized that domestic full employment was prerequisite to u.s. foreign policy goals.

Second, these plans embodied the continuity of the older producerist tradition in a new mass production setting. The alternatives that workers believed they had were not uniquely determined by technology and corporate hierarchy. The Auto Workers' industry council plan was informally known as the Reuther Plan, named for its chief proponent, Walter Reuther, director of both the union's General Motors Department and Skilled Trades Department, who developed the plan with toolmakers at GM and with friendly administration officials.

Reuther grew up in a Wheeling, West Virginia family and was instructed in the Debsian socialist politics of his brewery-worker father. After Reuther moved to Detroit in the 1920s, he was active in the League for Industrial Democracy and in debates among social-democrats and assorted left-wing factions, which were intensely active in the area. Reuther, as had Sidney Hillman before him, abandoned independent Socialist party politics in the later 1930s and, at the urging of Hillman, focused on pragmatic steps to democratize and "modernize" the social relations of industry.[51]

Third, union leaders were serious about the plans. Industry councils continued to provide the reform framework of the (eventually) dominant wing of the CIO. The CIO urged adoption of industry councils throughout the 1940s and, in 1951, called them a "permanent" part of labor's reform agenda.[52] Because of the history of factional conflict within the CIO between Communist party unionists and anti-Communists, which became very serious during the defense period and persisted until the breakup of the CIO in 1949, some observers have labeled the plans "conservative"—because they were proposed by the anti-Communist unionists—and made for merely tactical advantage—as an alternative to socialism. But the roots of the industry council plans go deeper, as already indicated. It is true that in respect to the positive use of government authority, the CIO's social-democratic producerism overlapped with Catholic social teaching—some of which was very "conservative" and ideologically procapitalist—and American Progressivism. Reuther himself gained the support of the Association of Catholic Trade Unionists during the factional fights, and he adopted the rhetoric of Progressivism once he left the socialist milieu. But in another respect, the plans were firmly within the range of contemporary alternatives that were debated at the end of the 1930s about how to have government planning without government domination and tyranny. In this sense, the CIO plans were typically pragmatic in their emphasis on problem solving, absence of rhetoric about capitalism and socialism, and in their proposals for combining government controls with private collaboration and decision making. At the same time, the CIO plans appeared to employers as nothing less than revolutionary.[53]

Wartime Standstill

The consequences of seeking a broader basis for the labor movement, nonetheless, were decidedly mixed. At first, as the economy and the Roosevelt administration geared for war in 1940 and 1941, labor's role, and especially the CIO's role, improved. The CIO won public approval in comparison with industrialists who resisted the effort and were more interested in the new opportunities for profit making. And, during the war, government support of labor-management cooperation compelled employers to recognize unions and to participate in collective bargaining. The ranks of CIO and AFL unionists increased tremendously. A new UAW organizing drive finally led to the unionization of Ford in 1941. Autoworkers' membership doubled between Pearl Harbor and V-E Day.[54]

But commitment to Roosevelt Democrats and war mobilization did inhibit the reform program in its popular, legislative, and social aspects and stymied the internal dynamics of the trade unions. A straw in the wind was that Hillman, in his role in the war administration, rejected arguments by some unionists that he was labor's representative (as Gompers had been during wwi) and the war mobilization should be decentralized into the hands of unions and industries. Instead, he envisioned the proper role of government to be to authoritatively direct the mobilization. Hillman loyally backed the government's suppression of an organizing strike by the uaw in California aircraft plants in 1941, the outcome of which for internal uaw politics was to further split the Communist wing, which led the organizing campaign, from the Reuther wing, which supported Hillman and the government.[55] Moreover, the administration authorized a policy of loosely applying the nlra to defense employers. But despite Hillman's cooperative support for Roosevelt's policies, shortly after Pearl Harbor in January 1942, the president scrapped the defense set up and Hillman himself and put a new War Production Board (wpb)into place.[56] The wpb rejected a proposal from Murray for joint labor-management administration of the new agency. GM president, C. E. Wilson, declared, apparently without irony, that "to divide the responsibility for management would be to destroy the very foundation upon which America's unparalleled record of industrial accomplishment is built."[57] The board was dominated by employers and the army. The broad and the intense hostility that the administration's tergiversation generated among labor leaders eventually led to the creation of additional agencies—including the National War Labor Board (nwlb) and the War Manpower Commission (wmc)—with tripartite representation of management, unions, and government, to deal with more narrowly-conceived, though still very important, labor issues. Labor's role in production planning remained sharply limited by managerial opposition to war plans that might act as a "wedge" for social reform and by acquiescence in this by government leaders who put greater value on wage stability, increased production, and maintenance of business support for the war than on continuing the reform of the society that the war effort would protect.[58]

As labor was increasingly squeezed out or by-passed in national policy making, it sought new forms of leverage. But labor leaders (with the spectacular exception of John L. Lewis and the umw, which now was an unaffiliated union) were constrained to preserve industrial peace by the "no-strike pledge" that they had made to the country after the Japanese attack on Pearl Harbor. Moreover, repeated congressional threats of a "labor draft" was held over them as a club. What made this new "union responsibility" for social order especially trying for labor leaders was the growing impatience of rank and filers, who had great potential power to win concessions from employers due to wartime full employment and the accumulated grievances over the lag of wages behind the cost of living. The UAW was one of the focal points in the CIO for many of these developments. Although the UAW leadership coalition still was rife with ideological tensions and disputes over how to respond to the clear business domination of the war effort and wartime attempts by companies like GM to undermine the union's presence in the plants, it held together against rank and file direct action tactics. The issue came to a head when the rank and file movement organized at the union's convention in September 1944 in Grand Rapids, Michigan, to have the UAW renounce the no-strike agreement. This movement was only deflected at the convention by a decision to hold a union-wide referendum on the question in early 1945—in which the pledge was reaffirmed in a very low turnout— but the partial defeat of the official position reflected the readiness of the rank and file to assert a major role in industrial politics.[59]

On the one hand, the War Labor Board eased the union leaders' predicament somewhat by absolutely insisting on company and union discipline of rank and filers to preserve the no-strike pledge and, on the other, rewarding compliant unions with contractual "fringe" benefits; new means of security for their organizations against both employers and insurgent memberships; and by helping set up grievance procedures so problems in the shop could be settled without strikes.[60] Ultimately the rank and file movements to break the no-strike pledge were held in check by a solid popular-front coalition among labor leaders, which again included Communist party activists who had joined the war effort after the German invasion of the Soviet Union.

The real locus of CIO political leverage was supposed to be the CIO Political Action Committee, created in 1943. Hillman was its director and he sought both to establish an autonomous labor political organization that could put friendly pressure on Roosevelt and intervene in elections and to preserve the popular front by forestalling pressures for a labor party. The PAC achieved some notable successes in the Congressional and presidential elections of 1944, temporarily stopping the rightward lurch that emerged in the 1942 elections and in simmering congressional hostility over its loss of authority.[61]

Reconversion to What?

The changing balance of power during the war helped create a more bureaucratic style of unionism, and this was, to a large degree, an outcome of government policy that favored managerial control of wartime production and managements' designs for industrial order. Some labor experts, such as George Taylor, argued that the wartime labor relations structures decisively influenced the postwar labor system. There was no doubt that the War Labor Board wanted to establish precedents and that certain of its policies, especially the addition of fringe benefits in collective bargaining contracts, were resumed after the war. But as union leaders and managers foresaw military victory, they turned their minds to the terms of industrial peace.

In 1945, Cooke and Murray readied a new edition of their book on industrial democracy, and Reuther presented an updated version of his industry council plan in a journal published by CIO and AFL union leaders. Reuther called for the creation of councils on which would sit representatives of workers, managers, and government and, in certain industries, also farmers and consumers. This "multipartite" governing structure was to ensure that the operation of industry would reflect the interests of society. The councils would make strategic plans for investment, products, and prices. The industry councils would be supported by company-level and plant committees of workers and managers and by a national government economic planning board.[62] The National Planning Board, again with "multipartite" membership, would set "social priorities" for production and distribution. Victor Reuther wrote that it would help transform "a formless, anarchic economy into a rational industrial society."[63] The basic conception of national macroeconomic management was based on analyses of underconsumption and the newer ideas of American Keynesians.[64] The economy was based on mass production—high volume manufacturing of standardized goods at a low unit costs and stable prices—and profits and wages both could be high as long as the market was extensive, thus allowing small profit margins to aggregate into great masses of financial surplus. However, top corporate managers would either over accumulate profits and not expand capacity to meet new demands or they would drive down wages relative to profits and thus undermine mass markets. Either way individuals were made economically insecure and were excluded from crucial decision making. The solution was to "compensate" for the shortfall in investment or mass purchasing power by high government spending for social insurance (for example, unemployment benefits, pensions) and investment (plant, education and training), coupled with high taxes on the wealthy and a strong labor movement to directly redistribute income.

The plan was distinct from Keynesianism in its attention to microeconomic issues. Whereas the implementation of the cio plan clearly would shift control of industry from management to labor, consumers, farmers, and government officials, Keynesian policy was compatible with the industrial status quo. Indeed this quality was not lost on some of its leading advocates among large corporations and in the U.S. Chamber of Commerce and the Committee for Economic Development, which wanted to stabilize labor-management relations.[65] The plan proposed a radical restructuring of industrial and political power. Reuther proposed the creation of "technical commando units" of skilled labor—noncompetitive "pools" of engineers, draughtsmen, and designers; tool and die workers; and maintenance trades—to service all companies in a region and to guarantee "flexible production." The plan also proposed a government research agency to license and spread scientific and technological information and to plan industrial modernization, including public ownership of "life and death" industries (e.g., utilities), high-risk experimental production, and "yardstick" plants in highly concentrated industries to promote technological change and price stability.

The cio also lobbied for "nationalization" of the u.s. Employment Service in order to tie national economic planning to local job creation and the establishment of a Labor Extension Service modeled on the U.S. Agriculture Department's Extension Service.

The UAW helped create and run a pilot program for the service in Michigan at the end of the war. The CIO (and some AFL unions) later testified in Congress on behalf of a law creating an Extension Service that would provide worker training in production methods and new technologies, economics, and labor history as a means of improving productivity and work force solidarity.[66]

To most industrial managers the New Deal had been a revolution that called for drastic measures to fight back against labor and "socialist" government. Yet, during the war, even the holders of this peculiarly American managerial reaction to liberal reform discovered that government power could be an effective stimulant to economic expansion. After all, business managers had taken the reins of planning and control of the "total war" domestic mobilization, side by side with the Army, and they claimed the largest credit for its obvious successes in sheer production and new wealth. Moreover, the no-strike pledge worked and the possibility of peaceful negotiations with union leaders became less threatening to an increasing bloc of employers. Nonetheless, management's postwar position seemed anything but assured. Most experts predicted renewed depression with reconversion to a peacetime economy, citing World War I experience to buttress arguments that the vast increase in industrial capacity created conditions of over supply. Also, business leaders claimed that war conditions (including cost-plus government pricing) undermined their internal cost structures and insisted that to survive and profit in a postwar competitive buyers' market, government should end all price controls and managers should regain mastery of production costs by increasing labor standards, lengthening hours of work, and dismissing the less productive workers. Labor costs loomed most threatening because the Labor Board had enhanced the political security of union leaders and vastly expanded the rolls of union membership. Employers were threatened by the breathtaking scope of the CIO reform agenda.

Corporate leaders, such as GM's Sloan, made clear that the acknowledged need for policies (private and public) to stabilize their operations did not entail loss of control over their companies to unions and government. And while the wartime U.S. Chamber of Commerce, parts of the Business Council, and the newly created Committee for Economic Development largely had abandoned laissez-faire rhetoric and had adopted a conservative version of Keynesian macroeconomic analysis, the Little Steel companies, most of the auto industry, and farm equipment manufacturers represented by the National Association of Manufacturers, local Chambers of Commerce, and the Automobile Manufacturers Association, provided the backbone of reaction to reform and vehemently opposed federal assumption of responsibility for economic performance. Both of these wings of employers' opinion were intent upon maintaining their authority to set wages and prices and preventing unions from using the state to restructure the economy and raise taxes. Manufacturing leaders, argued Sloan, had to broaden their claims from control in the arena of production to political and social leadership in order to prevent the "socialization of enterprise" which would come about from "nonbusiness" influence on government planning.[67]

The Committee for Economic Development (CED) was probably the most liberal group of businessmen, if not the most influential. Organized by Studebaker president, Paul Hoffman, and insurance executive William Benton in 1942, with encouragement from U.S. secretary of commerce Jesse Jones, CED grouped together the heads of mostly very large corporations who also were members of the Commerce Department's Business Advisory Council, in order to make plans for the postwar economy and to proselytize small business. The group wanted to use the tax code, monetary policy, and trade to achieve "high" rates of national employment and to smooth out business cycles without redistribution of income or infringement on traditional management prerogatives. These policies, they argued, could be achieved relatively "passively" and without much popular participation through the new powers for macroeconomic management that the federal government had acquired in Depression and war. For example, existing mildly progressive taxes and the introduction of payroll withholding made possible automatically increasing revenue with economic growth which, in turn, would act to slow down demand-push inflation on the high side of the business cycle. Moreover, export demand from Europe would absorb the productive "surplus" made possible by the enormous expansion of plant capacity during the war without redistributing income and recasting the composition of production. CED, favored "automatic stabilizers" like the tax code because it did not believe the government had the capacity for hands on, timely execution of a more interventionary policy, but CED, with the National Association of Manufacturers and the Chamber of Commerce, made sure the government did not develop such a capacity. The wartime U.S. Chamber of Commerce under Eric Johnston, a building construction executive, also accepted a role for the federal government in stabilizing the business cycle. Like the CED, it preferred to keep this role as limited and as politically insulated from popular influence as possible. Its primary goal for labor-management relations was stability based on recognized spheres of managerial and union action.[68]

In fact liberal businessmen differed little from the hard-liners when it came to issues of control inside the enterprise and, in any case, they were politically outweighed by them. Most employers, regardless of ostensibly broad business agreement on "free collective bargaining" and use of grievance procedures and conciliation methods[69], wanted to restore management control in the firm, which they believed had drastically declined during the war due to aggressive union demands and government meddling. The voluntarism of the Wagner Act and the reliance on evolving court decisions and Democratic administration policies were rejected by the NAM and, in particular, by the Big Three auto manufacturers who wanted new statute law to control labor.

The essential vision of these hard-line mainstream corporate leaders was a managerialism in which production was organized as an efficient bureaucracy with a single line of command from the chief executive's office to the shop floor. The corporation was not pluralist and corporate leaders, like GM's Sloan, explicitly rejected "cooperation." Management hierarchy was necessary for efficient operations and management control was based on property rights and delegation of authority to managers: managers had sole control of the disposition of the economic surplus and responsibility to increase revenues and profits. Automobile Manufacturers Association spokesmen, in 1945, opposed even the "job conscious" unionism long associated with the AFL that focused on wages, hours, and working conditions: rights to hire, fire, assign, promote, discipline, and classify workers, not to mention decisions about investment, products, technology, production standards, and scheduling were well beyond the proper scope of union concern. At best unions could express their opinions and grieve ex post facto management decisions.[70] As GM president Charles E. Wilson claimed, collective bargaining had to be contained in its proper sphere. Otherwise, "the border area of collective bargaining will be a constant battleground between employers and unions, as the unions continually attempt to press the boundary farther and farther into the area of managerial functions." GM's labor strategy was to firmly and decisively resist a union role in business planning with whatever resources were necessary.[71]

CHAPTER 4

Settling for Pluralism

Management's fear that collective bargaining is a Trojan Horse . . . is a nightmare of management's own making. Management has no divine rights. Management has only functions, which it performs well or poorly. The only prerogatives which management has lost turned out to be usurpations of power and privilege to which no group of men have exclusive right in a democratic nation.
                              —*Walter Reuther, undelivered speech, 1948*

I ndicative of industrial workers' continued influence after the 1930s was the rise to the presidency of the United Auto Workers Union of Walter Reuther, an autoworker of dynamic ambitions who, with his activist brothers Victor and Roy, had struggled through the factional wars on the labor left. By April 1946, when he was narrowly elected UAW president, Reuther was poised as the leader of the largest union in the CIO to take the side of older leaders like Sidney Hillman, Philip Murray, David Dubinsky (ILGWU), John L. Lewis, and William Green (president of the AFL).

In the context of labor union politics in the 1940s, Reuther distinguished himself, not so much as the unique advocate of national economic planning and social reform, but for the public prominence he gained by proposing specific and detailed reforms for industrial organization and by his perspicacious use of a wide variety of tactics as a UAW leader to achieve them. It was in this spirit that Reuther, a master toolmaker by trade, and his brother Victor had worked in the Soviet Union for over a year in the early 1930s and instructed Russian workers in mass production techniques. It was in this spirit as well that Reuther proposed in 1940 to the National Defense Advisory Commission his plan for the conversion of the automobile industry into one that mass produced airplanes. And it was in this spirit, in 1945, that Reuther outlined, in an in-house labor theoretical journal, his proposal for peacetime planning.[1]

Reuther's plan was consistent with CIO policy. CIO leaders believed that a popular government could guarantee the flexibility and responsiveness of the industrial order to social needs. The postwar 1940s economic policy debates over wages, prices, and profits were the substance of their daily business. The basic analysis was that the wartime experience of full employment was an aberration of the war and that no structural changes had taken place to prevent a return to depression conditions. Once wartime savings were spent, in two to five years, oligopoly firms would maintain or raise prices and cut production to preserve profits, tipping off a downward spiral of reduced employment and consumer demand and further production cutbacks. An economy based on mass production industries needed mass consumer markets, and only the government had the incentive and indeed the capacity to ensure they existed. But, unavoidably, union leaders were also deeply enmeshed in the micro relations in factories and offices across the economy, and they persistently proposed to link solutions to micro problems of organizing work with national policies.[2] Reuther's and the CIO's social-democratic vision of how the government should go about coordinating production and consumption was not fulfilled after the war. What the government did do, however, had a major influence on industrial relations and on the internal politics of the unions.

In 1945, the UAW–auto industry relationship still was dynamic and unsettled on the shop floor, in collective bargaining and in basic entitlements to authority to make decisions that affected the public. In this respect automobile labor relations shared a condition with almost all other industries. The AFL unions had more firmly established routines in the workplace, but the AFL, the railroad brotherhoods, and Lewis' independent Mine Workers Union shared with the CIO a basic political insecurity. Yet, the bitter animosity that top AFL leaders and Lewis felt for the CIO and the craft unions' antipathy to compromising their historic volutarism blocked labor unity on a social-democratic program and electoral realignment. The CIO tried and failed to gain support from the government, employers, the AFL, and John L. Lewis for using union-management bargaining relationships as a structural element in the management of the economy. But the labor system was not, thus, left "as is"; it took several more years of political struggle before labor-management relationships and government policies were devised that stabilized the balance of political forces and established new forms of cooperation.

A focused look at the UAW–auto industry relationship shows that the auto industry was often the central arena in which these struggles were waged. Also crucial was steady pressure from determined employers and an acquiescent government whose Democratic president agreed that labor was a subordinate partner at work and in politics. The settlement of auto labor-management relations at the end of the decade is a story of the narrowing of alternative producerist and managerialist industrial designs toward what became called industrial pluralism and interest group liberalism. The auto settlement and the settlements in other industries patterned on autos determined the boundaries of the New Deal's industrial order. The settlements reflected strategic successes and failures shaped by specific managerial incentives and counterstrategies, internal political dynamics of the unions, and patterns of Democratic party support and government organization. The ways in which labor-management conflicts were settled is crucial for understanding the subsequent institutional development of the industrial order because the settlements created incentives to maintain the forces which shaped them.

Creating the Postwar Bargaining Climate

With the end of the war with Germany anticipated in the spring and with Japan later in the year, the apparent necessity for labor-management cooperation on the old basis was gone. The leaders of the CIO and AFL acted cautiously, however, fearing a collapse of the postwar economy—as they knew and a few well remembered had happened after World War I—and with it a collapse of union membership, and they sought to continue the peaceful approach of wartime labor policy through voluntary action. Yet, the top union leaders increasingly found themselves rebuffed by employers and the government. By the end of the year, union organizations turned to direct action, and one of the greatest strike waves in American history.

Philip Murray and William Green signed a Charter for Industrial Peace with Eric Johnston of the u.s. Chamber of Commerce in March 1945 that proposed extending war-time labor-management cooperation during reconversion of the economy to civilian conditions. The charter had just seven points, but a committee was established to work out details. The members of the continuation committee included Sidney Hillman, Robert Watt, and George Meany for the AFL, R. J. Thomas of the UAW, Paul Hoffman of Studebaker, Henry Kaiser of Kaiser Industries, Otto Sevferth of Western Michigan Steel Foundries, E. J. Thomas of Goodyear, and J. D. Zellerbach of Crown-Zellerbach. The charter called for "management-labor unity" and a "practical partnership" based on the charter's principles. The Charter's strongest advocates included the Catholic Church and the Communist party. The *Daily Worker* argued that the charter's principles were only the start of a process.[3] George Taylor, the chairman of the War Labor Board, gave the agreement his blessing. The first principle was that "increased prosperity" should be based on full production, "improved productive efficiency, and technological advancement" and "advancing" wages. The charter endorsed "private competitive capitalism" as the "foundation" of the national economy; management's "inherent right" to "direct the operations of an enterprise," recognized by labor and government alike; union rights to organize and bargain collectively; social welfare provision; increased foreign trade; and collective international security through the United Nations. Implicit was a new union no-strike pledge and a promise by managements to avoid lockouts. The agreement was silent about the government's role in industrial relations and said nothing about shop-floor participation by workers. Because of these omissions and the implicit no-strike pledge, and yet hoping to show "good faith" to the public, the UAW mildly endorsed the charter in April.[4]

The official UAW position did overlap that in the charter, however. As outlined in its report "The Auto Industry After the War," the union was determined, in the quoted words of Franklin Roosevelt, to "use for abundance . . . the powers we have developed in production for war."[5] The greatly expanded plant that the government created during the war should be used at full capacity after the war to keep everyone employed—something at which company executives scoffed. To do so, a much larger product market had to be maintained through price controls, wage increases, public investment in public works and new industry (such as aircraft and prefabricated housing), government policies to stimulate "technological improvement" in the auto industry by, for example, fostering "real competition," foreign trade, and "sound industrial relations." The union also proposed a veteran's wage bonus and urged the government to continue production planning, including pooling skilled labor. Finally, the UAW advocated creation of a tripartite national economic council to recommend economic policies. The union's report warned employers that if they repudiated the Charter for Industrial Peace, they should know that the "full power" of the union "[would] be mobilized." However, neither the AFL executive council nor the NAM, behind the resistance of Chrysler executives, would support the charter and the agreement died.[6]

At the same time, the UAW and CIO worked closely with federal officials in the Office of War Mobilization and Reconversion, the Office of Price Administration, and the Labor Board to extend government controls over wages and prices.[7] They wanted the government to develop a conversion policy that boosted mass-consumer purchasing power so that the workers would not have to engage in strike action. Both the CIO and the AFL believed that wartime policy had not been just to labor, and both wanted a postwar boost in workers' wages to make up for lost real income during the war and for the decline in weekly wages as work hours were cutback from wartime levels, but the CIO wanted continued government controls on prices, whereas the AFL shied away for fear of parallel controls on wages.

Executive leadership, however, was in a disorganized state, partly because of the failure of wartime planning for reconversion and partly because of Roosevelt's death and the accession of Truman to the White House.[8] During this period, Truman's agenda was the object of widespread speculation. Truman, even less than President Roosevelt, was not a planner, nor did he favor "industrial democracy" of the CIO type. Truman's closest advisors in the early years of his presidency were businessmen who counselled quick decontrol of the economy, balanced budgets, and a return to market determination of prices and wages. His key labor policy advisors were John

Steelman, who favored conciliation by neutral experts, and Lewis Schwellenbach, who favored social-democratic labor policy, but who was ill for most of the time and consequently was a weak policy advocate. Liberals took heart in the belief that Truman was an old Progressive of the antimonopolist stripe. As senator, he had established his reform credentials by his investigation of military-business control of the war effort and by his endorsement of Roosevelt's Economic Bill of Rights.[9]

Throughout the summer and early fall, the CIO and its official allies, such as William Davis and Chester Bowles, counselled Truman to adopt as government policy that wages should increase without price increases. At first Truman rejected continued controls, and the administration quickly ended most of them after the victory over Japan in August. But, in September, Truman announced a policy favoring wage increases if they were given without price increases. At the same time, Truman desired to cut back the enormous wartime growth in the federal budget deficit, and he resisted general revenue tax cuts; in fact, he supported payroll tax increases to pay for social welfare programs. This policy implied a squeeze on profits and was in contrast to the utility pricing of wartime. It appeared that Truman, at least implicitly, was following a Keynesian path, although it is doubtful that the Truman administration perceived their policy as a deliberate profits squeeze.[10] A quick transition to "free collective bargaining" was fraught with dangers, and Truman's actual policy vacillated between conservative prescriptions and liberal hopes. The ambiguous situation resulted, in part, from Truman's failure to realize that labor and employers would not voluntarily settle their disputes and that the failure to develop the governmental means to do so would create an economic crisis. Government authority over the issue was already weakened by the end of the no-strike pledge and superannuation of the NWLB administrative structure. Corporations ignored the administration's wage-price policy with impunity; they argued they could not afford wage increases without price increases. GM's Charles E. Wilson suggested that if labor wanted to earn more, they should work more, and he proposed amending the Fair Labor Standards Act to make the forty-five-hour week the national norm.

Congressional Democrats showed that they were in no mood to

pick up where reform had left off before the war. Democratic majorities in 1945 and 1946 repeatedly rebuffed the CIO's agenda. It abolished the excess-profits tax, cut income taxes, rejected a bill to improve and extend social security benefits (including national health insurance and unemployment insurance), did not extend minimum-wage coverage, did not pass an employment discrimination bill, and adopted legislation that gave veterans privileges over war workers in the competition for postwar jobs. On the other hand, for a time in the spring and summer, it appeared that the Congress would approve legislation that would commit the federal government to peacetime planning, the full employment bill, initially introduced in January by Montana Democratic Senator James E. Murray. The analysis of what was wrong with the American economy that lay behind the full employment bill was widely accepted within the broad New Deal liberal Democrat network, but debate over how to craft legislation to overcome the problems revealed a division between popular and elite versions of planning.[11] Essentially, the analysis, developed by Alvin Hansen, was the "stagnationist" version of Keynes' theory, that had also influenced the work of the National Resources Planning Board's wartime manifesto and Roosevelt's Economic Bill of Rights. Hansen argued that the American economy had exhausted the relatively easy opportunities for investment that an expanding frontier and population had afforded and that technological change associated with mass production industries was not enough to sustain growth.[12] To ensure growing employment and improved living standards, the government should compensate for the shortfall of private investment with public investment. The bill declared that full employment was the goal of national economic policy. It required the president to present an annual budget that would estimate the gap between private investment and the investment needed to ensure full employment. Then a budget plan would follow to fill the gap through incentives to private investment and, since that was expected not to be forthcoming in sufficient quantities, public investment in infrastructure and social needs.

The Senate began debate on the bill in May, but the CIO gave it only a lukewarm endorsement because it failed to address the problem of corporate power as it emphasized fiscal policy. The UAW's Washington office reported with dismay back to Detroit that the proposed legislation did not include industry councils. Philip Murray testified that the bill was "quite moderate" and called on the Congress to boldly remake American "social and political institutions" in ways that could take advantage of the "extended technology" of production.[13] "The gap" between production and consumption "has been enormously widened just when we had begun to close it somewhat by New Deal legislation. Now we must have another, larger New Deal all over again." Murray argued that the purpose of the bill should not be to compensate for the failures of capitalism, but to plan for full potential from the start. Economic plans would be developed in conjunction with labor and management in industry councils. Reuther sent Senator Wagner a copy of his article "The Challenge of Peace," and he urged amendment of the bill to include a multipartite production board that would be the arena for social coordination and that would have a "major part" in the government's budget planning. The UAW sent drafts of alternative bills, but the Senate passed the full employment bill virtually as proposed in September.[14]

The House became the scene of furious opposition to the Senate version, led by auto manufacturers as part of an increasingly massive business coalition. Many argued that full employment and government spending would create inflation and provoke further government controls. Sympathetic southern Democrats rewrote the bill according to specifications developed by the U.S. Chamber of Commerce and reported it out of committee in December.[15] Treasury Secretary Fred Vinson guided the administration's efforts and kept away from the remaining planners in the government; he accepted the House amendment that separated the president's economic analysis from the annual budget plan. The final legislation passed by Congress as the Employment Act of 1946 closely followed the House version and it qualified the goal of national policy to "maximum" employment "consistent with free enterprise," deleted the full employment budget and plan and substituted an annual Economic Report of the President, and prevented the planning function from being centralized in the Budget Bureau under presidential control by creating a three-person Council of Economic Advisors appointed by the president with Senate concurrence.[16]

While the debate on the employment bill was going on in the

ANGMBERG

House, the CIO sought to reach a national agreement on wage and price relationships at the President's Labor Management Conference in November. The purpose of the conference, said Truman, was for the leaders of giant enterprise and labor unions to voluntarily decide how to compose their relations. The president himself did not attend, and Truman's position was certainly obtuse. The war had suspended consideration of the policy background for collective bargaining but, now that policy was again the source of great debate, so was collective bargaining's relationship to it. Top CIO leaders met with Truman before the conference and argued that what was needed was not a labor program, but a national program to solve domestic problems. Independent labor radical J.B.S. Hardman proposed that the Labor Management Conference invite consumer organizations to participate and become a permanent body, something like a "house of functional representation." The Inter-Union Institute for Labor and Democracy, publishers of the labor-intellectual journal *Labor and Nation,* sponsored its own conference in September.[17]

At the president's conference, the AFL and United Mine Workers joined the employers' associations to reject the CIO's cooperative vision and, more particularly, to prevent placing wage-price relationships on the agenda. Management representatives, such as Charles E. Wilson, who dominated the conference's committee on Management's Right to Manage, took a hard line against recognition of the "public interest" dimension of corporate decision making. The conferees were unable to resolve such basic questions of the scope of collective bargaining (both CIO and AFL wanted no limits on bargaining subjects and scope; they wanted to prevent rigid requirements so that labor-management relations could evolve as circumstances demanded) and what workers could be unionized (especially white-collar workers and factory foremen). The conference only managed to agree on general principles of support for collective bargaining (which was significant since the NAM previously had not clearly done so) and that "peaceful" administrative means of a fortified Federal Mediation and Conciliation Service should be used before the parties resorted to economic force.[18] As the conference came to an ignominious end, strikes broke out all across mass-production industry. They were the first battles in a renewed test of economic might over the shape of the postwar regime. They also were the fruit of employer resistance to union cooperation and of Truman's claimed neutrality: union leaders gave in at last to mounting rank and file pressure for direct action.

The First Round

The Truman administration's economic policy apparently rested on two different presumptions: namely, that the peacetime economy could be stimulated by maintaining consumer demand (via higher wages) and by private investment (which would occur automatically after the decontrol of production and prices). In the context of the New Deal coalitional debates of the previous fifteen years, virtually all of which began with the presumption that corporate misuse of authority was at the root of the depression, this policy was incoherent.[19] All the pragmatism of the New Deal economic analysis and prescription seemed irrelevant to the president who, instead, acted as if driven by an ideological imperative for "free enterprise": decontrol, no direct involvement in labor-management relations, balanced budgets, and protection for bond holders. Moreover, when his policy began to fail badly in the spring of 1946, Truman temporized with the big corporations and lashed out at the unions. This switch deeply alienated organized labor— CIO, AFL, Mine Workers, and railroad brotherhoods alike—and undermined the Democratic party in the fall Congressional elections.

CIO leaders, in 1945, had clearly preferred negotiated and political solutions to economic problems but, now spurned, they turned to strike action to gain wage increases demanded by the rank and file, whose current income had suffered a major cut from wartime levels as work hours declined, and whose employment prospects had narrowed with massive layoffs in the wake of defense contract cancellations. One hundred seventy-five thousand GM workers began to strike at the close of the labor-management conference on November 22 and continued for 113 days until March 13, 1946. The steel strike by over five hundred thousand USW (United Steel Workers) members began in January. There also were strikes of CIO Oil Workers, Meatpackers, and Electrical Workers and hundreds of thousands of others in trucking, textiles, and the glass industry, plus major strikes by the Mine Workers and the Railroad Brotherhoods in the spring of 1946, creating the greatest strike year since 1919.

The Truman administration's first response to the industrial crisis was to try peaceful conciliation and active mediation by government agents. In response to the disruption of the pivotal auto industry, President Truman asked the Congress for authority to appoint a "fact finding board" in the dispute. When the Congress ignored him, Truman just went ahead anyway and in December appointed a board to make recommendations for a settlement based on a determination of the "facts." But just which facts were to be considered was at stake. Reuther sought to have the UAW strike linked to the government's wage-price policy by insisting that GM's finances be reviewed during collective bargaining. The union demanded that GM open its books and prove its inability to give wage increases without price increases. If the company could so prove, the union said, it would scale back its wage demand accordingly. GM vigorously rejected this. The company made thorough counterdemands to narrow collective bargaining to the lines advocated by the NAM. GM demanded withdrawal of nineteen wartime-imposed contract clauses, including elimination of union security; reimposition of incentive wage plans; limits on union free speech; union responsibility for shop discipline, and uninterrupted production; reduction of the number of grievance committeemen; and a "management rights" clause that clearly limited collective bargaining only to wages, hours, and direct conditions of employment and prohibited negotiation on prices, profits, products, and powers to hire, fire, promote, transfer, and discipline. C. E. Wilson blamed a "government-built labor monopoly" and "class warfare" for "industrial anarchy."[20]

The union's position was widely popular beyond the ranks of labor. The UAW and Walter Reuther, who ran the strike as the director of the union's GM Department, organized support across the nation from consumer organizations, farmers, the professional middle classes, and others. The demand that GM "open the books" and demonstrate that it needed to increase prices was compellingly direct and pragmatic.[21] After all, Reuther said that if the company could prove the need, the union would not argue the point further. Moreover, the UAW's attempt to use the strike to further the public

interest in price stability and to support the government's economic policy seemed to present a new opportunity for government
economic management. Responsible unions, perhaps, were the
long sought means by which the federal government could stimulate the economy through fiscal policy without sectoral or firm-
level controls to prevent corporations from exploiting increased
demand. The unions could check the authority of corporate decision makers to recoup losses to wages through price increases.
After all, as Murray had argued during the debate on the Full
Employment Bill, workers were consumers, too; not just nominal
wages, but real wages were a legitimate concern of unions in
collective bargaining. *The New Republic* commented that the union
movement was "on the brink of assuming new and important
public responsibilities. . . . From now on, the most advanced unions
will act not only in the interest of their members, but in the interest
of sound national policy as well." *The Nation* argued that "Reuther
is fighting the government's battle and the consumer's battle."[22]

The UAW at first was cool to the proposal for a presidential fact
finding board because it seemed to be a type of compulsory arbitration in which GM workers would be required to return to their jobs
under the status quo while the board determined the issues. The
top UAW leadership, including Thomas and Reuther, already were
hard pressed to retain control of the rank and file movement; the
GM strike was extremely popular among the workers. In addition, it
was the only strike the union had: the UAW executive board had
decided to strike GM only. The union made "interim" settlements
with Ford and Chrysler in January, hoping to add pressures on GM
from competitors who could get into the marketplace sooner. The
contracts at Ford and Chrysler were concessionary on wages and
shop-floor power—they included "management rights" clauses and
provisions that raised the costs for union locals of protecting wildcat strikers—which made it hard for the union to back down at GM.
Moreover, during the course of the strike, Reuther attracted increasingly vocal criticism from parts of the socialist-left for both the
one-at-a-time strike strategy and the ability-to-pay demand. Therefore,
it was only once Truman appointed the Board members—Lloyd
Garrison, last head of the NWLB, Justice Stacey of the North Carolina Supreme Court, and Milton Eisenhower, president of Kansas
State College—that the union agreed to fact finding, apparently

confident that these men would be sympathetic to labor's case, though the GM workers still refused to return to work. Yet GM management opposed Truman's "outside" interference and, when it became clear on December 20 that the board would consider GM's ability to pay wages, it boycotted the Board's hearings. GM asserted that questions of profits and prices were beyond the board's capacity, and it charged that union demands that these were bargaining issues reflected the union's "socialism," which Reuther cheerfully admitted. The board continued its work nonetheless, and on January 10, 1946, recommended on the key question that GM pay a 17.5 percent (19.5 cents per hour) wage increase without a price increase. (The other issues would be remanded to collective bargaining.) The union accepted these terms, though the wage increase was substantially less than its original demand, but the company rejected it, arguing that any wage increase had to be reflected in increased prices. Truman then rejected his own board's recommendation and the strike continued.[23]

With the auto strike reached a stalemate, the administration's attention shifted to the steel industry where the United Steel Workers Union was set to go on strike January 14. For months leading up to the strike, U.S. Steel, as the principal employer and price leader for the industry, had stood firmly against price controls. It would only give wage increases if it could pass them on in prices, plus enough additional price to maintain profits in what the company assumed would be a depressed postwar market. U.S. Steel executives, led by Benjamin Fairless, carried on intense private negotiations with John Snyder, the director of the Office of War Mobilization and Reconversion who was sympathetic to management's demands. Chester Bowles, director of the Office of Price Administration and a liberal friend of labor, tried to resist price increases.[24] As he had in autos, Truman appointed a fact finding board in steel which was accepted for the USW by Philip Murray, who then postponed the strike deadline until January 21. The company made clear that regardless of what the board recommended, it would insist on a large price increase. The steel board soon recommended an 18.5 cent wage increase, but without addressing the price issue. Murray then caved in on the price issue and accepted the board's proposal, hoping to avoid a bruising showdown with the industry and a government that was clearly unsympathetic to the CIO's thinking about the need to balance prices, wages, and profits. But U.S. Steel rejected the proposal because it did not have an explicit guarantee for price increases. The steelworkers struck as scheduled. Snyder, James Byrnes, Fred Vinson, Bernard Baruch, and Truman himself became personally involved in negotiating with U.S. Steel, eventually settling, in February, on a price increase of more than twice what Bowles considered the maximum defensible "on the merits" to accompany an 18.5 cent wage increase. On February 14, the government announced a new price standard that included the steel "bulge" as the official anti-inflation line. The steel strike ended the next day.

The price line was thus broken and all industries made claims for comparable increases. The CIO unions already had made agreements with companies for 18.5 cents, pending the GM strike outcome, but, now, that became the maximum increase. GM offered the UAW the same 18.5 cents, which Reuther rejected. But there was little that the UAW could do, given that Truman and Murray had abandoned the fight and that the other automobile companies had also settled their wage negotiations with the UAW. The auto strike dragged on another month and was finally settled March 13 without union concessions to "management rights" and with an 18.5 cent wage increase. Both sides claimed victory, but the union clearly lost the policy point. However, Reuther turned his highly visible role as leader of the fight into a successful campaign at the April UAW convention to beat R. J. Thomas for the union's presidency.

The administration's new price policy was not a viable solution to problems of economic reconversion since it provoked strikes and fueled an inflationary spiral. The government began to directly intervene in labor-management disputes to prevent disruption of production. Its neo–laissez faire analysis was that pent up consumer demand, based on wartime savings, would begin to chase scarce goods in the market, driving up prices and, eventually, leading to a collapse of demand and employment. If workers and managers stayed on the job and produced sufficient goods for the market, then inflation might be prevented. Truman's advisors seemed to ignore the New Deal analysis of administered prices and income inequality. Corporate announcements, by GM and Chrysler among others, that they were profitable at just 50 percent of plant capacity found little response in the White House. The administration, instead, believed strikes to be the cause of lagging reconversion to civilian production and sought to control labor disputes through seizures of struck industries and repressive labor legislation. Truman's labor control policy played into the hands of congressional conservatives, who were in a more militant mood. Not only did they want to remove the remaining price controls on food and consumer goods and remove legal support for unions, they proposed legislation to end strikes through court injunctions and imposition of union financial liability for breach of contract.[25] It took almost a year for the Truman administration to realize its political error and begin to improve its ties to labor.

In the meantime, shortly after the settlements in steel, autos, electrical machinery, and other CIO bastions, two major labor disputes raged outside the CIO in coal and the railroads and broke open the fragile alliance among unions and between them and the Democratic party. Four hundred thousand soft-coal miners struck on April 1, while the Railroad Brotherhoods were set to strike later in the month. The Mine Workers sought a private welfare plan to be financed by a royalty per ton of mined coal, which ultimately would be paid by coal consumers, while the rail strike threatened to tie up the whole national economy, despite special railroad labor legislation precisely tailored to prevent such strikes through government mediation. John L. Lewis, who in January returned the UMW to the AFL after five years of unaffiliated status, strongly opposed what he called CIO plans for a "corporate state" and sought to regain his past leadership of labor by out bargaining both the CIO and the timid AFL. According to Lewis, wages should not be set according to the price level; prices were management's business. On the contrary, Lewis adhered to traditional AFL policy that high wages force modernization of industry. And mineworkers were going to get a pension for themselves, regardless of congressional action on social security.[26] Despite his CIO bashing, many CIO activists were attracted to Lewis' apparent militancy.[27] The AFL leadership was counselling moderation, until the postwar economy stabilized, to its affiliates. In the meantime it favored new social welfare legislation.

By the second week of May 1946, coal shortages had forced slowdowns and layoffs in steel and autos as the Bituminous Coal

Operators completely rejected the miners' demand for an employer-financed welfare and retirement fund controlled by the union. Many progressives outside of labor were torn by the UMW's struggles because of Lewis' autocratic control of the union and the conservatism of his pension demand. Truman intervened directly in the talks but, unable to win employer consent, the president seized the mines on May 22 and put them under government operation. Then the government-as-employer signed a contract with Lewis creating a welfare plan, financed by a royalty on coal tonnage, plus vacation pay, a new federal mine safety code, and a "pattern" wage increase of 18.5 cents. The price of coal promptly went up without any objection from the government or Lewis. However, since the southern group of Coal Operators still would not agree to the contract terms, the government was compelled to continue to run the mines to implement its agreement.[28] Indeed, Virginia congressmen A. Willis Robertson and Howard Smith introduced legislation to prohibit welfare plans, which the next year became part of the Taft-Hartley Act, although the issue was not resolved until the United Steel Workers forced the issue at U.S. Steel in 1949, and the Supreme Court ruled that employers had an obligation to bargain over such plans. Yet Lewis' demand in 1946 for a welfare fund provided directly by employers resonated across the labor movement, including in the UAW where demands for a pension plan were made in 1946 and 1947 and became part of factional politics within that union.[29]

In the rail strike, the unions again were outside the UAW and CIO policy orbit. Truman seized this industry May 23, but the unions of engineers and trainmen refused to work for the government. The main issue was pay; the railroad unions wanted more than the "pattern" because their wages seriously had lagged behind those in other industries for many years. Truman and many in the Congress reacted to the railroad unions' demand to break the "pattern" with indignation. Truman called the continued strike a threat to the sovereignty of the government. Secretary of State Byrnes attended the negotiations and attacked the unions. The president made a dramatic appearance before the Congress and thoroughly castigated union leaders (not just the Railroad Brotherhoods), and he asked for stiff controls on strikes and unions in basic industries, including a proposal to draft railroad workers into the

Army during the current dispute. The House passed the proposal 306 to 13.[30]

At virtually the same time as the House was voting, the strike was settled according to the "pattern," and the Senate let the draft proposal die. But a newly antilabor Senate joined the House and passed the Case bill, an amalgam of conservative reforms of the Wagner Act. The unions, now, were seething with anti-Truman and anti-Democrat passion. The UAW damned Truman's draft proposal as "intolerable."[31] The president of the Brotherhood of Railroad Trainmen vowed to use his union's entire treasury to defeat Truman in the 1948 elections. To prevent a complete break with labor, Truman vetoed the Case bill with just five votes to spare in the House. Murray was mollified by the veto, but other union leaders began to discuss how to drop Truman from the Democratic ticket in 1948 or form of a new political party.

On the price front, the AFL and CIO lobbied vigorously for continued price controls and reportedly made an agreement with Chester Bowles (now as director of the Office of Economic Stabilization) for a new no-strike pledge conditioned on effective price stabilization. Although a no-strike pledge seemed unlikely, in the spring, Truman warmed to continued price controls on sensitive consumer goods.[32] The administration had slowed government spending and halted public works projects and, though it continued the drumbeat for "continued production," the only remaining policy option to fight inflation was reimposition of price controls. The remaining war price controls were due to expire in June 1946, but Truman requested Congress extend them yet another year to June 1947. Public opinion was very favorable to controls, and their continuation ostensibly would be to Congress' credit, but many producer and distributor groups had bailed out. For example, previous supporters, such as cotton producers, switched sides, as, for the first time, they were to be covered by the controls proposed by the administration, while their subsidies were to be cut. Also intensely hostile were automobile dealers, who turned their anti–price control campaign into direct political power in Michigan where they took over the Republican party and elected a right-wing governor in November. The Congress debated the issue throughout the spring and finally passed a very weak bill in July that allowed wage increases to be passed on to consumers.

Labor's Fallback Strategy

With the conclusion of collective bargaining in 1946, the UAW and other unions had seen their economic position go from bad to worse and their policy initiatives ignored by the president. On the other hand, they survived the first year of economic reconversion; most of the large employers did not try to destroy the unions, which was something like progress. Moreover, the UAW and CIO did not feel defeated. They acted cautiously to be sure, but, during 1946, union leaders developed a two-part strategy to deal with what they considered their major problems in order to carry on the fight for their reform agenda. The new strategy did not emerge all of a piece as a plan, but gradually, from the unions' industrial circumstances and the changing political conditions of the labor movement during the next two years.

Still desiring a larger role in what they perceived as the necessary public management of the economy, union leaders had to contend with a crisis in their ranks that threatened to undermine the solidarity needed to carry on effectively. Not only were there grievances that could be addressed by worker direct action, but there was ample ideological reinforcement for doing so. Though the wage rate increases were an effective "feed back" for worker solidarity, in 1945–1946 real income lagged—made evident in price increases, although also related to diminished work hours—and large numbers of workers lost their jobs. Also, many workers were altogether left out of the wage increases obtained from the larger firms, while still others employed in the big companies, such as Kelsey-Hayes, Ford, and Chrysler, had some important issues compromised in the fight with GM. Although the sacrifice of some specific interests for the collective good is an inevitable part of large-scale unionism—and the UAW in 1946 still had some seven hundred thousand members—public debate was infected with an aggressively antiunion message that blamed labor leaders for the reconversion difficulties and that further undermined worker solidarity. In the UAW, some of these problems were reflected in an increasingly contentious leadership fight for control of the union.

The battle between Reuther and his supporters on the one side and R. J. Thomas and George Addes, the union's secretary-treasurer, and their supporters on the other has been characterized in

labor histories as a critical episode in the turn to the ideological right by the cio and, moreover, by the entire country in the
later 1940s and 1950s.[33] Indeed it was a critical episode in many
ways. The Reutherites became known as the right wing while the
Thomas-Addes group became known as the left wing, largely because the Reutherite social-democrats and Catholics opposed the
Communist party, which was supporting Thomas-Addes. But the
labels should not obscure the fact that both factions were left wing
in the broader context of American politics. Just as important is
that both leadership factions sought to impose new discipline on
union members to follow their leaders. The dilemma that Reuther,
Thomas, and those leaders who initially fell outside the bilateral
fight faced—and by extension the dilemma that leaders of other
unions faced as well—was that imposing rank-and-file discipline
and support for leaders can undermine the change of individual
consciousness toward solidarity that is associated with engagement
with other workers and which, in turn, is needed to sustain collective action. Both factions were aware of the problem, but the
internal dynamics of the union were conditioned by company
strategies to reassert authority over the shop floor and by hostile
government policy.

The broadly accepted managerial conception of its "prerogatives" was, as Howell Harris has carefully reconstructed it, rooted
in two reinforcing doctrines.[34] One was that property right and
common law gave to management the sole authority to determine
all conditions of employment, work rules, materials, machines,
labor, and disposition of the company income that contribute to
the production of goods for market. But, since unions had incon-
trovertibly gained legal recognition and the boundary between
union and management rights was contentious, managers also
turned to functional arguments. Managerial authority was based
on the superior efficiency of hierarchical command organizations.
Indeed, the war agencies and military had proved that some "classes of people" had to "decide" and some had to "carry out." And,
increasingly in 1946 and 1947, federal and state government officials were inclined to back the managers. The union leaders'
dilemma was that as long as workers' income lagged and working
conditions deteriorated, they were pressed by the rank and file to
strike, but striking raised the wrath of Truman and the conservative

coalition in Congress, which was in no mood to acquiesce in labor voluntarism. Yet, if organized labor followed a policy of industrial restraint, union leaders were likely to lose mass support and have to make concessions in working conditions.

What the union leadership decided, with Reuther a leading proponent, was, first, to take much of the routine conflict of micro labor relations out of play by regularizing dispute resolution procedures, much as Hillman and sympathetic labor experts, such as George Taylor, had urged for years. This meant serious commitment to grievance mechanisms and the development of the committeeman role. The new Reutherite director of the UAW's GM Department, Art Johnstone, became known for his insistence on the nicety of grievance procedure. Still, union leaders quickly discovered that the companies were hostile to pragmatic problem solving and to mediation by outside neutral experts. The companies wanted to establish an industrial common law of precedent in order to dismiss many complaints and to restrict arbitrators to interpretation of contract language after facts were presented to them in hearings rather than allow mediators to investigate a dispute and help find a solution. Ford and GM had considerable success with establishing this sort of grievance system, but at Chrysler, where the informal shop steward system was stronger, workers retained substantial authority on the shop floor.[35] Secondly, CIO union leaders—and both factions in the UAW—recommitted themselves to the coordinated collective bargaining they had attempted in 1945–1946. The CIO would establish the broad goals for collective bargaining in all industries, including wage rate increases, as well as determine the economic and political strategies to achieve them.

Thus, the UAW in 1946 first sought again to play a pivotal role in the CIO's advance. With the end of price control imminent, Chrysler workers were eager to take direct action, goaded on by the company, which was raising production standards and reclassifying workers to lower their pay.[36] Indeed, Chrysler workers probably had the most effective and militant shop organization of the Big Three auto companies, and many were eager to improve on the GM settlement. Chrysler was the UAW's immediate target because its contract, unlike those with GM and Ford (and other CIO union contracts settled in early 1946), had a "reopener" clause, which the union could activate if prices increased. The UAW notified Chrysler and "government and industry" that it wanted wage talks, but promised that if the government acted to control prices—the Price Control Act was put in effect August 20—the UAW would reevaluate its wage demands. The UAW's "basic economic concept" was that the public interest required that "the mass productive power of America must be matched by our purchasing power, if we are to achieve and maintain an economy of abundance. Accordingly, our task is to increase real wages by insisting that wage increases be paid out of the economies of advanced technology and not passed on to the consumer in the form of higher prices."[37]

The UAW not only was worried about price control and lagging real wages, but about employment and membership, which was down a half million from 1.2 million in March 1945 (its wartime peak). Strikes in the auto parts industries, such as springs, were compounding the problems of employment at the main car manufacturers, who were in no hurry to resume full consumer production in any case. In July 1946 GM and Chrysler reported they had passed their break-even points at just 50 percent of prewar production. The union was trying to improve and standardize wages and working conditions and had created special intra-union councils, for example for workers producing castings; springs; gears, axles, and transmissions; piston rings; bearings; as well as special corporation councils for Bendix; Borg-Warner; Thompson Products; Mack Truck, and so on. But it was difficult to do so when demand from the main manufacturers was soft. Steel production also was lagging, and steel executives refused to expand, which hurt the auto companies. It looked like textbook monopoly practices to the UAW. The UAW demanded "sustained production" along with new price controls to prevent a "low-level equilibrium" in which high prices and profits make low production and employment feasible for the companies. The UAW, in July, called a Full Auto Production Conference and invited all the auto assembly companies. Only the small producers Studebaker, Willys-Overland, and Kaiser-Fraser participated; GM and Ford refused to come and claimed the union's own supplier strikes were the cause of lagging production. The conference only produced a request that the federal government begin a program to collect scrap iron.[38]

Murray opposed any Chrysler strike threats because of the

uncertain political climate; the USW was going to wait until December. On August 15, the CIO held a wage-policy conference in Washington and endorsed the UAW's wage strategy, but with Murray's reservation that strike action should be postponed. The CIO created a Wage Research Committee to prepare a brief to guide collective bargaining by the unions and to detail to the public why CIO policy was in the public interest. The UAW agreed to drag out negotiations past the fall Congressional election and even to the first of the new year (which they did in fact) partly in deference to the CIO, partly because the union was strapped for money, and partly because the Thomas-Addes controlled UAW executive board opposed the one-at-a-time collective bargaining strategy proposed by Reuther. Nevertheless, during the long consideration of the Chrysler situation, Reuther gained an important ally in the factional wars in the person of Chrysler Department director, Norman Matthews.[39]

Without effective controls, the cost of living promptly increased 6 percent in July and another 13 percent by November. In November, controls on everything except rent were abandoned as futile. To cap off the period, the president's party took the blame at the polls for inflation and vacillation. The Republican slogan was a sneering "Had Enough?" Southern racism during the election campaigns took a violent lurch back to the days of lynching.[40] Moreover, the 1945–1946 strike wave and the reaction to it had led to a breach between the unions and the party and undermined labor support for the Democrats. The Wayne County (Detroit) CIO Council did no real campaigning. Turnout was unenthusiastic, and many agreed with the AFL's Dan Tobin, president of the powerful Teamsters and the labor representative on the Democratic National Committee, who had predicted that workers would stay at home on election day rather than vote for a "reactionary Republican or for a reactionary Democrat."[41] Republicans won a majority in both houses for the first time since 1928: in the House by 246 to 189 Democrats, including 109 Southern Democrats, and in the Senate by 51 to 45. Many leading liberal-left Democrats were defeated, while Republicans such as Richard Nixon and Joseph McCarthy were elected for the first time.

Although these election results were not unexpected, the reality of defeat reinforced the reassessment by labor leaders of their position. Reuther became more cautious and cool in his public rhetoric about the important role of government in democratizing industrial organization. The previous spring, in contrast, Reuther had turned around what later became the most powerful symbol of ideological cold war to the benefit of domestic social reform. Reuther argued on national radio that an "iron curtain" was being drawn around the labor movement by American industrialists and "reactionaries" who were using scare tactics by invoking the image of totalitarian government. But after the election, in December 1946, Reuther cautioned against an all-powerful central government, mindful of a business-controlled government inimical to labor's interests.[42] This source of Reuther's caution was reinforced in the next two years by American reaction to expanding Soviet control in eastern Europe (which Reuther and other top labor leaders watched intensely) and by the persistent hostility of reform opponents.

The second side of the new CIO strategy was to realign the coalition of forces that made up the Democratic party. The CIO did not accept the political boundaries of 1946. Union activists had reason to believe that the party would swing back to the left, given the widespread criticism of Truman by nonlabor liberals and the exodus of disgusted government officials. Moreover, congressional liberal Democrats debated proposals to reform the legislative process to make it more policy oriented and to shift toward a model of responsible party government. Although the reforms that were passed as the Legislative Reorganization Act of 1946 fell short, the notion of party reform was common currency along the New Deal network.[43] CIO leaders maintained that an active prolabor federal government was critical to sustaining industrial unionism and to enabling the unions to play their role in stabilizing the economy. The experience of the White House lamely sitting on the sidelines during the Labor Management Conference and then double-crossing the unions when they supported the president's wage-price policy was one they did not want to repeat. Also critical was the president's power to nominate to the federal bench and regulatory agencies, chiefly to the NLRB. The CIO's determination to change political direction was continuously fed during 1946 by the government's increasingly harsh battle with John L. Lewis and by such acts as the president's appointment of anti-union members to the Labor Board.[44] Moreover, the five-vote margin by which the Congress sustained Truman's veto of the Case bill was uncomfortably narrow. The unions needed to control a minimum of 33 percent plus one seat in the Senate to prevent backward steps; to go forward with new reforms, they needed much more. The CIO aimed high.

In March 1946 the CIO opened a "southern front" by launching a union organizing drive in the old Confederate states to eliminate the southern wage differential with northern industrial areas and to force a realignment of southern politics and thus undermine the conservative bloc in Congress. Murray called the southern drive an example of "substantive" political action.[45] (The AFL then also launched a southern drive to remain competitive with the CIO.) The plan was that southern unions would break the racially based, business dominated regional politics of the southern Democracy and swing the party to the left. The CIO and AFL put over $1 million into the drives in the first year.[46] The CIO also tried to establish a national popular alliance of workers, farmers, consumers, and small businesses behind price controls and consumer purchasing power and against "monopoly." Labor's social democrats and liberals continued to advocate practical alliances between workers and farmers based on organizing cooperatives to provide food and housing.[47]

The organizational locus of their electoral strategy was the CIO-Political Action Committee. The CIO–PAC had been organized to oppose a third party and to encourage leftists to vote for Roosevelt. Now it became the bulwark of an advancing New Deal program. In May 1946 the CIO–PAC joined with the National Citizens PAC and the Independent Citizens Committee of the Arts, Sciences, and Professions (ICCASP), whose executive director was Harold Ickes, to coordinate actions for the congressional elections. In September, the three organizations held a conference of "progressives" and issued a ringing declaration of support for New Deal economic and social programs and denounced the conservative coalition in the Congress. The conference also praised Henry Wallace, who had just been sacked by Truman from his post as secretary of commerce.[48]

But as the CIO moved tactically in the emerging political conditions, old conflicts with the AFL and some nonlabor liberals came to the fore and put the purpose of the organization in doubt. Some unions like the ILGWU (AFL), liberal organizations like the Union for Democratic Action (UDA), and Catholic activists had never accepted Sidney Hillman's wartime popular front strategy for the CIO–PAC because of the prominence of Communist party members. During the 1946 election, the Catholic hierarchy, the Chamber of Commerce, and the Republicans were whipping up anti-Communist sentiment and tarring both the CIO for its wartime coalition and the Democratic party for its connection to the CIO. In fact, the Communist party had adopted a new strategy, in April 1945, which reversed its recent support for the Charter of Industrial Peace. Party secretary Earl Browder was ousted and a new emphasis on revolutionary eschatology informed a no-compromise stance. Its trade union cadres had begun to agitate for mass direct labor action, which conflicted with Murray's strategy, not to mention the AFL's. The Communists' reversal confused debate among many nonlabor liberals and a large proportion of union activists who wanted the CIO–Political Action Committee to remain autonomous from the Democratic Party. This was Murray's position as well, although he did not want to seem to break completely with the Democrats. For example, the USW convention in May 1946 reendorsed the two-party system while the UAW's executive board supported independent candidates.[49]

The defeat of the Democrats in the 1946 congressional elections forced the issue. Many more unionists and nonlabor liberals now agreed with Max Lerner, James Loeb, Eleanor Roosevelt, and other New Dealers outside of government that the Communist-left was a liability that would prevent them from returning to power.[50] After the November election losses, the wartime alliance of liberals, social-democrats, and Communists broke into two pieces, partly embodied in the Progressive Citizens of America (PCA), created in December, which maintained the popular front and distanced itself from the Democratic party, which PCA denounced as dominated by Jim Crowism and machine pols, and the anti-Communist, Americans for Democratic Action, created in January 1947, whose most prominent issue was opposition to the Soviet Union. Murray initially joined the PCA before the ADA planners announced their intentions. Reuther, Emil Rieve (Textile Workers), Jim Carey (Electrical Workers), and David Dubinsky participated in the founding meeting of ADA with Bowles, Leon Henderson, Gardner Jackson,

Eleanor Roosevelt, John K. Galbraith, other New Dealers, and former UDA leaders. However, Murray was not ready to politically split the CIO and insisted that all union leaders leave the PCA and the ADA, which they did.[51] In 1948, under the mounting pressure of the presidential election, they rejoined and made an alliance for realignment.

The Second Round

During the winter of 1946–1947, the CIO leaders adopted a new collective bargaining agenda that reasserted the links between industrial relations and government policy. The CIO's "National Wage Policy for 1947" was authored by Stanley Ruttenberg of the USW and Robert Nathan, a professional economist formerly with the federal Office of War Mobilization and Reconversion, who made a macroeconomic-focused argument for a large 23.5 cent per hour wage increase in basic industry. Coupled with this, in February 1947, the CIO leadership decided to bargain collectively for welfare benefits until federal legislation could be passed.

In the Nathan Report and a related brief sent to the newly operating Council of Economic Advisors (CEA), the CIO argued that the maldistribution of income, because of high prices and "exorbitant" profits sought by "Big Business," was undermining consumer income and, thus, the high demand needed for sustained employment and production. The Report concluded that "the salient facts of the wage-price-profit situation in American business today indicate that the national interest requires a major general increase in wage rates. It is most important that this general wage advance be achieved without crippling work stoppages."[52] The government should help ensure that employers give appropriate wages increases, or else it should expect strike actions. It was crucial that wage rate increases occur without a general rise in prices. The report went on to underline the critical role of government as a necessary force in ensuring economic balance and growth, but it said virtually nothing about micro relations.

Throughout 1947 the CIO carried out a policy of avoiding strikes and sought the administration's support for a new mechanism to coordinate decisions over wages, prices, and profits.[53] On the one side, government should concert wage-price agreements, perhaps through a labor-management conference; tax excess profits and eliminate tax loopholes for the wealthy; pursue antitrust action; enact social security, health, and medical care laws; create a permanent Fair Employment Practices Commission; pass public housing and housing finance programs; subsidize small farmers; and prepare a "backup" public works program. On the other side, the Big Three CIO unions—the UAW, the USW, and the United Electrical Workers (UE)—would coordinate their collective bargaining to win industry-wide wage standards, a guaranteed weekly or annual wage, a "cost of living" wage increase and "stop gap" welfare programs. The CIO executive council established a Full Employment Committee, consisting of Murray, Reuther, Rieve, Jacob Potofsky (ACW), Albert Fitzgerald (UE president), and Ruttenberg, and began monthly meetings with the CEA in May. The Full Employment Committee discussed the entire range of economic policy issues with CEA members and staff but found little response during 1947. CEA chairman, Edwin G. Nourse, had solicited the CIO's opinions, as he had of other economic forces, during the preparation of the first "President's Economic Report," but he conceived of labor as an interest group, writing to Murray that the CEA would "consider the labor aspects of our Report with you" and he persistently expressed doubt about the macroeconomic policy role of organized labor. He opposed a new labor-management conference to settle aggregate wage-price relationships: such "efforts thus far have failed." He and his staff urged the unions to focus on the specific conditions of their industries when making wage policy.[54]

The CEA continued to counsel Truman for fiscal restraint, which cut against two standard analyses, by economists outside government and not associated with organized labor, of what the federal government should do. Alvin Hansen argued that fiscal stimulation was a necessary part of establishing business confidence in future market demand.[55] Also, the ADA's Committee on Economic Stability suggested that the federal budget had a surplus by mid-1947 and was dragging the economy down.[56] They wanted wage rises; price cuts negotiated by a Price Adjustment Board; and fiscal stimulation through increased unemployment compensation, housing, and foreign lending. The CEA continued to reject price controls, although it was concerned about price increases. The CEA disagreed with business representations that the impetus for price increases was the anticipation of sluggish markets. Another standard prescription was that the government should take action to broaden economic development. The CEA, in fact, considered various means of doing so, including increasing the minimum wage, antitrust action, small business tax breaks, new industries, like aircraft, regional development, and antidiscrimination actions, some of which were relatively cost free and depended on encouraging market competition. At the same time, Nourse noted to himself that although the CEA was aiming at policies that would extend economic growth to new areas, Truman continued to be attracted to legal reform of industrial relations.[57]

More importantly for the CIO's success, the Truman White House reassessed its electoral prospects for 1948, found them poor, and began a conscious "move left" to establish Truman as a true New Dealer.[58] To be reelected, wrote presidential aide Clark Clifford, Truman had to recapture the support of labor leaders, western state "progressives" and farmers, and black voters, and to rebuild big city party organizations. The southerners could be taken for granted; losses in the South were less important than making gains in the cities and the West. Clifford judged that rank-and-file workers were "not yet" politically conscious and, therefore, the party did not need to appeal to them with class rhetoric.[59] This electoral strategy was directed by an unofficial administration political program group with which the CIO developed regular contacts in 1947 and 1948. A key player in the group was CEA member Leon Keyserling.[60] By 1948, Truman's legislative program was similar to the CIO's.

But as CIO leaders and the White House were reestablishing an electoral alliance, employers took the initiative. The new managerial counteractions sharpened conflict within many unions over strategy and control and shaped second round labor-management settlements. The NAM and the Republicans took the 1946 election results as a popular mandate to stop a New Deal revival and to pass laws to restrict labor action. Employers took angry exception to the Nathan Report. *Business Week* correctly identified the CIO program as shifting income from ownership to wages and warned that business would resist attempts to maintain wartime wage levels and lower profits by raising prices. At its December 1946 Congress of

American Industry, the NAM rejected internal pressure from the auto companies and many steel firms for outright repeal of the Wagner Act, but committed itself to new controls on the "monopolistic power" of unions and the spread of unionism.[61]

The NAM was well connected to the Republican-controlled congressional committees that rewrote the Wagner Act and produced the Taft-Hartley Act in 1947, which differed only marginally from the NAM program. Prominent congressional advisors came from GM, Chrysler, UAW-organized agricultural implement manufacturers like J. I. Case and Allis-Chalmers, and from steel firms. The CED's opposition to detailed legislation specifying the scope of labor-management relations was swept aside.[62] The Taft-Hartley Act easily passed in July by 308 to 107 in the House, including 90 southern and border state Democrats voting yes, and by 68 to 24 in the Senate, including 20 southern Democrats voting yes. Even the Democratic National Committee's sentiment was split: 95 for a veto, 64 to sign it, and 4 to let it pass without signing; 86 of proveto votes were nonsouthern, while 33 of the 64 prosign votes were from southern state members. President Truman, in a reprise of the Case Bill scenario, vetoed the act, but the Congress swiftly overrode it.[63]

The act narrowed the scope of collective bargaining by conceiving union-management contracts as defining the limits of agreement rather than as a charter for continuing cooperation. The act invited the parties to try to write all-embracing documents that could prescribe for all contingencies, to insist on rigid contract observance, to adopt defensive tactics to protect historical interests and, generally, to distrust in situations that call for cooperation. This conception was embodied in the U.S. Steel contract proposal for 1947, in which Murray understood that

> all conditions of employment, where they are not incorporated into local agreements or covered by the national agreement, would be terminated and management would be free to change them at will. . . . The new approach . . . will compel the union to negotiate into the contract the manifold working conditions outstanding in the various plants . . . such as in the auto industry.[64]

He added that this "would invite chaos." Nonetheless, big corporation employers sought this sort of labor management system as their own second best choice. The act also withdrew incentives for worker solidarity. It restricted interunion cooperation and barred most industry-wide and multi-employer bargaining schemes; outlawed "secondary boycotts"; gave managements new rights to intervene in employee unionization; limited union security and protected the worker's right not to join a union; limited worker rights in so-called "economic" disputes by allowing employers to hire permanent replacements; and imposed financial liability on unions for strikes during the contract term.[65]

The act had several immediate consequences. It made it easier for nonunion firms to resist unionization and put large areas of the country off limits to unions by allowing state governments to pass even more restrictive laws than the federal one. Southern employers, especially, forced unions to engage in expensive litigation, which caused the AFL to abandon its southern organizing drive and put more resources into its Washington headquarters. CIO unions already had found it hard to maintain the financial commitment to the drive before Taft-Hartley.[66] Also, the unionization of foremen was crushed (see below), and the act undermined unions and locals with Communist leadership by forcing Communist party members to quit their posts. It also compelled non-Communist union leaders to emphasize discipline among the ranks to ensure victory in the newly mandated annual representation elections (later modified) and to prevent direct action tactics in contract disputes which might leave union treasuries legally vulnerable.[67] Finally, the act prohibited organized labor from participating in electoral politics (later found unconstitutional), blocking the door to attempts to reverse this legislation.[68]

Even as Taft-Hartley eased management fears, it figured prominently in labor's debates as the worst of several Congressional actions setting unions back, and it created a siege mentality among union leaders who called Taft-Hartley a "slave labor" act. Other setbacks were the failure to reorganize and fortify the Department of Labor and the slashing of the NLRB's annual budget and staff. The Taft-Hartley Act's blatant assault on political rights went to the social-democratic unionist's heart. The CIO reacted quickly to this part of the bill and overturned the provision's implementation by making endorsements in two special congressional elections, inviting prosecution and then winning the case in 1948. Now more than ever, the top leaders believed, unions needed to unify behind a Democratic electoral campaign to win back control of the Congress and repeal the legislation. The new political conditions reinforced a strategy to tie industrial action even closer to immediate political feasibility.[69]

A further consequence of the new political realities and labor's response was that second round contract settlements in 1947 were far inferior to labor's strategic goals. Steel took the lead as the UAW deferred to the USW. But, when U.S. Steel objected to the USW demand for "portal-to-portal" pay (to cover the time travelling from the gates of huge steel works to specific work sites) and refused to discuss wages until the USW gave up this demand, Murray personally extended the contracts in steel for seventy-eight days.[70] Both UAW leadership factions had connived to prevent rank and filers at its national wage and GM collective bargaining conferences from committing the union to specific demands that might lead to a strike, and negotiations at GM dragged on without resolution. With the big two unions tied up, the UE then set the "pattern" in April 1947, settling with Westinghouse and GM for 11.5 cents and six paid holidays plus a corporation commitment to bargain later on pension and health plans. The total value of the settlement was about 36 percent less than that put forth in the Nathan Report. One of the reasons for the quick settlement was that the electrical industry had seen its profits plunge with the end of the war while the union and workers had depleted their resources in the 1946 strikes (e.g., although UE had settled quickly at GM and GE, it had a long strike at Westinghouse).[71] Steel, next, quickly settled for about 15 cents and company agreement to a dues check-off. The USW gave a two-year no-strike pledge and, while the company and union agreed to "continuous" bargaining to solve problems as they arose, the contract prohibited mediation. GM then offered the UAW an 11.5 cent an hour increase plus 6 paid holidays, or 15 cents total, but GM rejected the union's demand for pension and health plans. The UAW executive board, in late April, agreed to GM's terms plus a vague commitment from GM to bargain later on health and pensions. Chrysler settled on a similar package a few days later but, true to its "brass hat" reputation, without the commitment to bargain on health and pensions. The company, in 1947, was willing to take a strike, but the UAW was not. The UAW did win synchronous contract dates at GM and Chrysler and with UE–GM and won a financial commitment to move toward equal pay for equal work.[72]

It was during the Ford negotiations that the two sides of the new CIO leadership strategy came into conflict. Taft-Hartley raised the question of how reasonable it was to plan on government support rather than take direct industrial action. Both UAW factions were critical of the UE pattern, but they both supported the CIO strategy and the pattern was arguably an outcome of it. The problem was that under the current conditions, the companies were making headway in their campaign to wrest control of the shop floor, and the workers' best response was direct action. In the Ford negotiations in June and July, a firm managerial position, backed by the Taft-Hartley legislation, and a divided union led to further lost ground for the UAW.

Negotiations were complicated by a strike of the Foreman's Association of America (FAA), an independent union, which had won collectively bargained contracts in 1944 at Ford and a few other companies, and by passage of the Taft-Hartley Act during the strike, which removed statutory protection for foremen unionization.[73] The FAA strike at Ford raised the issues of labor solidarity and the worker's role in management, both for the union and for the revived postwar Ford management, which wanted to break the FAA as a part of its plan to reorganize itself in GM's corporate image. The foremen put up pickets and appealed to the UAW, the Teamsters (who trucked parts among auto plants), and the AFL crafts to honor them. For the building trades and Teamsters, which had traditions of unionizing foremen, the pickets did not raise unusual issues, but, for the mass production workers in the UAW, harsh experience with the foremen clashed with the opportunity to extend union influence and economic democracy. Would the UAW honor the picket lines and effectively shut down Ford and break with CIO policy? The impending Taft-Hartley Act did not legally recognize the foremen's union before the National Labor Relations Board nor could the foremen join the UAW without jeopardizing the UAW's status. On the other hand, on its own and without NLRB protection, the FAA probably would have to strike more often to win its demands and yet still rely on UAW members not to do foreman work.

The issue became part of the intense factional play within the

UAW leadership. The Addes faction was responsible for the UAW's continuing negotiations with Ford in the person of Ford Department director, Richard Leonard. They did not want to strike—and they claimed Murray's support—because they hoped for a later industry-wide strike. Although they rejected Reuther's argument that the UAW needed NLRB status, since they were opposed to recognizing the Taft-Hartley Act, the two sides did agree, in March, not to honor the FAA pickets. However, Ford Local 600 in Dearborn, the single largest local in the UAW, which was closely contested between the two factions although pro-Addes at the time, wanted the UAW executive board to change policies to honor the FAA's pickets. As the FAA strike lagged—Ford refused to meet with striking foremen—Reuther agreed with Local 600 and said that UAW members should not cross the picket lines in order to keep solidarity. But not only did the Addes-Thomas-Leonard group oppose this, so did pro-Reuther members of the board, who opposed foremen unionization in principle. Finally, the board decided to intervene in Ford-FAA negotiations with the threat of UAW retaliation if Ford was not forthcoming to the FAA in one week. In the meantime, however, Leonard reached a tentative agreement with Ford, which preempted the UAW from strike action. The FAA strike then quickly collapsed, and some twelve hundred foremen were fired and replaced by recruits schooled in a new management training program.[74]

In the proposed Ford contract, the company agreed to concede the union shop for one year (allowed under Taft-Hartley), abandon the right to sue the union for breach of contract (after Murray met with Henry Ford II, labor relations vice-president, John Bugas, and president, Ernest Breech, and convinced them that minor contractual violations were simply unavoidable in the real world of factory work), and agreed to a pension plan. However, the UAW Ford Department gave up "about twenty-three" demands, including future law suits for portal-to-portal pay, contract dates synchronous with GM and Chrysler, and a twenty-minute paid lunch period which had covered over 50 percent of Ford workers. Reuther opposed the pension plan, which did not require full vesting of pensions, beside the costs to workers in concessions, and he won the IEB's (International Executive Board of the UAW) agreement to offer Ford workers a choice of the pension plan plus a 7 cent wage increase or no plan and a 15 cent an hour increase: workers followed Reuther and took the wages.[75]

The poor Ford contract was one of several issues that contributed to the Reuther group's taking virtually complete control of the union in late 1947. The other principal issues in UAW factionalism were the loss of an eleven-month strike at Allis-Chalmers; the scurrilous tactics of Reuther opponents during the union election campaign; the failed merger of the UAW with the Farm Equipment Workers Union (FE), the largest union in that industry; and how to respond to the Taft-Hartley Act.

In the Allis-Chalmers strike, the UAW executive board and Reuther (with Murray's advice) tried to maneuver around a viscerally hostile management, which refused to follow the first round wage increases and which insisted on changes in the internal life of the Allis local union, which was led by elected Communist-oriented officials.[76] When the complicated negotiations and public relations tactics failed in January 1947, the UAW's two major factions erupted in mutual recriminations, which the Reuther group turned to its own advantage. Next, in June 1947, the executive board passed an Addes-Thomas plan to merge with the Communist-led FE, an action that would have boosted the voting strength of the Addes forces in the fall UAW convention. Yet, the detailed provisions of the merger proposal were so heavily weighted in favor of the FE that the Reuther group was able to turn the issue to its favor on the grounds that it violated the principles of industrial unionism. Moreover, the Catholic allies of Reuther forcefully made a case against merger with a "Communist union."[77] In a membership referendum in July, the Reuther forces campaigned throughout the union on this and other factional issues and defeated the merger proposal by 2 to 1.[78] The FE campaign probably helped shift the executive board in Reuther's favor on Taft-Hartley compliance, and certainly laid the groundwork for his smashing victories at the UAW convention in November.

Reuther favored compliance with the act until its repeal for the factional and organizational advantages such a course offered. The act would force Communist allies of Addes out of office, and the Addes group would be more closely identified with Communists. Moreover, the union's industrial position would be safeguarded from competing AFL unions, which had already complied with the act and which, therefore, could get on a representation election ballot in a contested organizing drive while the UAW could not, as long as it did not comply with the law. Competition was especially hot in the aircraft industry with the Transport Workers and Machinists unions and with the AFL building trades in Detroit for the maintenance workers at the auto plants.[79] Finally, Reuther argued, the UAW had hundreds of unfair labor practice cases pending with the NLRB, some involving fired organizers, and they would all have to be abandoned. In short, Reuther and his allies argued that there was too much to lose and that the act should be resisted through electoral mobilization and legislative action. On April 24, the UAW had shut down the auto plants in Detroit to hold a mass rally against the Hartley Bill passed by the House. When GM threatened to discipline workers who were going to participate, the Addes group favored a showdown with the company. Reuther argued against this, saying that workers could grieve any unjust discipline. The rally, he and Emil Mazey said, should be aimed at the government in a coordinated campaign with their legislative allies.[80]

The Addes group wanted to boycott the NLRB. They claimed that Reuther supported Taft-Hartley and published a newsletter called *FDR* that reported that Taft and Reuther would team up on a ticket in 1948. More sensibly, the pro-Addes Percy Llewellyn, of Local 600, argued that union strength is based on "the militancy you create among the minds of the workers."[81] In July and early September a slim majority on the UAW executive board voted against compliance with the act. Practically, the union remained stalemated until November when the Reuther forces swept both the UAW convention and all but four seats on the newly elected board.[82]

In the meantime, at the AFL and CIO conventions in October 1947, each national federation adopted union "autonomy" on compliance with Taft-Hartley, which meant that they *would* comply and not use mass industrial action to break the law. Although by the time of the convention ten CIO unions had decided to comply with the act, the Communist-influenced unions were strongly in favor of noncompliance. For example, James Matles, vice-president of the UE, argued for direct rank-and-file action and mass demonstrations. Simultaneously, at the AFL convention John L. Lewis made a dramatic appeal for resistance, but the AFL convention voted to comply after Tobin took the wind out of Lewis' rhetoric by saying he was happy to line up against Communism. The UMW then disaffiliated itself from the AFL. The CIO convention, essentially, made the same choice as the AFL. The majority CIO leadership's calculation was fundamental doubt about whether industrial unions could persist under the act, especially with unions bearing financial liability for disciplining the ranks. They doubted they could withstand the costs, and Murray was not anxious for a test of economic strength and rank-and-file militancy to find out. He was proud of the CIO's bargaining strategy in which wage gains (although nominal) had been won without strikes. Combined with this argument was the fact that workers were not anxious to strike, given inflation and the draw-down of savings; the pivotal factional issue of Communist party certification, which applied only to the union leadership; and the belief of the CIO's dominant leadership that a strategy of electoral mobilization was a viable alternative.[83]

The so-called left wing opposition found itself marginalized by the refusal of most of the CIO to support mass defiance and creation of a labor political party and by Truman's "left turn." When, in November 1947 after the union conventions, former vice-president and commerce secretary Henry Wallace declared his candidacy for the presidency on a Progressive party ticket, Murray immediately wired all affiliates to withhold any and all endorsements until the CIO executive council could meet on January 22, 1948. There the council resolved to oppose Wallace after very acrimonious debate, as did the AFL, in February.[84] The anti-Communist provision of the Taft-Hartley Act made it easier for Murray and Reuther to put pressure on Communist party-oriented unionists to choose "union" or "party" loyalty, a disingenuous argument at best since the CIO majority had settled on a rigidly Democratic course. More to the point, a Wallace candidacy for president could not elect a Congress to repeal Taft-Hartley. Moreover, Truman's veto of the act had convinced Whitney, of the Railroad Trainmen, to abandon his previous promise of substantial financial aid to defeat the president in 1948. The CIO, in March 1948, moved to enforce political unity and to organize labor behind the Democrats for the November elections.

The CIO now had to develop more systematically a stance toward the Democratic party that was supportive, but also constructively critical. In June, a "Statement of Political Policy" was developed and later, in 1949, amended and delivered to the CIO convention that foresaw a realignment of the ideological and voter bases of the Democratic party.[85] It reviewed the record of the PAC's progressively developing strategy for independent labor political influence. "At the beginning, the CIO called for a series of progressive measures in the fields of industrial relations, equal rights, social security, economic stabilization and foreign affairs . . ." The CIO developed "political techniques which have strengthened the hand of progressives," including complex and extensive means to register and get out the "labor and liberal" vote. Then it moved on to the selection of candidates, lobbying, court challenges, and systematic political education. Yet, despite members gaining "invaluable experience" and "understanding,"

> it is clear, however, that the democratic forces which made the name of the New Deal the watchword of human fellowship . . . are no longer influential in our national government. . . . The first need . . . is a suitable national political organization. . . . Whether or not the newly reorganized political party which ultimately emerges bears the name of any existing political party is unimportant. . . . The Realignment we propose must be based upon a fusion of the honorable and constructive elements in the major parties, the exclusion of reactionary or communist-ridden political organizations, and the destruction or elimination from political power of venal and racketeering old-time political machines.[86]

CIO partisanship led leaders to yeoman work for the administration's pet issues, which were shifting to the primary arena of presidential power, namely foreign affairs. For example, labor leaders had criticized the Truman Doctrine, announced in March 1947, according to which the United States would provide military aid to anti-Communist forces in Turkey and Greece, and the administration's intention to monopolize nuclear power. The European Recovery Program (ERP), proposed by Secretary of State Marshall in June, however, provided the opportunity for labor social-democrats to part company with Communist party–influenced unionists and Henry Wallace, who opposed the Marshall Plan, and align with the administration.[87] The CIO could support the Marshall Plan, including direct food aid, financing increased exports, and reconstruction of European economies, as compatible with its own internationalism, even though the issue split the World Federation of Trade Unions to which the CIO belonged. For the administration, however, the specific conditions of this program now were reversed. Government leaders had argued that foreign markets were needed to resolve domestic problems; now domestic support was needed to guarantee global peace. Thus Secretary of State Marshall made it clear in a speech to the 1947 CIO convention delegates that domestic economic stability and political unity were prerequisite to the success of the Marshall Plan. The "productivity of American farms and factories" were "the basic problem" confronting the program and were the "responsibility" of "every American." Labor discipline was needed at work to prevent scarcities from turning into inflation (since "excess" production was shipped to Europe) and in politics to bolster the program against traditional isolationists.[88]

The CIO did not accept all the bland assurances about the European Recovery Program's humanitarian purposes. Indeed, Reuther criticized the ADA in a speech to their first annual convention in February 1948 for failing to press the administration for broader control of the program (and for their tepid domestic agenda). However, with Walter Reuther and Jim Carey (of the anti-Communist faction in the UE) in the lead, the CIO adopted the position that liberals should support the ERP idea and then pressure the administration to make the ERP a truly democratic program. Reuther argued that the ERP was an "idea" up for grabs. "I say the choice is not between Communism and the narrow, selfish exploitation of Wall Street monopoly capitalism. The choice of the world is between totalitarianism and freedom."[89] In November 1947, in testimony before the Harriman Committee, which Truman had appointed to develop the Marshall Plan, CIO representatives made the following points. Aid to Europe should carry no restrictions on the types of politics and policies of the governments of the countries receiving aid (especially it should allow Socialists in government), the aid commitment should be long-term to allow governments to plan, European societies should develop their own capacity to produce and export (and not be dependent on the United States— or Russia), labor should have policy-making positions in its administration, and related policies should be developed to prevent domestic price inflation (e.g., force increased steel production and impose price controls). Nonetheless, when the ERP legislation did not include these last two points, the CIO still reported that it was a major victory.[90]

Holding out for Wallace were CIO opponents of the Marshall Plan: the Longshoremen, UE, FE, the Mine, Mill and Smelter Workers, Office and Professional Employees, Fur Workers, Communications Workers, Food and Tobacco, and Transport Workers. As the majority of the executive board was against them, the leaders of these unions argued for autonomy for affiliates, just as the CIO had done with Taft-Hartley six weeks earlier, to support whomever each union chose in the presidential election. This position was unacceptable to Reuther and the CIO majority now. Murray and Reuther vilified these unions and claimed the Communist party and its union allies were pursuing a policy of tacit alliance with reaction by splitting the labor vote in the United States and perpetuating misery in Europe.[91]

There then ensued throughout 1948 a bitter fight among the factions to control the PAC organization and money. The UAW board diverted political action monies from pro-Wallace CIO–PACs to pro-Truman UAW regional directors to prevent locals and districts from using money for Wallace. Also, in June 1948, the UAW invited the national CIO to take over the Wayne County (Detroit) Industrial Union Council–CIO for having endorsed Wallace. This council was one of several around the country, including state councils in California and Minnesota, that the CIO set out to bring into line behind the Democrats. The CIO placed an administrator over the Wayne County Council, ousted the leftists and, in 1949, new elections to the IUC board were swept by the right wing. All IUCs and local PACs were ordered by the CIO executive board to support only national PAC policy. As for postelection interest in a third party, it evaporated when Truman squeaked by Thomas Dewey and the Democrats regained control of Congress.[92]

The Third Round

Increased political unity of labor in 1948, including AFL involvement in national electoral politics, and Truman's need for labor and liberal support helped break both management's "united front" against wage increases in the third round and the administration's hold-the-line policy against inflation. The beginnings of a broader union-industry settlement emerged. And with the Democratic victory in November, the new CIO strategy now seemed to begin to pay off.

During the fall of 1947, the Truman administration had settled upon an anti-inflation program to counteract the stimulus of new military spending and aid commitments in Europe, steel shortages, and poor agricultural harvests. Truman emphasized, in an October nationwide address, that the real danger of inflation was the depression which would follow and that the problem was rooted in "structural imbalances" among sectors and between wages and prices.[93] The president called a special session of Congress, in November, on foreign policy, but also demanded action on his domestic agenda: voluntary wage and price stability in highly organized sectors, rent control, price ceilings on critical materials and food stuffs, agricultural export and transportation controls, an increase in the minimum wage (mostly for nonunion workers), and a so-called "cost of living" tax abatement for low incomes, credit and commodity exchange controls, an excess profits tax, and regional economic and natural resources development. The Congress agreed to virtually nothing, which Truman called "pitifully inadequate."[94] Privately, the White House was not completely disappointed: the Republicans were falling into a Democratic trap and setting themselves up to take the blame for inflation in the 1948 elections.[95]

In early 1948 corporate leaders were determined to resist the administration's anti-inflation policy and the third round of collective bargaining. The *New York Times* and National City Bank argued that Truman's new defense preparedness program required government retrenchment. The bank's newsletter noted the high profits that manufacturing firms were earning, but argued against new corporate taxes and for emphasis on increasing productivity. Strikes and featherbedding had to end and shares of national income should be stabilized.[96] GM economist Rufus Tucker attacked the CEA's second annual report as "Marxist" for its apparent commitment to the income distribution analysis.[97] Top executives formed a united management front against wage increases.[98] On January 1, GE announced a small price decrease and vowed not to give wage increases. Other manufacturers followed GE's lead, including Ford,

Westinghouse, and U.S. Steel. Jones and Laughlin Steel raised
prices, but then its president, Ben Moreell, held several meetings
with CEA chair, Nourse, and agreed to cut prices back if the USW
would hold the line on wages. Nourse agreed that third round
wages increases should be held in check.[99] He argued that steel
should focus instead on increased productivity, an argument that
Moreell made to the USW. Moreover, GM reneged on its written
agreement to bargain on pensions and tried to implement a program unilaterally.

    In contrast, at the start of the year, the unions looked weak.
The CIO and AFL were not working together. The coal miners and
the Railroad Brotherhoods went on strike again without coordinating their actions with the labor federations. Within the CIO, there
was great dissension over the candidacy of Henry Wallace and
American foreign policy that threatened to split the "progressive"
labor ranks come November. Also, not more than half of UAW
members in Detroit were registered to vote.[100] The UE was too
internally torn by left-right struggle to fight management, including GM where it had thirty-seven thousand members and GE, which
was leading the new hard line policy. The USW's two-year 1947
agreement with U.S. Steel only allowed thirty-day talks on wages,
but no requirement for resolution of wage demands within the
contractual no-strike pledge and no promise to resolve the welfare
fund issue. Packinghouse workers launched an industry-wide strike,
but gave up after nine weeks. Moreover, the unions under Taft-
Hartley had to expend energy to hold union representation elections and reorganize plants. The UAW estimated that there were
some sixty thousand "free riders" at GM.[101] To meet all these circumstances, the Reuther leadership in the UAW redoubled its efforts
at organizing the already organized workers in the industry. Union
officers planned a disciplined economic struggle with the major
employers, which would respond to immediate demands of the
membership and avoid entanglements with partisan politics.

    The union targeted Chrysler; when the company refused to
give any wage increase, Chrysler workers went on strike. Ford
publicly asked for a wage cut in May. The UAW then turned its
sights on GM, threatening "no contract-no work" when the existing
agreement expired May 28. Within the UAW in January and February 1948 there had been agitation for a rank-and-file–directed

strategy relying on direct action and large increases in wages. Sources of this were presidents of five large locals in Flint, plus scattered Communists and Cannonite-Trotskyists in Detroit and Cleveland. They wanted a pension and a wage increase to make up for the wage shortfall, since 1945, behind the increase in the cost of living, which they connected to Truman's policies. Reuther's strategy now was to keep "political" issues separate from collective bargaining and he vigorously criticized factional opponents for connecting Truman and the Marshall Plan to wage policy though, of course, he himself continued to do so from within the Democratic party network. Reuther rejected left-wing demands for a general strike and a cost-of-living wage formula. He said these were unlikely to work and, in fact, would be harmful to the ranks' "bread and butter": for example a COLA (cost-of-living adjustment) could lead to wage reductions. The union could win increases, he argued, without the "fireworks" of an industry-wide strike. The objectives adopted by the executive board's Policy Committee, nonetheless, followed the specific rank and file demands: a 25 cent an hour wage increase, 5 cents for a health and hospitalization plan, a 40-hour guaranteed weekly wage, 3-week vacation pay, a fund to reduce wage disparities within occupations, and a pension plan. The union also demanded extensive job control concessions from the company.[102]

The UAW–GM National Negotiating Conference amended the Policy Committee recommendations after Reuther urged it to put 10 of the 25 cents into a pension; the Ford Committee did the same. Leftists and other militants, including Chrysler Department director, Norman Matthews, argued this meant the workers would have to finance their own pensions and diverted the rank and file from a "clear cut" struggle to discussion of pension plan details. They forced the executive board to call a new GM conference, but they were defeated a second time. After the official union objectives were set, sixteen locals with thirty-eight thousand members voted against strike action, including the Communist party–oriented Flint Buick Local 599 and Fisher 23 in Detroit.[103]

Nonetheless, GM became convinced that the UAW had the organizational strength to launch a debilitating strike (as they were doing at Chrysler). The UAW was on its way to winning the Taft-Hartley representation election at GM with 89 percent of the vote.[104]

The trade-off of lost production during introduction of its first new postwar model for wage stability seemed to be not worth the cost. Earnings were good now and promised to be better; the company's financial problems were solved. On May 25, GM made concessions on wages.[105] The UAW and General Motors agreed to tie wages to changes in the national price level, or COLA, and to changes in the national rate of increase in productivity through an annual improvement factor, or AIF. Although COLA was a demand of Reuther's opponents, UAW negotiators, with Reuther himself hospitalized at the time of the negotiations, were in favor of it under the inflationary conditions of the time. The union also accepted GM's proposal for AIF (the concept had been in the air since the war).[106] Also, the agreement made GM's insurance program part of the collective bargaining contract, pending outcome of a UAW appeal to the NLRB of GM's unilateral plan and court review of the issue, both of which were decided in the union's favor in 1949. The union and company agreed to committeeman representation of workers in discipline cases, to rate-setting authority for the grievance umpire on new jobs, to some language whose intention was to reject a common law or precedent-based approach to grievances, to make it harder for union members to drop out of the union, and to cut in half the probationary period for seniority.[107]

The 1948 agreements accomplished several goals. The wage formulas guaranteed that wages would keep pace with inflation (and price deflation, which happened in 1949; thereafter GM agreed that wages would not be lowered even if the price index fell) and that workers would share in productivity advances. It ensured workers of wage increases every year and committed the union to a management program to increase productivity through management efficiency and technology which, in any case, the UAW had not opposed. Reuther commented that he believed Wilson was finally understanding what the union was talking about. The UAW negotiators, especially secretary-treasurer Emil Mazey, believed that AIF was "a foot in the door" to shifting the distribution of income to labor from capital. And, in fact, the record of the following years shows that the UAW was able to increase the AIF even when measures of productivity lagged, thus shifting income.[108] Alfred Sloan preferred to call AIF a "merit increase" which would help introduce an "element of reason and of predictability into our wage program."[109] Sloan agreed that the measurement of productivity was not exact and was somewhat arbitrary, but the point was to have a rule that would produce stability in labor-management relations. Steady increases in wages also worked well for union leaders as a political shield from factional opponents and rank-and-file discontent. At the same time, the union was continuing to professionalize the services it provided to union locals to solve grievances and avoid direct action. The two-year term of the contract also contributed to stability as did a two-year freeze on wage adjustments among job classifications, although the company had wanted a five-year contract.[110]

The UAW and CIO actually were far from satisfied with the 1948 settlements. As Kermit Eby, the CIO's director of education and research, reported, the sentiment of the CIO Full Employment Committee was that the GM settlement actually meant there would be "settlements" rather than a pattern.[111] Also, the wage increases were too low, and the UAW had given up important demands for union security and steward representation. UAW negotiators failed to win several fundamental demands concerning authority in daily worklife, including strict seniority in job assignments, employee consent to reassignment, negotiated production standards, recognition of the union steward system, and negotiation of subcontracting. The UAW called the agreement a "holding operation" in the "context of today's economic and political reaction."[112] It recommended that GM workers accept the agreement as "their contribution to industrial peace." The COLA/BLS (Bureau of Labor Statistics) formula was accepted "only because most of those in control of government and industry show no signs of acting in the public interest. They are enforcing a system of private planning for private profit at public expense." Reuther looked to the CIO's realignment strategy to change the balance of political power to enable reform of industrial authority. A CIO strategy memorandum, during the 1948 campaign, expressly linked the "planned realignment" of the political parties with a "program for industrial democracy and planning." Industrial planning was "needed to tie the reorganized party together and stimulate action." Meanwhile, the Full Employment Committee met with the CEA about low wages and again urged it to support the industrial council plan.[113]

For its part, the administration considered that its hold-the-line campaign against the third round had failed.[114] Economic conditions were "good" in 1948, although inflation was mounting and the production of goods had hardly increased since the war. The experts continued to worry about the longer-run economic prospects, and the national elections provided another opportunity to develop arguments for continued government management. The UAW–GM contract was given intense scrutiny by the CEA. The council was encouraged by the use of COLA and AIF formulas. The use of COLAS was not new in American collective bargaining history; rather, the CEA's main concern was that the UAW–GM COLA formula was too sensitive to price changes. The AIF was the most novel aspect of the agreement since it allowed increases in real income and was a recognition by the company of its employees' rights to a share of productivity gains. However, Nourse did not believe that the 1948 contract was more than exceptional: the CEA still hoped to achieve price stability, making COLAS unnecessary, and it was doubtful that other companies would have the confidence to make a two-year bargain with guaranteed wage increases.

Indeed, GM's wage agreement with the UAW shifted responsibility for inflation back to the federal government and led to pattern wage increases for the UE in the electrical industry, at Chrysler and Ford, and even in the packinghouse and steel industries, although the COLA and AIF wage rules were not adopted. CEA member John Clark argued that the event that breached the business front was Truman's March 17 speech to Congress, after the Communist coup d'etat in Czechoslovakia, when the president requested universal military training and a draft.[115] This had been followed, on April 1, by an administration request for a $3.3 billion increase in arms and procurement and by a National Security Council recommendation, with which the Senate concurred, that a military alliance with Europe should be formed. All of these actions promised steady business in autos and other basic manufacturing industries and made wage concessions both feasible and a hedge against labor shortages.[116] With the wage breakthrough and redoubled prospects for military spending increases, the CEA and Truman's White House advisors shifted attention to other aspects of its economic stabilization and electoral programs.

Keyserling, who was elbowing Nourse aside as the most influential person on the CEA, argued from inside the Truman administration for the establishment of an "institutional" mechanism to tie collective bargaining, corporate price policy, capital markets, and production decisions to national economic policy. These private decisions were the "core problems" of the economy. He argued that unions and companies needed to be able to see beyond their own specific situation to "the economy as a whole". He said he was not suggesting that "the people who operate our economy are expected to turn into angels. It only means that they can still grow—that they have not reached the limit of their capacity. To say that this is impractical would be to reject the possibility of combining democracy and reasonable economic stability."[117] Others outside the administration were making similar suggestions. John T. Dunlop, economics professor at Harvard, noted that

> A national wage policy awaits instrumentalities to formulate and administer it. . . . Logically, the bodies essential to a national wage policy could be developed in one of two ways. First, the scope of collective-bargaining organizations could expand to the extent that a group of top union leaders and employers would negotiate a national wage pattern and policy. In so far as certain key bargains come to be recognized as leaders by the rest of the economy, these key negotiations would set a national wage policy without resort to any more formal association. Second, one side or the other could secure political power and use governmental authority to formulate a wage policy.[118]

Dunlop went on to observe that the Labor parties of Europe provided the means by which individual unions concerted their wage goals, but that this option was probably unlikely in the United States. He counted the Taft-Hartley Act as a very unfortunate attempt to go down the political road because of its detailed specification of labor-management relations. Instead, he suggested the creation of national advisory boards to help formulate national collective bargaining policy.

The Congress, however, was still in the hands of Republicans, who had announced, after their 1946 election victory, that their number one priority was a 20 percent cut in income taxes, which was backed by the CED, Chamber of Commerce, and the NAM. Truman had strongly opposed a 1947 Republican tax cut bill, as had the CIO, and Truman's veto was sustained by just two votes in the House. In 1948 the Republicans introduced a new tax cut bill that had enough concessions to House Democrats to pass over another Truman veto. Members of Congress also attacked labor standards directly by rejecting the administration's proposals to re-integrate the U.S. Employment Service and the unemployment compensation programs into the Department of Labor and by threatening to create new exceptions to the wage and hour laws in exchange for a token increase in the minimum wage. Also in 1948 Truman resisted, successfully, a campaign by CED and commercial banks to "free" monetary policy and raise interest rates. In this struggle the UAW was vitally involved in supporting the administration, which proposed, instead, to impose a CIO-backed excess-profits tax to make up for revenue lost from an income tax cut for lower income citizens. But the president did not expect this tax plan to pass the Congress—and it did not. Truman continued to play symbolic politics throughout 1947 and 1948 on domestic policy to gain leverage in the presidential election.[119]

Truman campaigned on the antimonopoly theme that business and the Republicans were responsible for price inflation: "only the man who has the money is able to get the necessities of life."[120] If private enterprise did not act responsibly, he warned, controls would be necessary. A similar theme was sounded by CIO leaders, liberal economists, and in Democratic campaign documents. Emil Rieve wrote that Truman's program was "startlingly" like the CIO's.[121] Liberal Keynesians outside the government published a volume called *Saving American Capitalism: A Liberal Economic Program*.[122] The minority report by liberal congressional Democrats on the Joint Committee on the President's Economic Report was a combination campaign document and detailed argument for Truman's economic program.[123] The common ideological theme was that businessmen were too shortsighted to know their own best interests, the consequence of which would be "socialism." This Democratic campaign rhetoric did not hide the fact that "liberal" congressional Democrats outlined a social-democratic program to prevent depression: natural and human resource development, including skill training and retraining, social services, education, urban and regional development, greater aid to labor-management cooperation, and policies to prevent "concentration of economic power in private hands" and to promote "free competitive enterprise."

The Truman administration successfully carried out most of its election plan. Wallace was pinned by Truman et al. as a fellow-travelling Communist, a key point in Truman's appeal to urban and union ethnics, while his "progressive" constituency, especially in the western and eastern states, was appealed to with rousing anti–Wall Street rhetoric—this was the "give 'em hell, Harry" campaign—and promises of western resource development. Blacks were promised a permanent Fair Employment Practices Commission (FEPC) and labor-liberals from the ADA at the Democratic convention won a strong civil rights plank) which alienated southerners, who bolted to the States Rights party, but the electoral vote losses were, in fact, sustainable.[124]

Settlement

The president's Economic Report of January 1949, written by Keyserling over Nourse's objections, outlined the elements of what became the administration's Fair Deal program: the repeal of Taft-Hartley, an increase in corporate taxes, further credit controls, an increase in the minimum wage, extension of unemployment insurance, national health insurance, new TVA-like (Tennessee Valley Authority) infrastructure investments, federal aid to education, public housing, authority to intervene in and compel expansion of crucial manufacturing materials such as steel, and free trade. The Congress, now with a Democratic, but not more liberal majority, rejected virtually all of the president's reform program in 1949, including Taft-Hartley repeal, the FEPC, as well as the International Trade Organization treaty. It even cut defense by more than $1 billion, although it increased "mutual defense assistance" $500 million and expanded housing finance.[125]

The CIO quickly found it futile to push Truman to fight for a more social-democratic policy in 1949. Indicative was the economic expansion (or Spence) bill, co-written and promoted as a logical forward step from the 1946 Employment Act by Rep. Brent Spence, Sen. Murray, Keyserling, Bertram Gross, the UAW, ADA, and others. The bill would have created a multipartite National Economic Cooperation Board, appointed by the president, that would have been advisory and would have worked with the CEA. It would have provided the missing "mechanism" to coordinate private and public economic decision making. The sponsors foresaw the board as using all the planning techniques envisaged at the time of the full employment bill in 1945.[126] Businessmen were aghast at the "socialist" planning and "class warfare" of labor-liberal Democrats.[127] Truman ordered Keyserling to desist lobbying for the Spence Bill.[128] Later in the year, the same labor-liberal group and seventeen cosponsors backed a new economic expansion bill but, without the president's support for institutional reform, there was really nowhere to go with it.

Truman wanted congressional conservatives to support his foreign policy and did not intend to "waste" his influence with them fighting for the broad reform agenda and otherwise scaring them with the prospect of economic controls as a price of military preparedness. National security planners were beginning a drumbeat for a massive military buildup to contain Communism, though the policy debate was not clinched for a large increase until the Korean War broke out in June 1950. The Soviet Union exploded an atomic bomb in September 1949; China "fell" in October. Security planners clearly outlined both a hardened containment policy and the domestic benefits of military-based Keynesianism.[129] The North Atlantic Treaty, ratified in early 1949, led to a boost in military expenditures while Marshall Plan aid was finally flowing fully in 1949. Military and economic aid spending increased from $17.3 billion in the second half of 1948 to $20.2 billion in the first half of 1949. As for the slumping economy, although virtually all Senators, whether Republican or Democrat, liberal or conservative, still favored cutting spending to match reduced tax revenue, Truman's foreign policy program and the automatic stabilizing features of fiscal policy led to "passive" deficits and actual countercyclical forces.[130]

A more congenial solution for Truman was to adopt Keyserling's emphasis on "growth," rather than stabilization of wage-price-profit relationships or labor management reform. The United States could have "prosperity and progress for the worker, the farmer and the businessman" plus development of underdeveloped regions and employment for marginal workers. Those who disagreed that all groups could progress together were "unwitting spokesmen of class against class."[131] Growth rather than income distribution, would provide the mass markets that large-scale industry needed. The administration withdrew its tax increase proposal; partially "liberated" monetary policy, which now was a drag on an economy in a downturn since it kept interest rates up; proposed eleven mildly expansionary measures; and passively accepted the "automatic" deficit as revenues declined with decreasing economic activity.[132]

Reuther explained to the UAW executive board that defense spending was being used by some as an economic panacea, which he rejected, but the union lacked the power to influence defense budget planning. "That is out of our reach." Instead, the union "can get into direct contact with the problem and try to steer it in the direction we think it has to move if we are going to solve this problem of gearing the economy and the abundance it can create to the needs of the people . . . through collective bargaining."[133] The 1948 CIO convention had reaffirmed that pensions and social security were part of labor's 1949 agenda for the "fourth round." The UAW considered holding off a collective bargaining demand for a health and hospital fund, pending congressional action, but union leaders predicted that Congress would not act at all or, at best, would pass a bill with benefits too low. The UAW planned to build on federal standards through collective bargaining "supplements."[134]

The Reuther leadership in 1949 still was fighting a two-front battle with antilabor forces and factional opponents. The 1948 contract with GM allowed for decreases in the cost-of-living adjustment and, when prices did drop in early 1949, so did autoworkers' wages. Even though Reuther had opposed COLA and the left had favored it, Reuther was blamed for the wage cut. Also, the buyers' market and new models at GM and Ford led the companies to "speed up" the work pace, in the fall of 1948, and to further factional charges that Reuther had agreed to this with the productivity formula. The union, in fact, had complained bitterly to GM, in the fall 1948, about the speed up and corporation stalling on settling grievances. At Ford, in April 1949, the union had belatedly sanctioned a massive three-week anti–speed-up wildcat strike in Detroit where over eleven hundred grievances had accumulated.[135] Opponents capitalized on rank-and-file dissatisfaction and defeated Reuther slates in key local elections at Federal Mogul, Chrysler Local 227, Chevrolet Forge, Chevrolet Gear and Axle 235, Amalgamated Local 205, Flint Fisher Body #2, and at Cleveland Local 45, while splitting control at Dodge Local 7 and Bohn Aluminum in Detroit.[136]

At the UAW's February 19, 1949, economic conference, Reuther, Emil Mazey, and Art Johnstone made a spirited defense of their wage strategy and record while their opponents unsuccessfully proposed a general strike (partly to press Taft-Hartley repeal) and a thirty-hour week and 30 percent wage increase, the latter two of which were similar to demands by other CIO unions, the AFL, and the UMW. Reuther rejected a general strike and argued that the expectation that an industrial crisis would force Truman to intervene was improbable, and in the event the government did seize control of the industry, the lesson of the previous few years was that "they never intervene for us."[137] The UAW executive board planned to strike one of the Big Three to win a pension plan. Reuther rejected Ford's claim that the recession was a reason to keep wage costs down. He called this a "classical" example of "capitalistic economics" and managerial control of resources that would undermine mass purchasing power. Reuther argued that the return of a buyers' market, in 1949, made the individual companies vulnerable to strikes. (In fact the Big Three had lost market share since the war to the so-called independent auto companies.) Reuther advised the conference that the union should "take advantage of what somebody said are the contradictions inside of a capitalistic economy" and exploit competition among the companies. And, as for the plight of small companies, which could not afford a fully-funded pension plan, well—that was another contradiction of a system that rewarded profitability and not car-building capacities. The union leadership upheld the position before the delegates that those companies would have to swim with the rest or sink.[138]

The steel contract expired in July, before the auto contracts, and U.S. Steel refused the USW demand for company-financed pension and health plans and a 20 cent wage increase. Ford and GE rejected similar demands from the UAW and UE. Truman asked the USW and U.S. Steel to extend their contract sixty days while a presidential fact finding board investigated the issues and made recommendations. The steelworkers accepted, but U.S. Steel publicly insisted that any recommendations would be advisory only and carried no moral obligation for the company to accept them. When the board, on September 10, recommended company-financed pension and health plans, Murray accepted for the USW, even though the board also recommended there be no general wage increase in steel and, by implication, elsewhere. But U.S.

Steel and other steel companies rejected the recommendations and the steelworkers then went on strike October 1 to win acceptance of the board's recommendations.[139] Republican member of Congress Clare Hoffman (R., Mich.) declared that the fact finding board was "phoney," "red biased," and "a plot against the people" that would lead to a "fascist labor government."[140]

On September 29, the UAW settled with Ford, which had conceded the principle of such plans in 1947, for a company-financed pension based on the steel board's recommendations. Despite some strong rank-and-file opposition, rooted in dissatisfaction with the settlement of the speed-up strike, the contract was ratified.[141] The rubber industry then agreed to a pension and, finally, in the second week of November 1949, first Bethlehem Steel, and then U.S. Steel, settled with the USW for a company-financed pension and jointly-financed health plan. The steel, rubber, and Ford pension plans were based on a formula tying them to federal social security, such that if and when social security was increased, company contributions would decrease. This was supposed to provide an incentive for manufacturers to join labor to lobby Congress.[142] Later, in 1950, Chrysler settled after a hundred-day strike. GM did not need the prodding: its net income in 1949 had set a record for a U.S. corporation, and it could afford to be generous without fear of investor reaction. The company agreed to a pension plan with no reduction in company contributions. GM also agreed to a union shop and raised the productivity formula, while the UAW agreed to a five-year contract with no wage reopening clause, but with COLA protection. The union "got no significant concessions" on work rules from the company, although it retained the right to strike on production standards. The UAW then returned to Ford and Chrysler to make their contracts also for five years, also with COLA and AIF. *Fortune* magazine called this the "Treaty of Detroit." It also was a gamble by the Reuther leadership that economic and political conditions would be stable for five years.[143]

The Liberal Order

The CIO and UAW–Reuther leadership had begun the period with a vision of industrial democracy in which workers would participate in decision making on the job, at the industry level, and nationally. This was rooted in the older producerist and Debsian socialist traditions, in the practice of skilled workers, and in Catholic labor teaching. The basic idea was that the means of production were being misused by corporate power, that a democratic society based on equal rights to participate could fulfill managerial functions better, in part by redistributing the economic surplus and in part by liberating workers' capacities from managerial domination on the job. The quick and massive rebuff of the CIO program by employers, Republicans, and most Democrats in the federal government created tactical confusion and turmoil within the CIO. The USW and the UAW retreated to a more traditional American union stance, though not completely the same as the AFL's. Like the old AFL, the USW and UAW redoubled their emphasis on government protection of "free collective bargaining" and a firm contractual basis for union and workers' security. They adapted traditional union policies for seniority and job classifications in a mass production setting to stanch the postwar losses to job and income security, and they compelled large corporate employers to forsake managerialist dreams and deal pragmatically with unions.

Their tactical retreat was aided by prolabor liberal industrial-relations experts who helped, for example, to rationalize (and preserve) the job-wage structure in the steel and meatpacking industries, just as the UAW had agreed with Chrysler and GM to stabilize wage classifications.[144] Prominent liberals, such as War Labor Board chairman George Taylor, Wayne Morse, and Supreme Court Justice William O. Douglas, advised that the lines between management and labor at work be preserved and formalized and that collective bargaining should focus on mutual adjustment. But the process of formalizing labor contracts and industrial common law hollowed out the idea of a producers' community and substituted procedural relationships within management-determined boundaries. Nonetheless, an industrial pluralism based on contractual union security and grievance procedures also protected union organizations. Under assault for what looked like their very existence, unions dug in their heels to prevent integration into the "common enterprise." For many liberals, the producers' community carried a profound challenge to American society since it envisaged a community of worker-managers carrying out society's work and, as such, would pit the producers against the owners of the

means of production. Thus, William O. Douglas opposed the unionization of foremen, arguing, in a dissent that was vindicated by the
Taft-Hartley Act, that labor-management collaboration would pit
the "operating group" against "the stockholder and bondhold-
er."[145] It was better to have a pluralistic "miniclass struggle," as
George Meany called it, between union and management in the
plants, than a political class struggle that union leaders were sure to
lose.[146] By 1950 the UAW and its sympathizers called off the political
campaign to establish a direct institutional tie between industrial
relations and national economic policy that would have enabled
labor to participate in governing the economy. The CIO and UAW
did not abandon completely the broader vision, though the extent
of labor-management cooperation became confined largely to high-
level private relationships between union and corporation leaders,
rather than an element of rank-and-file aspiration given the new
structure of incentives.[147] Still, the exhaustion of the unions ratified
then-current frontiers of labor-management authority and the evolving
practices of regulated dispute resolution. It also deprived the federal government of an alternative means of influencing the performance of industry. In fact, the postwar system was based on freezing
labor and management positions and subjecting disputes to arguments over contractual rules.

To many liberals and social democrats, labor political unity
had been tied to the need to better wrest reform from employers
and "reactionaries," but it became a rationale for demobilizing
factional opponents, enhance union prestige, and securing the
social basis for organizational stability. The two-party strategy led
to internal repression of union dissenters. Within the CIO, Reuther
and other "right-wing" leaders pressed Murray to act against
"internal" foes of the CIO, namely, the "left-wing" Communist-
linked unions. Reuther sounded the theme at the July 1949 UAW
convention that the "left" was responsible for the failure to repeal
the Taft-Hartley Act that spring and for the flagging southern
organizing drive. The "left" was again condemned for opposing
the Marshall Plan and supporting Wallace in 1948.[148] At the CIO
executive board meeting in May, the right-wing leaders worked to
convince Murray to expel the left and by the November 1949 CIO
convention, a purge had been agreed upon.[149] The UE, the largest
expelled union with over three hundred thousand members, tellingly

charged the CIO with subordinating labor's interests to the Democratic party and partisan politics. But many liberals believed expulsions were part of the national party realignment necessary to implement a reform program; Truman Democrats had already expelled states' rights Democrats from the Democratic National Committee.[150]

Yet the Democratic party simply did not develop a positive program for labor. Democratic allies merely held off the worst excesses of Republican and employer reaction, and they did not enact a reform program. The Democratic administration's domestic economic management policy came to an accommodation with labor's new collective bargaining agenda, but probably was unaffected by labor's specific demands because Truman only wanted and needed union electoral support to implement his own plans. The southern Democracy remained a bulwark against legislative reform and formation of a national labor movement. The immediate consequence was to reinforce incentives for union fragmentation and sectorally based welfare.

In the years to follow, economic growth and pluralistic industrial relations indeed did appear mutually dependent, as most organized workers steadily increased their wages and unions their memberships. On the other hand, private-sector unionization, as a percentage of the potential membership, hit its postwar peak in 1955. The blocked expansion of unions blunted labor's claim that its strength at the workplace was crucial for economic success. But in the long run, evidence that the relationship was more complex emerged from the experiences of workers for whom the postwar settlements undermined their industrial positions in the 1950s and 1960s and ultimately in the 1970s and 1980s in the face of competition from nations with more flexible forms of industrial order.

CHAPTER 5

Creating a
Special Interest Group
The Skilled Auto Workers

The success of American manufacturing industry in the twenty-five years following the postwar settlements stands in sharp contrast to the chronic problems that have beset unions and corporations since the early 1970s. Then the unprecedentedly long boom reinforced labor-management stability with payoffs of steadily increasing wages and profits while, in recent years, these historical industrial relations practices have stood as obstacles to the reorganization of industry widely perceived as necessary for future market successes. There is virtually universal agreement that a higher level of skills is desirable for American industries faced with intensified international competition in order to increase productivity and to maintain high standards of living. One basic concern is to increase the productivity of American industry, which otherwise cannot hope to compete with extremely low-wage countries in a free trade regime. Another concern is that competitive success now depends less on investment in new physical capital (because production technologies are available to virtually all competitors) than on the ability of managers to deploy labor to use and adapt technologies as market conditions fluctuate. A third concern arises from evidence that the blue-collar work force promises to become increasingly black and Hispanic, and these are precisely the social groups that currently obtain the least amount of schooling and training. Finally, for unionists and those who believe that effective worker representation is critical, not only to a successful economy, but to political democracy, there is growing appreciation that broader education and training may play a crucially important role in the job security of workers and, hence, in the future of unionism.[1]

In an upskilling strategy, workers and managers would cooper-

ate in training programs in which employees would learn new skills
and take responsibility for a broader range of workplace tasks than
traditionally assigned. A more capable work force, in turn, would
undergird a corporate market strategy based on flexible process
technology and rapid and efficient product innovation.[2] One of the
key obstacles to reorganization commonly cited, paradoxically, is
the persistence of historical craft jurisdictions and craft autonomy.[3]
Part of the reason for this is that skill development is linked closely
to an array of other concerns about work reorganization and job
loss. Broad agreement on expanding the capabilities of blue-collar
workers obscures disagreements about just what kinds of skills are
needed or wanted, and about how workers are to obtain greater
education and training, as well as about the effects of different
answers to these questions on the balance of power at the workplace and the declining share of the labor force that is organized.
While skilled workers conceive their skills as enhancing their capacity, authority, and autonomy in varying work contexts, they
perceive that managements want to cut labor costs and fit the
worker more snugly within the organizational hierarchy of specific
firms.[4] The apparent recalcitrance of the already skilled to cooperate in the new managerial strategy, in turn, acts as confirmation for
employers that highly trained workers are untrustworthy and inef-
ficient.

Whether or not flexibility of job assignments and cooperation
can be solutions to current problems depends, in part, on confronting the basis of the skilled trades' persistent disruptive power. This
chapter argues that the rigidity of craft work in the automobile
industry is an outcome, partly, of past defeats of the aspirations of
skilled workers. Skilled autoworkers played a crucial role in unionizing the industry and challenging the old partisan politics and
industrial order. But skilled manufacturing workers were compelled to narrow their purview in the 1940s and 1950s during
successive applications of a conception of work that overdrew the
lessons of mass production under postwar political conditions. As
firms lengthened the division of labor, skilled tradesmen sought to
broaden the role of the autonomous workman. But they were
blocked by the new labor management system and their second-
best alternative was to preserve as much of what they had as
possible.

As we saw in chapter four, the UAW and major automobile manufacturers, in the postwar 1940s, negotiated rules that helped stabilize relationships in the shops between production workers and supervisors and in politics between industry and society. Collective bargaining established the means of resolving shop-floor disputes without disrupting production through grievance procedures, of ensuring steady increases in workers' incomes by tying wages to increases in national rates of productivity and the cost of living, and of establishing that productive efficiency depended on managerial actions and new technology. Moreover, both union and companies supported government policies to promote economic growth. The postwar settlements were not made to resolve problems of skilled tradesmen, but they committed the union, managements, and government to courses of action that came to shape the politics of skilled work. Postwar labor management severely limited the scope of worker participation in the production process and largely reaffirmed managerial initiative and control as it shifted labor-management relations toward contract administration and firm-specific welfare benefits rather than the substance of work.

It was the common sense of the day that mass production methods entailed the demise of skilled work and premium craft wages. The passing of craft autonomy was a price of technological progress, while broadening the distribution of income helped ensure the realization of society's abundant productive potential. Both mainstream liberal and Marxist authors agreed that technological modernization was the principal explanation of the crafts' recalcitrance and "conservatism," namely, that skilled workers' resistance to inevitable rationalization of work is an attempt to protect archaic craft privileges.[5] The persistence of craft workers in manufacturing was explained by the political needs of managers.

According to Stanley Aronowitz, mass production technologies made advanced manufacturing craft skills unnecessary. What explains the persistence of skilled labor in manufacturing is the political threat that mass production poses to managerial control. Precisely, by reducing the qualifications for employment to practically nothing, the entire work force is unified in a common industrial destiny. Therefore, employers, with the support of the outmoded craftsmen, reestablished "the hierarchical division of labor within the factory" to prevent a challenge to management control. The "aristocracy of labor" was maintained in several ways, among them ethnic and racial antagonisms, separate seniority lists, wage differentials, and apprentice training.

> One way of providing justification for the position of the skilled worker or that of the industrial "professional". . . was the formalization of training. The informal methods of apprenticeship gave way gradually to formal schools that granted credentials. . . . Such training became the material substratum of the ideology of skill, and disguised its ephemeral character at the point of production.[6]

Nevertheless the privileged position of skilled workers was one factor that led craftsmen to become the leaders of the industrial union drives of the 1930s and 1940s. But after the Second World War, skilled workers reverted to their true interests in hierarchy and began to reestablish their separate role. "But it did not take long for the skilled workers to recognize that, despite their adherence to the new unionism, their interests were not served by its egalitarian ideology."[7] The primary way that skilled workers accomplished this was by gaining the right to separate representation elections of which, "naturally, employers were strong proponents."[8]

Aronowitz ably reflects the perspective that mass production technologies and the creation of unskilled work were the most efficient forms of production for employers to establish. Skills were obsolete and skilled workers and apprentice training were structurally reactionary. Industrial unions are progressive because they integrate the working class. Yet much historical research presents a picture of a less uniform march to mass production industrial organization and the wholesale devaluing of workers' skills. Moreover, contemporary comparative research on the labor forces of the advanced industrial countries finds that those economies that created and maintained extensive forms of worker skill development are the most capable of taking advantage of product market opportunities and, thus, most able to maintain full employment and income.[9] High levels of blue-collar skills now seem to be associated with those outcomes that the postwar labor system based on low-skill mass production work was created to most efficiently achieve. The American system, precisely, is the one that has experienced the most difficulty in responding flexibly to the new conditions of competition, which highlights the American system's specific historical character. The actual influence of background conditions—

the extent of the market and the balance of political power—on work organization, then, is a matter of some judgment and is not merely a technical question. Extensive deskilling is only one way to efficiently organize work. The emergence and continuing dominance of Tayloristic methods of work is based on the power of managements to do this profitably, not on superior efficiency.

As against the model that foresees craft work reduced to a set of task-specific job classifications and skilled automobile employment as a lost cause, it makes sense to reconceive skilled work as a viable, but lost opportunity. This notion is reinforced by the actions of skilled workers themselves, who sought to preserve and expand their role in the auto industry. Deskilling shapes the jobs of all workers, skilled, nonskilled blue-collar workers, and white-collar workers in service industries alike but, because of the historically autonomous position of manufacturing craft workers, they have been at the cutting edge of technological change and, hence, of the workers' struggle with employers. Skilled manufacturing workers have persistently been leaders of movements for workers' control and less readily succumbed to the appeals of consumerism to focus on income and life-style opportunities away from work.[10] For over twenty years, beginning in the early 1930s, trades activists sought to substantially shape industry. Not only did they compel employers to bargain collectively, but it was a vision of a regional cooperative economy that informed their outlook. As it turned out, their ambitions were unfulfilled and their demands were recast in an interest group framework. The protection of their truncated positional advantage then placed them at odds with the liberal prosecution of civil-rights demands.

The Reemergence of Manufacturing Craft Unionism

The regulation of skill and the role of craft workers in manufacturing by the 1920s was based on substantial corporation self-regulation. Firms continued to extend the division of labor, creating extremely simple, repetitive jobs. Nonetheless, craft work survived. With the success of GM's design-led product market strategy in the mid-1920s, employers' demand for skilled labor increased. To fill the balance of their demand for skilled labor, big employers maintained corporation schools, although they and smaller companies also relied on skilled immigrants from northern and western Europe. Much work was performed by these small companies. They provided dies and tools to the auto manufacturers, and they operated on a traditional system based on broad skills and general purpose machinery. Individual tradesmen "bounced around" among the independent "job shops" and the manufacturers' "captive shops" seeking better pay and working conditions.[11]

After consumer markets collapsed, the automobile firms sought a new market strategy—sometimes called Sloanism[12]—of enhanced product differentiation. Indicative of the strategy was General Motors' introduction of a new standard vehicle, the all-purpose road cruiser, which packed more style and luxury. Components of the strategy included annual model changes, the adoption of all-steel car bodies (the turret-top) and the introduction of a new generation of machine tools. Following the depression, the auto companies continued to differentiate products based on this standard. As postwar consumer markets stabilized, they began to automate their production lines by linking them with transfer machines and, in the 1960s, with the introduction of electronically-controlled tools. These and other innovations in autos and elsewhere helped reduce the need for production labor, but led to increased demand for toolmakers. Employment of toolmakers increased nationwide by 19 percent from 1930 to 1940, by 62 percent from 1940 to 1950, and by another 19 percent from 1950 to 1960.[13] Employers' deskilling and disinterest in apprentice training in the 1920s put them in a difficult spot, explained a leading journal of metalworking. "New industries, new processes, new machinery, new materials require great numbers of skilled workers. . . . particularly since the pre-Depression era was characterized by over-specialization."[14] Employers' increasing needs for skilled workers created a new skilled labor shortage by 1934 when auto production regained levels achieved in 1929, but the resolution of the problem was different from that of the prewar era. The federal government asserted a more sustained interest in industrial relations with the National Industrial Recovery Act and skilled tradesmen allied with production workers to form industrial unions.

The NIRA encouraged firms to use apprentices as one technique to stabilize the labor market. Training standards would be established through the code authorities for each industry. Federal investigators determined, however, that employers refused to negotiate with employees' union representatives over industry standards and that the employer-dominated approach led to "exploitation of youths, at the expense of unemployed adults."[15] After the NIRA was declared unconstitutional, the Congress passed the National Labor Relations Act in 1935, which, not only entitled workers to bargain collectively over "wages, hours and other terms and conditions of work," but led to the rule that each work site would have just one union in order to prevent company-dominated unions from dividing the work force, thus effectively throwing together skilled craftsmen and production workers. Whether low-level supervisors and foremen, traditionally often drawn from the ranks of apprenticeable skilled trades, also could join the union remained a live issue until the Taft-Hartley Act of 1947 removed such employees' rights to organize from the protection of the NLRA.

At the same time, federal government officials continued to see apprenticeship as a valuable program for regulating labor standards, and they convinced President Roosevelt to issue an executive order to create a Federal Committee on Apprentice Training to develop a youth training policy.[16] Within weeks after the Supreme Court found the NLRA constitutional, in April 1937, the U.S. House of Representatives passed the Fitzgerald Apprenticeship Act, partly based on the recommendations of the federal committee. The act provided for federal support for skill development programs established through collective bargaining.

At the congressional hearings on the Fitzgerald Act, federal committee members testified that the apprenticeship training policy should be aimed at solving several problems having to do with the supply of skilled labor for industry and with the need to develop citizenship. Labor supply concerns included the stabilization of labor markets by channelling youth away from "overcrowded" trades and into new occupations; the lack of common standards for skill from one part of the economy to another; and the dearth of employees who were thoroughly trained in manufacturing and who could be employed either in blue-collar craft work, white-collar technical jobs, or managerial positions. The public members of the committee went further to declare that apprentice training was an important part of citizenship development (as much as liberal arts education). It was a "measure toward social security" that enabled individuals "to absorb or overcome technological changes, to adjust themselves to changes more quickly, so that they can make shifts within their occupation or even within closely allied occupations in times of falling off of employment." Apprentice training "is a preparation for . . . taking their place as citizens who are going to make sane, intelligent decisions on matters of public importance."[17] The public schools were the logical center for a broad program. But a major evaluation of the federal vocational education was highly critical of the program, and both employer representatives involved in the federal committee's work and the AFL opposed government "dictation."

The AFL feared an over-supply of craftsmen, but beyond concerns about the rate of unemployment, the AFL's position reflected a learned suspicion of government authority that led it to advocate public action only where it endorsed the decisions of voluntary groups, such as itself, no matter how narrowly organized.[18] The final form of the act built on federal collective bargaining policy. A new Bureau of Apprenticeship and Training in the Department of Labor would help develop apprenticeship standards, project labor market needs, and foster joint union-employer agreements on apprentice programs. The federal government would work through state committees to gain the voluntary cooperation of unions and companies to carry out apprenticeships subject to local conditions.

The CIO sent no representatives to the House hearings on apprentice training. Yet, it would be a mistake to assume that unionists in the mass production industries had no interest in apprentice training. As discussed in chapter three, skilled autoworkers formed the Mechanics Educational Society of America in 1933. In their vision of a reformed industrial order, a prominent goal of MESA was to establish apprentice training programs.[19] For the craftsmen, the programs were much more than just a job training mechanism, they were the key to the trades' position and crucial devices for industrial regulation. Apprenticeship, as the preferred (but not only) path to skilled jobs, regulated the labor supply and helped preserve the crafts' bargaining power and their authority in the plant. Apprenticeship rates (the ratio of apprentices to journeymen) could be adjusted periodically in collective bargaining contracts and in firm-level negotiations to meet industry and employer needs for more labor. Collectively bargained training also helped solve a collective action problem for firms: no single firm had an incentive to underwrite the training of workers who could end up working for competitors, a very common occurrence. But once all firms were required to jointly pay for training, all firms could come out winners and none carry a disproportionate burden.

Yet, even with collective bargaining rights, skilled and production workers encountered determined management resistance to negotiated cooperation. MESA battled with employers during the NIRA period and, in 1938, won contracts with the job shops that included apprentice training. MESA activists also were pivotal in the unionization of the big automakers, after they joined the UAW–CIO in 1936 and formed UAW Locals 155 and 157 in Detroit. They continued to bargain jointly with the ATDMA for a regional contract and for the right to participate in collective bargaining at the big firms. At GM and at Ford, when it was unionized in 1941, contracts included apprenticeships.

But then, during the war, the skilled trades came under special government controls. In fact, skilled workers accepted the government's manpower plan even though it sidestepped skill development through apprentice training. The government's war needs generated a tremendous and immediate demand for war materiel coming from the automobile plants and for skilled labor. To prevent the trades from "taking advantage" of the situation, the government regulated workers' wages to slow increases, prevented job actions and job mobility, and won skilled trades' agreement to upgrade production workers into specialized jobs that were pieces of historical craft work for the duration of the war.[20] At the end of the war, both factions of the UAW proposed plans to "pool" skilled labor. In Reuther's version, workers would be organized into noncompetitive "technical commando units" to service the entire industry or industrial area irrespective of company and product, but this, and other union proposals, was shunted aside.

Craft Aspirations and Postwar Politics

Looking back, in 1949, over the previous ten years, toolmaker activist James Bowden reminded a Detroit regional meeting of tool and die makers engineers and maintenance tradesmen that the skilled workers' "vision was disrupted" by the war. Now they had to regain the initiative in the "postwar situation."[21] Acute concerns about wage rates and the managerial hard line against workers' control led to a transformation of the structure of skilled trades' preferences. Before the war skilled workers had been leaders of an expanding coalition of labor involvement in managing industry, from which all workers would gain; with the defeat of a New Deal revival after the war and with what they perceived as a retreat by top union leaders, skilled workers tried to shore up their own position.

The leaders of the Detroit tool and die councils called on the UAW to create a "tool and die local" to which all tool and die makers in the region would belong.[22] Tool and die leaders adopted a program to mobilize the traditional sense of pride in craft work and professionalism in common concerns among rank-and-file craftsmen to push for greater trade autonomy within the union. Their program included wage increases; "bona fide" apprentice training; industry-wide vesting of pension benefits; organizing the unorganized; greater education of production workers about skilled trades issues; and greater representation in the union through a union sanctioned skilled trades conference, skilled trades representation on collective bargaining committees, and a charter for a tool and die local in Detroit.

Skilled trades unionists faced immediate employment security problems. First, the dumping of hundreds of thousands of government-owned machine tools onto the market plus the postwar layoff of skilled workers had led to a proliferation of small unorganized job shops. Toolmakers wanted the UAW to support an organizing drive in the Detroit area.[23] But they became increasingly frustrated by the direction that Reuther's leadership took in collective bargaining to equalize wages between production workers and skilled workers: why should unorganized workers join the UAW to earn less? Second, as postwar demand increased by 1948 as the auto companies retooled for the first postwar car models and because of the Cold War military commitments, employers filled trade jobs with wartime upgraders and subcontracted construction work on new plant.[24] The Big Three's own captive tool rooms paid lower wages than the job shops and could not readily attract skilled journeymen. Rather than raise wages, corporation managers unilaterally continued the wartime upgrader program. The corporations could quickly expand their "skilled" labor force and keep down their wage bill at the same time. Although the trades had agreed to it during the war, under the new conditions—a couple of years of high unemployment for skilled workers and a chance to regain lost ground—upgrading seemed to distribute benefits disproportionately to employers. Tool and die makers argued that upgrading diluted the trades and was part of management's plans to gain greater control over skilled labor by creating new job classifications. The answers seemed to be to reassert the primacy of apprentice training as a prerequisite to access to skilled jobs and to increase skilled worker wages in the captive shops. Maintenance workers similarly argued that the union should prevent construction subcontracting to nonunion and AFL-organized firms, which paid higher wages. Again the answers were union organizing and tougher collective bargaining on wages and working conditions.

The new strategy recalled the trades' traditional concerns. Skilled workers wanted to establish a largely autonomous craft sphere within the existing collective bargaining framework. They proposed to accomplish this initially by creating a regional pool of skilled labor in the industry that would free workers from control by or dependence on any one employer. The AFL building trades and longshore work historically was organized this way. The idea appeared eminently practical for tool and die makers, too, given the fact that these craftsmen continued to be highly mobile. A Bureau of Labor Statistics study of Detroit in 1951 found that 43 percent of tool and die workers had worked in more than one industry in the previous eleven years (not to mention how many different firms within an industry).[25] According to the study, 26 percent of all tool and die makers worked in the tool and die jobshop industry—machine tool accessories, 17 percent in machinery, 15 percent in electrical machinery, and 21 percent in the motor vehicle industry. Further, wage rates would be tied to skill level, not one's occupational niche; job and income security would be maintained by work sharing and managing the volume and quality of skill training; and industrial relations would be based upon the substantive nature of the work (i.e., the broad range of skills that craft workers had would ensure them of authority to deal equally with management in deciding how to carry through projects).

The reassertion of craft power was first of all a response to employers' strategies. But it also was a challenge to the UAW's emerging industrial pluralist self-conception and commitment to a regulatory regime that favored labor relations stability. Despite union disapproval, the skilled tradesmen had the resources to assert their sectional interests in their independent skilled trades councils and their control of craft knowledge.[26] Yet, a narrow assertion of craft interests was potentially divisive vis-à-vis production workers. The "zero-sum" possibilities were evident in their demands for priority for apprentice training programs and enforcement of agreements against upgrading production workers into skilled jobs, for elimination of rules that allowed seniority production workers to bump into skilled jobs, and for wage increases greater than those won for production workers.

On the other hand, skilled workers had been champions of the UAW and very much wanted to remain part of it. Moreover, skilled workers depended on the strength of the union. As a minority within the union, skilled workers especially needed an effective means of influencing union policy, and they did so through the top leadership of the International union. For example, they helped amend the UAW constitution to give the leadership a veto of local contracts that did not conform to union policy, and they championed company- and industry-wide solutions to problems of training and organizing nonunion shops.[27] A crucial weakness in the skilled trades position inside the union was that leading tradesmen were supporters of the so-called "left-wing" group within the UAW organized around George Addes, R. J. Thomas, and Richard Leonard. For example, the Communist party's whip in the union, Nat Ganley, was a business agent in the east side tool and die Local 155. W. G. Grant, a toolmaker and one-time president of Ford Local 600 (the single largest local in the union), ran against Reuther for the presidency in 1949.[28] This complicated the skilled trades' task because it placed them at loggerheads with the "right-wing" group that provided majority support for Walter Reuther's drive to consolidate his control of the union in the postwar years. Orrin Peppler, one of the MESA organizers and a leader of the UAW toolmakers, called on Reuther to remember his "close association with the Detroit–Wayne County Tool and Die Council."[29] However, the Reuther group ran local campaigns against tradesmen who were "left wing," including an intense battle to oust Communist party member John Anderson as president of the east side Detroit tool and die Local 155. In the face of the Taft-Hartley Act, Anderson defeated the Reuther candidate in 1947, but was forced to resign because of the non-Communist provision of that law. The toolmakers lost some of their most experienced leaders in this way.[30] After the Reuther group placed its supporters in local leadership positions and the union's policy became focused upon national wage formulas geared for production workers and on plant-level dispute procedures, the skilled trades leaders became political supporters and bureaucratic dependents of the union. This made them vulnerable to rank-and-file dissatisfaction.

The UAW IEB, for its part, was committed to industrial unionism and in no way wanted to see craft workers leave. This, and historical ties with skilled trades leaders, made some of the board members sympathetic to skilled trades demands. But the IEB's attention was focused on production workers, who constituted about 85 percent of the membership. There was no love lost between production and skilled workers, and the UAW did not want to appear to be favoring the skilled trades. The union leadership demanded fair working conditions and distribution of national income, but did not demand the upskilling of jobs. They thus contained skilled trades problems within the union. The union's Achilles' heel was reliance on employers to respond favorably to bargaining demands and on Democrats to ensure progress toward the Keynesian welfare state. If companies and the government did not come through on what workers considered fair, there was less reason for rank-and-file consent to management's workplace authority and to union discipline.

The UAW did agree with skilled workers that the upgrading issue was essentially a question of "cheap labor."[31] The IEB was concerned, too, with competition from AFL building trades unions and the small, but persistent, remnants of MESA. The union negotiated a "journeyman-upgrader" agreement in 1948 with the auto manufacturers that put some limits on their ability to do this.[32] The 1949 UAW convention endorsed apprentice training, after many years of encouragement from the federal Bureau of Apprenticeship and Training and such labor intellectuals as Joseph Scanlon and Clinton Golden, while UAW leaders proposed an alliance with other unions in manufacturing to increase and coordinate apprentice

training programs.[33] The IEB also agreed to assign two extra organizers to tool and die organizing in Detroit; called an international
skilled trades conference, and appeared to win some limits on
subcontracting.[34] Moreover, in 1950, an area-wide pension plan was
won in contracts between UAW job shop locals and the ATDMA, and
skilled workers won an extra nickel wage increase over production
workers at the Big Three. The wage premium was taken as "the
first strong indication that organized pressure can bring results."[35]

UAW leaders rejected demands for a tool and die local, charg-
ing supporters with "craftism," and suppressed the skilled trades'
edition of the union's newspaper in late 1950.[36] The top UAW
leadership was, at best, divided about the role of skilled labor in
industry. The Reutherite leadership shared a popular perception
that industrial modernization was squeezing skilled trades workers
between the semiskilled mass production workers on the one side,
and the growing ranks of technical white-collar employees on the
other. For the same reasons, they believed that the full development
of the forces of production was a progressive development, not the
least quality of which was to create the basis to equalize conditions
of employment. Ultimately, the UAW was willing to protect the
trades from management assaults, but they were opposed to extending skilled trades authority or according them special status in
the union.

Stalemate and Coexistence

Skilled trades activists continued their campaign throughout
the 1950s. This was conditioned by labor market demand, at first
favorably affected by the Korean War and then by the Big Three's
product market strategies of the mid-1950s, and by the interest of
the union leadership in shoring up its influence in the industry and
national politics.

The Korean War helped cement bipartisan congressional support for "containment militarism,"[37] although it vitiated much of
the domestic reform program. The war experience also clarified
some shortcomings of the UAW's policy and temporarily threw both
the AFL and the CIO back into an oppositional political stance. The
war buildup spurred demand for labor and put upward pressure on

prices as industries scrambled for supplies. Inflation led to demands for wage and price controls and for ways to ensure that there was sufficient skilled labor to do all the tooling to convert industry for military production. The UAW reacted quickly and positively to the Korean War, and, with the AFL and the CIO, it asserted a claim to a major role in directing the domestic side of the war. Skilled worker leaders found themselves in a stronger bargaining position as a result of both the government intervention and the inflation-related wage militancy of rank-and-file workers.

Auto manufacturers first tried to meet the demand for labor by creating "trainees" and implementing new upgrading programs. Skilled trades leaders sought wage increases and agreements to prevent future company exploitation of production–skilled worker differences after the war. The UAW's Skilled Trades Committee developed a changeover policy with skilled trades concurrence and began to negotiate it with the companies.[38] The policy allowed the upgrading of production workers to either single-task machines in tool and die and machine repair, or as helpers in maintenance. These workers, known as "changeovers" at Ford and Chrysler and NDE's (for National Defense Emergency) at GM, would be required to sign waivers of future claims for skilled trades seniority. Seniority would accrue to their production classification and no upgraders would be allowed to receive permanent journeyman status. The union's policy was to urge locals to negotiate apprentice agreements where there was need for more skilled workers. Since virtually no auto plants had apprentice training programs, the union's stress on apprentices amounted to a wedge under company policy.

At the same time the UAW, CIO and AFL had a rude political awakening in Washington. Once President Truman had declared a national defense emergency on December 15, 1950, the CIO and AFL presented him with their program for labor leadership in the defense mobilization bureaucracy. They believed they had earned this by their staunch Democratic support, but they quickly learned this was not to be.[39] Not only was direction of the mobilization put into the hands of General Electric's Charles Wilson and other corporation executives, but price and profits controls were rejected. Instead, the government's economic stabilization program emphasized controls on wages: it precluded regular cost of living benefits, the annual improvement factor, and health and welfare benefits. Moreover, the Wage Stabilization Board (WSB) announced a wage freeze in January 1951.[40]

Reuther and all other labor leaders resigned their positions in the war agencies in February and began to mobilize political pressure on Truman. The AFL and CIO held a joint conference in Washington to air grievances and roundly denounced the President. The UAW convention in April debated repudiation of the Democratic Party and the creation of a labor party, although the leadership was careful to conclude that the time was not ripe for independent political action. The Truman administration and corporation leaders then offered compromises to allow contractual COLA, AIF, welfare payments, and a 10 percent wage increase and to include government mediation of some labor disputes. On April 30 the union leaders voted to return to their positions.[41]

Included in the compromises was the creation of tripartite panels to negotiate special wage increases in the aircraft and tool and die industries and to make recommendations on health and welfare benefits. The UAW representative on the Tool and Die Panel, Joe Piconke, and other "labor" members were able to win over the "public" members to the UAW's program on skilled trades upgrading and wage increases only by making major concessions on capping job shop rates and forgoing national wage standards. Labor and the public then out voted "industry" for a package of recommendations to the full Wage Stabilization Board. But the public members on the full board sided with industry and rejected the recommendations. UAW leaders were incensed by what looked like a double cross and suspected the handiwork of General Motors. The WSB ignored the UAW's good faith and put the union's leaders in a difficult situation with the ranks, both skilled and production. They had had to convince tool and die leaders to provisionally accept its compromises. Now, without the government enforcing special wage increases for skilled workers, they had to come out in the open for them.[42]

Reuther decided the UAW was no longer bound by bargaining norms and planned to take direct action with the help of the skilled trades. Together the IEB and a twelve-man committee of skilled trades leaders decided on a five-point program: 1. endorse the Tool and Die Panel report; 2. seek CIO support for it; 3. organize mass meetings about it; 4. win the changeover agreements; and 5. refuse to work overtime and to train upgraders.[43] However, the leaders and the IEB discovered the ranks were not completely behind them nor was the CIO willing to take action to back them up. Tool and die job shop workers in Detroit and elsewhere around the country did not want to fight for the compromise Tool and Die Panel's recommendations, which included a cap on their wages at a time of inflation. Moreover, when changeover agreements were complete at Ford and Chrysler, it was discovered that the negotiators had made further compromises.[44] Another reason many skilled workers rejected the compromise program was that they only mildly supported the Korean War, the underlying purpose of wage stabilization.[45] Moreover, at the March 1952 IEB meeting, Vice-President Gosser pointed out that sentiment for a multiunion general strike was undercut by the lack of rank-and-file solidarity and by the Steelworkers, who were hedging industrial action because of the upcoming 1952 presidential election. The tool and die agitation fizzled.[46]

The UAW then moved to solidify its ranks. It helped skilled trade leaders to organize workers into more skilled trades councils around the country and unionize tool and die job shops around Detroit. It negotiated 260 local apprentice training agreements and more than doubled the staff of the UAW Skilled Trades Department. The IEB began informal, private talks with GM, in September 1952, to gain wage increases for skilled trades and production workers despite the fact that their contract did not expire until in 1955.[47] Finally, as the UAW leaders continued to feel pressure from below, they removed John Fairbain, a former MESA organizer and Local 157 member, from the GM negotiating committee after the following craft appeal to the next skilled trades conference.

> I think we have to get everything we can. . . . We have inaugurated the Changeover Agreement, Improvement Factor and all that sort of thing. . . . Well, God bless the production workers. GM can show us that percentage-wise the skilled workers are above the production workers. [But] we need a wage increase. . . . This is not Utopia. You work at your skills and you get paid for your skills.[48]

The UAW did win wage increases in 1953—with Reuther arguing that contracts were "living documents"—and backing the claims with direct action tactics. But the return to civilian production in

1953 and tight monetary policy created a very competitive consumer market and more aggressive management strategies to increase efficiency through new process technologies and to manage product markets. It also led to major unemployment among production workers, followed by a slowly increasing, but steady demand for skilled workers.

Work Reorganization and Craft Revolt

In the post-Korea buyers' market, working conditions began to undergo rapid change. Auto companies increased the number of models they offered and rapidly automated their plants. Between 1947 and 1959, General Motors' investment in fixed assets was $8.893 billion, of which $5 billion was invested from 1953 to 1958, and $2.2 billion was for special tooling. Ford invested $2.2 billion between 1954 and 1958. Total car, truck, and bus production increased from 4,797,621 to 7,220,000 or by 50.5 percent between 1947 and 1957. At the same time, blue-collar employment in the industry increased just .5 percent although the skilled trades proportion increased by a third.[49]

A few examples will illustrate the situations the workers increasingly faced in the 1950s. Ford built a much heralded engine plant in Cleveland, in 1951, in which engine blocks were machined by an automated fifteen hundred foot line of machine tools, which performed more than five hundred boring, broaching, drilling, honing, milling, and tapping operations. One hundred fifty-four blocks were machined per hour by 41 workers compared to the old manning level for the same rate of production by 117 workers, yielding a labor saving of 65 percent. Stamping operations also were automated by Ford, for a company-wide productivity gain of 300 percent, while 5,000 workers were laid off from the supplier firm that had supplemented Ford's stampings.[50] While jobs were lost, other jobs were simply changed, made easier or more demanding of skill. A 1956 UAW report described changes in skilled trades jobs:

METAL BODY BUILDING—A newly recognized trade and is highly skilled. The demand forced by competition of curved body lines on autos and the many different types of bodies with lighter but stronger chassis.

DIEMAKING—Big dies that previously took months to develop only take weeks now.

DIESINKING—The new Keller machines finish the die so accurately that the tedious hand work on the bench has been greatly eliminated.

TOOLMAKING—The skill of the Toolmaker has had to keep pace with the technical developments and the higher precision requirements. The new field of plastics, as in diemaking, is not yet progressed sufficiently, to be positive of its affects on the trade.

PYROMETRY AND INSTRUMENT REPAIR—This work also has increased in volume as well as improvement of the instrument. They are now used in so many places and forms to test material for strength, for heat temperature, gas and air pressure, as indicators on production lines in Assembly for tabulating output, heat treat of metals etc. . . . The accuracy registered by those instruments is very important so they must be repaired, maintained and installed by well-trained skilled mechanics.[51]

The union's policy toward these developments was to use collective bargaining to redistribute income from increased productivity directly to workers and to resolve disputes among workers over work assignments.

One of the union's major bargaining breakthroughs of the 1950s, supplemental unemployment benefits (SUB), is indicative. The origins of SUB were the demands raised in the 1930s for better production planning to stabilize employment. In the 1940s the union had formulated this into a demand for guaranteed wages that would provide incentives for employers to stabilize employment. By 1955 guaranteed wages had been reformulated as supplemental unemployment benefits and the UAW won SUB in the auto negotiations that year. SUB would be financed by company contributions of five cents per employee per hour, up to a stated maximum, to guarantee laid-off workers 60 percent of after-tax pay for up to twenty-six weeks (in the late 1950s). The union hoped to induce the companies to avoid unemployment and, because SUB payments were supplemental to state unemployment benefits, to lobby to raise the latter so as to limit its own contribution.[52] SUB was another element of the political formula in which sustained income was traded for consent to managerial designs for efficiency.

Moreover, the union sought to negotiate new (if fewer) job classifications with higher wages that took into account changed job content so as to maintain individual worker income. For example, Ford's new stamping plant in Chicago, which opened in June 1956, had just 101 classifications, compared to 315 at its old Dearborn plant, and included an automation classification. Workers objected that Ford was simply trying to gain control over the content of skilled work, but Ford management insisted that both production and skilled worker classifications be consolidated because "the complexity of the equipment made it mandatory."[53] But whatever the company's goal, as Ken Bannon and Nelson Samp, director and assistant director of the UAW Ford Department explained, the union had two goals in cooperating with the company's reorganization. The first was to gain, for the production workers directly involved, increased wages from productivity improvements and, for those still employed, greater job security through broader job categories. The second was to mediate the conflict between production and skilled workers over the breakdown of traditional trades, which threatened the skilled workers' authority at work. Production and skilled workers had to show solidarity by not competing for each other's work.[54] However, there was no unifying point of view to justify a common approach to work organization that preserved the crafts since the union defined unionism to mean the income-control bargain. The union's claim that skilled trade knowledge was essential for the long-term strength of the industry and, therefore, should be protected was as oft-repeated as unexplained. After all, did the union have an alternative to the low-skill organization of work?

When skilled workers demanded enhanced apprentice training to reinforce craft status, the issue was settled inside the union by pressure politics, complicated by the fact that the wide variation of classification and actual work done by company and plants provided unclear guides to action. What was happening, in part, was that some changeover workers were allying with workers in so-called "bastard" classifications—fractions of skilled trades—to win their way into the skilled trades and earn higher pay.[55] Many locals were sympathetic to the changeovers' claims. Supporters argued that separate apprenticeships were needed to win the support of the workers in these classifications, given that they were already active in the union and the companies were ignoring the Changeover and apprenticeship policies. Militants of both job and captive shops opposed creating separate apprenticeships for craft fractions and advocated instead a "condensed" tool and die apprenticeship no matter what the job title.[56]

Militants then demanded greater representation for skilled workers in the locals. Thus, Walter Dorosh, a tool and die worker at Local 600 at River Rouge and a rising star as recording secretary of its four thousand plus Tool and Die Unit, took up the demand for a guarantee of skilled trade representation at all levels of negotiating and a veto on special skilled trade agreements. At the same time, maintenance workers acted more like their AFL brethren, who were then fighting over craft jurisdictions and taking each other to court. For example, hydraulically controlled machines had become very important with automation, but they combined elements of work from several existing crafts. "The electric power is maintained by the Electrician. The machine power is maintained by the Machine Repair. The air power is maintained by the Pipefitter. The hydraulic power is maintained by the Hydraulic Repair."[57] Maintenance workers insisted on taking jurisdictional disputes through the grievance procedure to arbitration, against the advice of both the union and skilled trades leaders, since the procedure was incapable of dealing with substantive issues and would just ratify management's right to assign labor.[58] Negotiations were preferred.

The administration of apprenticeship programs reveals the continuing dependence of skilled workers on the UAW leadership in industry-wide problems. The auto companies were recruiting tool and die makers from among "displaced persons" from Europe rather than increasing training. Some tradesmen wanted restrictions placed on the practice although the militants favored testing such workers to make sure they were indeed skilled and then inducting them into the union. Others argued for lowering the immigration quota, requiring proof of a labor shortage, or taking political action against company parts imports. The union promised to refer the issue to a moribund CIO committee. Finally, as local apprenticeship programs were negotiated, prominent skilled trades leaders, such as Ray Kay, president of the Detroit Maintenance Council, reversed long-held positions for local control and supported International union control of journeyman cards to prevent administrative chaos.[59]

Throughout 1954 the UAW held conferences and conventions to mobilize rank-and-file support for the 1955 collective bargaining round and the SUB demand. Nevertheless, a result of the contract settlements in July was a mass movement by skilled workers to disaffiliate from the UAW. After the proposed contract was read to a mass meeting outside the River Rouge complex by Local 600 president, Carl Stellato, both production and skilled workers, walked off the job. Most production workers returned to their jobs during the next few days, but the skilled workers apparently, were dissatisfied by the small increase in straight hourly wages, which seemed to have been "sacrificed" to finance SUB, and they stayed out. As the Detroit Tool and Die Council had warned in June: "Failure to win for the skilled workers a decent level of wages or achieve the rest of their reasonable demands will create dissatisfaction."[60]

The "rest" of the demands had been debated at a skilled trades conference in January which, under International control, had rejected proposals from the Detroit Tool and Die Council for "wage equity" (equalize captive and job shop rates, a 10 percent wage increase, double time for overtime, and triple time for Sundays and holidays), an end to compulsory overtime, area-wide seniority, and elimination of single-purpose job classifications. Instead, the conference supported the International's policy rejecting "rigid" rules against overtime, apprenticeship ratios, and subcontracting, and favored retraining, more holidays, early retirement, prior notice of subcontracting, and work reorganization, eliminating changeover employees, ending wage spreads within classifications, and continued wage homogenization of production and skilled labor via flat rate increases.[61]

Rapidly mobilizing sentiment against the contract among skilled workers culminated in a mass meeting in Flint on July 17, called by rank and filers from GM Flint Ternstedt Local 326 and Buick Local 599. Leaders from the Detroit Tool and Die and Maintenance councils were spurned and participants created an independent International Society of Skilled Trades (ISST). Leaders of the ISST won meeting support to register with the National Labor Relations Board for separate union status.[62]

The IEB immediately set out to stop the separatist movement.

Its Skilled Trades Committee met with the Flint ISST leadership in early August, and won over the new organization's president and two others, much to the chagrin and anger of other ISST activists.[63] The IEB also launched an extensive internal campaign of spying on, and contesting the arguments of, the secessionists in the shops. The ISST continued to mobilize skilled workers in large numbers, however, both in Flint and in Detroit. It claimed about fifty thousand members throughout southern Michigan in November, nine thousand of whom were in Detroit. If true, this represented about 20 percent of the skilled trades membership of the UAW.[64] During the next six months, the ISST presented a model of a federation of crafts, independent of both the CIO and AFL. The latter were criticized for becoming "industrialized." The ISST claimed not to be anti-industrial union, but procrafts. There seemed to be little difference in the specific workplace demands of ISST members or sympathizers and UAW tradesmen.[65]

Skilled trades leaders actively opposed ISST organizing and Ray Kay kept close tabs on ISST meetings and membership for the IEB. They also attempted to regain the initiative on skilled trades issues. In a September 28, 1955, meeting of the officers of the Detroit councils, it was agreed to present a four-point program at the IEB's next meeting, in October, and to hold a mass meeting afterward to decide next steps. The four-point program gave prominent place to the demand for greater autonomy within the union. The points were: 1. separate contract ratification for skilled tradesmen; 2. an immediate reopening of contracts to negotiate a 10 percent wage increase, and a commitment to percentage wage increases in the future; 3. more local representation for skilled trades issues by the Skilled Trades Department; and 4. unity between production and skilled workers.[66] A delegation, headed by Ray Kay, was chosen to present the program to the IEB. At the October IEB meeting, the delegation reaffirmed its loyalty to the UAW, but they stressed that the skilled workers had real grievances which had been outstanding for years.[67] The GM contract was completely inadequate, they said. The UAW had not won at GM (as at Ford and Chrysler) recognition of the journeyman program: apprentice training still was task oriented, apprentices did not receive journeyman cards (which "killed" attempts to unionize apprentices), and the contract gave journeyman status to changeover workers with only four to six years experience instead of ten, which violated the union's policy and disrupted wage relationships. Moreover, there had been no progress on equalizing captive and job shop rates nor an end to the wartime cap on captive rates, the subcontracting clause was inadequate, and the IEB had connived with Ford to create the new automation classification, which, they argued, was used by the company to control other trades classifications.

When the IEB voted against the four-point program, the skilled trades leaders were faced with a dilemma. At the previously scheduled mass meeting, October 23, the four-point program was reaffirmed. The "living document" theory of collective bargaining contracts, used by Reuther to open the agreements in 1952–1953, was invoked to justify their demand to reopen the current contract in 1956. On November 4, a joint meeting of the Detroit councils' officers was held to plan a strategy, but the Maintenance Council officers behind Ray Kay backed down from the four-point program, splitting the joint meeting 15 to 13 to rescind the wages campaign.[68] Although the Tool and Die Council continued to agitate, the combination of the IEB's rejection of the four-point program and the Detroit council officers' reversal of the October 23 mass meeting decision were fuel for the ISST fire. The councils were criticized in ISST leaflets for "switching sides." On November 6, the Wayne County chapter of the ISST held a meeting of some four hundred workers and decided to petition the NLRB for representation elections.[69]

Taming the Trades

The legal basis for craft representation "carve outs" from industrial unions went back to Wagner Act disputes in the late 1930s between the AFL and CIO. The NLRB had not settled the question of whether skilled workers could secede from an industrial union chosen by majority rule in which they were a minority. The NLRB twice reversed regulatory direction on these issues. Going back to 1937, in *Globe Machine and Stamping Co.*, federal labor regulators had decided that craft workers had the right of self-determination and could opt out of industrial unions to form their own craft organizations.[70] However, in the years following the case, the board had granted a number of exemptions to the Globe doctrine that blocked "craft severance" in industries that were characterized by a high degree of "integration of operations."[71] The Taft-Hartley Act seemed to settle the question in the affirmative, however, as part of employers' strategy to limit industrial unionism. The auto companies had been strong proponents of Taft-Hartley, but they came to oppose craft severance in the 1950s. Following Taft-Hartley, the Eisenhower board declared, in 1954, in *American Potash and Chemical Corporation* that it would no longer block craft severance on the basis of integrated operations. Whether or nor craft severance resulted in "a loss of maximum efficiency" was not the primary issue to decide but, rather, the main issue was to determine if there was a community of interests of the craft workers. "An excellent rule of thumb test of a worker's journeyman standing is the number of years' apprenticeship he [*sic*] has served."[72]

When ISST petitions for craft representation elections were filed from GM plants in early 1956, it seemed that the workers would have a good chance for a favorable ruling from the Eisenhower NLRB. But the Michigan regional Labor Relations Board dealt the secessionists a halting blow in late February. The board heard ISST petitions from GM AC Sparkplug Local 651 and Flint Ternstedt and rejected them on the procedural ground that a hearing was only possible during the six months preceding the termination of a contract; meanwhile a bona fide contract had priority. This ruling reflected the "contract bar" doctrine that the national board had developed as a means of controlling rank-and-file self-help and of stabilizing union-company relations. In short, the ISST would have to wait until the 1955 UAW–GM contract ran out in 1958 to petition for elections.

The temporary demobilization of the ISST that this caused in 1956 encouraged the IEB to take a more ameliorative position and to soften the get-tough policy it had adopted with the skilled trades. The IEB had instructed local unions, in March, to expel from office any local officer who was a member of the ISST and the Detroit Tool and Die Council had been told to stop its wages campaign or be taken over by the IEB. But in October the Ford and GM national councils voted to endorse the skilled workers' demand for representation in negotiations and in December, at the Fifth International Skilled Trades conference, the IEB announced that it would recommend constitutional changes at the 1957 UAW Convention along the lines advocated by skilled trades leaders.[73]

They would allow skilled trades separate voting rights on those parts of contracts dealing solely with the skilled trades, the right to strike separately with IEB approval, and separate election of skilled trades representatives to local and national negotiating committees. The IEB also promised that priorities in 1958 collective bargaining would be improved apprentice training and retraining programs, and elimination of wage spreads, subcontracting and the cap on captive shop rates. At the April 1957 UAW convention, delegates ratified the IEB's proposals after long debate and created the eleven functional subcouncils, including an industry-wide tool, die, and maintenance council. The IEB presented the proposed changes as necessary adjustments to the new technological context of industry, not as palliatives to a rebellious minority of skilled workers.[74] Leonard Woodcock, director of the GM Department, argued that the proportion of technical, white-collar, and professional workers was increasing with industrial modernization and, if the union wanted to organize them, delegates should recognize the organizing value of greater direct representation in the union for nonproduction groups. The minority report opposed the changes, and argued, with some reason, that the issues involved in the skilled trades revolt were worker-management issues, not internal union representation problems.[75]

In May 1958, the NLRB came specially to Detroit to hear some of the more than forty ISST petitions and the arguments against them by the companies and the union. When the board announced its decision to deny the petitions later in the month, it had combined elements from both *National Tube* and *Potash*. Already by 1958 the Board had become concerned about the ISST. In a case in mid-1956 involving an ISST petition at the Fort Die Casting Corporation, an auto parts supplier, the board had ruled that a craft organization, in the meaning of the term in labor law, meant crafts organized singly and not as part of a federation of crafts, which was the ISST model.[76] Now in 1958, the board recalled that decision, but went on to deny the petitions on even more prohibitive grounds. The ISST petitions failed the "coextensive" rule which required petitioners for craft severance to request elections in bargaining units that were coextensive with existing units of the bargaining relationship. The board reasoned that GM was a single integrated unit, exemplified by centralized national collective bargaining and by the functional union subcouncils that the UAW had just created. So, because the ISST petitioned in just forty of GM's plants, all were dismissed.[77] The NLRB veto, combined with massive unemployment in the auto industry that began in late 1957, ended the ISST.

In early 1959 the loyal skilled trades leaders were taken into camp by the IEB. During 1957 and 1958, the skilled trades leaders had actively sought the changes in the union's constitution which were passed at the 1957 convention, as well as a five-point program for 1958 collective bargaining. The UAW officially adopted the skilled trades' program as part of its ambitious 1958 agenda. However, the IEB decided to rein in the union's demands because of the deep recession, which had begun in late 1957, and the potential political harm from public criticism of "wage push" inflation. For example, liberal congressional Democrats on the Joint Economic Committee were working on a benchmark economic study (released in 1959) that argued that the stagflation of the Eisenhower years was a result of both oligopoly "administered pricing" and wage demands in a few core industries like steel and autos, which outstripped productivity gains. Democrats reendorsed a growth strategy and new proposals for sectoral aid for "structural unemployment" and wrote them into their 1960 national platform.[78]

At a special convention in January 1958, Reuther won support for a more modest bargaining agenda, including a new demand for profit sharing and deferral of a previously approved demand for 40-hours pay for 30-hours work. But at the Sixth Skilled Trades Conference in February, skilled trades leaders insisted on the original program and a big wage increase, a halt of foreign sourcing of tools and dies, rank-and-file review of the conference recommendations at mass meetings, elimination of overtime until there was full employment, a one-year wage agreement, and negotiation—not arbitration—of classification disputes.[79] On April 28, 1958 at a mass meeting of skilled workers in Detroit, the City-Wide Skilled Workers Committee was formed to monitor and pressure collective bargaining negotiators. (It also was formed with an eye on tradesmen who then were signing up with the ISST.) Once the union reached tentative agreement with the auto companies, another mass meeting was held, on September 21, at which skilled trade leaders urged workers to reject the Ford and Chrysler contracts.[80] Rejection would be symbolic, the officers of the Tool and Die Unit at Local 600 argued, since enough other Ford plants had ratified the agreement to make their vote moot and because Ford (and General Motors) had refused to recognize skilled workers' rights to strike separately. It was important, nonetheless, to preserve "our identity and the righteousness of our cause" and to signal Ford the "battle" was not over. This tactic was strongly opposed by the Local 600 leadership. The contract was ratified by the local as a whole 15,084 to 3,977 while the Tool and Die Unit passed it 912 to 850.[81]

After the contract was signed the City-Wide Skilled Trades Committee created the City-Wide Unemployed Production and Skilled Workers Committee. They staged a demonstration at UAW headquarters in downtown Detroit, in November, which brought the IEB's wrath upon them. The IEB had had enough of the pressure tactics and abruptly abolished all thirty-eight regional skilled trades councils. In their place, the skilled workers were organized into industry bargaining subcouncils and the Skilled Trades Advisory Committee to the IEB was set up under Skilled Trades Department control.[82]

Fragmenting Skill Development

After 1958 skilled workers, with few individual exceptions, operated within the framework of the postwar labor system. An attempt to revive the ISST in 1966 failed miserably. There were still left-wing organizers, especially among tool and die workers, some of whom became prominent in the 1960s and later, but skilled tradesmen almost solely engaged in militant actions to demand more wages and protect existing job classifications. They became a pressure group promoting their own interests in the union. This, of course, did not mean that skilled workers always agreed with the union policy. On the contrary, they persistently perceived that the top leadership gave their demands short shrift and their militancy renewed factionalism.

One consequence of limiting the workplace role of skilled workers and the scope of skilled trades organization was to narrow the purposes of apprentice training. Apprenticeship became isolated from work organization and technology developments and changes in the composition of the labor force. Emphasis was placed on its "credentialing" qualities and on controlling access to the trades. Nonskilled workers who were excluded fought for equal access, while employers increasingly sought alternative forms of employee training. But as long as the industrial order created incentives for stability, there was little incentive for union negotiators to do more than tinker around the margins of the automobile training system.

The stable system of mass consumption and production encouraged automobile manufacturers to redouble their efforts at standardization and specialization.[83] While the companies transformed work, the 1960s boom did create an acute supply problem for both skilled, and what became known as technical, workers.[84] Typically for the New Deal order, the issue was dealt with locally and by collective bargaining. But skilled workers and union negotiators continued their collective bargaining routines whose formulas were too narrowly focused to challenge the emerging division of labor. The union leadership was most concerned with which union members would do the work—production workers versus skilled trades—and not with issues of how production would be organized. The same was true for most skilled workers, too: only a few left-wing tradesmen raised the issue of controlling new technologies and expanding apprentice training; most were interested in gaining premium wages and improving benefits.[85]

Thus, during the 1964, 1967, and 1970 auto industry collective bargaining negotiations, employers demanded increased numbers of apprentices and creation of specialized, single purpose jobs. The UAW leadership shared the general perception among labor economists and industrial-relations specialists that a bottleneck in the skilled labor market could choke economic expansion. In 1964 the International UAW agreed in advance to allow locals and companies to increase the number of apprentices at work. They relaxed some seniority rules and the prerequisites for entering apprenticeship programs in order to expand the pool of eligible workers (especially to increase the opportunities for black production workers), while the amount of classroom instruction was reduced at Ford in 1964 and at GM in 1967.[86]

Also, the tool and die locals agreed to recognize "temporary" journeymen, workers who moved into skilled jobs for specific purposes and learned the trade on the job. Their seniority could be merged with that of the bona fide craftsmen after eight years. Despite these concessions, some specialty firms withdrew from the apprenticeship program, although they still participated in other parts of the regional bargaining system. Other employers demanded specialized jobs such as die barber and punch finisher that required less training. The UAW was willing to compromise. Locals 155 and 157 agreed to the creation of a "tool machine operator" that firms wanted to employ on smaller machines like shapers. Workers still would go through apprentice training and receive higher pay, but the training was focused on a far narrower range of tasks and, presumably, was more cost effective. But, of course, these workers were less able to switch to other types of work if demand declined for work from the machines they operated. For this reason apprentices objected to the narrow training, while union locals built "seniority fences" around specialized jobs to prevent employers from shifting these workers to other jobs that would displace all-around journeymen.[87]

Similarly, the union showed little interest in extending the careers of skilled workers. The UAW failed to expand the skilled worker classifications by capitalizing on favorable grievance umpire rulings that recognized as toolmaker work the programming required for the new automated machine tools. Ford had argued vainly that this new type of tooling work should be shifted to nonunion technical staff.[88] Instead, the union (including most skilled workers, it should be said) apparently saw the situation as an opportunity for wage increases and compromise on labor supply rather than as a job control issue. Not surprisingly, then, the union's apprentice administrators showed little interest in advanced courses in programming that were developed by training instructors.[89]

Nor did most educators and policy-makers see a need to emphasize all-around training or the upgrading of jobs. The new computer-controlled technologies were conceived as dedicated tools that could be operated by unskilled button-pushers. A study of manpower needs in Michigan for vocational programs projected a huge increase in the use of numerically-controlled machines, but recommended that no new training programs were needed because "unskilled personnel" would operate them. Gardner Ackley, the chair of the President's Council of Economic Advisors, urged

employers in 1966 to "economize on scare skills" and begin "breaking down jobs or redesigning processes" so that individuals without
training could be employed.[90]

Instead, with a ceiling on skilled workers' careers at work (at
least if they wanted to stay in the union) and emphasis on promotion of production workers, a conflict burst into the open over
access to the trades. Organizations of black workers, such as the
UAW-based Trade Union Leadership Council (founded in 1957),
were pressing for greater participation for blacks in union policy
making. Apprentice programs gained notoriety as a focus of equal
employment opportunity initiatives. The Johnson administration,
with the help of allies among the national leaders of AFL–CIO
unions, began a program to voluntarily integrate apprenticeships
in the virtually all-white male skilled trades, especially in the
construction industry, a litmus test for whether the liberals' equal
opportunity commitment extended to "good" jobs. Jobs for so-
called marginal workers had opened as the national unemployment
rate dipped below 4 percent, but civil-rights groups recognized that
the only jobs available were entry-level positions on the internal
labor market job ladders. Unless minority workers could break into
craft, technical, and professional jobs, they would be the first fired
in a recession and would have few skills on which to fall back.[91]

But the limited progress of the cooperative approach eventually led civil-rights organizations into pressure tactics against the
unions and to court mandated affirmative action. For example, the
Boston Urban League sponsored the United Community Construction Workers' Union, which broke off from the voluntary
Boston program and set up the Third World Jobs Clearinghouse
based on federal court mandates for a certain percentage of construction job referrals.[92]

Unlike some of the building trades, the UAW was strongly
committed to the Democratic party and civil rights and it responded with an outreach program to encourage minorities to apply to
the auto industry apprentice program. Yet, because by the 1970s
the numbers were still small, the union established a preapprenticeship
program to prepare blacks (and women) for the apprenticeship
qualifying test. But there was an outcry from skilled workers when
it was discovered that union instructors were teaching students the
test answers.[93] The whole exercise only seemed to confirm the

common sense that "working class careers" was an oxymoron and to further undermine union solidarity and labor political influence.

Another consequence of the narrow scope of apprentice programs was that employers increasingly turned to nonunion technical education programs to fill their needs for highly trained personnel. In the 1940s and 1950s employers and educators began to agree on the need for a post–high school technical curriculum located at two-year community colleges. At the time, however, most community colleges were bridges for low-income students who wanted to go to four-year institutions.[94] What was distinctive about the debate that ensued was the relative lack of interest by educators and business planners in trade education. Instead, projections of labor force needs emphasized the growth of white-collar "preprofessional" occupations between those of craft worker and professional. What employers wanted was to define the new jobs they were creating as technical white-collar, nonunion jobs.

For example, in 1952 Ford asked the Dearborn school board to write a proposal to take over the Henry Ford Trade School campus and equipment and to reorient its community college program to technical education.[95] But, in 1951, students at Dearborn Community College, located close to Ford's world headquarters, preferred college transfer courses by 4 to 1. Only 21 percent were in terminal programs in technical subjects. Nonetheless, the Dearborn school board hired a leading educator, Algo D. Henderson, director of the Center for the Study of Higher Education at the University of Michigan and associated with President Truman's Commission on Higher Education, who recommended a preprofessional approach as the path to the future. What the Board proposed to Ford was to double Dearborn's enrollment and double the proportion of students taking the terminal two-year technical course.[96] The company accepted and the school was renamed the Henry Ford Community College.

From Ford's point of view, the community college provided an appealing alternative to expanding union involvement in the workplace. Although the Fitzgerald Act mandated joint union-management administration of apprenticeship, programs could be kept focused on historical definitions of craft work. As discussed earlier, skilled workers were adamant that companies and unions establish such programs and that only workers who had graduated from a bona fide training program (or who had accumulated ten years experience) could perform work in skilled job classifications. Yet, the new apprentice programs simply added another piece to the fragmented system of American education and training and soon proved how little skilled workers had gained. All apprentice programs combine on-the-job and classroom instruction. But trade instruction at Henry Ford Community College was not integrated into the broader technical curriculum. The apprentice curriculum hardly changed over the next two decades, despite the changing nature of work and technology and despite development of new courses by the college for apprentices to take. Classroom work was focused on getting people through a standard number of hours of coursework. Apprentice programs were managed to preserve the status quo in labor-management relations.

Political Rigidity and the New Flexibility

Since the early 1970s, product market instability has plagued the pluralist industrial order as American manufacturing industries have been increasingly exposed to foreign competition. Some are optimistic that changing world markets will compel companies to discover that a highly skilled work force is more capable of flexibly shifting work tasks as product market conditions demand and is more capable of high quality and value-added production. Similarly, workers and unions will realize that an expanded definition of skilled work provides more long-run employment security. But such deterministic thinking runs against the historical legacy of low-skill jobs, the skilled trades struggle to persist, race and gender discrimination, the liberal arts traditions of public education, the decline of independent worker representation through unions, and a broken-down political capacity to deliver full employment. Even as some employers have shifted toward a new flexible strategy based on interfirm collaborations and greater "skills" required by both blue- and white-collar employees, they have encountered not only resistance from skilled workers who worry about employment security as jobs are broadened, but a dearth of workers with enough capability or even the capacity to readily learn the new manufacturing style.

As the unionized manufacturing sector experienced crisis beginning in the early 1970s, the American system for apprentice training went into decline. The total number of metalworking apprentices reached its highest level ever in 1970. In 1969 Michigan and the surrounding states had accounted for 70 percent of all graduated toolmaker apprentices nationwide and 39 percent of all machinists. By 1971 the number of new toolmaker apprentices dropped to the lowest level since 1963. After 1979 apprenticeships in automobiles took a plunge to the lowest levels since the late 1940s. And, other than apprentice training, blue collar workers receive only a minuscule proportion of corporation training investment.[97]

The big auto companies first tried to extend the division of labor and standardize products globally, increase overtime and subcontracting, gain financial concessions from the UAW, and substitute computerized process technologies for both unskilled and skilled labor. Skilled autoworker militants demanded a contractual ban on compulsory overtime. When the companies offered to trade overtime for upgrading, the skilled trades called it a new Taylorism. At Ford the skilled trades rejected the contract in 1973 and threw the UAW into crisis. Throughout the 1970s they challenged "management's rights" to make unilateral decisions on plant closings and products and called for a new union effort to mobilize members to devote their skills to producing quality products in the United States. However, the UAW's responses were based initially on standard collective bargaining routines to preserve income and legislative lobbying to secure foreign investment in the United States. But the crisis deepened and changed for the union and the companies. Now the crisis is about a low-skill, hierarchical organization of work and its coordination with other institutions of society.[98]

The job shop sector was one of the first casualties of the overextension of the old model. A major element of manufacturing flexibility is widely recognized to be the existence of an independent tooling industry whose companies can provide special services to the center firms, ranging from the supply of extra machining capacity to engineering consultations. The center firms themselves then do not need to invest in specialty tool-making equipment and engineering services that would only be employed part time. Equally valuable is the ability of the tooling industry to adapt to new demands: the organization of the industry combines high skills, firm-specific product specialization, and industry-wide cooperation reflected in layers of subcontracting among firms. The variety of products involved is diverse, but the principal products of the job shops in 1972, in dollars, were special dies and industrial molds. In the Detroit area, the automakers relied on the job shops to provide them with such crucial pieces as the dies used for stamping car body parts.[99]

Nonetheless, after the mid-1950s, the tooling industry went into a long-run decline from which it has not recovered. The independent Detroit tooling industry collapsed from 28.8 million hours worked in 1956 to 14 million hours in 1958 and 10 million hours in 1961. Then the general upturn in the national economy and military spending in the mid-1960s caused an increase in tooling business and in work hours and employment. However the 1960s peak was just 16 million hours. By 1973 work hours had declined to 7.6 million.[100] It is common today to blame imports for the industry's crisis, but the decline far antedates the current situation. The complete explanation is beyond this study, but part of it is the contrary consequences of stability for production innovation, and part of it is the practices of the labor system initially designed to suit mass production work and transferred to skilled work.

With the demise of the vision of a regionally deployed skilled metalworking labor force in which individual tradesmen would shift with industrial needs within an industry-wide agreement, a countertrend was established. The principal change was decisions by the Big Three to build their own body dies in the 1950s and 1960s. The firms, then, were vastly increasing the number of car models, and they argued that body shapes were "trade secrets." The Big Three came to rely less on the flexible expertise of the job shop and increased the capacity and employment of their captive shops. Job shop wages lagged behind those of the automakers in the late 1960s and capital investment was low; at the same time job shop workers pushed the union to raise company-paid benefits to match the Big Three. A crisis emerged within the Detroit Tooling Association (the new name for the ATDMA) caused by the collapse of

206 — STEPHEN AMBERG

member firms and led to a bitter industrial conflict with the UAW tooling locals in 1971, which resulted in the breakdown of regional cooperation.[101]

Despite escaping much of the union presence, specialty firms still suffered the jolting passage of the economy in the 1970s and 1980s. Now, with some revival in this sector, the center firms that specialty companies supply are placing much greater demands on these companies for precision and fault-free parts and on the ability of suppliers to work together. But specialty firms are faced with a dearth of skilled labor and few resources to train workers.[102] At the same time, the partisan political framework that supported a degree of negotiated cooperation among unions and firms was disrupted and has not been reestablished. Although the Carter administration Labor Department was an effective advocate for apprentice training, the Reagan administration evinced little interest in programs that involved unions, even dropping a number of statistical series tracking skills and, instead, eased the immigration of skilled labor.[103]

CHAPTER 6

Boundary Maintenance
at Studebaker

The New Deal's formulas for industrial order among the major players in the economy also shaped the economic behavior of more minor players among small companies and competitive industries. Studebaker Corporation's abandonment of the automobile market in the early 1960s demonstrates both the power and limits of the postwar settlements. With the cooperation of the United Auto Workers and the encouragement of outside management consultants, Studebaker managers, in the 1950s, sought to transform their firm into one whose labor relations and market strategy conformed to that of industry leader General Motors. Their failure to do so sheds light on one of the key industrial dilemmas of the 1990s. Can firms construct an alternative form of work organization capable of producing an economically viable, flexible response to the stagnant mass markets and heightened product competition that have come to characterize much of American manufacturing? Or are mass production firms in high wage regions doomed to lose out to companies that reap cost advantages by producing for mass consumption in world markets and locating their factories in low wage countries?

This chapter claims that at Studebaker Corporation, a small firm in a mass production industry dominated by giant organizations, pieces of an alternative producerist flexible-specialization strategy were already in place when financial crisis enveloped the firm in the 1950s.[1] A fully realized flexible-specialization strategy combines a flexible production process with a product strategy aimed a filling market niches overlooked by mass producers. As a locally controlled producer with a long history of production in

— 207 —

South Bend, Indiana, Studebaker might have been able to capitalize on the growing segmentation of the auto products market and the high degree of labor solidarity in its plants. Such a strategy would have avoided a head-on clash with Ford and GM and concentrated the firm's energies on a strategy which proved more viable when the first wave of small car imports arrived in the mid-1950s. But the formulas which had come to govern industrial politics foreclosed an exploration of any such unorthodox solution to Studebaker's dilemma. To the contrary, the firm's effort to mimic GM and Ford locked its managers, workers, and bankers into an insoluble conflict, which reduced Studebaker to near bankruptcy. As this strategy backfired, management pursued the orthodox alternative: disinvestment and diversification into other products. Studebaker became a successful conglomerate in the 1960s, but only after it closed its South Bend factories and left the auto business.

Work and Society at South Bend

The pattern setting UAW–GM contract settlement of 1950 helped codify the new industrial order by establishing wage rules that linked workers' purchasing power to the rising prices and productivity of the U.S. economy. Although an increasingly elaborate set of work rules and grievance procedures protected workers from the foreman's full authority, the postwar era saw the gradual reassertion of management's "right to manage." Legal limits on the scope of collective bargaining, the "management rights" clauses inserted into manufacturing industry union-management contracts, and the accommodative policies pursued by the leadership of most large trade unions laid the groundwork for the resurgence of management power that began in the 1960s. For producers like GM and Ford, the new order was a boon. Government macroeconomic demand stimulation and pattern increases in wages guaranteed a mass market for standardized products and a payoff for expensive labor-saving investment. GM produced 3.4 million cars and trucks a year during the mid-1950s, and its most popular model, Chevrolet, sold over a million and a half units in each year of the decade. In 1955 its market share stood at over 50 percent; its return on investment was over 30 percent during 1953–1957.[2] Given its enormous market strength, GM adopted product innovations only after they had proven themselves elsewhere. Instead, it focused its resources on improving production methods and passed on any increased costs to consumers.

In contrast, Studebaker had an incipient flexible-specialization strategy. The company had a radically different relationship to its market. Its market share was 2.6 percent in 1946 and 4.0 percent in 1950 when it sold 268,000 cars. After 1953 its share declined to 2.4 percent in 1954, 2.1 percent in 1955, and 1.1 percent in 1957.[3] As a consequence, small changes in the quality of demand could have a large impact on its cash flow and profitability. To flexibly shift with changing markets and efficiently produce comparatively small batches of products, its employees took on a broader range of work tasks and responsibility. Rather than driving to standardize products and the production process, Studebaker management emphasized distinctive product design and quality.

Studebaker had first adopted a specialist strategy in the early 1920s, when it began production of the Light Six, a high quality low-priced car with distinctive styling. Yet, a disastrous policy of liquidating operations to maintain dividends bankrupted the company early in the depression. But after coming out of receivership in 1933, the company again sought a market niche. Studebaker's strategy proved very successful in the 1930s and, except for 1938, the company made money. Strong sales of its new economy Champion model in 1939 promised growing success on the eve of World War II. During the war, Studebaker built amphibious vehicles, big trucks, and aircraft engines. Government officials even suggested that Studebaker management take over Ford, which was faltering in its production commitments.[4]

In the postwar consumer market, Studebaker was first among all companies with a new model. Market share stood at 5.4 percent in 1951, its best year ever. Studebaker also expanded abroad in order to broaden its sales base. It sold cars in dozens of countries in 1953 and operated or licensed manufacturing facilities in twelve countries in 1955. Again, in 1953 Studebaker set the new car pace in the industry, adapting Chrysler's novel power steering to its model line and introducing the long, low body style which later came to dominate the industry. In 1953 its sales were $594 million.

Moreover, the company had invested in new plant and machinery at a rate equal to the Big Three after World War II, and its production facilities were up to date.[5]

Paul Hoffman, who had been a star salesman for the company in Los Angeles and its vice-president for sales, presided over the rebirth of Studebaker after its depression era bankruptcy. Taking over in 1935, Hoffman sought to capitalize on the company's tradition of product quality and historical roots in the South Bend community. According to Hoffman, the company could only compete in the larger auto market if it took full advantage of the "intangibles entering into value—and particularly those which did not cost us money. Morale and good will of the working force were two such intangibles."[6] Under Hoffman, Studebaker emphasized pride of workmanship in its product marketing and traded on its one hundred years of manufacturing experience in South Bend. The company boasted that over one-third of the work force were father-son-daughter "teams."[7] This was more than advertising gimmickry, for Studebaker's economic position was too precarious after 1933 to withstand the strikes and job actions that characterized auto industry labor relations during the late depression years. Thus, Studebaker readily accommodated itself to the rise of industrial unionism in the 1930s. It bargained with an AFL federal local in the mid-1930s and recognized, without a strike, UAW Local 5 in 1937.

Hoffman's politics also differed markedly from those of most other automobile executives in the 1930s and 1940s. He was a leading internationalist Republican and served as first chair of the Committee for Economic Development.[8] By 1948 Hoffman's stature was such that President Truman appointed him director of the European Recovery Program. In the early 1950s he was president of the Ford Foundation and a founder of the anti-McCarthyist Fund for the Republic.

In the immediate postwar years, Studebaker's unique style of labor management seemed to provide a basis for a flexible-specialization manufacturing strategy, which might enable the company to compete with its larger rivals. The company did not fight the union over wages or institutional security. Studebaker historically had followed the wage pattern set in Detroit and, in 1945, it willingly granted the union a 12.5 percent wage increase and promised to match any further increase won from GM. Although UAW Local 5 did not have a union shop, the company voluntarily agreed to a dues check off during the war and, in fact, encouraged workers to sign up with the union. And until the mid-1950s, no management rights clause existed in the short and generally word-ed UAW-Studebaker collective bargaining agreement.[9]

The scope of bargaining was "almost unlimited," remembered one local union president. Management could act unilaterally, though both sides consulted with each other on important issues. For example, the company went to considerable lengths to accom-modate union plans for revising wage rates and job assignments to achieve greater equity among local members. Disputes were han-dled by a grievance system, as elsewhere in the industry, but there were no written grievances, little adherence to "common law" precedent, and no arbitration. The company's top officials held a problem-solving, pragmatic approach to labor relations issues, which they saw as a part of, rather than distinct from, production ques-tions. Compared to GM, the firm had an extremely thin personnel department, so its top management, including Presidents Paul Hoffman (1935-1948) and Harold Vance (1948-1954), frequently bargained directly with union officials, "talking out" difficulties in a relatively flexible give and take fashion. "The logic of production has been the logic of industrial relations," reported two academic observers in 1947. "And the solution of production problems has been immediate, forthright and to the point."[10] The system seemed to pay off in "mutual trust" and "glass-smooth labor relations." Surveys of grievance cases at Studebaker and General Motors in 1944 and 1945 found that just 5.5 percent of grievances at Studebaker were complaints about unfair treatment from supervisors com-pared to 20 percent at GM.

Studebaker workers combined a solidaristic tradition of active unionism with a strong sense of allegiance to the company. Their local had played a key role in founding the UAW–CIO in the mid-1930s and had supported independent political action.[11] Democrat-ic and highly participatory, Local 5 supported a wide range of cooperative and union sponsored social services in the following decade, including a credit union, food store, lending library, and housing cooperative. It was one of the few CIO locals to demand and win from management a union controlled pension fund in the 1930s.[12]

Although Studebaker workers would prove themselves extremely militant when it came to a defense of what they considered customary work norms, these same workers were intensely loyal to the company itself. Compared to Detroit area auto workers, they were an older and more often home-owning group who overwhelmingly thought Studebaker the best place to work in South Bend. Jealously guarding their autonomy, Local 5 conducted its affairs, including negotiations with Studebaker, almost entirely without aid or interference from the International staff of the UAW. During the 1930s the Studebaker local, not only refrained from calling any strikes, but kept discipline at work. In 1939 the union even did some independent advertising for the new Champion model.[13] Then in 1946, when stoppages at auto supply factories threatened to disrupt Studebaker's effort to get a production jump on the Big Three, Local 5 used its UAW connections to provide the company with information about the timing and likely duration of these supplier strikes.[14]

On the shop floor level worker collaboration with management rested upon the local's extensive influence over operation of the company's group piece rate system and its control of an elaborate seniority scheme. Studebaker was one of a handful of auto industry companies that had kept a piece rate system rather than switch to measured day work (hourly rated). Although the International UAW had campaigned against the piece rate system in the 1930s and 1940s as a principal cause of "speed up" and unhealthy working conditions, Studebaker workers insisted on its retention because their influence in the factory enabled them to exercise control over the actual operation of the system. Workers ran the jobs themselves, a local member recalled, and supervisors were "just clerks."[15] Studebaker workers regularly joined together to control the work pace and their wages were higher and work effort lower than in Detroit factories.[16] Local 5 shop stewards were the linchpin of this system. There were proportionately five times as many at Studebaker as at GM and Ford. It was standard practice for shop stewards to meet every morning to plan their approach to the day's work and to monitor the composition of work groups to ensure equitable individual effort, group morale, and pay.[17]

The seniority system provided the second pillar of shop floor union strength. Seniority rules at Studebaker, as elsewhere in mass production industry, were designed to provide an equitable method for deciding who should be laid off, recalled, transferred, or promoted, in such a way as to prevent political manipulation by supervisors favoring apple polishers, rate busters, or younger workers. To long-tenure workers, seniority rules also provided short-run job and income security. Compared to other auto companies, seniority rights at Studebaker were unusually extensive. Workers in South Bend had the right to transfer to any job anywhere in the plant and "bump" a current job holder with less seniority. Layoff and recall operated the same way. In contrast, seniority rights at the Big Three usually were limited to bumping only lowest seniority workers and bidding on jobs only within a given task or skill group (noninterchangeable occupational classifications). At South Bend and Detroit bumping rights could be exercised only if the worker could qualify for the new job, but at Studebaker workers had won generous qualifying periods and options for further bumps.[18]

Toward Industrial Pluralism

In the post–Korean War years, a buyer's market returned, and the first casualties were firms in the auto industry. GM and Ford engaged in a market share and production war, and rapidly automated their plants, which put pressure on the so-called auto independents: Nash, Hudson, Willys, Kaiser-Fraser, Packard, and Studebaker. Except for Nash and Hudson, which merged to form American Motors, all went out of business in the next ten years. As financial difficulties quickly mounted, top Studebaker management came to believe that the company's problems were rooted in its insufficiently orthodox business strategy. There were two basic elements inherent in this analysis: first, they thought the company was too small to reap the needed economies of scale in the auto industry. It would have to increase production and sales and compete head to head with the other major auto producers in order to reduce unit costs. Second, labor practices and productivity would have to be brought into line with Ford and GM. Studebaker management had exhibited "poor judgment" in attempting a flexible accommodation with its workers, argued labor economist Robert MacDonald. Its "weak, complacent and short-sighted (managers) virtually relinquished control of their plants."[19] The company, thought most observers, needed to adopt a managerialist strategy to survive in the more competitive auto market of the 1950s.

Studebaker began a significant change in its long-time corporate strategy in 1953 and 1954. The company merged with the Packard Motor Company in June 1954, and under the presidency of Packard's James Nance, who had spent much of his career as a GM manager, began to shape Studebaker–Packard's (S–P) labor and product policies to make the firm conform to the GM model. Major features of the new strategy were to abandon the distinctive styling required for a niche strategy, field a full line of cars to cover the entire market, expand the dealer network, and integrate product components and production to gain greater economies of scale.[20]

But rather than reviving the company, the new strategy was the beginning of the end. Although S–P's combined production capacity stood at 470,000, which was well above what most economists considered the minimum level necessary for efficient production, sales never came near this level. Studebaker–Packard's new product strategy followed the industry pattern by filling the market with 33 cosmetically different models of four basic cars in 1955, and 25 models in 1956 (up from 17 models in 1953).[21] Moreover, unlike a flexible-specialization strategy, the company did not produce small batches of different cars on the same production lines. Instead, it maintained multiple production facilities—Studebaker's plus Packard's—which was an enormous financial drain without volume sales. But, as one business editorialist observed, Packard was an "ex–car of distinction" and Studebaker designs were "dolled up" to industry norms.[22] Studebaker's chief designer still argued for new products to meet the "market emerging for specialized cars," but S–P rejected his counsel.[23] Its prices were slightly above those of its Big Three competitors in 1955, so without a distinctive product the merged company lost $29.7 million on sales of 148,000 that year. Despite a rapid increase in foreign car imports, Studebaker's sales dived to 105,000 in 1956 and red ink splashed to $103.3 million. These losses, combined with the large new debt taken on to deploy the full line strategy, contributed to the company's virtual insolvency by the end of that year.[24]

The strategic turnaround also disrupted the old Studebaker management hierarchy. Under Nance's presidency, a thorough corporate reorganization was begun, which brought a phalanx of Packard managers to South Bend, split industrial relations from operations management, and rigidified Studebaker's traditionally informal authority structure.[25] Lower- and middle-level Studebaker managers resented and resisted the new regime, and Nance's relationship with Paul Hoffman, who had returned to the new firm as chairman of the board, quickly deteriorated.[26] Finally, the new management focused its energy on production engineering and the rationalization of the production process.

These difficulties made Studebaker managers all the more determined to impose GM-style shop discipline and convinced them that a radical reduction of labor costs was essential to corporate survival. In a report commissioned by the firm in the summer of 1953, Anna Rosenberg and Associates reported that Studebaker's labor relations system needed a thorough overhaul. Rosenberg was deeply enmeshed in the liberal Democratic network. She had been a labor relations trouble-shooter for President Franklin Roosevelt and an assistant secretary of defense under Truman, she was a political confidant of business liberals Chester Bowles and William Benton, and she joined the effort of the Committee on the Present Danger to commit the United States to containment militarism. Her report for Studebaker recommended stronger contract administration, a foreman training course, and a "communications" program aimed at production workers.[27]

Studebaker managers were determined to bring the firm's production standards "up" to those at GM. To do so the number of direct and indirect labor hours per car would have to be cut by 34 percent, which required a sizable reduction in the labor force and an increase in the amount of work performed by the remaining employees. Studebaker–Packard wanted a completely new labor contract that would include a management rights clause like that at GM, a union shop, a grievance procedure ending in arbitration, tough anti–wildcat strike language, management-controlled production standards, and a pay cut of 10 to 20 percent.[28]

In its efforts to transform shop floor labor relations, S–P management sought to abolish the group piece work system and thoroughly reform the local's elaborate seniority arrangement. In 1954 management demanded that the local agree to replace the longstanding incentive pay system with a day work pay schedule. Under the day work arrangement, a worker is paid a basic hourly rate and is expected to meet a standard of production per hour, which is set by an engineering department time-and-motion study of the operation performed. Managers thereby gain much greater discretion to control the pace and volume of work. Note that the worker is paid in exchange for a "fair days work": the job itself is determined by management. In freeing wages from production of particular pieces and emphasizing production flow and time, management can easily change the process and organization of work.

Studebaker–Packard management also complained vigorously about the seniority system because it inflated employment and training costs.[29] The system triggered great chain reactions of bumps during large layoffs. As manning levels in various departments were cut, workers bumped into jobs in other departments. Those who were bumped then bumped others, who bumped others all around the plant. During the time workers had to qualify, jobs were double-manned. If the worker could not qualify for one job he or she was allowed more bumps. Not surprisingly, people were "lost in the bumps":[30] either management could not keep track of all the changes, or a department supervisor might ask a bumping worker to temporarily perform a different task, after which the worker would never return to the previous job. In the meantime, workers drew more pay and held onto their jobs while management footed the bill. In 1954 management insisted that abuse of this system could only be curtailed if Local 5 agreed to a limitation of job transfers: three per year interdepartmental and two intradepartmental.[31]

Officials of the International UAW, including Walter Reuther, had met with management over the winter of 1953–1954 and were convinced that Studebaker was in desperate straits.[32] The union had made a study of Studebaker's market position and, in a reversal of its position that weak companies had to swim or sink, apparently accepted the view that more formal labor-management relations could help insure the firm's survival under the new competitive conditions. More broadly, Reuther argued before the Joint Economic Committee of Congress that the root problem was the rationalization of the industry: "automation in Detroit is creating unemployment in South Bend."[33] The further development of the means of production and the concentration of market power in a few huge companies was the cause of problems for small companies and communities. Until new policies were implemented, the UAW agreed with Studebaker management that the company's contract should be put on an equal footing with the Big Three and that Studebaker workers' superstandard wages were keeping production costs uncompetitively high. This was consistent with the UAW's historic position in favor of industry-wide standards, although applied for a novel purpose, and managerial initiative in work organization. Moreover, the union had long opposed piece work and this was an opportunity to get rid of it at Studebaker. The top leadership put great pressure on the Local leadership to be accommodating and to sell the membership on the new contract.[34]

Shop Floor Politics

On the shop floor level, Local 5 members fought Studebaker to a virtual standstill. They used slowdowns, wildcat stoppages, official strikes, and "abuse" of the bumping system to resist the managerial work reforms. For five years in the mid-1950s they kept Local 5 in turmoil, but no alternative strategy emerged from any of the leadership factions that managed to take control of the local in this period. Some leaders upheld the International's position against their own private inclinations, while opponents promised only more vigilant bargaining. But when the opposition was elected to local office, their defensive posture proved ineffective against the company's long-term plan for further concessions.

The blockage of social democratic unionism in the postwar era and the failure to institutionalize labor participation in decision making about work organization provides part of the explanation of Local 5's inability to formulate a coherent response to the management onslaught. Organized by George Hupp, Ray Berndt, and J. D. (Red) Hill, a self-described "right wing" faction took over the local in 1945 and, thereafter, dominated the local officialdom. It had a strong rank-and-file base among the workers added to the labor force during the war and probably relied heavily upon Catholics for much of its support. Red baiting their opponents, the Hupp faction had attacked local president Bill Ogden for splitting his time between the local and the state capitol, where he sat in the legislature, and they campaigned successfully to purge the regional UAW staff of "Communist" supporters of the George Addes group competing for control of the union.[35] They became influential in city and county politics, but less so state-wide. In the state CIO (and later AFL–CIO) Council, they were largely unsuccessful at uniting the labor movement behind a liberal program, largely because AFL and some CIO unions would not participate in a common political organization with UAW militants.[36]

The right-wing program was centered on defending and extending workers' job rights, which right-wingers believed the Communists were willing to sacrifice for labor participation in corporatist planning schemes like the Charter of Industrial Peace.[37] Yet personality and fiefdoms characterized Local 5 politics after the victory of the right wing. One right-wing stalwart volunteered that they dominated the local "like the one-party South."[38] And in fact, like one-party regimes, the local opposition was reduced to a rump organization which gathered together at local election time to set a slate of the "outs" against the "ins."[39] Shop stewards became practically autonomous in their attention to ad hoc deal making with shop management; they were uninterested in a debate on the larger role the union might play in production. One local president recalled that departments were "unions unto themselves."[40]

Although union officials adopted a generally defensive posture toward managerial reform initiatives in the late 1940s, they were not unwilling to make some concessions. Hupp and other local officials counselled the company to take a more principled stand in grievance bargaining and maintenance of work standards. They were also willing to entertain some reform of the union's complex seniority system, if only to protect workers from too frequent job changes.[41] But, in fact, there was little cooperation these local officials could offer Studebaker without appearing to "give in" to management.[42] Their claim to legitimate power rested on defense of workers' job interests. Indeed job control was an important source of union solidarity, especially after 1950 when employment at Studebaker became increasingly erratic.[43]

Although Local 5 members agreed to reopen the contract in 1954, union leaders were very apprehensive about the reception rank and filers would give the company's proposals. After reaching a tentative agreement with the company in August, local president

Louis Horvath simply dumped the detailed contract reforms in workers' laps and called for a "yes" vote. The members rejected it. The company immediately announced it would lock out the workers, so local leaders quietly encouraged rank-and-file petitions for a new vote. At a massive school field rally held to reconsider the concessions later in August, workers passed the new contract on a voice vote.[44]

During the next year workers refused what they had ostensibly voted for, namely that management had sole control over the organization and content of work, while their job control rights were sharply diminished.[45] Studebaker workers were willing to take a pay cut—they already were working only every other week—but they balked at the newly asserted management rights over working conditions, effort norms and job transfers. A steward later charged that these would "tear the heart out of the union".[46]

At first local and International leaders were able to convince the rank and file to avoid resistance and see how the system would look once in place.[47] Then in January 1955, the company began to build up its inventory as it anticipated a strike later in the year when new contract talks were scheduled and when further concessions would be demanded. Workers began wildcat strikes and the stewards organized a slow down to the old rate.[48] The management sent the whole line home January 6, asserting that "operating schedules" were a "management function." The stewards replied that management should "cooperate" with the union and negotiate the standard or the workers would set it unilaterally.[49] The company refused and for several days slowdowns were followed by mass one-day suspensions. Then, on January 17, the local voted strike authorization 7,188 to 806 and prepared for an actual strike. Studebaker began intensive negotiations which led to modification of the standard in the union's favor.[50]

A few months later the company girded itself for new negotiations, fully expecting a strike. President Nance talked to Reuther "several" times in advance to reconfirm the International's perception that the company needed concessions. At the same time, the company began a systematic department-by-department program of standards enforcement and "force reductions." The number of man-hours per unit fell from 160 to 122.5.[51] Workers resisted with a one-day plant shutdown in mid-May after the union refused to order an absent worker back to work when there were no relief workers to replace him. Ten days later there was another plant shutdown.[52]

By early July 1955, the International UAW had to send Studebaker Department representatives to South Bend to prevent a breakdown of local negotiations over "speed up and layoffs."[53] On July 8 the company laid off 1,700 workers, about 17 percent of the work force, and canceled all bumping rights. The next day the local scheduled a strike vote. The UAW Studebaker Department and local president, Horvath, criticized the company, but wanted to keep negotiations going. They opposed a strike over the layoffs and canceled rights and successfully, if "narrowly," defeated the motion to strike.[54]

Local union elections scheduled for that same July were a kind of referendum on the new industrial relations, but they offered only one thing: to ratify rank-and-file frustration with their impotency. Local politics were constrained by the fact that Studebaker had already made the decision to pursue the new strategy without local consultation. A second constraint was the opportunistic character of Local 5 factionalism. Thus, although the workers believed their stake in the company was threatened and that management had broken its trust, the election simply led union leaders to fight over local office and a militant defense of contractualism. In effect, the union had accepted the parameters of the New Deal industrial order.

The right-wing faction maneuvered to avoid responsibility for concessions and to keep control of the local by slating Les Fox for president, a right-winger who had singularly opposed the concessions.[55] But Local 5 members were so provoked by the new work regime that they rejected this ploy and decisively defeated Fox, and most of the rest of the right-wing slate, in favor of Bill Ogden.[56] Yet the former oppositionists offered no coherent plan to change the situation and now tried to stick to the contract. Rank and filers continued their own opposition (now with help from the right-wing faction) and rejected Ogden's plea to avoid wildcat strikes, act "responsibly," and use the grievance procedure.[57]

When official contract talks began August 5, 1955, the company again demanded major changes that would bring S–P's internal plant regime close to that of General Motors' and would sharpen the division within the plant between management and managed.

Their proposal would reduce the number of stewards by two-thirds, restrict seniority bumping to noninterchangeable occupational groups with no bumping at workers' discretion, create a division-wide (all South Bend) unskilled labor pool, create company-wide social insurance (i.e., merge Studebaker's plan with Packard's inferior one) with joint control (instead of unilateral union control at Studebaker), deunionize plant guards, allow foremen to reassign workers within job categories out-of-seniority, limit seniority in layoff and recall, reduce relief time, and eliminate contractual standards for break-in time on new jobs, among other demands.[58]

Members put intense pressure on the union negotiators to resist management demands and contract talks reached an impasse in September. However, the International would not authorize a strike and, after the negotiations dragged on for another three months, it took over from the Local. The UAW Studebaker Department director, Norman Matthews, who was the founding president of Packard Local 190 in Detroit and then the Chrysler Department director, agreed with the corporation to most of the changes. The new contract was narrowly ratified in a low turnout election in January 1956, 2,456 to 2,139.[59]

Management believed it had a very good contract. President Nance reviewed the "successes" of 1955 for the board of directors. Studebaker had made its labor costs competitive with the industry. Labor hours were down to ninety-six per unit in January. The "right of management to manage" had been won. Studebaker had adopted the GM-style divisional management structure, and it had restyled its product lines. "Now our problems are the problems of the industry," he asserted.[60]

Studebaker workers' resistance was seriously undermined, but not over. Throughout 1956 wildcat strikes continued, especially over the revision of cleanup and relief time. Stewards from all departments organized "mass relief" in defiance of the contract. When one department continued wildcatting and supervision discharged them, laid-off workers refused to hire-in to replace them. Stewards refused to follow the griever model, according to which workers must follow orders until grievances are settled. They argued that the company should write a grievance if it disputed the workers' application of the contract: the company was forced to back down, at least temporarily.[61] Over the next several years

Studebaker's labor relations settled into an adversarial pattern typical of unionized heavy industry.

The electoral merry-go-round continued. Ogden was defeated for reelection in 1957 by Forrest Hanna, a former vice-president under Horvath who temporarily split off from the right wing. Yet Hanna also lost a re-election bid in 1959 and was replaced by Fox who, as vice-president from 1961 to 1964, became a chief negotiator. On the one hand, the new management's hardball tactics created a lasting "bitterness" among the rank and file and stewards.[62] Fox argued that the union's financial "sacrifices" were not appreciated and workers simply ended up "sharing scarcity and misery" and "subsidizing" the company. On the other hand, Ogden claimed that "mismanagement" and management "cronyism" caused s–p's plight, including the "loose production standards." Fox and Ogden each later explained that production standards were a "power situation" in which stewards represented workers' demands to protect jobs and income by keeping the pace of work reasonable.[63] It was management's "responsibility" and "right" to resist them and tighten standards, said Fox. But management's new wage system changed the local leaders' situation by removing problem solving from the shop floor. Attempts by stewards to leverage influence through militant job control tactics were unavailing with the new authority structure and without International support.

National Industrial Politics

UAW strategy in this crisis was two-fold. On the one hand the International used collective bargaining to win fair distribution of gains from the rationalization of production at GM and Ford. The UAW had won employer paid supplementary unemployment benefits in the 1955 national contract negotiations, but it did little for Studebaker workers. Benefit levels in the 1950s were too low; they did not help high seniority workers, especially at Studebaker where SUB was paid to both laid-off and short-week workers; Indiana disqualified SUB recipients from unemployment compensation until 1957; and in 1958, the UAW agreed to let Studebaker defer its SUB contribution for fifteen months.[64]

On the other hand, as it cooperated to make Studebaker competitive (much as it did at American Motors and Chrysler in

1958),[65] the UAW sought to transform the workers' demands for job
security and local control into a public obligation for local redevelopment aid and into evidence of the need for vigorous Keynesian
growth policies. The UAW campaigned to draw national policy
attention to unemployment and community disinvestment during
the 1950s. The union effort was inconclusive, at first because of
uneven AFL–CIO interest, and then because of Congressional factionalism and Eisenhower administration opposition to all but the
barest macroeconomic management.

In 1955, Senator Paul Douglas (D., Ill.), an influential independent economist for twenty-five years before becoming Senator, and
a prominent ally of labor liberals, introduced legislation, supported
by Reuther and the AFL–CIO, to provide capital and planning for
"distressed" high-unemployment communities.[66] Reuther and the
CIO urged Congress to establish a federal community development
authority that would target local areas for special treatment by
federal procurement authorities for technical assistance and public
works and that would create a federal unemployment account
through the unemployment insurance system for individual retraining and moving expenses. However, the prospect of national-
izing the unemployment insurance system as well as coordinating it
with both the vocational education and apprentice training agencies was unlikely, and the CIO agreed that, given high national rates
of unemployment, labor mobility was less important than creating
new jobs where people already were.[67] The Douglas bill proposed
creation of a federal loan and grant fund that would buy land and
machinery and provide public works and manpower training assistance. Also, though superficially similar to the structural reform
proposals of the 1940s, the distressed areas proposal conformed to
the compensatory model of social welfare in that it did not address
problems of authority in industry. It did propose that, in conjunction with a new federal agency in charge of administration, there
would be local "public advisory committees." In South Bend this
would have meant participation by the heavily Democratic and
union-staffed local government. But the South Bend Committee of
100, the leading employers' boosters association, refused to join a
national committee created to lobby for the legislation, which
suggests that local cooperation between labor and managers would
have been problematic in any case.[68]

Douglas's bill passed the Senate in 1955 with the help of a

liberal coalition that included the leading machine tool industrial-
ist, Senator Ralph Flanders (R., Vt.), and the Committee for a
National Trade Policy, an influential group of liberal businessmen
who sought to reinforce labor support for free trade by support for
programs to compensate those hurt by broadening competitive
pressures. The administration blocked the bill in the House with
the aid of the conservative faction of the Democratic party, but the
steady, slow increase in the number of congressional Democrats in
the late 1950s led both houses to pass it in 1958 and then again in
1959. President Eisenhower vetoed it both times. It was not until
1961, after John Kennedy was elected, that the bill, now known as
the Area Redevelopment Act (ARA), was passed into law.[69]

Nonetheless, the administration very much wanted to prevent
Studebaker's bankruptcy, apparently for fear of its impact on financial markets and the combined impact of these at the polls. As a
candidate in 1952, Eisenhower had endorsed the liberal consensus
that the federal government had a responsibility to counteract
serious inflation and unemployment. As president, he followed a
neo-Keynesian policy based on the essential soundness of the private forces driving the economy. The government's role was to
ensure growth through the macroeconomic tools of balanced budgets and monetary policy. Hence, the Justice Department approved
mergers among the small auto companies while allowing GM to
increase its market share above 50 percent. Studebaker's employment had fallen from twenty thousand in 1950 to ten thousand in
1954. By early 1956, S–P's precarious existence had become the
object of special attention in the White House.[70]

Studebaker management's strategy, at the time of its merger
with Packard, had been to rely on defense contract profits to bridge
the company over to its full-line product strategy. But the Eisenhower
administration, through former GM president and now secretary of
defense Charles Wilson, was reducing military spending as part of
its policy of fiscal restraint, and it was cutting back its supplier base
to fewer large companies, which undercut Studebaker's plan. Paul
Hoffman now busied himself lobbying the Defense Department
and his good friend Eisenhower for defense contracts. The president was responsive because Studebaker had a good defense production record, moreover, this kind of aid could be considered ad
hoc rather than a departure from administration economic policy.[71]

The UAW supported these efforts. Local 190, the former Packard local in Detroit, voted to support Hoffman. The UAW Studebaker Department appealed to Wilson to give defense orders to S–P, while Democrats urged greater government spending on the military.[72]

At the same time, Studebaker sought to secure more capital from the firm's creditors and/or find another merger partner to perform both of these functions.[73] The banks did want the company to survive somehow, if only because the company's assets were so devalued they would be insufficient to pay back even preferred debt. But First National City Bank, Chase Bank, and Metropolitan Life Insurance Company refused further funds in January and February 1956. The New York Federal Reserve Bank was cool to a loan and eventually said no. The U.S. Federal Reserve would not guarantee a loan, and they blocked any talks between S–P and American Motors, formed in a 1954 merger of Nash-Kelvinator and Hudson.

In August 1956, the Defense Department awarded contracts to Studebaker, which "sold" them to Curtiss-Wright, a major defense contractor, who also leased Studebaker's two most modern plants. In addition Studebaker sold its subsidiary in California, which had a contract for the Dart missile. As another part of the deal, President Nance resigned, the Packard line was dropped, and elements of the old Studebaker management took control.[74]

With the money thus earned, Studebaker paid off its creditors and launched its new compact Lark in 1959, which was very profitable. It also earned about $10 million as the marketing agent for Mercedes-Benz. But rather than continue its specialty market strategy, Studebaker managers used its profits to diversify into other product markets by acquiring a dozen manufacturing companies in the next three years.[75] In doing so, a former Studebaker fleet sales manager argued, they failed to develop auto market niches for police cars, taxis, and luxury designs, one of which proved profitable in the hands of independent producer Avanti.[76]

In late 1963, Studebaker suddenly announced it was suspending all car production. It left behind 7,200 active Local 5 members, a $30 million unfunded pension obligation, and a 9.1 percent unemployment rate in South Bend. Yet, in other ways it was a favorable conjuncture for Local 5 workers because the national economy was broadly expanding. Not only did the rate of unemployment in South Bend soon decline to the national average, but Local 5 survived by organizing the companies that bought the old Studebaker plants.[77]

Triumph of Industrial Orthodoxy

In retrospect, Studebaker's crisis was not so much caused by high product prices, loose production standards, or a management effort to GMize industrial relations, but by a broader political institutional limit on the alternatives available. The root of the problem was the postwar failure to establish labor and community roles in industrial decision making. The postwar settlement that did emerge truncated the vision that the UAW and other CIO unions had of an economic system in which labor would directly participate with management in production planning under state supervision. Instead, the unions were compelled to concede the shop floor to management and direct intervention in the structure of the economy for government management of the business cycle.

Of course there were legitimate strategies both of cooperation and dissent in the postwar order. Legitimate cooperation took place at the highest level of national collective bargaining and economic policy. Union dissent involved participation in the Democratic party to win social reforms to boost growth and insure workers against economic insecurity. The latter were not guaranteed success, however, nor did reform advocates always observe the boundaries of legitimate action. The political stalemate of the late 1940s continued in the 1950s—exemplified by the distressed areas legislation—and reinforced strategies for private bargains, managerialist solutions, union defensiveness, and "market" outcomes. The companies' orthodox alternative strategy was disinvestment and diversification. The postwar settlement provided incentives for Studebaker management to emulate the Big Three's high volume, standardized strategy with all that that means for the internal organization of work. But a strong local union and strong postwar markets masked, until 1953, the incoherence of Studebaker's actual market and labor conditions. When the crisis began management hardly seemed to hesitate to adhere to orthodoxy. It protected its leading investors first and foremost and cut labor costs while diversifying into other products.

A managerialist strategy was adopted at Studebaker in the post-Korea period, but the cut in labor costs did not save the auto company. Their real problem was that the company did not have crucial prerequisites either for managerialism or for producerist flexible-specialization. It could not readily implement the former, first because of the militant job control unionism it provoked from Local 5 and, second, because a high volume strategy was impractical given its relatively small market. At the same time, the political conditions for a flexible-specialist policy were missing, given the lack of federal support for industrial planning.

CHAPTER 7

The Liberal Democratic
Reform Cycle

*Collective bargaining . . . has lifted, directly and indirectly, a whole class
of abused and deprived Americans into a new status of active economic
and political citizenship [but this] is significantly reduced in value by
what is lost through the inequities and inadequacies of the public bargains
that are struck through the current political process.*
— *Leonard Woodcock, "USA," 1974*

With the election of John F. Kennedy to the presidency in November 1960, many unionists, liberal activists, labor experts, and Democratic officials believed
they had a new opportunity to advance the reform
agenda left overhanging from the Truman administration. President Kennedy promised to "get the country moving again" after
several sluggish years of brief economic expansion and recession
and of nasty and diversionary public debates about Communist
subversion. The Kennedy administration adopted a more
interventionary approach to the economy and sought to coordinate
executive branch policy making with leaders of unions and corporations. But what seemed promising in 1960 became almost twenty
years of frustration as these reformers repeatedly attempted to
extend the liberal industrial order with only marginal successes. By
1980 reform had been stymied and a new ultraconservatism committed to managerialism was poised to take power. In fact, throughout
the era American unions found their room to maneuver to protect
their members' interests increasingly constricted. The changing
conditions of work and unionism contributed to a shift in labor's
political strategy. During the early and mid-1960s, the AFL–CIO was
expansive and provided critical support for civil rights and the War
on Poverty; in 1980 unionists seemed to be split from unorganized

workers and their organizations were under siege at work. But because industrial relations had been carefully shielded from electoral politics, these developments were largely unappreciated by the active public. By 1980 many nonlabor Democrats seemed to lack any idea of "what unions do" for the economy, and society, and party. Indeed, many Democrats had been won over to the views of newly resurgent employers that what unions do "to" the economy was what was wrong with it. Nonetheless, the emergence of a new managerialism was fatal to the governing capacity of Democratic party officials. The failure to reform the basic components of the New Deal industrial order in ways that helped unions serve workers meant that the institutional parties to the industrial order were going to go down with it.

Reform cycles such as this have been identified in many western democratic capitalist nations, but normally social scientists have left the United States outside the analysis. The logic of the omission was that the European reform cycles were rooted in the aspiration of laborist and social-democratic political parties to peacefully transform the capitalist economies of their societies, and in the United States there was no such political party. In Europe, the electoral road to social democracy was blocked by the crises induced in economic performance by reform policies for welfare provision and full employment. The argument was that a capitalist economy simply could not operate under these conditions, would begin to stagnate, and would present a dilemma to the reformist parties: should they press on with reform regardless of cost and commitments to peaceful change, or should they submit to the disapproval of voters who cared less for the long-run transformation than for the short-run conditions of life? The democratic reformers accepted the latter judgment; they could aspire to power at the next electoral turn. Thus, the apparent structural contradiction between electoral democracy and capitalist economy created a cycle of reform. A few researchers realized that, on this sort of structural argument, the United States also had a reformist party— the Democrats—with a strong base among the organized working class as well as a capitalist economy and that the two eventually were going to clash if the Democrats continued to add costs to production through deficit spending, taxation, and regulation.[1]

This chapter conceives of the American reform cycle in two

different ways. First, comparative evidence suggests that the progress of reform is historically specific to particular nations. Sweden, the former West Germany, and Japan were countries that were able to maintain virtually complete employment in a capitalist context. In the United States, the reform cycle was rooted in strategic and ideological failures in the management of the New Deal industrial order. Organized labor was the linchpin between society and politics: unions aggregated the direct economic interests of citizens at work and mobilized workers for the Democratic party; one role depended on the other. Thus, unions were the officially designated representatives of employees' interests at work and they were, moreover, designated to accomplish certain tasks: to gain employee consent and to raise working class incomes to match the production potential of industry. Arriving at agreement on just what was sufficient income was a major issue in winning consent; the process of getting to agreement was collective bargaining at the company level. The parties to collective bargaining could agree or not, in which case the union could strike to test its claims to resources, and the employer lockout, to test its abilities to hold out in the marketplace. An agreement at a major company in a major industry—a General Motors or Ford or a U.S. Steel or a Hormel—could set a pattern for agreements elsewhere. On the other hand, disputes had to be company-by-company: no pattern strikes were allowed, for example. Moreover, employees had few effective rights at work until they unionized. This historically specific industrial relations system was reconceived as a modern, rational rule-based system, namely industrial pluralism.[2] The observation of the rules by unions and employers was supervised by the NLRB and the federal courts with the object of keeping conflict carefully within bounds in order to achieve the substantive goals of consent and economic performance.

In addition, the AFL–CIO (the merged federation that was established in 1955) had turned its Committee on Political Education (COPE) into a prime electoral organizer for the Democratic party. The unions almost uniformly supported the Democratic party—no serious thoughts about independent political action now—even though differences still existed among labor leaders. It was clear that the AFL was the dominant force on the AFL–CIO executive council, but the former CIO unions grouped themselves into the federation's Industrial Union Department, headed by Walter Reuther.

Union members' emphatic electoral support for national Democrats waned with Eisenhower at the head of the Republican ticket, but was almost two-thirds for Kennedy in 1960 and 80 percent for Johnson in 1964.[3] Union campaign organization, money, and votes won elections and ensured that government officials friendly to the liberal industrial order stayed in office.

But industrial pluralism was an ideal, not an accomplished reality; it demanded considerable effort to manage it relatively smoothly; advancing the boundaries of the system required additional political resources, especially a politically capable union movement. Thus, the specific qualities of the American reform cycle were not wholly determined by the institutional structures of economy and polity, but also arose despite the structures and had the quality of threatening the stability of the practices that partly embodied them. There were two major internal challenges to the liberal industrial order. First, the collective bargaining system was hobbled by the Taft-Hartley restrictions on union activity; the authority of unions in the workplace could be effective, but was in no real sense comparable with managements' strategic control. As managers increased the pace of industrial change after the 1940s by recomposing the division of labor, moving to nonunion states and investing abroad, the unions often were left scrambling for adequate responses. Closely related was the scope of collective bargaining. About one-third of the blue-collar labor force was unionized in 1960, mostly in northeast and north central states. A huge number of workers were outside the system in the south and west, in the public sector, and in service industries. Moreover, even though the memberships of the industrial unions associated with the CIO, plus a few old AFL unions, included comparatively high percentages of minority workers, the question of scope became increasingly racialized and genderized in the 1960s and 1970s.

The industrial order also was challenged from without. The collective bargaining system was inflationary by design. This was one of the benefits of the system and was not a serious problem for employers and government agencies to manage so long as the United States was a protected market. Once foreign-based producers gained access to American markets, there was a real problem with lower-cost competition, loss of macroeconomic management capabilities, and increased unemployment and underemployment.

The national government had embraced free trade in 1936, but it was not until twenty years later that very many American firms experienced serious foreign competition and, then, special international agreements were made, such as the Multi-Fibre Arrangement governing textile trade. But the problem became a chronic one. The AFL–CIO was pro–free trade. On the other hand, if unions were going to remain a key part of the Democratic coalition for an expanding economy, the government would have to adopt additional compensatory policies

Two alternative worlds of possibility emerged in the 1960s. One was creation of a Keynesian welfare state and the other was managerial self-regulation. In fact, the election of John F. Kennedy to the presidency was part of the reform momentum that had gathered at the end of the 1950s to more aggressively prosecute creation of a Keynesian welfare state. The UAW generated some of the most active members of the reformist wing of the Democratic party that sought to bring to fruition the reforms planted earlier. The union's leaders, prominently Walter Reuther and his successors as president of the union, Leonard Woodcock and Douglas Fraser, remained among the most committed to the reform agenda when many others had given up. For example, in the 1950s Reuther was on the executive board of the Conference on Economic Progress, Leon Keyserling's policy planning group, which argued for "Keynes plus": incomes policy, Keynesian macromanagement, plus active labor market policies targeted on hard-to-reach groups. Keyserling was the key author of Democratic Advisory Committee on Economic Policy statements that were circulated privately before the 1960 election.[4] Also in the 1950s, the academic field of labor market policy opened up with congressional concern with "distressed areas," reflected in the creation, in 1960, of a permanent Senate subcommittee on employment and manpower. In the late 1950s, liberal Democrats in the House formed the Democratic Study Group to solidify the reform bloc in Congress. By 1973, the group claimed membership of one-half of House Democrats. Still others criticized over-emphasis on general economic stimulation. John Kenneth Galbraith argued that sole attention to stimulating the private sector had led to private opulence and public squalor.[5] The "baroque" designs of cars coming out of Detroit were a favorite example of misplaced priorities. Such groups as the Americans for Democratic Action and the National Planning Association began to support the adaptation of Swedish, British, and French experiments with incomes policies and indicative economic planning.[6]

Managerial self-regulation was the direction indicated by the "old right" of the Republican party, associated with Senator Barry Goldwater, for whom organized labor ran a close second to the Soviet Union as the embodiment of political corruption, and with the multitude of employers who had never accepted the legitimacy of unions.[7] The world of managerial self-regulation was a union-free environment and a night-watchman state. This reactionary ideal gained adherents throughout the 1960s and 1970s and Ronald Reagan (elected governor of California in 1966) became its champion.

The conditions for successful reform in the 1960s were to resolve the challenges to the liberal industrial order. Unionists had to build and maintain support among individual union members for collective bargaining negotiations and contract settlements. The problem that emerged was not rank-and-file loyalty to the unions, but the limited scope of labor rights at work. Also, the geographical scope of the collective bargaining system had to be expanded. Union organization had to spread out of its regional confines, which entailed winning labor law changes from Congress. As CIO founders, Reuther, Hubert Humphrey, Chester Bowles, and other liberals had long before realized, this in turn required realigning the southern Democracy by allying with southern blacks and civil-rights groups, an alliance not only of convenience but of "substance," as Philip Murray had said. Finally, reformers had to seek unity among national unions for coordination between union collective bargaining policy and the Democratic administration. Labor union unity was fragile because of the nonrepresentative character of the AFL–CIO executive council; members unions retained their autonomy on collective bargaining. In turn, sympathetic Democratic officials would have to devise ways for the party to overcome the interest group- and sectional-orientation of national politics. Instead of success, however, after a few years of progress, a breach opened between organized labor and nonlabor Democrats, as the result of conflicting presidential priorities, intraparty disagreements, racial conflict, and the Vietnam War, although none of these was structurally determined. Organized labor began to lose its ability to play its aggregative role which, in turn, shifted the balance within the Democratic party away from unions and created space for managerialism to emerge.

Making the System Work

The incoming Kennedy administration was faced with two obstacles to carrying out an expansionary macroeconomic policy. The first was its probable effects on the balance of payments and the second was the institutional conditions for growth.[8] Beginning in December 1958, European currencies became fully convertible with the dollar in recognition of Europe's recovered industrial strength. European central banks had, by then, accumulated dollars via NATO (North Atlantic Treaty Organization) and economic aid programs, precisely as planned by American policy makers in the postwar 1940s. On the one hand, American dollars provided the liquidity needed for investment and trade, on the other hand, foreign balances of American currency potentially weakened the value of the dollar. Central bankers could exchange them for other currencies and gold, which would undermine the value of the dollar and make more expensive the foreign purchases of the U.S. government and American corporations, which hindered the pursuit of American economic and political goals. In 1959 the United States had its first dollar crisis. Rather than hold and use their dollar balances, European central bankers traded them for gold, leading to a run against U.S. reserves. Thus, any U.S. government attempt to stimulate a longer expansion, apparently, was boxed-in by the necessity to protect the international value of the dollar, that is, economic expansion meant rising wages and prices which led to declining competitiveness in world markets, increased imports, and, ultimately, a balance of payments crisis. In order to restore the balance of payments and still protect the fixed rate of exchange, the government had to retrench and deflate the economy which, in turn, knocked out the mass consumption basis of the domestic expansion.

Though hardly pleased, the lesson that American treasury officials and the banking community learned was that European bankers would withdraw funds if and when the U.S. government deviated from orthodox fiscal policy. If the United States inflated,

REFORM CYCLE   — 235

ran deficits, and generally followed a liberal Keynesian program, the balance of payments would be put into the red. Some way had to be found to protect the dollar, and with it America's international power, while raising domestic economic activity.

The second obstacle was related to the first. One of the lessons Republican liberals and Democrats believed they had learned from the 1950s was that the u.s. economic structure had a tendency to "premature inflation." When economic activity picked up, corporations would take advantage of the strengthening market to raise prices, unions would seek to raise wages, and the two together contributed to inflation that choked expansion of consumer demand and new investment. These relationships were summarized by British economist A. W. Phillips in the Phillips Curve: there was a trade-off between increases in wages and prices and employment. To managerialist businessmen the key impediment to high production and employment was the "monopoly" power of trade unions to force wages up and keep them there even during recessions. This prevented supply and demand from operating to reset price levels and forced employers to agree to trade high wages for less employment. Organized labor also had a structural analysis, in which "administered pricing" by oligopoly industries kept prices artificially high while labor market problems were linked to technological unemployment, distressed areas of declining industrial sectors, and bottlenecks in the supply of critical materials and skilled labor. As for wage increases, the collective bargaining system was supposed to keep wages up to a level to clear product markets.[9]

The new Democratic administration had arrived in office very much as a consequence of a revival of the liberal-labor wing of the party in the late 1950s, but Kennedy had also gained the support of conservatives in Congress and some business leaders, and his administration responded to both camps. Its strategy was three-fold.[10] First was fiscal stimulation of aggregate demand, as per Keynesian prescription. The administration's preference was to create a deficit by spending more money for area redevelopment, public works, unemployment compensation, manpower and education, and accelerated military purchases, but most of the spending programs were blocked in the Congress and the administration shifted to tax cuts instead. To meet the political obstacles to fiscal stimulation, the administration had proposed two other policies. The first was an array of marginal money policies, keeping within the existing international monetary system, to pool gold with European nations to spread the costs of protecting the dollar, raising short-term interest rates to keep money in the United States, while keeping long-term rates low to encourage capital investment (the monetary "twist"), concerted cooperation from commercial bankers to cap the export of u.s. capital, and inauguration of trade talks aimed at opening foreign markets for American manufactured goods.

Finally, the president's Council of Economic Advisors announced wage and price "guideposts," in the president's Economic Report in January 1962, to allay the fears of opponents of demand stimulation and its attendant inflation at the Federal Reserve, in Congress, and in the administration itself. The suggested standard for noninflationary settlements was to peg wages to national productivity increases, calculated by the CEA in 1962 at 3.2 percent per year. Although the CEA determined the specific figures, the administration did seek the endorsement of labor and management representatives. Kennedy created a Labor-Management Advisory Committee (LMAC) in early 1961, and the LMAC was called upon to endorse the guideposts, which it did, though with reservations.[11] The management members were Elliot Bell (Business Week magazine; McGraw-Hill), Joseph Block (Inland Steel), Henry Ford II, John Franklin (United States Lines), J. Spencer Love (Burlington Industries), Richard Reynolds (Reynolds Metals), and Thomas Watson (IBM). The labor members included Walter Reuther, George Meany (president of the AFL-CIO), David Dubinsky (ILGWU), David McDonald (USW), Thomas Kennedy (UMW), Joseph Keenan (IBEW), and George Harrison (Railway Clerks). No one wanted the guideposts to become a strict rule applicable in all cases. Labor members especially served notice it believed that labor's share of national income should increase to spur consumer demand and that specific collective bargaining settlements should also reflect equity. But they held off rejection, in part because they accepted the reality of structural imbalances and they expected that once the economy "got moving again" they would be able to do better. The Kennedy administration assured the committee that adherence to the guideposts was voluntary.

In fact, the LMAC was part of the "Keynes plus" agenda of organized labor and liberals, which was supported by the administration. The Department of Labor, under its secretary, Arthur Goldberg, formerly counsel to the CIO and the United Steelworkers

Union, was the focal point of the new thinking about collective bargaining and labor market programs that had emerged in the 1950s.[12] Goldberg was the chair of the LMAC and he and Reuther treated the committee as a quasicorporatist economic council to debate ideas and propose policies to the president. The LMAC started with eight staffers, and added many more, and, in 1962, had a budget of $300,000. The committee met monthly, the president came often, and it invited administration cabinet members, the CEA, and outside experts to make presentations and take part in discussions. After one of their earliest meetings about structural and cyclical unemployment, Clark Kerr, then chair of an innovative Automation Committee at the Armour meatpacking company and a member of the UAW's Public Review Board, urged reform of the U.S. employment service and suggested other public policies in the Swedish style to encourage retraining and labor mobility. Reuther seconded the motion that the LMAC study European policies. Goldberg then invited a delegation from the Swedish government to explain how they worked to the executives and labor leaders of the Committee.[13]

At the same time, some members of Congress and the Department of Labor proceeded to develop a program for active labor market policy. The Labor Department's ambition to make manpower an equal arm with macroeconomic policy placed it at odds with what the Keynesians at the CEA and its chair, Walter Heller, believed needed to be done. CEA economists treated collective bargaining, the guideposts, and manpower planning as decidedly secondary to fiscal stimulation.[14] They scoffed at the AFL-CIO's claims that technological unemployment was a serious problem: general economic stimulation and free labor markets would take care of that. At the CEA, the guideposts policy was called the "local version" of European incomes policy,[15] but unlike the social-democratic version, the American incomes policy assumed that supply and demand was the normal and legitimate arbiter of economic distribution and took the economic growth process for granted in the sense that it was a managerial responsibility. The administration's unemployment goal was set at 4 percent, the preference of the CEA, but it was called an "interim" target in deference to the Labor Department's more ambitious proposal for 3 percent.[16] Moreover, the CEA tolerated labor market policy if it meant more spending and, at the president's request, Heller began to think of ways through which the government could solve problems of chronic poverty.[17]

The Kennedy administration's economic strategy was modest, but promising, for organized labor, especially if the other challenges were addressed. The guideposts policy implied considerably more central guidance and public purpose for labor-management relations. Since collective bargaining was the major benefit of the liberal labor system for rank-and-file workers, the new policy seemed to undermine the role of unions in looking out for their memberships. On the other hand, if the unions could get organized through a formal mechanism, they could gain leverage on the government's program and win policy quids pro quo. Workers were not only interested in wage increases, but in employment, working conditions, and in such benefits as health care and social security pensions. Reuther, for one, was eager to make a political deal to strengthen the coordination between organized labor and the Democratic administration. In fact, he beat the CEA to their guidepost policy in his proposal in 1961 that the LMAC recommend the creation of a public board of review over wage and price decisions.[18] Critics William Gomberg and B. J. Widick warned that the unions' priority should be the rank and file, and they castigated labor leaders who would trade collective bargaining independence for the policy promises of the party.[19] On the AFL–CIO executive council, Meany led doubters about corporatistic arrangements that would limit union autonomy. Reuther's proposed public review board gained qualified support from the USW's David McDonald (and from public and business members Bell, Love, Watson, Cole, and Kerr), but Meany and most of the AFL–CIO executive council were willing to acquiesce in the guidepost policy if it was clearly voluntary and if progress was made on the rest of the program.

Progress was made. The administration's guidepost policy met with fairly easy success. The first two major industries were autos and steel, both of whose unions were led by men sympathetic to the guideposts. In 1961 Reuther told the CEA that he would hold back auto wages in that year's collective bargaining contracts if auto prices and steel wages in 1962 also were restrained.[20] In fact the three-year auto contract was modest and the steel union leadership, after the USW's bruising four-month strike in 1959 and after an appeal by Goldberg, accepted an agreement with the steel companies that was fully a third less than the government's guidepost.

Later in 1962, President Kennedy had to browbeat the U.S. Steel corporation into price compliance, which made the union look virtuous, but the administration's program looked on-track, and the unions were encouraged.[21] Even when the UAW renounced the guideposts in 1964, backed by Meany, and then negotiated a wage settlement greater than 3.2 percent, the CEA was unruffled because the wage contract was within the bounds of automobile industry productivity increases.[22]

Also, the Department of Labor pressed the labor market program within the administration and with the LMAC. Most of the business members of the LMAC, with the notable exception of Henry Ford II, tried to find areas of agreement with the labor members and the secretary of labor.[23] AFL–CIO leaders strongly favored programs to lower the high rates of unemployment, then at postwar record levels, and they feared that new investment in automated technologies would aggravate the situation by displacing workers. The leaders acknowledged that the private means for settling labor-management claims, namely collective bargaining, could not resolve the basic problem of how to create jobs.

> The problems of automation and technological change clearly cannot be solved just by private parties in the collective bargaining arena. Such efforts can point the way toward constructive answers, as indeed they have. But automation and technological change are having a profound and far-reaching impact and they have generated problems which require government action.[24]

Only the government could help the community get a handle on this problem. Union leaders backed policies to increase public employment, domestic investment, and exports of manufactured goods, but the AFL–CIO also challenged the direction of technological changes and campaigned for domestic policies to compensate workers "displaced" by economic development. Goldberg charged the LMAC in 1961 with the task of studying the question of unemployment and automation. LMAC's January 1962 report, "Benefits and Problems Incident to Automation and Other Technological Advances," accepted the link between labor-saving investment and unemployment and proposed a mix of private and public policies. These included the commercial Keynesian tax cut for general economic expansion, plus public works and extended unemployment compensation; private and public programs for retraining and education; prenotification to workers of plant closings and reliance on attrition for work force reductions; and improved employment service programs. However, the LMAC report rejected the AFL–CIO's demand that the federal government become "employer of last resort" and that employers move toward a thirty-hour work week (at forty hours pay) to spread the available jobs.[25] By early 1963, Willard Wirtz, who became secretary after Goldberg was nominated for the Supreme Court in August 1962, and such academic labor experts as Frederick Harbison had helped move the LMAC toward a focus on manpower planning that challenged the CEA's macrofocus.[26] Virtually all of the LMAC members were more pessimistic about economic growth than the CEA, and they were quite critical of Kennedy for being timid in economic affairs. Wirtz argued to Heller that even though auto factories were working at full capacity, the unemployment rate in Detroit was stalled at 5.5 percent.[27] The Labor Department brought the Swedish delegation to the LMAC in late 1962 and again in 1963 in its search for ways to extend labor's influence on economic change beyond collective bargaining.[28] The Swedes outlined the operation of their Labor Market Board and Price and Cartel Agency after which Reuther urged the LMAC members to consider similar labor- and management-representative institutions for the federal government.[29]

In addition to the LMAC action, President Kennedy announced, in January 1962, an executive order favoring unionization by federal employees, which spurred rapid organization of the public sector throughout the decade. Congress passed the Trade Expansion Act with a provision for compensation ("trade adjustment assistance") for workers who lost their jobs as a result of free trade. The Congress also passed the Manpower Development and Training Act (MDTA) to respond to problems created by "dislocations in the economy arising from automation or other technological developments" and to fill the need for "improved planning . . . to assure that men, women and young people will be trained and available to meet shifting employment needs."[30] The Act funded skill and occupational programs for workers already employed or in the labor force, such as the steelworkers in the Pennsylvania district of MDTA's House sponsor Elmer Holland. It was meant to lay the foundation of manpower planning and it created an annual Manpower Report of the President (parallelling the Economic Report), a National Commission on Technology, Automation and Economic Progress, and an Office of Manpower, Automation and Training in the Department of Labor. Finally, the Congress passed the Keynesian tax cut in 1964.

The extension of industrial pluralism and realignment of the political parties also were boosted by the increasingly supportive alliance of liberal Democrats and the civil rights movement. The civil-rights movement had already shown its mettle in southern struggles and its ability to bring thousands to march in Washington in the late 1950s. Labor activists had been closely involved with the movement going back to the 1930s and now they were being pushed by black trade unionists. The Negro American Labor Council was formed in 1960 and led by AFL–CIO executive council member A. Philip Randolph.[31] Black autoworkers formed the Trade Union Leadership Council (TULC) and successfully promoted their own candidate for mayor of Detroit over the UAW-backed choice in 1961. The positive involvement of the unions was reflected in the UAW's financial support of Martin Luther King, Jr. Reuther was on the podium at the huge 1963 March on Washington at which hundreds of union locals were represented. Federal officials began to support racial equality, too. Liberal judges decided against segregation, and, then, Presidents John Kennedy and Lyndon Johnson actively intervened in conflicts on the side of the movement. Johnson announced a War on Poverty in the spring of 1964, and the Democratic Congress passed the Civil Rights Act later that year. Finally, after Democrats had made these policy choices, Johnson was elected president in a landslide over Barry Goldwater, who opposed the Civil Rights Act and unions, despite the loss of several deep South states to the Republicans. The Democrats won more than two-thirds of the seats in both houses of Congress.

Trouble in Paradise

The exhilaration of these successes continued for a time, but existing differences among Democratic factions were aggravated by the weaknesses of the party as a vehicle for social change.

President Johnson acted to aggrandize his personal power and that of the presidential office at the expense of the development of party and governmental capacity. Into the breach between the mounting popular demands for change and the administration stepped labor activists, and they got hammered.

Already before the election in 1964, this scenario had been played out. At the Democratic party convention a bitter conflict had taken place between the Johnson campaign and the Mississippi Freedom Democratic party (MFDP)—the civil rights shock troops in that state who had formed a loyalist party—over who should sit at the convention. The regular Mississippi Democrats resisted integration and would not pledge to support the national party ticket. The situation was ripe for realignment. Johnson, however, sought a personal triumph in the November election—polls already showed the Democrats trouncing the Republicans—and wanted to seat the regulars in his wall-to-wall coalition. The MFDP and its allies among SNCC (Student Nonviolent Coordinating Committee) and the Congress for Racial Equality (CORE) were outraged and threatened to disrupt Johnson's plans. The president then called on labor leaders—Walter Reuther in particular—and northern liberals—especially Hubert Humphrey—to get the MFDP to back off and compromise for a couple of token seats and promises that 1968 would be different. But the MFDP would not back off; 1964 was late enough to deliver on civil rights. An already militant civil-rights movement was radicalized by the Democrats' temporizing and organized labor earned their distrust.[32] Liberal and social-democratic unions became lumped together with unions with segregationist policies. The absence of blacks in high-level union officialdom was a highly visible reflection of the slowness of reform.

What did labor leaders get for their yeoman work for Johnson? The Civil Rights Act of 1964 was a dramatic and far-reaching political act and everyone knew it. Johnson reportedly remarked that by signing the law, he was giving up Democratic control of the South. Such sentimental heroics ignored the realignment strategy. Votes lost from racists and conservatives were supposed to be replaced by blacks and unionized workers. Granted, in 1964 there were precious few of either, the program was to create them. One step in the right direction was the Voting Rights Act of 1965, which provided for federal supervision of problem voting districts in southern states. The next step was not taken, namely overturning state "right to work" laws by repealing section 14(b) from national labor law. Doing so was at the top of the AFL–CIO agenda for the new Congress in 1965, but, again, organized labor was called on to serve the president's interests.[33] Johnson administration officials would not spend their influence for cloture of an expected Senate filibuster, despite a Democratic supermajority, and insisted that the unions agree to postpone repeal in deference to ostensibly broader issues like health care. The AFL–CIO did agree and repeal never happened.

Organized labor got very little from the administration in labor market policy. The War on Poverty was greeted by unionists and labor market policy activists as a very modest program. "Hardly a first small step" said the AFL–CIO.[34] Reuther testified in March 1964 at the congressional hearings on creating the Office of Economic Opportunity (OEO) that the antipoverty program was "wholly inadequate" and that more resources should be expended as part of a national economic plan. The UAW's national convention shortly afterward established a $100,000 fund for its own antipoverty effort.[35] In fact, the administration's antipoverty effort was beset with substantive and resource problems. Substantively, the War on Poverty was part of the administration's macroeconomic policy. The CEA conceived it as a means to expand the labor supply as the economy reached full employment.[36] The administration conceived the War on Poverty as programs for black people, primarily, with the objective of overcoming the disadvantages of poor backgrounds for labor market participation. The programs were far narrower than the structural changes that labor market policy advocates had been discussing. They failed to connect the need for jobs and income with the existing institutions of the economy that created low-skill, low-pay work. Moreover, because Johnson wanted to keep control over the effort, the programs were administered separately from the Department of Labor.[37] The War on Poverty was Johnson's claim to history. The very limited objectives of the programs—despite the rhetoric of "war"—created widespread frustration among blacks, confrontations between antipoverty activists and local authorities and, within a few years, a backlash to limit further federal efforts, in which the president himself joined.

Indeed, the administration's economic advisors did not think that there was anything fundamentally wrong with the economy that had to be reformed. The expansion of the economy had solved most of the problems of dislocated workers that worried the AFL–CIO, just as the CEA had argued, at least in the short run. To the CEA, to keep the economic expansion going meant actively confronting the structural unemployment apparently embodied in "disadvantaged" workers with low skills, inadequate education, and little work experience, many of whom were minority racial and ethnic groups, women, and youths. This approach endorsed neoclassical labor market theories and supported a policy focus on remedial and "treatment" programs for individual sufferers of poverty to improve their labor market performance.[38] In contrast, in 1965, when the tripartite National Commission on Technology, Automation and Economic Progress made its recommendations to the administration, the CEA showed little interest. Even while the commission was working, the CEA undercut their work. The unions and its Labor Department allies reacted angrily, in the spring of 1964, to CEA-sponsored regional LMAC meetings called to discuss "private" collective bargaining techniques of worker adjustment to technological change.[39] William Batt, Jr., an administrator at the Area Redevelopment Administration (ARA) and a pioneer of labor market programs in Pennsylvania in the 1950s, argued that the government should use the Employment Service "like the Swedes do."[40] The ARA (like the Douglas distressed areas bills) was based on the notion that the government should help workers find jobs in their communities and that communities should diversify their industrial bases. But now, Batt was convinced, given that the economy was moving close to full employment, unemployed workers should be given incentives to move to high-demand areas. He was encouraged that IBM and the steel industry collective bargaining contracts included moving allowances and portable job rights. Batt wanted to nationalize the employment service and to induce more labor and industry mobility. Reuther again made a "very strong pitch" for a manpower-oriented economic policy, which the LMAC endorsed, but the CEA successfully resisted.

The Automation Commission's consensus final report, "Technology and the American Economy," made clear that there was agreement that displacement was a necessary price of economic progress and technological change.[41] But it made equally clear that the federal government had a responsibility to enact policies to see that the gains of change were equitably distributed and to reduce workers' resistance to change. A two-part package of policies was recommended to ensure economic security for all Americans: growth for leading industrial sectors and skilled labor and public opportunities and income maintenance programs for those less able, or unable, to compete in the marketplace. With problems of economic security reduced, the government then could pursue policies to increase efficiency and employment. These policies included improved and expanded education and broad-based skill training, reform of the U.S. Employment Service to provide on-the-job training, and policies to end discrimination. However, the failure of the commission to endorse national economic planning drew criticism from the labor members and from public members Daniel Bell and Whitney Young, who argued that "it is our firm conviction that some form of democratic national planning is essential in the United States" not only for "sustained full employment" but to assure "proper allocation of economic resources." Yet, despite the orthodoxy of the commission's recommendations, the report's publication, in 1966, met with little policy response because the administration had shifted away from concern with full employment and toward programs to fight inflation.[42]

Indeed, the administration's economic policy increasingly turned toward restraining collective bargaining. The policy contributed to internal turmoil in and among many unions. Already, in November 1963, after the assassination of Kennedy, the CEA had warned President Johnson that the government should "strengthen its anti-inflation policy" and insist more vigorously on the use of the guideposts.[43] In their January 1964 report, the CEA asserted that the guideposts would enable the economy to avoid the Phillips Curve trade-off as economic growth continued; the President's Economic Report fully endorsed the guidepost policy. The administration focused most of its attention on the auto negotiations that year, but it did not pressure the parties very diligently, perhaps because it was an election year. But then, after Johnson steeply escalated the war in Vietnam in July 1965, the economy reached 4 percent unemployment in December, and the CEA and Federal Reserve began to urge an economic slowdown.

The CEA and other government officials already were actively intervening in wage and price decision making by corporations and unions, but, although the administration had some notable successes, such as the can industry, steel prices continued to rise (and steel imports continued to mount) and, although officials were entirely resourceful at bending rules and regulations to pressure private actors, the policy was ad hoc and under stress. President Johnson reactivated the LMAC in December 1965 to gain their support for restraint.[44] The new membership was Wirtz, John Connor (secretary of commerce), Arthur Flemming (president of the University of Oregon), Howard Johnson (president of MIT), Page Keeton (dean of the University of Texas Law School), George Taylor (Wharton School), Walter Reuther, George Meany, I. W. Abel (USW), W. A. Boyle (UMW), David Dubinsky, George Harrison, Joseph Keenan, Donald Burnham (Westinghouse), Henry Ford II, Henry Kaiser (Kaiser Industries), J. Ward Keener (Goodrich), W. B. Murphy (Campbell Soup), Thomas Watson (IBM), and Stuart Saunders (Pennsylvania Railroad). The administration asked the LMAC, in early 1966, to consider either higher taxes, wage and price controls or perhaps stricter adherence to the guideposts, or higher interest rates and lower money growth. The CEA, headed now by Gardner Ackley, wanted unions to stick strictly to the wage guidepost. The UAW and AFL–CIO argued that the guideposts mainly held back wages, which the government's own figures confirmed. As a proportion of national income, wages had declined and corporate income increased during the economic expansion.[45] They also opposed a tax increase and higher interest rates: they wanted domestic expansion to continue. They argued that controls on prices and a profits tax would be a more equitable way to halt inflation.

Labor leaders now openly objected to the assumption in the guidepost formula that workers' incomes should be held to a constant share of national income, especially while profits raced ahead with increased factory utilization and dividends were excluded altogether. The automobile companies, for example, reaped huge returns on equity on record sales volumes:[46]

Table 7.1

AFTER-TAX RETURN ON EQUITY

	1964	1965	1966
General Motors	22.4%	25.8%	20.6%
Ford	12.6%	15.7%	13.0%
Chrysler	19.1%	14.7%	11.1%

PRODUCTION OF PASSENGER CARS

1963	7,600,000
1964	7,700,000
1965	9,300,000
1966	8,600,000

The industry was garnering an increasing share of consumer income for automobiles by upgrading and making standard previously optional equipment, for which they charged higher prices. They were able to comply formally with the guideposts however, despite a fierce, if arcane, debate among consumer advocates, the UAW, CEA and the Bureau of Labor Statistics, because the CEA and BLS considered the price rises noninflationary if they "delivered more car" for the money.[47]

In early March 1966, Reuther met with President Johnson and recommended a Price-Wage Public Review Board and a "progressive spending tax," a kind of value-added tax commonly employed in Europe. He told the president that the executive was overburdened by the demands of ad hoc incomes policy; it needed an institutional mechanism to concert private decision making. The new board would still be voluntary, though more effective than the guideposts, in part because it would publicize judgments about price and wage changes. The new tax would affect high income consumers hardest and thus ensure "equality of sacrifice."[48]

The LMAC began discussion of what kind of policy it should endorse, but many union leaders and industrial relations experts were unenthusiastic about Reuther's plan. The AFL–CIO executive council, in February, stated that *if* the president needed controls, they would have to cover all incomes equitably, but Meany would not publicly advocate an incomes policy.[49] The reasons that the AFL–CIO balked at incomes policy were three. First, Reuther and

Meany were engaged in a rivalry to lead the organized labor movement. Meany already was at retirement age and Reuther believed he should become the new president. Meany and the old guard AFL leaders abhorred the prospect. Second, during 1965, insurgent unionists challenged union leaders to take advantage of the tight labor markets to gain increased wages in construction and in steel, where they baited Steelworkers president McDonald with the UAW's big 1964 settlement.[50]

Third, from the labor experts' theory of wage determination, centralizing wage policy could not substitute for the collective bargaining system of local consent and equity.[51] Labor economists explained that a settlement in one industry had direct repercussions on internal politics in others because wage structures in part are based on wage comparisons among workers across industries. One key wage group is the skilled trades. The general economic expansion and the Vietnam war had raised demand for skilled construction workers to build new industrial, military, and commercial buildings. Building trades unions took advantage of this to rapidly raise hourly wages. And skilled workers in steel won a big increase in 1965 and helped I. W. Abel upset David McDonald for the union presidency.[52] Labor expert John Dunlop argued that wage restraint was possible only by close attention to the details of labor markets and union-management relations. Reuther's response was that wages were only part of the problem of inflation: the government needed to control all forms of income, something that collective bargaining could not do.[53] However, the CEA was not prepared to rely on labor experts who, the CEA was sure, would find reasons to raise wages beyond the guideposts.

After several months of debate, the LMAC issued a report, in August 1966, that reendorsed the principle of voluntary wage and price restraint and included a phrase proposed by Reuther that asserted that "we believe that in a free society any policy to achieve price stability will be acceptable and effective only if it bears equitably on all forms of income."[54] Reuther hoped thus to commit the LMAC and the government to a policy that regulated, not just wages and prices, but salaries, interest, and dividends. The LMAC continued to meet and discuss the specific measures that the government should take to implement its recommendations.

In the meantime, Reuther had other ways to influence policy.

The intensity of wage and working conditions claims continued to press union leaders' reluctance to support the administration's policy. In fact, union leaders in the steel, electrical equipment, and aircraft industries were voted out of office in 1965 and 1966 and there were major challenges within the UMW and Teamsters. As president of the AFL–CIO's Industrial Union Department (IUD), Reuther launched a program of "coordinated collective bargaining" through which many unions would appoint members to a committee to bargain with a common employer. The IUD acted as a clearinghouse and coordinating agency with a computerized information system on companies, markets, and contracts. In the first two years, over seventy such multiple union committees were set up. One of the purposes of the program was to help unions gain leverage by uniting against increasingly diversified conglomerate companies who, not only had many plants in any one product line, but had multiple product lines among which to switch resources and/or play unions off against each other. This agenda was notably traditional. Even conservative union officials, such as Roy Seimiller of the Machinists, were enthusiastic supporters of a program for more effective bargaining. Some old AFL unions even joined the IUD.[55] But another purpose of coordinated bargaining was to create the possibility of union-government cooperation by developing technical and political conditions for the federation to direct collective bargaining.

In autos, Reuther decided the rank-and-file skilled auto workers' demands for pay comparable to rates in the construction industry could be useful for pushing the administration.[56] Reuther had become impatient with Meany's refusal to take a public stand on a "positive" wage program. In something of a reprise of the Korean War tool and die scenario described in chapter five, Reuther ran out in front of the workers to head their pressure toward change of national policy. They were very willing to oblige. At the May 1966 UAW convention, Reuther and Doug Fraser, who were the codirectors of the union's Skilled Trades Department, met with skilled trades delegates and proposed a campaign to break open the auto contracts a year early to win a wage increase.[57] After the convention, skilled trades leaders organized the Dollar An Hour Movement among the rank and file to win a dollar wage increase. Leaders came from the GM Technical Center Local 160 in suburban

Detroit, Ford Local 600, and Detroit job shop Locals 155 and 157.
The movement quickly spread across the United States and Canada. Large demonstrations were organized; there was a one-day
strike of Local 600 skilled workers to attend a movement conference; and there was civil disobedience. The UAW demanded that
the Big Three and Detroit Tooling Association reopen the contracts that summer. However, by late August, the guideposts were
broken by coordinated bargaining in the electrical equipment and
airline industries, and Reuther called off the campaign for immediate wage increases in automobiles.[58]

Reuther's goal was to substitute an incomes policy for the
administration's guideposts. Yet, if the initiative was Reuther's,
inertia was on Meany's side. Given the voluntarism of the AFL–CIO
and that a quarter of the executive council leadership had no
"operating" or representative responsibilities with their home unions,
Meany only had to do nothing in response to Reuther to satisfy the
varied collective bargaining and political interests of the member
unions. Although Reuther supported smashing the guideposts, he
did not simply want to break them, but to replace them with a more
inclusive policy.[59]

The LMAC subcommittee on guideposts reported in December
and rejected "Keynes plus."[60] The report contained an interpretation of its August endorsement of Reuther's "equity" statement
that significantly differed from that of the UAW. Equity now meant
the "total involvement of segments of the nation—personal, institutional, and governmental"—in a policy of "restraint." No national policy was proposed on fair shares of income and their
relationship to the direction in which the social-economy should
move. Instead, it said government program expenditures were
reaching the limit of the economy's ability to absorb them and that
the existing system of micro–decision making should only be aided
by "behavioral goals" enunciated in the guideposts. If there were
"recalcitrant" sectors, perhaps special remedial government action
would be justified. In particular the report mentioned manpower
problems in skilled labor and service industries (especially the
health industry). Finally, the main "price stabilization" tools remained fiscal and monetary policy. In part the report reflected the
realities of postwar industrial relations, but it also seemed to mirror
the technocratic bias of the CEA and to ignore the need for reform
of labor-management institutions.

The UAW called the report of "no practical use," "confused and inconsistent," and based on the "dangerous and false assumption" that the root of economic crisis was "excess of demand."[61] The UAW's research department argued that unemployment still was too high and that the balance between consumer income and profits was unfavorable for sustained growth. The UAW said it was inconsistent to endorse involvement of all segments of the nation and then focus only on wage and price decisions; the report had favorably mentioned use of a "post-audit" procedure but still failed to propose that all forms of income be covered. Moreover, though the report noted that the guidepost policy had "not gone unchallenged," it endorsed the CEA view (reiterated in the 1966 economic report) that "discretionary power" had raised prices and wages beyond supply and demand, as though market results were the standard of justice. The UAW felt compelled to point out that redistributing income was one of the "legitimate" goals of unions in collective bargaining, and it argued that government policy should continue to be stimulative to reach those segments of the population and those physical resources still not sharing in growth and prosperity. At the December LMAC meeting Reuther again presented his proposal for a Wage-Price Review Board. There was "spirited discussion" of it, with W. B. Murphy of the Campbell Soup Company leading the opposition, but the administration, apparently, wanted to avoid the issue of prior notification of price changes and the AFL–CIO rejected interference with collective bargaining. Action on Reuther's related proposal to establish a tripartite economists' panel to study the question was deferred to the next meeting.[62]

Before the next meeting, however, Secretary of Labor Wirtz readied his own alternative of a merger of the Departments of Labor and Commerce.[63] This won administration support; the CEA asked the LMAC to endorse it. Crucial to the administration's support was concern about a balance of payments crisis implied in the breakdown of the guideposts. They feared the 1967 collective bargaining round and the weighty automobile negotiations. Although perhaps a timid step toward reform, the merger proposal also had substantive merit because it would tie labor market policies and the collective bargaining services of the Labor Department to the marketing and growth policies of the Commerce Department. It would allow the government to go beyond rigid macroeconomic policies.

Although initially in favor of the merger, the AFL–CIO executive council vetoed it. The crucial and only real objection to it was labor's claim that no administration would place a labor representative in charge of this new department because of the sensitive business programs involved.[64] Therefore, organized labor would lose its only cabinet representative. The Johnson administration gave mute affirmation to the claim and the proposal died. The LMAC in early 1967, then accepted the proposal for an economists' panel, but it was never appointed. Instead, Johnson formed the Cabinet Council on Price Stability, in February 1968, to focus attention on inflation, and it held joint meetings with the LMAC throughout the year, but again with no effect.[65]

Collapse of the Liberal Democratic Coalition

Johnson's preoccupation with the war and technocratic approaches to managing the business cycle overshadowed problems associated with managing a reform coalition, which were linked to problems of sustaining employment, revising authority relations in industry, and expanding the scope of the pluralist system. But the UAW was still in the game. At the 1964 UAW convention, Reuther had argued that organized labor needed realignment of the political parties. "They lack integrity and internal discipline essential to meeting their responsibilities." The union's staff and close allies were deeply involved in rewriting the party's rules before the 1968 convention, and they helped mobilize thousands of people to work in the South to make the Voting Rights Act a reality.[66] Reuther explained the situation to Willy Brandt, the Social-Democratic leader of Berlin:

> The achievement of democratic franchise and full citizenship rights by millions of southern Negroes will drastically shift the balance of political power in the thirteen southern states . . . a region . . . which historically has been represented by the most reactionary and socially backward forces. . . . This will accelerate the historic process of bringing about a fundamental political realignment of forces in the United States.[67]

In late 1964, the UAW, with Martin Luther King, Jr., James

Patton of the Farmers Union, and others, created the Citizens' Crusade Against Poverty (CCAP) to enhance the War on Poverty.[68] Reuther chaired the effort and the UAW sustained CCAP's operating expenses, spending over $500,000 of its own funds in four years, plus $100,000 from the AFL–CIO Industrial Union Department, and over $1 million from the Ford Foundation (of which McGeorge Bundy was president) and the Stern Family Foundation. CCAP trained antipoverty community organizers and sought to create a network for five thousand grass-roots poverty organizations, in part by helping tie together efforts into regional "resource pools." CCAP launched programs to aid southern tenant farmers and to highlight the need for government programs to end hunger. The UAW also actively engaged in VISTA (Volunteers in Service to America) and Headstart; helped recruit autoworkers from Appalachia and inner-city Detroit to suburban auto plants; signed a $2.1 million contract with the Labor Department to provide skill upgrading and retraining to workers in the auto parts and supply industry; campaigned to open up the skilled construction and metalworking trades to blacks; helped finance unionization of California farmworkers; supported the major black voter-registration drives in the South; promoted the organization of "community unions"; and aided the 1968 Poor People's Campaign and march on Washington, among many other projects.

Reuther called on the Industrial Union Department and the AFL–CIO's Building and Construction Trades Department to champion "Keynes plus" legislative programs and won broad agreement from them. And after the 1966 congressional elections ended the two-thirds Democratic majority in the Congress, Reuther, Abel, and other IUD leaders responded with appeals and organization to prevent cutbacks in the war on poverty.[69] The labor federation actively supported legislation for public employment, equal employment opportunity for minorities, national health insurance, skill upgrading, limits on overtime, and study of family allowances and negative income taxes. But, on the other hand, the unions became identified with the shortcomings of federal policy and with what might be called sectoral corporatism. The unions' strategy increasingly looked like not enough—it was not paying off for black workers, in particular. On all counts activists considered the successes too meager, and new fissures developed between the social movements and organized labor.

An explosive arena for these differing perspectives was the bitter conflict that emerged on opening the skilled trades to minority workers discussed in chapter 5. The increased demand for skilled labor during the economic boom raised the perennial question of how to supply it. There were two principal avenues: apprenticeship and breaking down craft skills or "lines of demarcation" into more basic, less skilled, tasks. Generally the labor movement and its academic allies favored increased apprenticeship. But there was a new issue added to this old debate, namely, the underemployment of minority workers and their severe under-representation in craft occupations. Many civil-rights activists viewed apprenticeship prerequisites and qualifying tests as a means of discriminating against minorities. That they had other, legitimate, purposes was not widely appreciated by nonlabor liberal professionals. This liberal view was reinforced by the CEA's technocratic desire to enlarge the labor pool and keep the economic expansion continuing without inflation. CEA chair, Ackley, urged managers to begin "breaking down jobs or redesigning processes in ways" that made it possible to hire the marginal worker who then would not require training.[70]

The Civil Rights Act mandated equal employment opportunity, and the Democratic party and national leaders of the building trades agreed to voluntary programs—linked at first with Model Cities—to increase the number of blacks in apprentice programs. But serious, and sometimes violent, three-way conflicts emerged between black workers, skilled trades unionists, and employers over apprenticeship standards and access. Years of conflict over implementation cracked local Democratic coalitions where liberal Republicans were available as alternative allies for blacks workers frustrated with continuing discrimination, as in New York City and Boston. Local divisiveness was a microcosm of the sharp conflicts that emerged over the enforcement of equal opportunity within the AFL–CIO top leadership and between them and civil-rights organizations.[71] Some progress toward patching up the liberal Democratic legislative alliance was achieved, reflected in passage of the 1968 Housing Act, but no agreement could be found on administrative and judicial supervision of employment.[72]

Inside the UAW, racism was also a problem, but the union leadership was firmly for integration. Yet the combination of weak local remedies for working conditions problems, a national government backing away from antipoverty efforts, and an International leadership apparently allied with management and the government all provided the impetus for the emergence of new rank-and-file opposition, the Revolutionary Union Movement (RUM)—mostly black autoworkers—and the United National Caucus (UNC)—an alliance of black production workers and radical skilled tradesmen. Both the RUM and the UNC challenged the UAW leadership by attacking the union's alliance with Democratic officials and their Vietnam war policy, racism in the union and plant managements, and labor contracts that traded wages and time off for continued managerial control of work. The RUM organized first at Chrysler's Dodge Main in Hamtramck (an enclave in Detroit) in 1968 and spread to other plants. Its confrontational tactics and bitter rhetoric spurred union and company to promote moderate black union officials and company supervisors, but this defused the movement, which split over internal disagreements. The UNC alliance was smaller and more cohesive. Its success was contingent on a labor market policy that would disallow task training and that would extend the "job ladder" for unionized skilled work by letting workers perform new tasks such as programming the new automated machine tools. Neither point was won and the multiracial alliance fell apart as white workers voted out their radical local leaders and the International ran campaigns against them.[73]

Meany and Reuther both were losing patience with the Democrats: they don't "deliver" on their promises to labor, said Meany.[74] But the two leaders were split over the federation's responsibilities for going ahead with reform without government leadership. Part of the split was the personal rivalry between the two men, but Meany's and his allies' fears of Reuther's power base in the IUD and of extraunion social movements also was based on a judgment that the existing labor system depended on continued Democratic control of government. Risking influence with government officials was an uncertain strategy. Meany backed away from coordinated bargaining and the broaching of political class struggle.[75]

Thus, coordinated collective bargaining had not only achieved some success, but also began to run into employer resistance, congressional investigation, NLRB hearings, and court proceedings. Machinists president Siemiller hailed the success in preventing aerospace firms from "whipsawing" unions against one another, but employers claimed it was illegal industry-wide bargaining. In fact, unions found that they could concert their bargaining strategies, but they still could not necessarily win a contract: they needed the government's support to overcome employer resistance. Apart from coordinated bargaining, the IUD found that the Johnson administration was reluctant to help them break the southern union blockade by denying government contracts to labor law violators like J. P. Stevens. The Justice Department's response that the government had to award contracts to the lowest bidder was "legal B.S.," said Reuther. "Do they want us or do they want Mr. Stevens? He is in the other party."[76] J. P. Stevens remained unorganized.

These conflicts in the AFL–CIO were compounded by Reuther's shift away from automatic Cold War consensus on international labor affairs and the Vietnam war. At the 1965 AFL–CIO convention, UAW secretary-treasurer Emil Mazey had attacked Johnson's war policy while Reuther's brother Victor, who was the director of the UAW's international affairs department, charged the AFL–CIO with fellow-travelling with the CIA.[77] Walter reinforced this charge at the 1966 UAW convention by criticizing Meany's preoccupation with anti-Communism to the detriment of a "positive" foreign policy and organizing workers in the United States. The criticism created a storm in the AFL–CIO council, but the council was able to deflect the charges to its own satisfaction. Finally, in February 1967, the UAW's International executive board, citing the lack of internal democracy in the AFL–CIO council and the need for the labor movement to "work as a responsible member of the community to help solve the problems of the total community," in particular by recommitting itself to organize the unorganized, voted to withdraw their officers from the AFL–CIO executive council and related labor committees and institutes.[78] At the same time, the UAW did not want to create an open breach in the labor movement before the 1968 presidential election and, therefore, did not secede from the federation. Instead, the UAW asked for a fundamental debate at the AFL–CIO convention in December 1968.[79] This, of course, placed UAW leaders in an increasingly untenable situation.

Another reason for postponing a showdown with Meany was the upcoming 1967 collective bargaining with the auto companies, the success of which was a continuing basis for Reuther's leadership. In fact, while the UAW leadership was sticking to the grand strategy, they, and other union leaders, were losing the support of the rank and file in the institutional core of collective bargaining. Working conditions had already risen to the top of the list of grievances during the 1964 auto industry negotiations when Reuther called the auto plants "gold plated sweatshops."[80] The industry's orthodox industrial pluralist response was a new contract that traded more pay and more time away from the job and more union grievance committeemen for continued management autonomy over the labor process. Employers and union alike were surprised when local members insisted on resolving local working conditions issues and held up auto production for weeks beyond the settlement of the national contract. The work force had changed since Eli Chinoy's famous study of autoworkers in the late 1940s had found that almost one-half thought of going into business for themselves. Twenty-five years later only one-tenth did so. Workers realized their careers were tied to auto work and job satisfaction was associated with job control.[81] At the same time, auto managements sought to reduce labor costs of production by increasing production standards, avoiding new hiring while requiring overtime, introducing automatic equipment, subcontracting and emphasizing task-specific worker training.[82]

Table 7.2

YEAR	AVERAGE WEEKLY AUTO OVERTIME	OVERTIME ALL MANUFACTURING
1962	4.2	2.8
1963	4.4	2.8
1964	5.0	3.1
1965	6.2	3.6
1966	4.9	3.9

In 1965, General Motors established a new division, General Motors Assembly Division (GMAD), to take over expensive, problem factories, which became famous equally for "driving" assembly line workers as for provoking local strikes.[83] GM's total grievance case load more than doubled from 106,000 in 1960 to 250,000 in 1969. Absenteeism rose dramatically, reportedly more than doubling at one of the Big Three during the 1960s, while a majority of unskilled new hires quit within one year. Finally, unofficial work stoppages at GM increased four-fold and days lost from production rose to five times the level of the 1950s by the end of the 1960s.[84] In February 1967, a wildcat strike by a local in Mansfield, Ohio, forced the shutdown of GM's production nationwide. Reuther had the International take over the local, but the issues remained.[85]

At the UAW's April 1967 Bargaining Convention, delegates approved the IEB's agenda for more daily relief time, more holidays, early retirement, higher skilled trades wages, plus a guaranteed annual wage, and a general wage increase of about 90 cents per hour, or a 6 percent total wage increase. The union also demanded the right to strike over subcontracting disputes. The Big Three concerted their strategies to hold the UAW and to limit cost-of-living allowances, as the Johnson administration advocated. The UAW struck Ford on September 6 and settled in October. At both Chrysler and GM there were local prebargaining strikes. The terms of the 1967 Ford pattern contract were mostly orthodox: major improvements in wages and benefits and increased time away from the job. At the same time, the union also agreed to cap COLA, a clear signal of the leadership's intention to act responsibly toward the Democratic coalition. The union won a guarantee of 90 percent of income for up to one year for laid-off workers with at least seven years seniority, two additional holidays, a company promise that no workers would be laid off as a direct result of subcontracting, broader transfer rights for senior workers, and a 33 percent increase in relief time for assembly line workers. The national contract had not resolved many working conditions issues, such as voluntary overtime and overtime equalization, skilled trades demarcation, discipline and production standards (it did win improved contract language to dispute changes in jobs), and grievance handling. Also, the union did not win the right to strike over subcontracting. Local strikes involved over half of Ford workers and local strikes at GM persisted into 1968.[86]

Yet, as extraparliamentary and nonunion forces were mobilized and the administration's commitment to the war in Vietnam escalated and its enthusiasm for domestic reform waned, the Democratic party was increasingly incapable of aggregating both new and traditional supporters. The administration began to reap the problems of its unwieldy domestic and international policies, and

President Johnson sought to postpone or avoid choices that might sacrifice any part of the coalition. The president, at first, backed away from the tax surcharge recommended by the CEA, apparently fearing the political repercussions in Congress. Nonetheless, mounting inflation provoked a new dollar crisis early in the year. The administration planned to resolve the payments problem by pursuing policies to ease deflationary pressures by expanding the liquidity of the International Monetary Fund and continuing the Kennedy Round of trade liberalization negotiations, which ultimately would help U.S. manufacturing exports.[87] However, the domestic structure continued to generate overheated, inflationary sectors while the political routines threatened to cut programs for the poor short.

The postwar system was beginning to impose a logic in which international balances were adjusted by deflating the domestic price level through reduced government expenditures, and/or monetary restraint, and/or wage and price stabilization. Since the latter was not forthcoming, the former seemed inevitable. The governmental agencies of deflation in the United States are largely autonomous from the executive branch—the Congress and Federal Reserve—but Congress was only too willing to oblige. The reform coalition lost its enormous, but necessary, partisan majority in the 1966 congressional elections. Moreover, the Great Society had become very unpopular with many Congressmen for raising new forces within their districts; the price that congressional leaders exacted for the costs of war was a halt to new social programs. Yet, because the Congress acted slowly, the Fed (Federal Reserve Board) first squeezed the money supply in late 1966 and then obliged the partisan status quo by expanding the money supply at a record rate in 1967 and 1968 to meet war and domestic financial demands.[88]

The loose monetary policy provided a little breathing room. The Johnson administration itself searched for a way to negotiate an end to the war and keep its electoral coalition together. The strong challenge within the party from Senators Eugene McCarthy and Robert Kennedy and Governor George Wallace threatened to create a Hobson's choice familiar in two party systems. If the insurgents lost within the party (either the nomination or some lasting institutional and policy role) they might stay home on election day or vote "no," and the party would lose to the only available alternative, namely the Republicans, which was worse.

When Americans for Democratic Action, chaired by John Kenneth Galbraith, jilted Johnson and endorsed Eugene McCarthy in February, most of the labor members of its executive board resigned. Spot surveys of autoworkers' support for Democratic primary candidates revealed a collapse of support for Johnson and split support for Kennedy and Wallace. Reuther began to give background support to Kennedy, and after Kennedy's assassination he switched to Humphrey.[89] The AFL–CIO executive council plainly saw the looming disaster and adhered more closely to Johnson and then, when the president took himself out of the race, to Humphrey, despite deep dissatisfaction and anger with the administration's economic policies.

Despite 191,000 AFL–CIO volunteers getting out the vote in the week before the November election and labor contributions of a record $7.6 million to the party, the Republicans won in a close election, which was marked by large southern white voter defections to George Wallace.[90] Half a realignment had made the Democrats and organized labor the losers.

Once the election was over, Reuther lost interest in the debate in the AFL–CIO. The UAW disaffiliated from the labor federation and formed a desperate pact with the independent Teamsters Union, one of the most aggressive organizers, but also the most notoriously corrupt labor union in the country, called the Alliance for Labor Action (ALA). The quixotic plan was to form a new union center in America that could gain the support of unorganized workers, students, and "liberal intellectuals," but the ALA went nowhere. At the same time, Reuther lined up the UAW behind a campaign to reform the Democratic party.[91]

Divide and Fall

Throughout the 1970s, union leaders sought to regroup the ranks of the Democratic coalition. They reined members' frustrations with direct conditions of work where they could and fought amongst themselves over new strategies to revive the party. On the one hand, workers were organized by insurgents in union after union in the early 1970s to challenge the leaderships' collective bargaining routines. In some unions, such as the Mine Workers, the insurgents were successful, but only after the insurgent candidate was murdered by agents of the UMW president. In most unions, the leadership was able to beat them back, as was the highly popular Ed Sadlowski campaign in the steelworkers union. The USW, in fact, signed a no-strike pledge in return for guaranteed annual wage improvements and arbitration. Inflation-protected wage settlements in other industries mollified some of the rank-and-file militancy. On the other hand, with Nixon in office, union leaders and Democrats were in the opposition, and policy supports for the union agenda were harder to come by.

The Nixon campaign and presidency deliberately took advantage of the disorganization of the labor–Democratic party coalition. The "new Republican majority" was based on electoral appeals to southern racists and cultural traditionalists bitter over Johnson's war and civil-rights policies,[92] while the Nixon administration and employers played hardball with the unions. Thus, Nixon engineered a recession and then, when faced with the chronic balance of payments situation and the prospect that he would enter the next national election without economic recovery, the Republican administration completed what Johnson began and, in August 1971, ended American commitment to the postwar system of fixed exchange rates.[93] The administration devalued the currency, imposed an across the board tariff, and froze wages and prices for three months. Once the freeze ended, it was clear that controls had not solved the economy's problems. Nixon established a tripartite Pay Board to control wage settlements. The AFL–CIO, the UAW, and the Teamsters rejected the administration's one-sided "incomes policy" that hit wages as the source of inflation.[94]

At this point the unions retreated to the courts. The AFL–CIO, UAW, and Teamsters took the government to court throughout 1972 because the board's rules abrogated collective bargaining contracts. That the board and the Nixon administration clearly ignored controls on sources of income other than wages and that it was firmly backed in this political assault by business groups were not capitalized on. The labor union strategy simply was to reject downward adjustment of the living standards of union members. Individual unions sought wage indexing via contractual COLAs. Between 1970 and 1972 the number of workers covered by COLAs nearly doubled; the UAW won back COLA in the 1970 auto negotiations.[95] Colas left nonunion workers to bear the brunt of the government's anti-inflation program. During the 1970s real wages of auto, construction, and steel workers exceeded the inflation rate, while nonunion wages lagged.

Another aspect of the AFL–CIO retreat from the broader reform coalition was the federation effort to control import competition and support of the neomercantilism of treasury secretary John Connally. They pointed out that the trade adjustment assistance program had not compensated a single worker since 1962. The AFL–CIO helped sponsor the 1972 Burke-Hartke bill that proposed to freeze imports at 1965–1969 levels. The UAW resisted tariffs, but it did join the AFL–CIO in urging federal licensing of American foreign investment. Leonard Woodcock, who succeeded Reuther as president of the UAW in 1970, also proposed that the new policy should be to get the Japanese to make direct foreign investments in the United States.[96]

The Nixon administration finally ended its series of wage controls in early 1974, but had no new strategy to coordinate the institutions of the domestic economy that were now responding to the sudden tripling of oil prices in the context of floating exchange rates. The Democrat-controlled Congress took some action, but the ability of Democratic party leaders to provide programmatic guidance, already limited, became even more so without control of the White House and because of the weakness of organized labor. The Democrats controlled Congress even after Nixon's landslide reelection and they pushed through new legislation to replace both MDTA and OEO, the Comprehensive Employment and Training Act (CETA). This became the main labor market program of the 1970s, but it was mostly a public employment program and a pale reflection of the labor market activism earlier envisioned.[97] With a weakened presidential wing, Margaret Weir argues, mayors became more important in the party and combined with members of Congress to establish a local focus for labor market programs, which not only made it difficult to establish a national strategy, but lay athwart the industrial organization of labor. In 1974, the Congress liberalized the trade adjustment assistance program, but this was mostly a sop to the unions to hold off protectionism.

Union and liberal Democratic legislative leadership sought to regroup before the 1976 presidential elections, but in the meantime ongoing industrial problems were generating sharper worker-manager conflicts. Disputes had already led to judicial restrictions of worker rights to "self-help" to deal with management strategies and to new initiatives to reach consensus between unions and firms at the plant and national levels. The changed international economic balance had not only led to a rush of imports to the United States, but had intensified American firms' cost-cutting strategies, which included vigilance against domestic labor costs, direct foreign investment, and foreign sourcing of raw materials and parts. Workers and unions attempted to compel managers to bargain over workplace changes. When employers objected, the federal courts increasingly tipped the balance of power to employers. Liberal Democratic judges, from William O. Douglas on the Supreme Court on down, previously had created a presumption in labor-management law for arbitration of disputes over contract interpretation and to limit the use of economic force. Moreover, employers only had a duty to bargain on matters that the court decided were "mandatory." By the early 1970s, the courts began to resume more direct supervision of labor-management relations. They opened up to suits from employees and employers that challenged union actions and issued injunctions against strikes that sought contract enforcement even when the object of the strike was to get employers to arbitration. And they made it clear that employers would not be compelled to bargain over decisions—in contrast to the effects of decisions—to subcontract work, close down part of a plant, invest in a new plant elsewhere, sell a plant to a nonunion firm, or introduce new technologies.[98] In a case involving General Motors and the UAW, the District of Columbia Appeals Court affirmed the following NLRB reasoning:

> Decisions such as this, in which a significant investment or withdrawal of capital will affect the scope and ultimate direction of the enterprise, are matters essentially financial and managerial in nature. They thus lie at the very core of entrepreneurial control. . . . Such managerial decisions ofttimes require secrecy as well as freedom to act quickly and decisively. They also involve subject areas as to which determinative financial and operational considerations are likely to be unfamiliar to the employees and their representatives.[99]

That all such decisions can decisively affect the conditions of employment of workers was put beyond the ideological boundary of the liberal industrial order. Collective bargaining would not expand to meet the new economic conditions.

The law was one thing; actual industrial conditions another. Companies might try to escape their current work force, but many firms could not be so footloose. GM pursued a "southern strategy" of moving plants south, but the UAW was able to organize all of them, while Ford and the UAW wrangled over the company's slow close-down of the massive complex at River Rouge throughout the 1970s. And the workers were still doing the work. Indicative of the souring plant-level situation was that, even though the 1973 auto settlements resulted in substantial wage and benefit improvements plus some limits on overtime, upgrading production workers to perform skilled tasks, and subcontracting, the contract ratification vote in 1973 at Ford was fairly close, with ten production worker locals voting against and the skilled trades members company-wide actually rejecting it. Chrysler workers did reject their contract. In 1976, the Ford contract passed by the closest margin ever; the skilled trades again rejected it. This time at Chrysler, the contract passed with about one-third against among both production and skilled trades members.[100] At GM the number of union demands in 1973 contract negotiations numbered 39,200 compared with 11,000 in 1958.[101] In fact, after a widely reported wildcat strike at GM's Lordstown, Ohio, plant in 1972, GM and the other companies and the UAW had agreed on a new program to prevent working conditions problems. The companies introduced new personnel management programs, generally known as "quality of work life" or QWL programs, to improve work performance through attention to the nonwage motivations of employees. Managers sought to make workers feel wanted and valuable members of the production team by listening to employee suggestions and being diligent in applying dispute procedures. However, these programs typically failed to establish new authority for employees and their relationship to collective bargaining was ambiguous.[102] When managers revealed that their top priority still was getting high volumes of work out of the factory door, they undermined the programs, although new, more sophisticated versions appeared in the 1980s.

Another track of voluntary cooperation was private high-level negotiations between union and corporate leaders. These began

after Nixon was forced to resign. Beginning in late 1974, John
Dunlop, President Ford's labor secretary, pursued his personal
version of societal corporatist bargaining over a broad range of
economic issues and established the president's Labor-Management Committee, whose members were appointed by Ford. The
committee met throughout 1975, but became "private" when Ford
vetoed the so-called Common Situs Bill after massive business and
"new right" mobilization defeated it and Dunlop resigned.[103] The
bill represented the kind of structural reform that labor experts had
been discussing for years. The common situs provision of the
Construction Industry Collective Bargaining Act had been proposed a dozen years earlier; it was an exemption from legal rules to
enable a construction union to picket an entire building site rather
than just a single subcontractor. What was crucial was that the
picketing provision was the quid pro quo for organized labor's
agreement to changes in the structure of collective bargaining that
would limit local union authority to push up wages. Ford's veto
destroyed the legitimacy of the presidential Committee, but Dunlop
re-formed it as a private group which continued to meet until 1978
when the increasingly effective political mobilization of employers
led them to forsake cooperation on structural reform.

In the meantime, however, the fallout from the Watergate
scandal returned the Democrats to the White House and to control
of economic management. However fortuitous this was, the party
was increasingly rudderless despite the efforts of union leaders like
Woodcock. Since 1964, liberal Democratic party leaders had tried
to avoid the turmoil of the Mississippi challenge to the party by
reforming the party's rules to broaden its base by opening up the
presidential nomination process, ensuring that "young people,"
blacks, and women would be able to participate in internal party
affairs, and by strengthening the program-responsibility relationship between the party's activists and elected officials in Congress.
Some modest gains were made by 1968, but the party organization
bosses in state and local government plus the AFL–CIO's COPE had
kept a firm rein on the nomination. Nonetheless, a Party Reform
Commission had been created at the 1968 national convention in
response to a report from the Eugene McCarthy camp that challenged the party to democratize itself. The commission was initially headed by Sen. George McGovern (D., S.D.) and then by Rep.

Don Fraser (D., Minn.). The McGovern-Fraser Commission's suggestions for opening the convention delegate selection process were adopted in time for the 1972 convention, which witnessed a significant increase in representation from younger party activists, blacks, and women.[104]

But since the party's nominee for president, McGovern, lost the election in a landslide, the opponents of party reform were able to come back and challenge the reformers over the kind of party the Democrats would have. The reformers wanted to press on with making the party a "responsible" party that was representative of the Democratic voters (by race and gender), programmatic, and accountable. Against them were the self-identified "mainstream" Democrats of the Coalition for a Democratic Majority (CDM) who opposed McGovern and included in their ranks George Meany and Al Barkan (AFL–CIO COPE director), cold warrior members of Congress like Sen. Henry (Scoop) Jackson (D., Wash.), activists like Ben Wattenberg (co-author with Richard Scammon of the clarion call for the nonblack, nonpoor coalition, *The Real Majority*), and political scientists Austin Ranney and Jeane Kirkpatrick, and some local and state party organizations.[105] Although reluctant, the AFL–CIO leadership had endorsed the outline of party reform before the 1972 convention, but they abhorred the "new politics" liberals in the McGovern camp who sought to represent the new domestic social forces and to back away from the Democrats' historic "forward" military position against the Soviet Union. On the other side were the Democratic Planning Group, formed in the fall of 1974 and financed by some supporters of the McGovern and Edmund Muskie campaigns and the UAW, several other AFL–CIO affiliated unions, including the Communications Workers of America (CWA), the American Federation of State, County and Municipal Employees (AFSCME), the Oil, Chemical and Atomic Workers Union (OCAW), the IUE, Hotel and Restaurant Workers, and the Graphic Arts International Union, the Congressional Black Caucus, civil-rights groups, feminist organizations, the ADA, and local party insurgents, such as the liberal-labor coalition behind Sen. Ralph Yarbourough in Texas.[106] There was, of course, overlap within the groups in each faction, such as black autoworkers in civil-rights groups and former UAW legal counsel Joseph Rauh Jr. in the Democratic Planning Group. The first opportunity to work through the conflicts was the scheduled midterm party convention in 1974, itself one of the reforms meant to make the party into a regular national organization rather than an episodic quadrennial scramble. The convention was slated to adopt a party charter, something which the Democrats never had had.[107]

The CDM was successful, with strong congressional Democratic support, in having the new party chair, Robert Strauss, postpone the convention until December, safely—so it was thought—after the November congressional elections. Then, at a planning meeting in August, the AFL–CIO was so aggressive that civil-rights representatives such as Willie Brown of California walked out. Strauss had added several AFL–CIO officials to the Democratic National Committee (DNC) and some fifty additions to the Charter Commission, which the AFL–CIO had actively sought. The "mainstreamers" also were successful in narrowing the purpose of the convention simply to the charter proposal; there would be no substantive policy debates or resolutions that might embarrass members of Congress or presidential aspirants.[108] These tactics may have been too smart; Nixon resigned in August and the Democrats swept the November elections; however, the party did not stand for anything except being innocent of Watergate.

The major issues of conflict over the charter were affirmative action and proportional representation.[109] The Meanyites strenuously opposed any language that could be remotely construed as requiring quotas in party affairs; they were not satisfied with proposed Charter language that expressly banned quotas, but encouraged affirmative steps to be inclusive. The real problem was loss of AFL–CIO influence on the party. Some local party leaders backed the COPE position for fear of national supervision of local party functions. Proportional representation meant banning historic party practice in delegate selection for presidential nominating conventions that gave votes to the top vote-getting candidate (the unit rule) and substituting a rule apportioning delegates roughly according to the percentage of the vote each candidate received. Again, the local party leaders were the source of opposition. However, the November election sweep and the real prospect of victory in the 1976 presidential election gave strong momentum to swing groups in the party that sought to compromise the more militant factions. Among the swing groups was the Democratic Governors and the UAW, which, with seven other unions, met with Strauss to emphasize that Meany did not speak for them. The UAW sought to focus the attention of all factions on party unity and the poor condition of the economy rather than on charter semantics and symbolic issues. Strauss himself moved toward the reformers and gained the support of some the congressional leadership.[110]

The December convention endorsed the proposed charter easily, including the contested (though compromised) provisions. However, Meany and Barkan were livid, threatened to take the AFL–CIO out of the party (which they could not do in any case because of the divisions within the council), and resurrected the old political voluntarism associated with Samuel Gompers. Michael Johnson, the Pennsylvania COPE director, claimed "our participation in the Democratic Party as officers is an anomaly. . . . Once we get inside the Democratic Party, we foreclose our right to ask other candidates for support." Johnson had endorsed Republican Senator Richard Schweiker for reelection, which had led to his exclusion from the convention. A Barkan aide commented that involvement in party affairs divided the labor movement: "ever since we've been there" (in the DNC) "we find ourselves fighting with other trade unionists. We're letting politicians come between us."[111] Of course the labor movement was already divided between one wing trying to move with the broader, realigning forces in American society and the other wing expressing the indignation of leaders whose would-be followers had moved beyond them. Jacob Clayman of the AFL–CIO complained "many of us have spent most of our adult lives fighting to boost the level of those who have been kicked around by our society. Now we are pictured as some kind of social neanderthals."[112] In fact, the proposed charter would dilute the influence of the Meanyites in the DNC. On the other hand, real political strength of the AFL–CIO was its ability to reach down and mobilize working-class voters. This quality was, apparently, taken for granted by many nonlabor reformers, but it was also true that Meany stood against any mobilization that would threaten his leadership and shift authority to labor's social democrats.

The compromise charter was adopted by the convention, but the reformers' efforts to win support for it from elected leaders continued, throughout the decade and into the 1980s, without much success. Accomplishments included considerably broadening

participation in the nomination process and gaining more authority for women inside the party. Yet, establishing a representative
midterm policy convention and holding federal officials accountable to a party platform never was accomplished. And although the
AFL–CIO had contributed some $3 million to congressional candi-
dates in 1974 and was the "best organized supporter" of Democrats,[113] Meany took the labor federation out of active party
participation and it sat out the 1976 presidential primaries. The
AFL–CIO continued to lobby Democrats in Congress, but the "check-
book" style of politics was rapidly overcome by the emergence of
Political Action Committees formed by organized business.

Woodcock, in contrast to Meany, endorsed Jimmy Carter for
president in the 1976 primaries well before most people knew much
about him. Indeed, closely tied to changing party formation and
procedures were the substantive issues that the UAW and others
wanted the party to champion. Woodcock told UAW members at the
union's March 1976 convention that the country needed a liberal
president and Congress as well as an economic plan to legislate. In
May, Woodcock urged the Democratic Party Platform Committee
to become a responsible party by writing a platform for the long
run, by declaring that the platform was what it meant to be a
Democrat, and then requiring candidates—for the presidency and
Congress alike—to pledge their support. "By such action, the
Democratic Party and its candidates would aggregate ideology
from among the diverse interests in the party, chart and retain
direction and deliver as promised. When the parties fail that responsibility, they discourage the interest and participation of the
voters."[114]

The economic plan was developed by the Initiative Committee
for National Economic Planning, whose co-chairs were Woodcock
and Nobel laureate economist Wassily Leontief.[115] The committee
gained the support of Dunlop. The economic planning envisioned
would go beyond Keynesianism by openly developing sectoral
option plans, adopting a multiyear focus, and taking a broader
view than the federal budget. Hubert Humphrey, now a senator,
placed their ideas before the Congress in 1975 as the Balanced
National Growth and Economic Planning Bill, mostly written by
Leon Keyserling and Bertram Gross, who of course had been
"present at the creation" of the postwar system. This bill was

joined, in March 1976, with another one, the Equal Opportunity and Full Employment Bill of Augustus Hawkins (D., Cal.), which sought to amend the 1946 Employment Act by making full employment (defined as 3% unemployment) a legally enforceable right. The government would be the employer of last resort and prevailing wages would be paid. Private interest advisory groups to the CEA would be formalized. The combination of these two bills became the Humphrey-Hawkins Full Employment and Balanced Growth Act of 1976.

Indicative of the strains of reform was the coalescence of organized labor and civil-rights leaders in an organization to mobilize support for the legislation. Coretta Scott King and Murray Finley (Amalgamated Clothing Workers Union) were the co-chairs of the Full Employment Action Council, which carefully composed its board from the leaders of major labor, civil rights and feminist organizations, plus a few professors and a couple of executives (from Xerox and the Urban Development and Investment Company). The UAW placed Vice-President Irving Bluestone on the council and used its Community Action Program to organize a nationwide petition campaign.[116] The AFL–CIO took part in the development of the bill, but the federation mostly asked for changes, such as removing the right to sue for a job, which Meany believed would sink the bill politically. Largely absent were Democratic congressional caucus leaders. There was little preparation of legislators for this measure, which would be fairly complicated to carry out if passed. And, in fact, Congressional Democrats did not pass it because the large freshman class of Democrats opposed dealing with it before the fall 1976 election. The "class of '74," carried into office on the wake of Watergate, and often enough from Republican districts, were conservative on economic issues. Moreover, prominent commercial Keynesian economists, such as Charles Schultz, strongly warned against the bill because of its inflationary potential. Reformers continued to push party leaders to develop a more programmatic and popular approach, but a contrary view, that the Democrats were too close to labor and that democracy was indeed undermining American capitalism, gained sway.[117]

The new Carter administration ran rapidly through the cycle of programs associated with the preceding administrations, including the debates between Keynesians (such as Charles Schultz, who

Carter appointed to the CEA) and structuralists (such as Ray Marshall at the Labor Department) before deciding to go with the Keynesians. Carter started with general stimulation—for example, doubling the number of CETA public service jobs in six months and dramatically increasing trade adjustment assistance payouts—but ended as the first Democrat to preside over a deliberate recession. Like Dunlop, Ray Marshall sought sectoral deals, but the Labor Department quickly lost influence with Carter to the CEA; Marshall was shut out of Carter's high level economic policy group in late 1977.[118] In addition, the Democratic Congress, including the entire Georgia delegation, actually defeated the Common Situs Bill it had passed two years earlier in March 1977. Then the Humphrey-Hawkins Bill was seriously diluted and never gained more than a symbolic endorsement from Carter to the congressional black caucus.[119]

Increasingly since the defeat of common situs, organized employers and the "new right" were using labor issues to divide congressional Democrats and get what they want on, not only labor issues, but other issues, too. Moreover, the leaders of large corporations who, in the past, had been willing to pursue consensual policies, dropped out of the coalition into the "new right" camp. Dunlop's labor-management group was still meeting, but it broke down as Carter apparently ran out of options. Its members were Stephen Bechtel (chair of Bechtel), Reginold Jones (General Electric), Thomas Murphy (GM), Donald Perkins (Jewel), Irving Shapiro (Du Pont), George Schultz (president of Bechtel), Edgar Speer (U.S. Steel), Rawleigh Norris (Mobil), Walter Wriston (Citibank), Murray Finley (Clothing Workers), Frank Fitzsimmons (Teamsters), Lane Kirkland (AFL–CIO), Lloyd McBride (USW), George Meany (AFL–CIO), Martin Ward (Plumbers), and Douglas Fraser (UAW). A top issue was labor law reform. A bill was introduced and passed through the House of Representatives in 1977. If passed by the Senate and signed by Carter, the bill would have speeded-up NLRB decisions and court enforcement of unfair labor practices cases, made it easier for workers to get an authorized union representation election, and stiffened penalties for labor law violators. In short, it was a procedural reform, which did not directly touch the issues of managerial control and workers' job control. Nevertheless, the bill became a lightning rod for the right wing.[120]

The bill came up for a vote in the Senate in January 1978, but Carter wanted organized labor and Congress to delay action. Instead, the president wanted the Senate to take up the Panama Canal Treaty. Presidential priorities resulted in a delay of five months, during which business lobbyists mobilized against the bill and succeeded in gaining enough votes to filibuster the legislation in June. Though the employers' mobilization was massive and very well financed, labor was mobilized, too; the real problem was the organizational and programmatic weakness of the party: not enough Democrats could or would take the heat.[121] Even the business members of the labor-management group actively opposed it, which provoked UAW president Fraser to resign angrily. Citing the defeat of labor law reform as the "most serious" and "latest breakdown" of union-corporation cooperation, which also included Humphrey-Hawkins, national health care, raising the minimum wage, social security finance, occupational safety and health, tax equity, and electoral reform, he wrote to the group that employers were waging a

> one-sided class war—a war against working people, the unemployed, the poor, the minorities, the very young and the very old and even many in the middle class of our society. . . . If corporations like General Motors want confrontation, they cannot expect cooperation in return from labor. [Republicans and Democrats] are weak and ineffective as parties, with no visible, clear-cut ideological differences between them, because of business domination.[122]

Indeed, both political parties had degenerated into election vehicles for individual candidates, while elected officials increasingly responded to those business and trade association PACs that financed them. But there still was not anywhere else for labor to go, politically.

The Carter administration's bid for a global Keynesian expansion coordinated with America's allies failed to gel in 1978, which quickened employers' and government policy-makers' shift to domestic deflation. In late 1978, the Carter administration used its Council on Wage and Price Stability (COWPS) to try to gain voluntary "restraint"; it just made people mad. As international pressures continued to mount in 1979, and a dollar crisis arrived, the Fed and the Carter administration chose the orthodox Keynesian macroeconomic alternative: slow down the economy, cut social spending, and raise interest rates. A last attempt to mend fences was announced in September 1979 when the AFL–CIO signed a national accord with Carter officials for voluntary pay and price restraint and fiscal discipline. The accord created a tripartite Pay Advisory Committee, headed by Dunlop, and a Price Committee, but the effort, again, was disconnected and incoherent. Even more than with Reuther's proposal in 1966, organized support to make voluntary controls work was lacking. In any event, what was needed was Democratic attention to the shortcomings of the industrial order and, especially, the declining place of labor in it. The new policy turn fractured what little remained of the Democratic mass base as social policy clients were cut loose and unemployment soared.[123]

Sour relations with organized labor and the electorally inco- herent economic strategy were the keys to Carter's failed reelec- tion. Voters faced three Republican choices in 1980: a Democrat pursuing a Republican economic policy, a Republican running as an independent (John Anderson), and a Republican running as a Republican promising to get the country moving again (Ronald Reagan). Reagan won with 50.5 percent of the vote in a low turnout election. Northern state voters turned out at the lowest rate since 1924; southern turnout was actually lower than in 1968. Blue-collar workers split 50 to 50 for Reagan and Carter; union households split 52 to 48 for Carter, down from 60 to 40 in 1976 and 66 to 33 for Kennedy in 1960.[124] The postliberal Reagan and Bush years witnessed the end of any pretense that labor was a partner in the national policy consensus. The UAW was thrown into concessionary contracts at the Big Three, pattern bargaining was disrupted, and all across unionized industry organized labor was in retreat. The old New Deal Democratic party was dead, but no new party was born.

CHAPTER 8

Reconfiguring
Work and Politics

A persistent and historical goal of unionism is to bring democracy into the workplace. The thrust of a true quality of worklife program includes a process in which workers, armed with ample information, exercise the democratic right to participate in workplace decisions including job structure and design, job layout, material flow, tools to be used, methods and processes of production, plant layout, work environment etc. In its broadest sense it means decision†making as to how the work place will be managed and how the worker will effectively have a voice in being master of the job rather than being subservient to it.
—*Irving Bluestone, "Human Dignity Is What It's All About," 1978*

For over thirty years, the UAW and other unions operated within a New Deal political framework. They sought to broaden the coverage of benefits included in collectively bargained contracts, press government leaders to stay the course of stimulative economic policy and social reform, and cope with the unresolved problems of workers' roles at work. This agenda placed unions firmly on the side of national progress and identified unions as allies of blacks and consumers. However, the virtuous circle of stable labor relations, high wages and profits, and Democratic dominance was disrupted at the end of the 1960s and collapsed in the late 1970s. Now the liberal industrial order seemed to be characterized by a vicious circle of government debt, high labor costs, unresponsive production lines, and lost markets.

This realization was thrust onto American consciousness by the rush of imported goods from European and Asian nations in the early 1980s. The high value of the dollar and enormous fiscal stimulation through the military budget, coupled with high domestic interest rates and antiunionism, reoriented both consumers and manufacturers toward foreign sources. Domestic automobile employment fell by 40 percent from 1979 through 1983, and foreign producers captured over 25 percent of the u.s. product market, which they have maintained until today. Suddenly the United States no longer obviously represented the successful modern society toward which everyone else was moving. The Germans, the Italians, the Japanese, and others were not beating the Americans in autos and other product markets with low labor costs, for the most part, but with the advantages of their own national systems for combining labor and capital. These turned out to be more capable of exploiting the new world markets, which were both more segmented into smaller submarkets and saturated with production capacity, for cars and other consumer and producers goods. Firm success now depended less on giant production volumes to drive down unit costs, and more on product distinction and performance and on developing the broad capacities of employees to restructure their interactions flexibly to meet market contingencies.[1]

Stating the problem was difficult enough, finding solutions has been harder. Persistent ideologies of states and markets have colored leaders' perceptions of the need to devise new formulas for work and politics. In contrast to claims either that unions are doomed by the operations of free markets or that, even if unions could craft a new role, the American government is incapable of contributing to innovation, the record shows that the New Deal state was innovative and capable, in large part because it reconfigured work and politics. The New Deal industrial order, founded on pluralistic industrial relations, which tapped the energies of blue–collar workers anew, was a specific alternative to market pathologies and to authoritative state interventions.

The United States has had analogous experiences with the transformation of democratic capitalism. What each sequence has in common is widespread reform of the relationships among people producing and distributing wealth. The craft–based industrial order was undergoing change by the time of the 1890s depression and was recomposed in ways that became known as welfare capitalism in the 1920s, but which was anything but a welfare state. The widespread rewriting of the rules of electoral democracy significantly weakened popular influence on decision making about who got to do what with what kinds of compensation. The new industrial order became characterized by oligopoly, authoritarian labor management, and, politically, a "broadly–based oligarchy" (as Walter

Dean Burnham describes it) rather than a democracy. The depression of the 1930s set the stage for democratic forces to get into the game, at least partly, and stay there for decades, as usual under specific historical background conditions. Liberal Democratic party leaders were pushed and convinced to make room for organized labor in industry and party politics as the procedural vehicle for the aggregation of the blue–collar workers' interests. Just as during the previous sequence, procedural changes were also substantive interventions that rearranged the rights and entitlements of all groups.

In all of the sequences industry is more or less ordered; there is no free market. Instead, there are differing institutional means to stabilize production relations and to coordinate industry and society to enable individuals to work and live with dignity. In the 1920s, Republican proponents called welfare capitalism "normalcy"; in the 1950s and 1960s, political scientists conceived the "normal vote" that made the Democrats the "majority party." Truly, if institutions establish stability, then individual interests and behaviors may be normalized. But an industrial order is still created and, in all the experiences, is, at best, partially determining of how people live. Individual motives and events external to the system are beyond complete control and contribute to the attenuation of established authority.

Thus, the liberal Democratic industrial order established by the New Dealers was built of the specific conditions that individuals faced in the 1930s and 1940s. The new order was based on the core of already existing large corporations with their internal hierarchies and on existing political party organizations. The New Deal changed the rules to reorder the place of corporations in society. What was distinctive of the sequence was the effective organization of workers in unions and the Democrats' use of organized labor to gain and keep the political power necessary to rein the power of corporate leaders and redistribute resources. Workers already were organizing to do something like this. What liberal Democrats did was constitutionalize industrial government. They extended civil liberties to employees to free them to elect representatives to negotiate a contract that would govern labor–management relations. The strategy, broadly, worked very well for a very long time. However, the specific institutional relationships that were established did not cover workers' full aspirations, and a dynamic of normal antagonism on the shop floor ensued. The key to the attenuation of industrial order was that the CIO and AFL alike conceived collectively bargained contracts as open–ended documents that reflected the extent of agreement between workers and managers on how to meet new contingencies, while employers, virtually unanimously, conceived contracts as defining the limits of union rights at work. The latter position carried the day with a Republican–dominated Congress, in 1947, in the Taft–Hartley Act. Disputes about the act that went to court enabled liberal Democratic judges to develop arbitration as a compromise position in the late 1950s but, then, increasingly, over the next two decades, federal judges and elected government officials shifted to the managerialist interpretation. Despite the vigorous efforts of the UAW and some other unions, in alliance with the broader network of New Deal Democrats and emerging social movements, the industrial pluralist system did not expand to meet new contingencies. On the contrary, the boundaries in the plant were hardened, and the perimeter of union organization shrank.

The ability of the New Deal industrial order to reproduce itself (to change with change) had been taken for granted in the formulas abstracted by students of the political economy. Industrial pluralism, interest group liberalism, and Keynesianism all were supposed to be pragmatic tools of adjustment and progress. But the thread that bound practitioners of adjustment was the political coalition that came to power in the 1930s, not any logic of industrialism. By the 1970s the fabric had unravelled. The institutions associated with the coalition, preeminently unions and the Democratic party, were no longer able to hold themselves together to successfully manage insurgent demands for more participation from rank–and–file, civil–rights, women's, and antiwar movements. These challenges were compounded by a series of crises that were associated with the adjustment of the American domestic economy to newly assertive and competitive foreign economic forces and that unleashed self–interested behavior in market and government.

From the 1930s to the 1970s the Democratic party had aggregated the interests of disparate groups and classes and enabled them to affirm their general political support for the liberal industrial order. The role of liberal Democratic unions was pivotal: successful collective wage bargaining and electoral support for its official defenders went together. The strength and, later, weakness of this configuration was the removal of labor issues from partisan politics to administration and adjudication. The alternative path of social collaboration at work—concerning substantive issues, not only of pay, but of the quality of investment, organization of work, product strategies—coupled with politically organized class conflict over the terms of competition was placed beyond the boundaries of legitimate politics. Institutions of democratic self–government, especially the political parties, but also government agencies, schools, and private organizations like unions, were underdeveloped. There were only fragments of a process in which citizens could rethink the requirements of the political formation of unions and corporations and other economic institutions that tie together micro and private and macro and public policies. This was unproblematic until the 1960s. But then problems of interest formation and aggregation and of economic growth became chronic. In the early 1970s, an elite movement emerged based on a new managerialist vision of industry and society, and it gained adherents among employers and the professional middle classes and influenced both major political parties. Issues of full employment and industrial democracy had few effective supporters as the public discourse focused on the costs of democratic government and on shifting authority and resources to the corporate leaders of the private sector. And with these issues has gone the need for the New Deal's consensual multiclass partisan style. Doug Fraser's 1978 protest against the "one–sided class war" by top corporate leaders made public the political crisis of the old order.

Creating a High–Participation Society

In principle, the Americans could do the same thing as their chief competitors, namely regain economic health, not by copying their rivals, but by learning how to adapt useful models to historic American practices. What might this be? and how could it be achieved? The chief candidate has been forms of managerialist cooperation among unions and managers and increased worker responsibility for plant competitiveness.[2] Managers pursue competitive success by driving firms to respond flexibly to shifting market conditions and to reduce production costs. Rather than guaranteeing productivity through high–volume output, precisely defined occupations, and dedicated equipment, the key is the absence of strict organizational hierarchy and the deployment of teams of employees to a changing menu of tasks and projects with general purpose technologies. Progress toward both objectives is achieved by winning workers' active support for management's definition of the firm's goals. The means of gaining workers' involvement is "cooperation" between employees and managers according to which workers take on new tasks, take initiative to solve production problems, and supply their particular knowledge about doing jobs to the company.

Thus, American–based auto companies launched programs to reestablish industrial relations on a newly flexible basis. In the 1980s they demanded and won concessions of wages and sectoral welfare benefits, including modifications of postwar wage rules. They also won agreements to transform the job structure by collapsing occupational categories into broader designations and reducing the importance of seniority and traditional skills. The new organization of work was built on the formation of teams of employees trained to cooperatively develop and carry out plans to increase productivity; a new emphasis on perfection of production; eliminating redundancy in the labor process (especially inventory and stocks of parts, but also "extra" employees); greater subcontracting; making plants compete with each other for the opportunity to produce certain parts or products; and tighter links with fewer supplier companies.

These ongoing managerial work reforms fit ambiguously with historical labor practices, whether those favored by workers or nonlabor liberals. On the one hand, the new workplace regime satisfies employee desires to be involved and make a significant contribution. On the other hand, it is a benevolent dictatorship.[3] Although some auto unionists reacted positively to the collaborative elements put in place, the first real internal opposition in twenty years, based on the perception that collaboration has not stopped managerial actions to close plants, permanently layoff large numbers of employees, and throw wages and working conditions into competition, has emerged. The programs that have been put in place (in automobiles and elsewhere) have, with few exceptions,[4] uniformly preserved highly unequal powers between employees and managers over virtually all major decisions that shape the organization of work. They do not, in fact, contribute, to any very great extent, to the fulfillment of employees' desires to participate. Instead, they tightly envelope workers in new managerial strategies. Work reforms introduced by management are structured to compete with collective bargaining and to isolate individual plants and their workers from other plants and make them compete with each other and, hence, to undermine labor solidarity.[5]

Yet, if workers' opposition to management's work reforms has been defensive and focused on preserving as much of the postwar system as possible, while unions have suffered continuing losses of membership and public prestige as forces of progress, then can labor do something else? Defensiveness affirms some important historical union values, but by itself does not save jobs or offer much guidance to how to link the protection of workers' interests at work to the problems associated with declining industry and a competitive economy. The historical producerist vision in American unionism suggests the outlines of a high–participation workplace and society that articulates a newly virtuous circle in which prolabor workplace reforms are linked to solutions to the broader society's interest in productive industry and democratic government. The beginnings of a new democratic producerist vision already exist, in principles developed in many local experiments and by some national officers in the AFL–CIO.[6] The producerist goals of democracy at work, enhancing the productive capacity of the work force, worker self–management, universal labor organization, government control of nonproductive speculation and irresponsible finance, and prohibition of vicious forms of competition (sweatshops and whipsawing) are the principles of a positive program of work reform.

The producerist world is implicit in ongoing industrial reforms, such as collaborative forms of production among firms (including the interfirm agreements noted above), within the firm among line staff (marketing, engineering, design), between a firm's staff and production (supervision and the unionized work force), and among the core firms and key suppliers. Rather than extend the division of labor geographically, production can be concentrated to gain economies of scope. The object is to share development

costs, improve product quality, craft products to regional tastes and
requirements, shorten product and process innovation cycles, expand the capacity or contribution of supplier firms, and secure
employment, at least, for the core work force.[7] However, the changed
background political conditions make its future more problematic
than the new managerialism.

One of the most thoroughgoing local experiments is the General Motors Saturn project, initiated in 1982, to produce a new
automobile from a clean slate: a new corporate shell, a new loca-
tion in Tennessee, a new product, new design and marketing
procedures, and new industrial relations. Throughout the 1980s,
before the first Saturn model was produced in 1990, the UAW and
GM formally collaborated on virtually all aspects of implementing
the project.[8] The Saturn corporation is characterized by teamwork
labor–management relations and extraordinary union participation in decision making about the organization of work, hiring,
subcontracting, marketing, and pricing. Union members receive
extensive human relations training to make the participative style
work smoothly. Limitations of the project are reflected in the
continuing control of investment at GM headquarters, local UAW
collaboration to deny subcontracts to underperforming unionized
companies rather than engaging in relational contracting, center-
ing new authority on the union and not on the employees, and the
isolation of Saturn workers from other union members. Other
experiments are trying to overcome some of these shortcomings.

At the UAW-organized Mazda complex south of Detroit, the
local has successfully enlarged the proportion of the work force that
gains employment security, and it has aggressively organized subcontractors. More ambitiously, regional UAW staff, union locals,
and auto–parts suppliers around Detroit are collaborating in the
Council of Independent Parts Suppliers to extend working–conditions guarantees while enhancing the competitiveness of the industry. This effort has been hindered by the 1990 failure of Michigan's
Democratic governor, who actively supported this kind of effort, to
win reelection and by the disinterest of the new governor. More
promising still, in part because of different political conditions, is a
statewide effort in Wisconsin, the historical home of craft manufacturing. The Wisconsin regional strategy enlists multiple unions,
including the UAW, and the metalworking firms, which employ

almost thirty thousand people, and has gained the support of state government behind a strategy for high–skill manufacturing that combines workplace collaboration with worker authority to participate in decisions that affect employment security.[9]

The producerist theme of real participation that does give workers more authority provides a means for labor to refocus political debates on competitiveness by stressing that the success of more flexible product strategies and forms of work depends on establishing new rights for workers in the workplace and the broader society. Anything less than a shift of authority from management to labor simply recreates inequality and fails to develop new capacities. By basing its contribution to competitiveness debates on how democracy enhances workplace capacities, unions can show how the government has a positive role to play in modernizing existing industry by providing incentives and guidelines for cooperation, not competition. Industry councils and a labor extension service, as once promoted by the CIO, could be created to promote best practices in labor–management relations and production processes. Their purpose would be to enhance government capacity to craft training and education programs for employees no longer firmly tied to an employer, to educate managers and workers about their industries and new technologies, to encourage development of production networks among firms, and to provide the institutional setting for representatives of labor, management, and the government to make more informed decisions. The government also could revise labor laws to legalize multiemployer industry–wide bargaining (beyond the current limits to construction, shipping, and garments) to enable the newly contingent work force to organize to develop and defend common interests.[10]

A vision of work that links plant–level experiments in collaboration to public debates about the proper relationship of industry and society also is an important piece of a new political movement to change the rules governing industrial decision making in ways that sustain that collaboration. Without policies to enhance workers' economic security and authority (among other goals), workplace reforms will be isolated, limited to core firms and their employees, and management dominated and, thereby, liable to worker distrust and resistance, unhelpful for union revival, and most likely to result in a Pyrrhic victory for managerialism. Already, when firms close plants that have been cooperative, there is reason to argue that workers and unions have to raise the quid pro quo for collaboration from more working days to influence over corporate strategies. A union campaign that combines extensive political education with popularization of exemplary cases of reform, including those plants that were closed despite union cooperation, would articulate an alternative understanding of the politics of industry and society and of workers' contributions to productive success. The producerist vision would help regain the confidence of nonunion allies among economic development officials, nonunion workers, civil–rights organizations, small supplier firms, and middle–class consumers who stand to benefit from an approach to public policy that emphasizes the productive capacity of workers and firms. Union initiatives in this area might make these groups supporters of the political coalition for public policies that make possible real worker cooperation.

Either future is possible. Although both ideal types include dangers for unions, the second, collaborative strategy is more likely to secure employment and income. On the other hand, the former seems more probable as long as American employers continue to limit employee authority against a partisan political background still not supportive of government industrial planning and policy supports for the development of working–class capacities. Yet, the electoral system has responded before: in cases of sudden devastating crises like the Great Depression and in long crises like the modernization of the ex-Confederate States. Similarly, the long crisis of mounting exposure to international economic competition is leading to political pressures that are rearranging alliances and transforming interests. The future outcome of these contemporary pressures is not determined. There is no guarantee that the actual future will be "functionally compatible" with the democratic freedoms we claim to cherish any more than were past responses.

Antinomies of Power

A paradox learned by liberals in the early decades of this century, but lost in the simplifications of post-New Deal politics is that cooperation and conflict go together. Productive cooperation requires symmetry of authority between workers and managers: only equals can freely make agreements and feel obligated to fulfill them. Inequality leads to domination, withdrawal of support, and the inefficiencies of mutual compulsion.[11] But even the New Dealers only went part way. This logic is reflected in those historically politically structured practices that sharply limit the extent and kind of participation employees can engage in. These are properly the objects of new reform debates.

Because New Deal industrial relations was procedurally oriented within a framework of preexisting management rights, initiative was politically and legally structured as an exclusive managerial prerogative. Although workers gained the right to organize and, in practice, managerial rule daily was violated informally, the basic inequality created disincentives to share knowledge because of distrust of the use of managerial authority. Similarly, the dilemma of labor leaders was structured by conflicting pressures to advance the immediate economic interests of the membership and to act responsibly within the rules maintained by government officials who managed the economy, whether well or poorly. If union leaders did not respond to rank– and–file demands, they risked their bargaining leverage, which depended on their ability to mobilize the ranks. At the same time, they had to gain member support for collectively bargained contracts to make agreements worthwhile for employers and political leaders.

Thus, when new conditions emerged in the 1970s, automobile workers reacted rationally—as they had been encouraged to do—and demanded inflation–protected wages, less work, and more controls on management discretion. Union officials perceived that such defensiveness was not sufficient if jobs were to be saved and societal equities protected. But, at the same time, the Keynesian policies of aggregate demand stimulation only seemed to price American products out of world markets and contribute to both inflation and unemployment; and the top UAW leadership encouraged local union participation in new managerial styles that encroached on collective bargaining. Although the UAW has continued to support a greater labor role in business planning and public policies that socialize the aggregate costs and benefits of industrial restructuring, it is not surprising that managers, and many Democrats, view unions as irrelevant and that membership opposition has appeared: after all, if collective bargaining to raise wages is harmful and unions forsake their contractually–based job rights in the plant, what is left for them to do?

In the broader society, authority was structured on the basis of political equality, although here, too, the rule was violated daily in practice. The chronic class–skew in electoral politics this century was modified by the creation of the industrial union movement. If not for the AFL-CIO, the Democratic party would not have had much popular organization. Without organized labor's capabilities and, later, those of civil–rights groups, feminists, and environmentalists, it would have been hard to get people to the polls. But, even then, turnouts were modest and have become more modest still. The American winner–take–all electoral system, with single–member districts and plurality elections, and the separation of powers in government, provide incentives for political leaders to muffle their messages and avoid responsibility for government performance. These conditions make it exceedingly difficult for most citizens to discover how the political system can serve their own interests. As popular organizations, such as unions, lose their membership bases and direct access to working–class voters, the situation becomes even more dire. Shortsighted and opportunistic candidates for office will adjust to the existing active electorate. The public policy reality is that the Democratic party has not supported popular economic policy to compete with the Republican alternative of increased managerial authority.[12] Workers who lose their jobs, whether from foreign competition, as a result of workplace reform, or anything else, face meager unemployment payouts, minimal and employer–dominated retraining programs, lost health insurance, part–time work, minimum wages and stagnation in job opportunities in traditional occupations.[13] The United States can be characterized as a low participation polity with the public policies and low–trust industrial relations to match.

The post-New Deal political conditions have so far tipped the balance of power even more toward managerialism. The dramatic reduction of union membership among private sector workers, to about 12 percent, has been accompanied by a massive mobilization of firms and industries in electoral politics. But the greater power of managers does not guarantee a workable solution to industrial problems. The historical record suggests that workers will reject a system that fails to be just as it purports to be efficient. "More democracy" seems part of the answer to how to ensure a sustainable economy. Yet under current conditions, the "more democracy" solution (i.e., more authority for workers and unions) seems to imply ratification of labor's defensive agenda. Hence, the managerialist alternative is to accept less democracy and more management control. Another is to establish new forms of politics that enable members of the community to participate in devising new settlements of labor–management and private–public boundaries of responsibility for investment and equity. The new politics implies not just "more," but a "different" democracy that admits an autonomous labor aspiration to shape the relationship of work to society.

Notes

AAD   Automobile and Accessories Division of the Employers' Association of Detroit.

ALHUA   Archives of Labor History and Urban Affairs, Walter P. Reuther Library, Wayne State University, Detroit, Michigan.

BW   *Business Week.*

CIO EB   Congress of Industrial Organizations executive board, Industrial Relations Collection, Littauer Library, Harvard University, Cambridge, Massachusetts.

CUA   The Catholic University of American Archives, Washington, D.C.

DHM   Discovery Hall Museum, South Bend, Indiana.

EAD   Employers' Association of Detroit, Historical Collection, American Society of Employers, Southfield, Michigan.

EN DD   Edwin Nourse daily diary, Nourse Papers, Harry S Truman Presidential Library, Independence, Missouri.

HFM   Henry Ford Museum, Dearborn, Michigan.

HST   Harry S Truman Presidential Library, Independence, Missouri.

IEB   International Executive Board of the United Auto Workers Union, Archives of Labor History and Urban Affairs, Walter P. Reuther Library, Wayne State University, Detroit, Michigan.

IR   Industrial Relations Collection, Littauer Library, Harvard University, Cambridge, Massachusetts.

IUD   American Federation of Labor-Congress of Industrial Organizations, Industrial Union Department, Archives of

Labor History and Urban Affairs, Walter P. Reuther Library, Wayne State University, Detroit, Michigan.

JFK   John F. Kennedy Presidential Library, Boston, Massachusetts.

LBJ   Lyndon B. Johnson Presidential Library, Austin, Texas.

NYT   The *New York Times*

OPM   Minutes of Office of Production Management meetings, National Archives, Washington, D.C.

SBT   *South Bend Tribune.*

SHSWA State Historical Society of Wisconsin Archives, Madison, Wisconsin.

TDE   *Tool, Die and Engineering News*, Industrial Relations Collection, Littauer Library, Harvard University, Cambridge, Massachusetts.

UAW FD United Auto Workers Ford Department, Archives of Labor History and Urban Affairs, Walter P. Reuther Library, Wayne State University, Detroit, Michigan.

UAW GM United Auto Workers General Motors Department, Archives of Labor History and Urban Affairs, Walter P. Reuther Library, Wayne State University, Detroit, Michigan.

UAW RD United Auto Workers Research Department Collection, Archives of Labor History and Urban Affairs, Walter P. Reuther Library, Wayne State University, Detroit, Michigan.

UAW ST United Auto Workers Skilled Trades Department Collection, Archives of Labor History and Urban Affairs, Walter P. Reuther Library, Wayne State University, Detroit, Michigan.

CHAPTER I

1. Influential social science studies in the 1960s began with a recapitulation of the standard model, e.g., Edward C. Banfield and James Q. Wilson, *City Politics* (Cambridge: Harvard University Press, 1963) and Robert Dahl, *Who Governs?* (New Haven: Yale University Press, 1964). The field of industrial relations was tied to the modernization framework through the InterUniversity Project, one of whose most influential studies was Clark Kerr, John T. Dunlop, Frederick Harbison, and Charles A. Myers, *Industrialism and Industrial Man: The Problems of Labor and Management in Economic Growth* (New York: Oxford University Press, 1964). Also see A. O. Hirschman, *Essays in Trespassing* (New York: Cambridge University Press, 1981); and Reinhard Bendix, *Work and Authority in Industry: Ideologies of Management in the Course of Industrialization* (New York: John Wiley, 1956).

2. Clark Kerr, *Labor Markets and Wage Determination* (Berkeley: University of California Press, 1977); Grant McConnell, *Private Power and American Democracy* (New York: Knopf, 1966); and Seymour Martin Lipset, *Union Democracy* (New York: Free Press, 1956).

3. Samuel P. Huntington, *Political Order in Changing Societies* (New Haven: Yale University Press, 1968), and Samuel P. Huntington, "The United States" in Michel Crozier, Samuel P. Huntington, and Joji Watanuki, *The Crisis of Democracy*, (New York: New York University Press, 1975), 59–118.

4. Walter Dean Burnham, "The Changing Shape of the American Political Universe" in Walter Dean Burnham, *The Current Crisis in American Politics* (New York: Oxford University Press, 1984), 25–57, and "Thoughts on the Governability Crisis in the West," *Washington Review of Strategic and International Studies* (1978); Theodore Lowi, *The End of Liberalism* (New York: Norton, 1969); J. Rogers Hollingsworth, "The United States," in *Crises of Political Development in Europe and the United States*, ed. Raymond Grew (Princeton: Princeton University Press, 1978); and William Nisbet Chambers and Walter Dean Burnham eds., *The American Party Systems: Stages of Political Development* (New York: Oxford University Press, 1975).

5. J. David Greenstone, *Labor in American Politics* (New York: Vintage, 1969).

6. Burnham, "Insulation and Responsiveness in Congressional Elections," in *The Current Crisis*; and Norman Nie et al., *The Changing American Voter* (Cambridge: Harvard University Press, 1976).

7. Burnham, "Theory and Voting Research," in *The Current Crisis*, 58–91; Philippe van Parijs, *Evolutionary Explanation in the Social Sciences* (Totowa, N.J.: Rowman and Littlefield, 1981); and Jon Elster, "Marxism, Functionalism and Game Theory: The Case for Methodological Individualism" in *Marxist Theory*, ed. Alex Callinicos (New York: Oxford University Press, 1989), 48–87.

8. Alfred D. Chandler, *Strategy and Structure* (Cambridge: MIT Press, 1962); and see Louis Galambos, "The Emerging Organizational Synthesis in American History," in *Men and Organizations: The American Economy in the Twentieth Century*, ed. Edwin J. Perkins (New York: Putnam's Sons, 1977), 3–15.

9. Lloyd Ulman, *The Rise of the National Trade Union* (Cambridge: Harvard University Press, 1955); Selig Perlman, *A Theory of the Labor Movement* (New York: MacMillan, 1928); John T. Dunlop, *Industrial Relations Systems* (Carbondale: Southern Illinois University Press, 1958); and David Brody, "The Emergence of Mass Production Unionism," in *Men and Organizations*, ed. Perkins, 58–85.

10. The tie between the standard model and the theory of democratic elitism has been noted many times. A good discussion is found in C. B. Macpherson, *The Life and Times of Liberal Democracy* (New York: Oxford University Press, 1977).

11. Steve Fraser, "Dress Rehearsal for the New Deal: Shop-Floor Insurgents, Political Elites and Industrial Democracy in the Amalgamated Clothing Workers," in *Working-Class America: Essays on Labor, Community and American Society,* ed. Michael H. Frisch and Daniel J. Walkowitz (Urbana: University of Illinois Press, 1983), 212–255; David Montgomery, *The Fall of the House of Labor: The Workplace, the State and American Labor Activism, 1865–1925* (New York: Cambridge University Press, 1987); Ellis W. Hawley, "Herbert Hoover, the Commerce Secretariat and the Vision of an Associative State, 1921–1928," in *Men and Organizations,* ed. Perkins, 131–148; and Philip Scranton, "Diversity in Diversity: Flexible Production and American Industrialization, 1880–1930," *Business History Review* 65 (Spring 1991): 27–90.

12. Mancur Olson, *The Rise and Decline of Nations: Economic Growth, Stagflation and Social Rigidities* (New Haven: Yale University Press, 1982).

13. E.g., Ronald Dore, *Flexible Rigidities: Industrial Policy and Structural Adjustment in the Japanese Economy, 1970–1980* (Stanford: Stanford University Press, 1986); Peter Hall, *Governing the Economy* (New York: Oxford University Press, 1986), 234–242f; and Paul Osterman, *Employment Futures: Reorganization, Dislocation and Public Policy* (New York: Oxford University Press, 1988), 108–134.

14. David Truman, *The Governmental Process* (New York: Knopf, 1971); and Nelson Polsby, *Community Power and Political Theory* (New Haven: Yale University Press, 1963).

15. See John Zysman and Laura Tyson eds., *American Industry in International Competition* (Ithaca: Cornell University Press, 1983), 23–32.

16. Peter Friedlander, *The Emergence of a UAW Local, 1936–1939: A Study in Class and Culture* (Pittsburgh: University of Pittsburgh Press, 1975); John Bodnar, "Immigration, Kinship and the Rise of Working Class Realism in Industrial America," *Journal of Social History* 14, no. 1 (Fall 1980): 56–58f; and Kristi Andersen, *The Creation of a Democratic Majority* (Chicago: University of Chicago Press, 1979).

17. Cf. Lawrence Mishel and David M. Frankel, *The State of Working America, 1990–1991* (Armonk, N.Y.: M. E. Sharpe, 1991).

18. Everett Carl Ladd and Charles Hadley, *Transformations of the American Party System* (New York: Norton, 1975).

19. Kevin Phillips, *The Emerging Republican Majority* (New York: Arlington House, 1969); Richard M. Scammon and Ben Wattenberg, *The Real Majority* (New York: Coward-McCann, 1971); and Kevin Phillips, *Mediacracy* (Garden City: Doubleday, 1975) introduction.

20. E.g., Edward Carmines and James Stimson, "The Dynamics of Issue Evolution: The United States," in *Electoral Change in Advanced Industrial Democracies,* ed. Russell Dalton, Scott Flanagan, and Paul Allen Beck (Princeton: Princeton University Press, 1984), 137, who admit that "we do not know . . . which particular mechanisms produce equilibrium" in the party system, but "we assume" that one "exists."

21. Seymour Martin Lipset ed., *Emerging Coalitions in American Politics* (San Francisco: Institute for Contemporary Studies, 1978); William Crotty and Gary Jacobson, *American Parties in Decline* (Boston: Little, Brown, 1980); and Everett Carl Ladd and Charles Hadley, *Political Parties and Political Issues* (Beverly Hills: Sage, 1973).

22. Lipset, *Emerging Coalitions*, 23.

23. Michael Goldfield, *The Decline of Organized Labor in the United States* (Chicago: University of Chicago Press, 1987).

24. Cf. Theda Skocpol, "Political Response to Capitalist Crisis: Neo-Marxist Theories of the State and the Case of the New Deal," *Politics and Society* 10 no. 2 (1980): 155–201.

25. Thomas Ferguson, "From Normalcy to New Deal: Industrial Structure, Party Competition and American Public Policy in the Great Depression," *International Organization* 38 (Winter 1985): 41–94.

26. Fred Block, "Beyond Corporate Liberalism," *Social Problems* 24 (1977): 352–361.

27. Claus Offe, "Competitive Party Democracy and the Keynesian Welfare State" in *Contradictions of the Welfare State*, ed. Claus Offe (Cambridge, Mass.: MIT Press, 1984); and James O'Connor, *The Fiscal Crisis of the State* (New York: St. Martin's Press, 1973).

28. Rhonda F. Levine, *Class Struggle and the New Deal: Industrial Labor, Industrial Capital and the State* (Lawrence: University of Kansas Press, 1988), 5, 13–15.

29. Jill Quadagno, *The Transformation of Old Age Security: Class and Politics in the American Welfare State* (Chicago: University of Chicago Press, 1988).

30. Alain Lipietz, *Mirages and Miracles: The Crises of Global Fordism* (London: Verso, 1987), 14.

31. Lipietz, *Mirage and Miracles*, 35; and cf. Montgomery, *Fall of the House of Labor.*

32. Samuel Bowles and Herbert Gintis, "The Crisis of Liberal Democratic Capitalism: The Case of the United States," *Politics and Society* 11, no. 1 (1982): 65–66; and David M. Gordon, Richard Edwards, and Michael Reich, *Segmented Work, Divided Workers* (New York: Cambridge University Press, 1982).

33. Arthur MacEwan and William Tabb, *Instability and Change in the World Economy* (New York: Monthly Review Press, 1989); Mike Parker and Jane Slaughter, *Choosing Sides: Unions and the Team Concept* (Boston: South End Press, 1988); Knuth Dohse, Ulrich Jurgens and Thomas Malsch, "From Fordism to Toyotism? The Social Organization of the Labor Process in the Japanese Automobile Industry," *Politics and Society* 14, no. 2 (1985): 115–146; cf. Paul Hirst and Jonathan Zeitlin, "Flexible Specialization versus Post-Fordism: Theory, Evidence and Policy Implications" in *Economy and Society* 20, no. 1 (1991): 1–56; and Charles F. Sabel, "Moebius-Strip Organizations and Open Labor Markets: Some Consequences of the Reintegration of Conception and Execution in a Volatile Economy," in *Social Theory for a Changing Society* ed. James Coleman and Pierre Bourdieu (Boulder, Co.: Westview Press, 1991).

34. Peter B. Evans, Dietrich Rueschemeyer, and Theda Skocpol eds., *Bringing the State Back In* (New York: Cambridge University Press, 1985); Margaret Weir, Ann Shola Orloff, and Theda Skocpol eds., *The Politics of Social Policy in the United States* (Princeton: Princeton University Press, 1988); and Hall, *Governing the Economy.*

35. Theda Skocpol, "Political Response to Capitalist Crisis"; and Kenneth Finegold and Theda Skocpol, "State, Party and Industry: From Business Recovery to the Wagner Act in America's New Deal," in *Statemaking and Social Movements: Essays in History and Theory*, ed. Charles C. Bright and Susan F. Harding (Ann Arbor: University of Michigan Press, 1984).

36. Weir et al., *Politics of Social Policy*, 23; and see the exchange between Theda Skocpol, Kenneth Finegold and Michael Goldfield, "Explaining New Deal

Labor Policy," *American Political Science Review* 84, no. 4 (December 1990): 1297–1315.

37. These types are similar to those employed by Michael Piore and Charles Sabel, *The Second Industrial Divide* (New York: Basic Books, 1984), namely flexible specialization and Fordism.

38. Lowi, *End of Liberalism*; Derek C. Bok and John T. Dunlop, *Labor and the American Community* (New York: Simon and Schuster, 1970); and Robert Collins, *The Business Response to Keynes* (New York: Columbia University Press, 1981), 39.

39. Arthur L. Stinchcombe, *Theoretical Methods in Social History* (New York: Academic Press, 1978), 40.

40. Roberto Mangabeira Unger, *Social Theory: Its Situation and Its Task* (New York: Cambridge University Press, 1987). See Unger, *Social Theory.*

CHAPTER 2

1. Doug Ross, "Enterprise Economics on the Front Lines: Empowering Firms and Workers to Win," in *Mandate for Change*, ed. Will Marshall and Martin Schram (New York: Berkeley Books/Progressive Policy Institute, 1993), 51–80; Barry Bluestone and Irving Bluestone, *Negotiating the Future* (New York: Basic Books, 1992); Robert L. Kuttner, "Labor Policy: The Case for a New Social Contract," in *Changing America: Blueprints for the New Administration*, ed. Mark Green (New York: Newmarket Press, 1992), 154–169; Lawrence Mishel and Paula B. Voos, eds., *Unions and Economic Competitiveness* (Armonk, N.Y.: M.E. Sharpe, 1992); and Ruth Milkman, *Japan's California Factories: Labor Relations and Economic Globalization* (Institute of Industrial Relations, UCLA, 1991).

2. Cf. Elinor Ostrom, *Governing the Commons: The Evolution of Institutions of Collective Action* (Cambridge, Eng.: Cambridge University Press, 1990); and Alan Fox, *Beyond Contract* (London: Faber and Faber, 1974).

3. Daniel Nelson, *Managers and Workers: Origins of the New Factory System in the United States, 1880–1920* (Madison: University of Wisconsin Press, 1975), 81–88, 196 notes 4, 8.

4. Cf., Stanley Aronowitz, *False Promises: The Shaping of American Working Class Consciousness* (New York: McGraw Hill, 1973); David Gordon, Richard Edwards, and Michael Reich, *Segmented Work, Divided Workers* (New York: Cambridge University Press, 1982); and Stuart Brandes, *American Welfare Capitalism* (Chicago: University of Chicago Press, 1976).

5. David Noble, *Forces of Production: A Social History of Industrial Automation* (New York: Oxford University Press, 1986); and David Montgomery, *The Fall of the House of Labor: The Workplace, the State, and American Labor Activism, 1865–1925* (Cambridge: Cambridge University Press, 1987). Cf. Philip Scranton, "Diversity in Diversity: Flexible Production and American Industrialization, 1880–1930," *Business History Review* 65 (Spring 1991): 27–90; and Gerald Berk, "Constituting Corporations and Markets: Railroads in Gilded Age Politics," *Studies in American Political Development* 4 (1990): 130–168.

6. Richard Franklin Bensel, *Sectionalism and American Political Development, 1880–1980* (Madison: University of Wisconsin Press, 1984); David Montgomery, *Workers' Control in America: Studies in the History of Work, Technology and Labor Struggles* (Cambridge, Eng.: Cambridge University Press, 1979), 48–55; Bayrd Still, *Milwau-*

kee: The History of a City (Madison: State Historical Society of Wisconsin, 1965), 321f, 337–339, 371, 453, 476, 486, appendix table 1; Howard Chudacoff, *The Evolution of American Urban Society* (Englewood Cliffs, N.J.: Prentice-Hall, 1975), 91; and Gerd Korman, *Industrialization, Immigrants and Americanizers: The View from Milwaukee, 1866–1921* (Madison: State Historical Society of Wisconsin, 1967), 78–79.

7. Edward R. Kantowicz, "Carter H. Harrison II: The Politics of Balance," in *The Mayors: The Chicago Political Tradition*, ed. Paul M. Green and Melvin G. Holli (Carbondale: Southern Illinois University Press, 1987), 17; Olivier Zunz, *The Changing Face of Inequality: Urbanization, Industrial Development and Immigrants in Detroit, 1880–1920* (Chicago: University of Chicago Press, 1982), 19, table 1.3; and Montgomery, *Workers' Control in America*, p. 57.

8. U.S. Census Bureau, *Fifteenth Census of the United States: 1930 Population* (Washington, D.C.: U.S. GPO, 1931) vol. 4, table 2; Zunz, *Changing Face of Inequality*, 19, 200, 292–293. Raymond R. Fragnoli, *The Transformation of Reform: Progressivism in Detroit—and After, 1912–1933* (New York: Garland Publishing, 1982), 133, 155 table 2; and Joyce Shaw Peterson, *American Automobile Workers, 1900-1933* (Albany: State University of New York Press, 1987), 16.

9. Martin J. Sklar, *The Corporate Reconstruction of American Capitalism, 1890–1916: The Market, the Law and Politics* (New York: Cambridge University Press, 1988), 20–21, 24.

10. Montgomery, *Fall of the House of Labor*, 183, 185–186, 192; Leon Fink, *Workingmen's Democracy: The Knights of Labor and American Politics* (Urbana: University of Illinois Press, 1983); Christopher L. Tomlins, *The State and the Unions: Labor Relations, Law and the Organized Labor Movement in America, 1880–1950* (New York: Cambridge University Press, 1985), 60–61f; and Victoria Hattam, "Economic Visions and Political Strategies: American Labor and the State, 1865–1896," *Studies in American Political Development* 4 (1990): 82–129.

11. Montgomery, *Fall of the House of Labor*, 206–207; Harless D. Wagoner, *The U.S. Machine Tool Industry, 1900–1950* (Cambridge, Mass.: MIT Press, 1966); and Gary Herrigel, "Industrial Order in the Machine Tool Industry: A Comparison of the United States and Germany" (Paper in the author's possession, 1989).

12. Montgomery, *Fall of the House of Labor*, 206, 210, 234, 247.

13. Wagoner, *U.S. Machine Tool Industry*, 22; Nelson, *Manager and Workers*, chapter five; Sanford Jacoby, *Employing Bureaucracy: Managers, Unions and the Transformation of Work in American Industry, 1900–1945* (New York: Columbia University Press, 1985), 88–90f; Steve Babson, "Pointing the Way: Skilled Workers and Anglo-Gaelic Immigrants in the Rise of the UAW" (Ph.D. diss., Wayne State University, 1989); and Gary Stewardson, "The Relationship between the Changing Technology and the Training of Machinists and Tool and Die Makers in the United States Machine Tool Industry: 1880–1980" (Ph.D. diss., University of Maryland, 1987).

14. Montgomery, *Fall of the House of Labor*, 259f, 266; Tomlins, *State and the Unions*, 70, 76–77; and Richard Jules Oestreicher, *Solidarity and Fragmentation: Working People and Class Consciousness in Detroit, 1875–1900* (Urbana: Illinois University Press, 1986), 241–242.

15. Montgomery, *Fall of the House of Labor*, 261f; and James Weinstein, *The Corporate Ideal in the Liberal State, 1900–1918* (Boston: Beacon Press, 1968).

16. Cf. Stephen Skowronek, *Building A New American State* (New York: Cambridge University Press, 1982); and William E. Forbath, *Law and the Shaping of the American Labor Movement* (Cambridge, Mass.: Harvard University Press, 1991).

17. Paul Kleppner, *The Third Electoral System, 1853–1892: Parties, Voters and*

Political Cultures (Chapel Hill: University of North Carolina Press, 1979); Walter Dean Burnham, "The Politics of Heterogeneity" in *Electoral Behavior: A Comparative Handbook*, ed. Richard Rose (New York: Free Press, 1973).

18.   Still, *Milwaukee*, chapter 14 and 296–300, 307, 311.

19.   Kantowicz, "Carter H. Harrison II," 17, 19, 21–22.

20.   Melvin G. Holli, *Reform in Detroit: Hazen S. Pingree and Urban Politics* (New York: Oxford University Press, 1969), 13, 15–16; Fragnolli, *Transformation of Reform*, 12–15; and Kleppner, *Third Electoral System*, 194f.

21.   "Place, Value and Importance of the Employment Bureau as a Necessary Activity in Association Work" (typescript, September 21, 1926); EAD Coll.; cf. Thomas Klug, "Employers' Strategies in the Detroit Labor Market, 1900–1929," in *On the Line: Essays in the History of Auto Work*, ed. Nelson Lichtenstein and Stephen Meyer (Urbana: University of Illinois Press, 1989); and Allan Nevins and Frank Hill, *Ford: The Times, the Man, The Company* (New York: Scribner's, 1954), 377–378, 514.

22.   Joyce Peterson, *American Automobile Workers*, 13, 95, 104–105; and cf. Don Leschoier, *The Labor Market* (New York: MacMillan, 1919).

23.   "Place, Value and Importance of the Employment Bureau as a Necessary Activity in Association Work," EAD Coll.; Stephen Meyer III, *The Five Dollar Day: Labor Management and Social Control in the Ford Motor Company, 1908–1921* (Albany: State University Press of New York, 1981), 72, 77–78.

24.   EAD minutes (February 21, 1905, February 19, 1907, February 22, 1910, and April 18, 1911); Paul H. Douglas, "American Apprenticeship and Industrial Education," *Studies in History, Economics and Public Law*, 95, no. 2 (1921): 320–324; Automobile and Accessory Division (AAD) of the Employers' Association of Detroit minutes (June 19, 1911), 4; and Detroit Trade School *Journal*, EAD Coll.

25.   R. B. Weaver, vice-president of the Timken-Detroit Axle Company, AAD minutes (January 3, 1911), 3.

26.   AAD minutes (January 3, 1911), 7f, (June 5, 1911), 12, and (June 11, 1911), 3–4.

27.   Fragnolli, *Transformation of Reform*, 16–28, 34, 38, 68, 73, 128f; Zunz, *Changing Face of Inequality*, 204–206; Melvin G. Holli, "Urban Reform in the Progressive Era," in *The Progressive Era* ed. Lewis Gould (Syracuse, N.Y.: Syracuse University Press, 1974), 138, 151; and Sidney Fine, *Frank Murphy: The Detroit Years* (Ann Arbor: University of Michigan Press, 1975), 31, 91–93.

28.   EAD minutes (April 18, 1911 and September 12, 1911).

29.   AAD minutes (June 5, 1911), 7; and EAD minutes (January 16, 1912, 10–15.

30.   David Noble, *America by Design: Science, Technology and the Rise of Corporate Capitalism* (New York: Oxford University Press, 1979), 300–302, 308–310; Arthur G. Wirth, *Education and the Technological Society: The Vocational-Liberal Studies Controversy in the Early Twentieth Century* (Scranton, Penn.: Intext Educational Publishers, 1972). Raymond E. Callahan, *Education and the Cult of Efficiency* (Chicago: University of Chicago Press, 1962).

31.   AAD minutes (July 17, 1911), 5f; EAD minutes (September 12, 1911), 8–9; *Histories of the Public Schools of Detroit* (Detroit: Board of Education of the City of Detroit, 1967) vol. 3, pp. 1380–1381, 1626–1627; Arthur B. Moehlman, *Public Education in Detroit* (Bloomington: Public School Publishing Co., 1925), 161–162, 216–218, 228–230. The EAD took credit for getting Detroit public schools to adopt

vocational education, but they were disappointed with the results, EAD minutes (February 18, 1913).

32. Matthew Woll, president of the Allied Printing Trades and spokesman for the AFL on training, speech to the National Society for the Promotion of Industrial Education, *Proceedings of the 10th Annual Meeting* (February 22–24, 1917), 69.

33. Holli, *Reform in Detroit*, 226 note 39; Zunz, *Changing Face of Inequality*, 111, 225–226; Melvin G. Holli and Peter d'A. Jones eds., *Biographical Dictionary of American Mayors, 1820–1980* (Westport, Conn.: Greenwood Press, 1981); Oestreicher, *Solidarity and Fragmentation*, 233–237; and Babson, "Pointing the Way," 117–118, 136f.

34. Fragnolli, *Transformation of Reform*, 13–15, 115, 133–134; Zunz, *Changing the Face of Inequality*, 107, 323; and Fine, *Frank Murphy*, 32f, 79–81.

35. Roger Keeran, *The Communist Party and the Auto Worker Unions* (Bloomington: Indiana University Press, 1980), 32–34; Joyce Peterson, *American Automobile Workers*, 112–114; Howell Harris, "The Snares of Liberalism? Politicians, Bureaucrats, and the Shaping of Federal Labour Relations Policy in the United States, ca. 1915–1947" in *Shop Floor Bargaining and the State: Historical and Comparative Perspectives*, ed. Steven Tolliday and Jonathan Zeitlin (Cambridge, Eng.: Cambridge University Press, 1985), 157.

36. Henry Ford Trade School Coll., boxes 1, 3, HFM.

37. Meyer, *Five Dollar Day*; Ottalie Leland, *Master of Precision: Henry M. Leland* (Detroit: Wayne State University Press, 1966); and Alfred P. Sloan, Jr., *My Years With General Motors* (Garden City: Doubleday, 1963).

38. Fragnolli, *Transformation of Reform*, 53, 62–63, 67, 71–72, 74, 83, 101–129, 138–140, 154, 166; and Holli, "Urban Reform," in *Progressive Era*, ed. Gould, 151. Election results from the *Detroit News*, various dates.

39. Zunz, *Changing Face of Inequality*, 313; Klug, "Employers' Strategies," in *On the Lines*, ed. Lichtenstein and Meyer; Joyce Peterson, *American Automobile Workers*, 18–22.

40. Joyce Peterson, *American Automobile Workers*, 59–70; and Brandes, *American Welfare Capitalism*.

41. Montgomery, *Workers' Control in America*, pp. 57-59. Robert Max Jackson, *The Formation of Craft Labor Markets* (New York: Academic Press, 1984), 256f.

42. Robert Ozanne, *A Century of Labor-Management Relations at McCormick and International Harvester* (Madison: University of Wisconsin Press, 1967), 52–70f.

43. *Chicago Daily Tribune*, November 9, 1904, p. 1; all election statistics are from the *Tribune*, various dates.

44. John D. Buenker, "Edward F. Dunne: The Limits of Municipal Reform," in *Mayors*, ed. Green and Holli, 34–35, 36, 48, 228 note 42.

45. Ibid. 42–45; Paul M. Green, "Anton J. Cermak: The Man and His Machine," and Maureen A. Flanagan, "Fred A. Busse: A Silent Mayor in Turbulent Times," in *Mayors*, ed. Green and Holli, 99–110, 54–55.

46. Maureen A. Flanagan, *Charter Reform in Chicago* (Carbondale: Southern Illinois University Press, 1987), 77–83, 103–104, 128–130.

47. Buenker, "Edward F. Dunne," and Flanagan, "Frederick A. Busse," in *Mayors*, ed. Green and Holli, 42, 47–49, 57–58; Julia Wrigley, *Class Politics and Public Schools: Chicago 1900–1950* (New Brunswick, N.J.: Rutgers University Press, 1982), 105–107; and cf. Paul Peterson, *The Politics of School Reform, 1870–1940* (Chicago: University of Chicago, 1985).

48. Douglas Bukowski, "Big Bill Thompson: The Model Politician," in *Mayors*, ed. Green and Holli, pp. 62–63, 66–68f.
49. Ibid., 63–64, 68; and Steven Fraser, *Labor Will Rule: Sidney Hillman and the Rise of American Labor* (New York: Free Press, 1991), 64f.
50. Wrigley, *Class Politics*, 50–54, 60–69, 78–83f.
51. Woll speech, *Proceedings*, 69.
52. Illinois State Federation of Labor, *Weekly Newsletter* (May 8, 1915), quoted in Wrigley, *Class Politics*, 86; and Eugene Staley, *History of the Illinois State Federation of Labor* (Chicago: University of Chicago Press, 1930), 527–531.
53. Wrigley, *Class Politics*, 83; and cf. Ira Katznelson and Margaret Weir, *Schooling for All: Class, Race and the Decline of the Democratic Ideal* (New York: Basic Books, 1985), 152–155, 159–160.
54. Wrigley, *Class Politics*, 139f; Staley, *History*, 361f; and cf. Paul Peterson, *Politics of School Reform*, 141f.
55. Staley, *History*, 364–384; and Melvyn Dubofsky, "Abortive Reform: The Wilson Administration and Organized Labor, 1913–1920" in *Work, Community and Power: The Experience of Labor in Europe and America, 1900–1925*, ed. James E. Cronin and Carmen Siriani (Philadelphia: Temple University Press, 1983), 197–220.
56. Staley, *History*, James Weinstein, *The Decline of Socialism in America, 1912–1925* (New Brunswick, N.J.: Rutgers University Press, 1984 ed.), 222–224; Tomlins, *State and the Unions*, 76; and Harris, "Snares of Liberalism," in *Shop Floor Bargaining*, ed. Tolliday and Zeitlin, 157.
57. David Brody, *Labor in Crisis: The Steel Strike of 1919* (Urbana: University of Illinois Press, 1987 ed.); Melvin I. Urofsky, *Big Steel and the Wilson Administration* (Columbus: Ohio State University Press, 1969), 284–291, 324–333; David Brody, *Steelworkers in America: The Nonunion Era* (New York: Harper, 1960), 275; Korman, *Industrialization*, 152, 162f; and Ozanne, *Century of Labor-Management Relations*, 111–114; and Joyce Peterson, *American Automobile Workers*, 60.
58. Still, *Milwaukee*, appendix; election statistics from the *Milwaukee Journal*, various dates.
59. Korman, *Industrialization*, 53.
60. Ibid., 51 note 22; Still, *Milwaukee*, 301, 304; and W. J. Fairbairn, "History of Wisconsin Apprenticeship Ancient and Modern" (typescript, c. 1923), Industrial Commission Papers, Apprenticeship Division, Administrative Files, SHSWA.
61. John H. M. Laslett, *Labor and the Left: A Study of Socialist and Radical Influences in the American Labor Movement, 1881–1924* (New York: Basic Books, 1970), 15–21.
62. Still, *Milwaukee*, 307. At the Social Democrat's 1900 city convention, 67 of the 147 delegates were union representatives.
63. Ibid., 310, 524–525.
64. Ibid., 315–316, 468, 521; Korman, *Industrialization*, 50; and Sally Miller, *Victor Berger and the Promise of Constructive Socialism, 1910–1920* (Westport, Conn.: Greenwood Press, 1973), pp. 69–74.
65. Still, *Milwaukee*, 516–519; and Daniel W. Hoan, *City Government: The Record of the Milwaukee Experiment* (Westport, Conn.: Greenwood Press, 1974).
66. Still, *Milwaukee*, 520–521, 522 note 4 where the *Milwaukee Journal* says the reform is anti-Socialist. The Socialists called the reform antiworker.
67. Ibid.
68. Stewart Scrimshaw, "A Personal Encounter with the Twentieth Century

Development of Industrial Relations" (typescript, 1968), SHSWA. Scrimshaw was the first state supervisor of apprenticeship.

69. George Hambrecht, "The Part-Time School Movement in Wisconsin," Hambrecht Papers, box 1, SHSWA; Stewart Scrimshaw, *Apprenticeship: Principles, Relationships, Teachers* (New York: McGraw-Hill, 1932), 189, 199.

70. Industrial Commission (IC) Apprenticeship Division, Administrative File: Apprenticeship Papers, 1917–1948. Initially the State-Wide Advisory Committee had 26 members, 13 from each group, and included major employers like Allis Chalmers and Kearney and Trecker—which provided the chair, the Milwaukee Metal Trades and Founders Association and the socialist leader of the Milwaukee Federated Trades Council, Frank Weber, who later became the president of the Wisconsin Federation of Labor. The later, smaller committee still included the employers' group, but not the Trades Council. Fairbairn, SHSWA. Cf. G. Soundara Rajan, *A Study of the Registered Apprenticeship Program in Wisconsin* (Madison: Industrial Relations Research Institute, University of Wisconsin, 1966), 23.

71. There were approximately 87,000 total journeymen, which works out to about 7:1 overall, although ratios were set by trade. IC Apprenticeship Division Administrative Files: Apprenticeship Papers, 1911–1916, SHSWA.

72. Ibid,; Scrimshaw typescript, chapter 5, 7–8; Rajan, *Registered Apprenticeship*, 42; and Scrimshaw, *Apprenticeship*, 207.

73. Ibid., 211; and Scrimshaw typescript, chapter 5, 14.

74. Ibid., chapter 3.

75. Scrimshaw, *Apprenticeship*, 186–187f; "Apprenticeship at Allis-Chalmers Co.," *The Wisconsin Apprentice* 7, no. 4 (April 1924), 1; Harold S. Falk, "The District Apprenticeship System," *The Wisconsin Apprentice* 9, no. 6 (October 1926), pp. 1, 3–4. Falk was the owner of a participating company in Milwaukee.

76. IC Apprenticeship Division Administrative Files: Apprenticeship Papers, 1911–1916, SHSWA; and Falk, "The District Apprenticeship System," 3.

77. IC Apprenticeship Division Administrative Files: Apprenticeship Papers, 1917–1948, SHSWA; *The Wisconsin Apprentice* 9, no. 3 (March 1926): 1. *The Wisconsin Apprentice* 12, no. 4 (April 1929): 1. Scrimshaw *Apprenticeship*, 212–213. Almost exactly 20% of the apprentices in 1929 were female according to the Board of Vocational, Technical and Adult Education, Director's File, 1917–, box 9, SHSWA. Harry Millis and Royal Montgomery, *Organized Labor* (New York: McGraw-Hill, 1945), 439–441.

78. Charles McCarthy, "The Social Influence of Continuation Schools" (speech, 1915); and Charles McCarthy, "Some By-Products of Industrial Education," *LaFollette's Weekly*, February 11, 1911, Charles McCarthy book file, McCarthy Papers, box 21, SHSWA.

79. Scrimshaw typescript, chapters 3–5; Scrimshaw, *Apprenticeship*, 189, 199, 201–202, 204-05; and George Hambrecht, "Charles McCarthy and His Relation to Education in Wisconsin," Hambrecht papers, box 1, SHSWA.

80. Korman, *Industrialization*, 168–9f, 174–182.

81. Stephen Meyer, "Technology and the Workplace: Skilled and Production Workers at Allis-Chalmers, 1900–1941," *Technology and Culture* 29, no. 4 (October 1988): 839–864.

82. Fraser, *Labor Will Rule*, Melvin Dubofsky and Warren Van Tine, *John L. Lewis* (New York: Quadrangle, 1977); and Tomlins, *The State and the Unions*, 79f.

83. Joyce Peterson, *American Automobile Workers*, passim.

84. Ibid. 102.
85. Babson, "Pointing the Way," passim.

CHAPTER 3

1.   David Brody, "The Rise and Decline of Welfare Capitalism" in *Workers in Industrial America: Essays on the Twentieth Century Struggle* (New York: Oxford University Press, 1980), 48–81; Joyce Shaw Peterson, *American Automobile Workers, 1900–1933* (Albany: State University of New York Press, 1987). 87–88; and Steve Babson, "Pointing the Way: Skilled Workers and Anglo-Gaelic Immigrants in the Rise of the UAW" (Ph.D. diss., Wayne State University, 1989).

2.   Emma Rothschild, *Paradise Lost: The Decline of the Auto Industrial Age* (New York: Random House, 1973); Ed Cray, *Chrome Colossus: General Motors and Its Times* (New York: McGraw Hill, 1980), 202f; Gerard Colby, *Du Pont Dynasty: Behind the Nylon Curtain* (Secaucus, N.Y.: Lyle Stuart, 1984); Alfred P. Sloan, Jr., *My Years with General Motors* (Garden City: Doubleday, 1963). The leading smaller auto companies expanded their share of the market throughout most of the 1920s even as GM, Ford and Chrysler expanded their combined share. Joyce Peterson, table 1-3; William J. Abernathy, *The Productivity Dilemma: Roadblock to Innovation in the Automobile Industry* (Baltimore: Johns Hopkins University Press, 1978); and Sidney Fine, *The Automobile under the Blue Eagle* (Ann Arbor: University of Michigan Press, 1964), 7.

3.   Cf. Lizabeth Cohen, *Making a New Deal: Industrial Workers in Chicago, 1919–1939* (New York: Cambridge University Press, 1991). E. E. Schattschneider, *Politics, Pressure and the Tariff* (New York: Prentice-Hall, 1935); Thomas Ferguson, "From Normalcy to New Deal: Industrial Structure, Party Competition, and American Public Policy in the Great Depression," *International Organization* 38, no. 1 (Winter 1984): 41–94; and Ellis W. Hawley, "Herbert Hoover, the Commerce Secretariat, and the Vision of an Associative State, 1921–1928," *Journal of American History* 61 (June 1974).

4.   Fine, *Automobile under the Blue Eagle*, 17–18, 115, 123.

5.   Stanley Aronowitz, *False Promises: The Shaping of American Working Class Consciousness* (New York: McGraw Hill, 1973), 174; and Benson Soffer, "A Theory of Trade Union Development: The Role of the Autonomous Worker," *Labor History* 1, no. 2 (Spring 1980): 151.

6.   Daniel Nelson, *American Rubber Workers and Organized Labor, 1900–1941* (Princeton: Princeton University Press, 1988), 143–150.

7.   Harry Dahlheimer, *A History of the Mechanics Educational Society of America in Detroit from the Inception in 1933 through 1937* (Detroit: Wayne State University Press, 1951), 28.

8.   Babson, "Pointing the Way," table 4, 167.

9.   Ibid., 396, 441.

10.   Roger Keeran, *The Communist Party and the Auto Worker Unions* (New York: International Publishers, 1986), 104, 106; and Mike Davis, *Prisoners of the American Dream* (London: Verso, 1986), 57–58.

11.   John A. Hobson, *Rationalization and Unemployment* (London: Allen and Unwin, 1930). American Progressive era reformer William F. Ogburn popularized

the concept of a "cultural lag" behind the development of the means of production. See Richard Pells, *Radical Visions and American Dreams* (Middletown, Conn.: Wesleyan University Press, 1973).

12. Cf. Kenneth Finegold and Theda Skocpol, "State, Party and Industry: From Business Recovery to the Wagner Act in America's New Deal" in *Statemaking and Social Movements: Essays in History and Theory*, ed. Charles C. Bright and Susan F. Harding (Ann Arbor: University of Michigan Press, 1984).

13. Fine, *Automobiles under the Blue Eagle*, 45–46; and Irving Bernstein, *The New Deal Collective Bargaining Policy* (Berkeley: University of California Press, 1950) 29f.

14. Fine, *Automobiles under the Blue Eagle*, 114–118, 127–139, 173, 185, 220–255, 386–399.

15. In December 1934, Leon Henderson held government hearings on the auto industry and, in January, recommended regularization of work schedules, guaranteed annual wages, unemployment insurance and hours regulation. Ibid., 350–363.

16. Ibid., 169; Keeran, *Communist Party*, 103; and Irving Bernstein, *Turbulent Years* (Boston: Houghton, Mifflin, 1969).

17. Christopher L. Tomlins, *The State and the Unions: Labor Relations, Law, and the Organized Labor Movement in America, 1880–1950* (New York: Cambridge University Press, 1985), 111.

18. Ibid., 113–115; and Peter Irons, *The New Deal Lawyers* (Princeton: Princeton University Press, 1982), 211–213.

19. *United States v. Weirton Steel Corp.*, 10 F. Supp. 55, 86–90 (District of Delaware 1935) discussed in ibid., 219–220.

20. Walter Galenson, *Rival Unionism in the United States* (New York: Russell and Russell, 1966).

21. Babson, "Pointing the Way"; and Steve Jefferys, *Management and Managed: Fifty Years of Crisis at Chrysler* (New York: Cambridge University Press, 1986), 63–67.

22. Eileen Boris and Nelson Lichtenstein, eds., *Major Problems in the History of American Workers* (Lexington, Mass.: D.C. Heath, 1991), 415.

23. William E. Leuchtenburg, *Franklin D. Roosevelt and the New Deal, 1932–1940* (New York: Harper, 1963), 104–105; and Marion Clawson, *New Deal Planning: The National Resources Planning Board* (Baltimore: Resources for the Future, Johns Hopkins University Press, 1981), 46.

24. Arthur M. Schlesinger, Jr., *The Coming of the New Deal* (Boston: Houghton Mifflin, 1958), 471, 486; and cf. Ferguson, "From Normalcy to New Deal," who discusses defections from the Liberty League to Roosevelt in 1936.

25. Sidney Fine, *Frank Murphy: The New Deal Years* (Chicago: University of Chicago, 1975) and *Sit-Down: The General Motors Strike of 1936–1937* (Ann Arbor: University of Michigan Press, 1969).

26. Morris Llewellyn Cooke and Philip Murray, *Organized Labor and Production: New Steps in Industrial Democracy* (New York: Harper and Brothers, 1941; reprint by Arno Press, 1971), 86–88, 188, 212–221, 242–246.

27. UAW GM Supplementary Agreement, April 12, 1938, re grievance procedure, GM Dept. Coll., box 1; Irving Howe and B.J. Widick, *The UAW and Walter Reuther* (New York: Random House, 1949); George Heliker, "Grievance

Arbitration in the Automobile Industry" (Ph.D. diss., University of Chicago, 1954); and John Brophy, *A Miner's Life* (Madison: University of Wisconsin Press, 1964), 272–273.

28. Report of the Committee on the Unauthorized Strike Clause, IEB minutes (June 17, 1937). Throughout 1937 and 1938, the IEB wrangled over the union's policy on production slowdowns and wildcat strikes and the union's 1937 acceptance of mutual responsibility with the company for them. According to the company, mutual responsibility was supposed to mean that the union either would discipline the union members or the company would suspend or cancel the contract. The IEB did not believe they could win member support for such a policy and argued that the company should instruct its plant supervisors to cooperate with employees and resolve grievances. IEB minutes (August 30–September 13, 1937), 5–7; also see IEB minutes (November 21, 1937 and January 12–23, 1938) where both main factions agree to more controls on wildcat strikes; IEB minutes (May 9–24, 1938), 65 where many locals protest IEB agreements with GM that the members have not ratified. For details on plant agreements and moves to standardize job control methods, see "Agreements, 1937–41" and "Minutes of a Conference—Fisher Body, August 20–22, 1938," Walter P. Reuther Coll., box 18. Still trying to impose discipline, the IEB agreed to temporary layoffs of wildcatters. IEB minutes (December 4–9, 1939).

29. Cf. Charles F. Sabel, "The Internal Politics of Trade Unions" in *Organizing Interests in Western Europe: Pluralism, Corporatism, and the Transformation of Politics*, ed. Suzanne Berger (New York: Cambridge University Press, 1981), 209–244.

30. Jack Skeels, "The Development of Political Stability within the United Auto Workers Union" (Ph.D. diss., University of Wisconsin, 1957); Martin Halpern, *UAW Politics in the Cold War Era* (Albany: State University of New York Press, 1988), 18, 23; Ray Boryczka, "Militancy and Factionalism in the United Auto Workers Union, 1937–1941," *Maryland Historian* 8 (Fall 1977); and Patrick Renshaw, "Organized Labour and the Keynesian Revolution" in *Nothing Else to Fear*, ed. Stephen W. Baskerville and Ralph Willett (Manchester: Manchester University Press, 1985), 229.

31. Babson, "Pointing the Way," 605.

32. John Barnard, "Rebirth of the United Automobile Workers: The General Motors Tool and Diemakers' Strike of 1939," *Labor History* 27 (Spring 1986); and author interview with Leonard Woodcock, December 10, 1982.

33. Melvyn Dubofsky and Warren Van Tine, *John L. Lewis* (New York: Quadrangle, 1977), 312–315; and Bernstein, *Turbulent Years*, 474–490.

34. D. O. Bowman, *Public Control of Labor Relations* (New York: MacMillan, 1944), 415f; Christopher L. Tomlins, *State and the Unions*, 158f; and cf. Karl Klare, "Judicial Deradicalization of the Wagner Act and the Origins of Modern Legal Consciousness, 1937–1941," 62 *Minnesota Law Review*: 265.

35. Ellis Hawley, *The New Deal and the Problem of Monopoly* (Princeton: Princeton University Press, 1966), 383–412; Cray, *Chrome Colossus*, 310–311, 345; Sloan, *My Years*, 201, 241; and Colby, *Du Pont Dynasty*, 354, 356, 358f.

36. Theodore Rosenof, *Patterns of Political Economy in America: The Failure to Develop a Democratic Left Synthesis, 1933–1950* (New York: Garland, 1983), 55, 93–95, 97, 100.

37. Sidney Hillman, *Production Problems* (CIO pamphlet, 1938), 1, quoted by Renshaw, "Organized Labour and the Keynesian Revolution," 230.

38. Cooke and Murray, *Organized Labor*; Philip Murray, "Industry Council Plan," July 7, 1941, CUA; Clinton Golden and Harold Ruttenberg, *The Dynamics of Industrial Democracy* (New York: Harper, 1942); Clint Golden, "New Patterns of Democracy," *The Antioch Review* 3, no. 2 (September 1943); "The Auto Industry After the War," Ford Dept. Coll., box 1; and P. Alston Waring and Clint Golden, *Soil and Steel* (New York: Harper, 1946).

39. GM Dept. Coll., box 1; Jack Steiber, *The Steel Industry Wage Structure: A Study of the Joint Union-Management Job Evaluation Program in the Basic Steel Industry* (Cambridge, Mass.: Harvard University Press, 1959); and Robert MacDonald, *Collective Bargaining in the Automobile Industry* (New Haven: Yale University Press, 1963).

40. A.D.H. Kaplan, *The Guarantee of Annual Wages* (Washington, D.C.: The Brookings Institution, 1947).

41. William Gomberg letter to Walter Reuther, May 7, 1943. Reuther Coll., box 9, ALHUA.

42. Howe and Widick, *UAW and Walter Reuther*, 20–28; Joyce Shaw Peterson, "Autoworkers and Their Work, 1900–1933," *Labor History* 22, no. 2 (Spring 1981); Allan Nevins and Frank Hill, *Ford: The Times, the Man, the Company* (New York: Scribners, 1954), and *Ford: Expansion and Challenge, 1915–1933* (New York: Scribners, 1957).

43. Sidney Fine, "The G.M. Sitdown Strike," *American Historical Review* 70, no. 3 (April 1965); and MacDonald, *Collective Bargaining*, 329–355.

44. Hawley, "Herbert Hoover"; and Rosenof, *Patterns of Political Economy.*

45. Donald R. McCoy, "The National Progressives of America, 1938," *Mississippi Valley Historical Review* 44 (June 1957): 76, quoted by Davis, *Prisoners of the American Dream*, 67.

46. James Patterson, *Congressional Conservatism and the New Deal* (Lexington: University of Kentucky Press, 1967). Leuchtenburg, *Franklin D. Roosevelt and the New Deal*, 252.

47. Dubofsky and Van Tine, *John L. Lewis*, 333; and Bruce Catton, *The War Lords of Washington* (New York: Harcourt, Brace and World, 1948), 58–59.

48. Dubofsky and Van Tine, 330–341, argue that Lewis's split with Roosevelt rested mostly on foreign policy disagreements. Maurice Isserman, *Which Side Were You On: The American Communist Party during the Second World War* (Middletown, Conn: Wesleyan University Press, 1982).

49. "1939–40," Reuther Coll., box 579, ALHUA; and *New York Times* (hereafter *NYT*), October 25, 29, 30, 1941.

50. Fred L. Block, *The Origins of International Economic Disorder* (Berkeley: University of California Press, 1977) chapter 3 ; cf. Irving Richter testimony for the UAW, "Trade Agreement Act of 1945," House Committee on Ways and Means, April 27, 1945, in "Foreign Trade 1945," UAW RD, box 13, ALHUA, which tied free trade to the IMF and the Charter for Industrial Peace (discussed in chapter 4).

51. Walter P. Reuther, "500 Planes a Day," in *Walter Reuther: Selected Papers*, ed. Henry M. Christman (New York: Macmillan, 1961), 1–12; see David Brody, "The New Deal and World War II," in *The New Deal: the National Level*, ed. John Braeman, Robert H. Bremner, and David Brody (Columbus: Ohio State University Press, 1975), 267–309; Victor Reuther, *The Brothers Reuther* (Boston: Houghton Mifflin, 1976); Steve Fraser, "Dress Rehearsal for the New Deal: Shop Floor Insurgents, Political Elites and Industrial Democracy in the Amalgamated Cloth-

ing Workers," in *Working Class America*, ed. Michael H. Frisch and Daniel J. Walkowitz (Urbana: University of Illinois Press, 1983), 212–255; and Matthew Josephson, *Sidney Hillman: Statesman of American Labor* (New York: Doubleday, 1952).

52. "Industrial Council Plan," John Brophy Papers, CUA; CIO convention proceedings (Cleveland, 1949; New York City, 1951; Atlantic City, 1952, pp. 311–314).

53. Douglas P. Seaton, *Catholics and Radicals: The Association of Catholic Trade Unionists and the American Labor Movement from Depression to Cold War* (Lewisburg, Penn.: Bucknell University Press, 1981); cf. Mark Starr, "Organized Labor and the Dewey Philosophy," in *John Dewey: Philosopher of Science and Freedom*, ed. Sidney Hook (New York: Barnes and Noble, 1967); Bernard Sternsher, *Rexford Tugwell and the New Deal* (New Brunswick, N.J.: Rutgers University Press, 1964); and Brophy, *A Miner's Life*, 81, 127, 150, 164, 299f notes that his support for coal nationalization arose from practical experience and socialist ideas. It was not until years later that he, though a serious Catholic, discovered Papal teaching on capitalism and corporatism.

54. Joel Seidman, *American Labor from Defense to Reconversion* (Chicago: University of Chicago Press, 1953); David Brody, "The New Deal and World War II," in *The New Deal*, ed. Braeman, Bremner, and Brody, 281–286; George Taylor, *Government Regulation of Industrial Relations* (New York: Prentice-Hall, 1948); and Victor Reuther, "Labor in the War—and After," *The Antioch Review* 3. no. 3 (Fall 1943).

55. Nelson Lichtenstein, *Labor's War at Home: The CIO in World War II* (New York: Cambridge University Press, 1982). Philip Murray was very critical of Hillman for not gaining for labor "executive responsible representation in the field of industry and in the field of government," "Address by President Philip Murray on the Industry Council Plan" (July 7, 1941), p. 4, Brophy Papers. CUA.

56. Catton, *War Lords of Washington*, 105; Josephson, *Sidney Hillman*; and *Industrial Mobilization for War: History of the War Production Board and Predecessor Agencies 1940–1945* (Washington, D.C.: GPO, 1947) vol. 1, 203–236.

57. OPM minutes, April 29, 1941, Record Group 179, National Archives, Washington, D.C.

58. "There was apprehension in some quarters that the Drive" to establish joint labor-management plant committees "might serve as a wedge for labor to enter the management of industry," War Production Board minutes, June 8, 1943, Record Group 179, National Archives, Washington, D.C.

59. UAW RD, box 12. Lichtenstein, *Labor's War*, 178–207.

60. George Heliker, "Grievance Arbitration," 96f.

61. CIO convention proceedings, November 20–24, 1944, 208–209; Josephson, *Sidney Hillman*, 637; Joseph Gaer, *The First Round* (New York: Duell, Sloan and Pearce, 1944); James Foster, *The Union Politic: The C.I.O. Political Action Committee* (Columbia: University of Missouri Press, 1975), 61; and Fay Calkins, *The CIO and the Democratic Party* (Chicago: University of Chicago Press, 1952).

62. Walter P. Reuther, "The Challenge of Peace," *International Postwar Problems* 2, no. 2 (April 1945); *Mill and Factory* (May 1944); and "The Freedom from Fear of Abundance: A Fifth Freedom for Postwar America," *The Progressive* 8 no. 25 (June 19, 1944).

63. Victor Reuther, "The Next Fifty Years," *Detroit* (June 1945), quoted in Frederick Harbison, "The UAW-General Motors Agreement of 1950," *Journal of Political Economy* 58 (1950): 404.

64.   J. Raymond Walsh, *CIO: Industrial Unionism in Action* (New York: Norton, 1937), 229–247. Walsh became director of the CIO Education and Research Committee.

65.   Herbert Stein, *The Fiscal Revolution* (Chicago: University of Chicago Press, 1969), chapters 5–8.

66.   William Green, "A Real Department of Labor," *The American Federationist* (June 1946); and "An Analysis of the Factors in the Closing of the University of Michigan's Workers Education Program" (Research paper, School of Education, University of Michigan, 1956); *NYT*, November 28, 1947, p. 48; and Hearings on the Labor Education Extension Service, Subcommittee on Education of the Committee on Labor and Public Welfare, U.S. Senate, 80th, 2nd session, February 16-20, 1948, and Hearings on Labor Extension Act of 1949, Committee on Education and Labor, U.S. House of Representatives, 81st, 1st sess., July 26–28, 1949, pp. 61–70; see John Gibson Papers, box 9, HST. Gibson had been president of the Michigan CIO in 1943 and then became U.S. assistant secretary of labor from 1946 until 1950.

67.   Sloan, *My Years*, and "Post-War Jobs" address to the Economic Club of Detroit, October 11, 1943; and cf. Robert Collins, *The Business Response to Keynes* (New York: Columbia University Press, 1981).

68.   Eric Johnston, *America Unlimited* (New York: Doubleday, 1944); Alan R. Raucher, *Paul G. Hoffman: Architect of Foreign Aid* (Lexington: The University Press of Kentucky, 1985), 51–59; and "Committee for Economic Development," Record Group 82, box 2186, National Archives, Washington, D.C. Reuther attacked CED planning as assuming mass unemployment, Reuther, "Freedom from Fear of Abundance."

69.   Howell John Harris, *The Right to Manage: Industrial Relations Policies of American Business in the 1940s* (Madison: University of Wisconsin Press, 1982), chapter 4.

70.   Sloan, "Post-War Jobs." Robert Scoville, Chrysler's labor economist, called collective bargaining "an assault on liberty," Harris, *Right to Manage*, 111. A contemporaneous liberal study agreed that hierarchy was necessary: the coordination of mass production "necessitates centralized determination of production standards," "Automobiles" in *How Collective Bargaining Works*, ed. Harry A. Millis (New York: 20th Century Fund, 1942), 576.

71.   Wilson quoted by Harbison, "The UAW–General Motors Agreement," 402; and Frederick Harbison and Robert Dubin, *Patterns of Union-Management Relations* (Chicago: University of Chicago Press, 1947).

CHAPTER 4

1.   Walter Reuther, "The Challenge of Peace," *International Postwar Problems* 2, no. 2 (April 1945); Victor Reuther, *The Brothers Reuther* (Boston: Houghton Mifflin, 1976); and Frank Cormier and William Eaton, *Reuther* (Englewood Cliffs: Prentice-Hall, 1970).

2.   Seymour Harris ed., *Economic Reconstruction* (New York: McGraw Hill, 1945); Alvin Hansen, "Reconversion and Post-War Needs," in *Full Employment: Proceedings of the Conference on Full Employment* (New York: CIO PAC, 1944); Irving

Richter, "Detroit Plans for Chaos," *The Nation,* June 30, 1945, 719–721; and CIO EB minutes, July 13–14, 1945, 302–318.

3.   *NYT,* March 29, 1945; *The Daily Worker,* April 7, 1945; UAW RD, box 16. The Communist party in fact had recently disestablished itself to reflect a shift toward advocacy from vanguardism; see Maurice Isserman, *Which Side Were You On?* (Middletown, Conn.: Wesleyan University Press, 1982).

4.   IEB minutes, April 16–22, 1945, 90; Irving Howe and B. J. Widick, *The UAW and Walter Reuther* (New York: Random House, 1949), 107–108.

5.   "The Auto Industry after the War," UAW FD, box 1; and IEB minutes, April 16–22, 1945, 90–104.

6.   AFL executive council minutes, April 30–May 8, 1945, 81–89 and August 6–14, 1945, 132f, IR; Howell John Harris, *The Right to Manage* (Madison: University of Wisconsin Press, 1982), 110.

7.   CIO EB minutes, July 13–14, 1945, 52–75.

8.   Ibid., November 1–2, 1945, 17–30.

9.   Gibson papers, box 21, HST, Robert J. Donovan, *Conflict and Crisis: The Presidency of Harry S Truman, 1945–1948* (New York: Norton, 1977), 26–27, 29, 107.

10.   Craufurd Goodwin and Stanley Herren, "The Truman Administration: Problems and Policies Unfold," *Exhortation and Controls: The Search for a Wage-Price Policy, 1945–1971,* ed. Craufurd Goodwin (Washington, D.C.: The Brookings Institution, 1975), 9–94; and CIO EB minutes, November 1–2, 1945, 18–30, 41–54, 113.

11.   Gerhard Colm papers, box 1, HST. Alvin Hansen wrote to Colm from the Bretton Woods conference on July 11, 1944 to urge the Democrats to include full employment planning in their campaign platform.

12.   Hansen and Colm were both very impressed with the British White Paper, "Full Employment in a Free Society." It's "200 proof," said Colm, but needs "to be diluted to 180 for American stomachs." He began work on what he called the American "pink paper," downplaying permanent government spending and emphasizing "business expansion" and that social programs were good "on the merits," memo from Colm to Weldon Jones (Budget Bureau) August 11, 1944, Colm Papers, box 1, HST. Full employment planning included policies across a wide spectrum: public employment, money supply, national debt, banking, security markets, industrial relations, wages, prices, regional development, mining, public health, taxes, income distribution and education. Bertram Gross (Interagency task force on the Employment bill) memo to Colm, February 24, 1945, Colm Papers, box 1, HST.

13.   Philip Murray testimony before the Senate Subcommittee on Banking and Currency, re: S. 380, August 22, 1945, 6–7, 15–16; and UAW Washington office, Donald Montgomery Coll., box 42, ALHUA.

14.   Ibid.; Frank Bender of the CIO addressed the Maryland delegation and urged adoption of the industry council plan. Truman Official File 170, HST.

15.   Stephen Kemp Bailey, *Congress Makes a Law* (New York: Vintage, 1950) observes that labor's low profile reflected disinterest. Some unionists purposefully adopted a low profile to help the legislation pass, Morris L. Cooke to Gerhard Colm (October 28, 1944). Colm papers, box 1, HST.

16.   Frank Pierson, "The Employment Act of 1946" in *Labor in Postwar America,* ed. Colston Warne (New York: Remsen Press, 1949); and Gerhard Colm memo to Weldon Jones, December 17, 1945, Colm papers, box 1, HST.

17.   Taylor, *Government Regulation,* 208–232; Montgomery Coll., box 23, ALHUA; and CIO EB minutes, November 1–2, 1945, 103–105.

18.   Howell Harris, *Right to Manage*, 114–118. "President's Labor Management Conference," David Stowe papers, box 1, HST.

19.   Leon Keyserling oral history, p. 75, discusses Truman's unsophisticated ideas and eventual development into a policy liberal, HST.

20.   Wilson quoted in *Cincinnati Times-Star*, December 5, 1946, cited in Kathyrine Groehn El-Messidi, "Sure Principles Midst Uncertainties: The Story of the 1948 GM–UAW Contract" (Ph.D. diss. University of Oklahoma, 1976), 40; *Monthly Labor Review* (January 1946): 86, April 1946: 537–542, and December 1946: 876–878.

21.   Howe and Widick, *UAW and Walter Reuther*, 136–148.

22.   Murray testimony op. cit.; and *The New Republic*, December 31, 1945 and *The Nation*, December 1, 1945 in Theodore Rosenof, *Patterns of Political Economy in America* (New York: Garland, 1983), 178.

23.   Reuther Coll., box 580, ALHUA; and Cormier and Eaton, *Reuther*, 229.

24.   John Snyder oral history, 232–239, 282-8, HST; and Chester Bowles, *Promises to Keep: My Years in Public Life* (New York: Harper, 1971).

25.   Goodwin and Herren, "Truman Administration"; and IEB minutes, October 18–20, 1946, 18.

26.   Melvyn Dubofsky and Warren Van Tine, *John L. Lewis: A Biography* (New York: Quadrangle, 1977), 454–462.

27.   Dwight Macdonald, *Politics Past* (New York: Viking, 1957, 189.

28.   Dubofsky and Van Tine, *John L. Lewis*. The government offered the coal operators a choice of a welfare fund based on tonnage or payroll. It also made the miners contribute to the hospitalization fund to check further demands, Gibson Papers, box 5, HST.

29.   Chrysler workers over age 65 were dismissed by Chrysler in the spring 1946. This provoked protests and the UAW executive board resolved to seek a company-paid pension, IEB minutes, April 16–26, 1946; and cf. IEB minutes, August 5–18, 1946. Alton Lee, *Truman and Taft-Hartley: A Question of Mandate* (Lexington: University of Kentucky Press, 1966).

30.   Ibid., 179.

31.   UAW letter to all CIO unions, June 7, 1946, CIO Departments, Philip Murray Papers, CUA.

32.   Allan Matusow, *Farm Policies and Politics in the Truman Years* (Cambridge, Mass.: Harvard University Press, 1967); Bowles, *Promises to Keep*; Barton Bernstein, "Clash of Interests: The Postwar Battle Between the Office of Price Administration and the Department of Agriculture," *Agriculture History* 41, no. 1 (January 1967); and Bert Cochran, *Harry Truman and the Crisis Presidency* (New York: Funk and Wagnalls, 1973).

33.   Max Kampelman, *The Communist Party vs. the CIO* (New York: Arno, 1957); Richard O. Boyer and Herbert M. Morais, *Labor's Untold Story* (New York: Cameron Associates/UE, 1955); and Martin Halpern, *UAW Politics in the Cold War Era* (Albany: State University of New York Press, 1988).

34.   Howell Harris, *Right to Manage*, 98–99. Recall the views of Sloan and the 20th Century Fund study cited in chapter 3.

35.   Reuther testimony before the Senate Committee on Labor and Public Welfare, February 21, 1947, UAW FD, box 2; UAW RD, boxes 24, 25, 57; and cf. Steve Jeffreys, *Management and Managed: Fifty Years of Crisis at Chrysler* (New York: Cambridge University Press, 1986).

36.   IEB minutes, August 5–18, 1946, 45–52, 198–204.

37. Ibid., 50.

38. Ibid., October 18–20, 1946, December 9–18, 1946, 60; "Full Auto Production Meeting 1946," Reuther Coll., box 100. ALHUA. Packard and Nash were willing to meet independently.

39. IEB minutes, June 4–5, 1946, August 5–18, 1946, 204–205, October 18–22, and December 9–18, 1946; and Halpern, *UAW Politics*, 188.

40. Donovan, *Conflict and Crisis*, 227, 243–245.

41. Selig Harrison, "The Political Program of the United Automobile Workers" (honors thesis, Harvard University, 1948), 125f; and Cormier and Eaton, *Reuther*, 243–244.

42. "Are We Moving toward a Government Controlled Economy?" (radio broadcast May 30, 1946) versus "Press Release from the National Foundry Conference" (December 7, 1946), Reuther Coll., box 582, ALHUA; and cf. *Ammunition* (UAW Education Department paper) September 1946 and Walter Reuther, "Our Social Setup Lags Behind Our Technological Progress," *Labor and Nation* (January–February 1947).

43. The American Political Science Association, *The Reorganization of Congress* (Washington, D.C.: Public Press, 1945). Joint Committee on the Organization of Congress, report pursuant to House resolution 18, 79th Congress, 2nd sess., report no. 1011, March 4, 1946; Robert Heller, *Strengthening the Congress* (Washington, D.C.: The National Planning Association, 1945); and cf. James Sundquist, *The Decline and Resurgence of Congress* (Washington, D.C.: The Brookings Institution, 1981), 179–189.

44. Marriner Eccles, Federal Reserve chairman, memo to Clark Clifford, November 27, 1946, Clifford papers, box 3, HST.

45. CIO EB minutes October 8, 10, 17, 1947, 246.

46. Ray Marshall, *Labor in the South* (Cambridge, Mass.: Harvard University Press, 1967).

47. Alston Waring and Clint Golden, *Soil and Steel* (New York: Harper, 1946); "The New Studebaker is Nice, But Have You Seen the Local? Rochdale Cooperation in South Bend in Creating Farmer-Labor Unity," UAW Education Department pamphlet #126; and UAW President's Quarterly Report, April 1948, IR.

48. Alonzo Hamby, *Beyond the New Deal* (New York: Columbia University Press, 1973), 154–155.

49. Donald F. Crosby, S.J., "The Politics of Religion: American Catholics and the Anti-Communist Impulse," in *The Specter: Original Essays on the Cold War and the Origins of McCarthyism*, ed. Robert Griffith and Athan Theoharis (New York 1974), cited by Donovan, *Conflict and Crisis*, 234; and Bert Cochran, *Labor and Communism: The Conflict That Shaped American Unions* (Princeton: Princeton University Press, 1977, 244f.

50. CIO EB minutes, May 16–17, 1947, 307–314f; and Irving Howe, *A Margin of Hope* (New York: Harcourt, Brace, Jovanovich, 1982), 83, 116.

51. Memorandum on Political Policy from John Brophy to Philip Murray, June 21, 1948, Brophy papers, CUA; and Hamby, *Beyond the New Deal*, 160f. Dubinsky (ILGWU), of course, was AFL and did not leave the ADA.

52. "The CIO National Wage Policy for 1947," December 1946, CIO report to the CEA, December 12, 1946, CIO secretary-treasurer Coll., box 68, ALHUA.

53. IEB minutes, October 18–20, 1946, 20, 39, April 22–28, 1947; and CIO EB minutes, May 16–17, 1947.

54. The guaranteed wage proposal was put aside until the president's Commission on Annual Wages, headed by Murray Latimore, could report, but then the CIO found it had to strenuously lobby Truman to keep the commission from dissolving without reporting in December, IEB minutes, December 9–18, 1946, 13; A.D.H. Kaplan, *The Guarantee of Annual Wages* (Washington, D.C.: The Brookings Institution, 1947); "Project on Annual Wage Study, 1947," Colm papers, box 1, HST; and Solomon Barkin, "Labor-Government Cooperation as Basis of Sound Price Policy," *Labor and Nation* (May–June 1947), 11f; EN DD 1946-5; Nourse letter to Murray, November 26, 1946, Nourse letter to Rieve, August 18, 1946, Bertram Gross (now assistant to Nourse) memo to Nourse, re: meeting with CIO Full Employment Committee (FEC) March 6, 1947, T. K. Hitch to CEA, re: meeting with CIO FEC, June 30, 1947, and CIO FEC letter to Nourse, September 26, 1947, Nourse papers, microfilm box 3, HST; and CIO EB minutes, May 16–17, 1946, 45–55.

55. Alvin Hansen, *Economic Policy and Full Employment* (New York: McGraw Hill, 1947).

56. "Report of the Committee on Economic Stability," May 15, 1947, Chester Bowles was the chairman; other members were Lauchlin Currie, William Davis, John Kenneth Galbraith, Richard Gilbert, David Ginsburg, Seymour Harris, Leon Henderson, Robert Nathan, Paul Porter, and Joseph Rauh.

57. ED DD 1946-5, 1946-7, 1946-9, and 1947-10.

58. "Political File—Confidential Memo to the President," 21–22, Clifford papers, box 21, HST.

59. "Labor Policy and Program," December 1946, Clifford memo to the president, Oscar Ewing papers, box 45, HST.

60. Keyserling oral history, 56–70. The other members of the group, said Keyserling, were Oscar Ewing, Charles Murphy (assistant counsel), Charles Brannan, David Morse, Girard Davidson (assistant secretary of the Interior), Donald Kingsley, and J. Howard McGrath; cf. Hamby, *Beyond the New Deal*, 191.

61. Clark Kerr, "Employer Policies in Industrial Relations 1945–1947" in *Labor in Postwar America*, ed. Warne, 55f; Harris, *Right to Manage*, 119–120; "The Facts versus the Nathan Report," NAM pamphlet no. 14, 1947, George Baker Library, Graduate School of Business Administration, Harvard University, Cambridge, Mass.; Sumner Slichter, "When Are Wages Too Low? When Are Profits Too High? An Answer to the Nathan Report" (New York: Bank of New York, 1947); and *Business Week* (hereafter, *BW*), November 30, 1946, 104.

62. Harry Millis and Emily Clark Brown, *From the Wagner Act to Taft-Hartley* (Chicago: University of Chicago Press, 1950) chapter 10; and CED, "Collective Bargaining: How to Make it More Effective," James Webb papers, box 18, HST.

63. Lee, *Truman and Taft-Hartley*, 67, 71; Gael Sullivan memo to Clark Clifford, June 14, 1947, Clifford papers, box 7, HST; Snyder oral history, p. 573, HST; and Donovon, *Conflict and Crisis*, 302.

64. Untitled memorandum, March 6, 1947, Mr. Murray's Confidential Memos, 1–2, Murray papers, CUA.

65. Millis and Brown, *From the Wagner Act*.

66. AFL executive council minutes, April 21–25, 1947, 34f, 77; and CIO EB minutes, October 7, 1947, 235–236.

67. William Andrew, "Factionalism and Anti-Communism: Ford Local 600," *Labor History* 20, no. 2 (Spring 1970): 238. In 1948 the USW amended its constitution

to forbid "any" member from "any action which constitutes a break of any collective bargaining contract," Lloyd Ulman, *The Government of the Steel Workers Union* (New York: John Wiley, 1962), 52.

68. The "legalization" of industrial relations demoralized those like Joseph Scanlon, Harold Ruttenberg, and Clinton Golden who wanted labor-management cooperation based on facts. Golden quit his post at the USW in 1946 and began planning for a series of studies sponsored by the National Planning Association on the "causes of industrial peace," Thomas R. Brooks, *Clint: A Biography of a Labor Intellectual* (New York: Atheneum, 1978), 225–236.

69. James Foster, *Union Politic: The C.I.O. Political Action Committee* (Columbia: University of Missouri Press, 1975), 109–110; and CIO EB minutes, October 8, 1947 and January 22–23, 1948.

70. IEB minutes, March 17–26, 1947, 16f.

71. Howell Harris, *Right to Manage*, 152; and Ronald Schatz, *The Electrical Workers* (Urbana: University of Illinois Press, 1982), 155, 159.

72. IEB minutes, April 22–28, 1947, 14–16, 60–61, 136–37.

73. Ibid., March 17–26 and June 2, 1947; and Allan Nevins and Frank Hill, *Ford: Decline and Rebirth, 1933–1962* (New York: Arno Press, 1976), 305–340.

74. IEB minutes, August 2, 1947, 7f, 33-39.

75. "Contract Correspondence 1947," UAW FD, box 1.

76. Roger Keeran, *The Communist Party and the Auto Worker Unions* (Bloomington: Indiana University Press, 1980), 278–280; and letter to all local unions from Walter Reuther, February 13, 1947, Emil Mazey Coll., box 5, ALHUA.

77. "Two Timing Catholics," *The Catholic War Veteran* (April 1947).

78. *Tool, Die and Engineering News* (hereafter, *TDE*) 11, no. 6 (August 1947): 2, IR.

79. IEB minutes, March 17, 1947 and March 1–5, 1948, 69; Reuther letter to Murray, April 7, 1947, to implement agreement to coordinate CIO action to "handle skilled trades problems," "United Auto Workers," Murray papers, CUA.

80. IEB minutes, April 22–24, 1947; contrast with Halpern, *UAW Politics*, 202.

81. Llewelyn quoted in the IEB minutes, August 2, 1947, 175.

82. Ibid., July 9, August 2, and September 22–24, 1947; *Ammunition*, UAW Education Department paper, July 1947; Mazey Coll., box 54, ALHUA. Reuther and the CIO right wing successfully defeated R. J. Thomas' reelection as CIO vice-president in October, *NYT*, October 12, 1947. New Reuther allies on the IEB included socialists Leonard Woodcock, Emil Mazey, and Martin Gerber, and Association of Catholic Trade Unionists activists Joe McCusker and Pat Greathouse.

83. The non-CP certificates may have applied to officers, but they effectively deprived union members of some of the leaders they had elected, CIO EB minutes, October 8–17, 1947, 60–63.

84. Ibid., January 22–23, 1948, 25–28; and IEB minutes March 1–5, 1948, 32f.

85. "Statement on Political Policy," Brophy papers, CUA.

86. Ibid., 4–5; and cf. Henry Brandon, "A Conversation with Walter Reuther," in *Labor and American Politics*, ed. Charles M. Rehmus and Doris B. McLaughlin (Ann Arbor: University of Michigan Press, 1967), 440–445.

87. IEB minutes, March 17, 1947; and Thomas Patterson, "The Quest for Peace and Prosperity: International Trade, Communism and the Marshall Plan," in *Politics and Policies of the Truman Administration*, ed. Barton Bernstein (Chicago: Quadrangle, 1970), 81–90.

88.   CIO convention proceedings, 1947, 260–262, IR.

89.   Ibid., 274–290; and Reuther speech in Reuther Coll., box 583, IR. Reuther rejoined the ADA in 1948.

90.   Frank Emspak, "The Breakup of the Congress of Industrial Organizations, 1945–1950" (Ph.D. diss., University of Wisconsin, 1972), 213f. Later, experience with the ERP, especially in Greece, led to critical labor reports, for example by Clint Golden, the labor liaison in Greece, and Paul Silver, a UAW representative in the ERP close to Reuther, IEB minutes, March 14–18, 1949, 801, 835, and April 24–28, 1950, 379–393.

91.   Ibid., March 1–5, 1948, 38, 43–48.

92.   Ibid., 420f, and November 29–December 2, 1948, 27f. Ousted from the Wayne County IUC were Tracy Doll (president), Sam Sage (secretary-treasurer), and Coleman Young (director of organization), Michigan CIO News Service press release, August 11, 1949, UAW RD, box 5; Emspak, "Breakup of Congress," 240–242; and Keeran, *Communist Party*, 285f; and Cormier and Eaton, *Reuther*, 252.

93.   Goodwin and Herren, "Truman Administration," 43–44, 47, 58–64; and Wilfred Lewis, Jr., *Federal Fiscal Policy in the Postwar Recessions* (Washington, D.C.: The Brookings Institution, 1962), 108–113.

94.   Truman press release, December 28, 1947, cited in EN DD, 1947-43.

95.   Confidential memo to the president re: the politics of 1948, November 19, 1947, Clifford papers, HST.

96.   National City Bank monthly letter on economic conditions, May 1948, EN DD 1948-12.

97.   Rufus Tucker, remarks reprinted in "An Appraisal of Official Economic Reports: An Evening with the Economists" (New York: Conference Board Studies in Business Economics, pamphlet, no. 16, April 1948), 10–12, copy in EN DD 1948-3. The economists' forum proceeded to have a long, sober discussion of how communistic the federal government had become.

98.   *BW*, May 22, 1948.

99.   Moreell letter to Nourse, May 10, 1948, EN DD 1948-14 and 1948-15.

100.   IEB minutes, April 24–28, 1950, 180.

101.   Ibid., March 1–5, 1948, 29–36f, 73f.

102.   Ibid., 33, 73; *Searchlight* (Local 659 paper), January 29, 1948, p. 6; and "Economic Objectives for 1948," UAW-CIO administrative letter, January 31, 1948, ALHUA.

103.   Nat Ganley (Communist Party whip in the UAW) in the *Michigan Herald*; Reuther Coll., box 101; and IEB minutes, June 7–10, 1948, 724–728.

104.   The UAW won the representation votes at Ford with a 92% turnout and 97.6% pro-UAW ballots (UAW FD, box 2) and at GM with a 87% turnout and 89% pro-UAW ballots (Harbison, "The UAW-General Motors Contract," 404).

105.   Wahley-Eaton Service (London), "American Letter," no. 1552, May 29, 1948, EN DD 1948-20; IEB minutes May 27–28, 1948, 8–11; and International Economic conference proceedings, February 2, 1949, 158, Reuther Coll., box 56, ALHUA.

106.   Alvin Hansen, "Wages and Prices: The Basic Issue," *NYT Magazine*, June 6, 1946, cited in Goodwin and Herren, "Truman Administration," 28.

107.   Only four locals voted against the GM contract. "Proceedings of the International Economic Conference," February 2, 1949, 155.

108.   IEB minutes, September 13–15, 1948, 339.

109.   Sloan, *My Years*, 395, 399–402; C. E. Wilson found opposition to AIF and

COLA from GM director George Whitney (J. P. Morgan partner) and the Du Ponts who did not want the formulas to be incorporated into national wage policy, El-Messidi, "Sure Principles," 91; Ford seemed to agree to the productivity bargain, see John Bugas speech of January 24, 1947 to the Mountain States Employers' Council, Inc., Montgomery Coll., box 70, ALHUA.

110.   IEB minutes, May 27–28, 1948, 58.

111.   Kermit Eby, director of the CIO Education and Research Department, letter to Murray, June 9, 1948, "CIO PAC," Murray papers, CUA.

112.   UAW press release, May 25, 1948, IR; Harbison, "The UAW–General Motors Contract," 399. Job control demands won included removal of the "gag" on union committeemen so they could act as advocates for workers to forestall otherwise automatic discipline and discharge (George Heliker, "Grievance Arbitration in the Automobile Industry," [Ph.D. diss., University of Chicago, 1954], 109), all grievance cases could be appealed to the umpire despite previous decisions in similar cases, and a dues check-off which, however, the UAW Chrysler negotiators did not favor, IEB minutes, March 1–5, 1948, 58–59.

113.   Minutes of the meeting of the CIO FEC with the CEA minutes, June 7, 1948, Reuther Coll., box 59, ALHUA; and CIO EB minutes, January 22–23, 1948.

114.   All three members of the CEA agreed in July that the third round policy failed, EN DD 1948-28.

115.   John Clark, "The Council, Business and Labor" (Unpublished manuscript), 19, J. M. Clark papers, box 3, HST.

116.   *BW*, May 29, 1948; and NE DD 1948–15 and 1948–28.

117.   Leon Keyserling, "Everybody's Problem: Prices, Wages, Profits" *Harper's Magazine*, March 1948. Keyserling and Nourse were facing off on their policy prescriptions, Keyserling memo to Nourse and CEA staff, May 26, 1948, noted in NE DD 1948-25, and Keyserling memo to Nourse, August 16, 1948, NE DD 1948–30b.

118.   John Dunlop, "A National Labor Policy," in *Saving American Capitalism: A Liberal Economic Program*, ed. Seymour Harris (New York: Knopf, 1948), 306–307; and cf. Sumner Slichter, "Wages, Prices and the People's Savings," *Proceedings of the Academy of Political Science* vol. 23 no. 1 (May 1948).

119.   Truman State of the Union Message, January 7, 1948; Goodwin and Herren, "Truman Administration," 46, 50; A. E. Holmans, *Fiscal Policy in the U.S. 1945–1959* (London: Oxford University Press, 1961), 58–64, 77, 80–94, 99; and IEB minutes March 1–5, 1948, 454–456.

120.   Goodwin and Herren, "Truman Administration," 55.

121.   Emil Rieve (CIO FEC) to all unions, August 16, 1948, "CIO PAC," Murray papers, CUA.

122.   Seymour Harris ed., *Saving American Capitalism: A Liberal Economic Program* (New York: Knopf, 1948).

123.   Joint Committee on the Economic Report, May 18, 1948, EN DD 1948-20.

124.   Donovan, *Conflict and Crisis*, chapters 41 and 43.

125.   CEA Annual Report, January 1949, 61–62; Charles S. Murphy oral history, 122, HST; Lewis, *Federal Fiscal Policy*, 119; and Holmans, *Fiscal Policy*, 105–107.

126.   IEB minutes, June 6–10, 1949, 48; EN DD 1949-29 and 1949-63; Holmans, *Fiscal Policy*, 118; Hamby, *Beyond the New Deal*, 331–332; and ADA Full Employment Conference report, July 19, 1949.

127. *Barron's*, April 1949, editorial.

128. Keyserling oral history, 187.

129. Jerry Sanders, *Peddlers of Crisis: The Committee on the Present Danger and the Politics of Containment* (Boston: South End Press, 1983), 28–29.

130. Holmans, *Fiscal Policy*, 116–117.

131. Leon Keyserling, "Prospects for American Economic Growth," speech to the Western Democratic Conference, San Francisco, September 18, 1949.

132. James E. Webb papers, box 18, HST; CEA annual report, December 1949; Lewis, *Federal Fiscal Policy*, 111, 113; and Bertram Gross and Wilfred Lumer, *The Hard Money Crusade* (Washington, D.C.: Public Affairs Press, 1954).

133. IEB minutes, March 14–18, 1949, 202.

134. *CIO Economic Outlook*, December 1948, CIO Convention Proceedings, November 1948, 56–57; IEB minutes, November 29–December 2, 1948, 171–182 and June 6–10, 1949, 48; and Harry Becker (director of the UAW Social Security Department), "Unions Move into Supplementary Security Programs Under Collective Bargaining," speech to the National Conference of Social Work, Cleveland, Ohio, June 15, 1949, IR.

135. "Report of the National Ford Department," November 1, 1949, UAW FD, box 2; and IEB minutes, September 13–15, 1948, 329, and April 28, 1949, 85–93. There were antispeedup strikes at a half-dozen other major plants as well, Howe and Widick, *UAW and Walter Reuther*, 182; and Richard Herding, *Job Control and Union Structure* (Rotterdam: Rotterdam University Press, 1972), 125. As a result of the strike, Ford committed itself to a constant line speed, notification of speed and production schedules, no requirement that workers make up production lost by management error, and recognition that body mix on the line could require extra manpower.

136. George Blackwood, "The United Auto Workers of America 1935–1951" (Ph.D. diss., University of Chicago, 1952); and *Counter-Action*, March 1949, Gibson papers, box 18, HST.

137. International Economic Conference Proceedings, February 19, 1949, Reuther Coll., box 56, .

138. Ibid.; and IEB minutes, January 10–11, 1949, 380 and March 14–18, 1949, 216–219.

139. Vincent Sweeney, *The United Steelworkers of America* (Pittsburgh: Pittsburgh University Press, 1956), 81–93.

140. Clare Hoffman, *Frame-Up in Steel* (New York: Constitutional Educational League, 1949).

141. Despite Ford's acceptance of a pension plan, they objected to fully vesting it. Bugas reportedly replied to the UAW Ford negotiators "I think your presentation . . . are (*sic*) definitely socialistic and I must say they follow the Karl Marx theory," "National Negotiating Bulletins," 1948, UAW FD, box 2.

142. *The United Automobile Worker*, October 1949, UAW RD, box 80.

143. Harbison, "The UAW–General Motors Agreement," 400–405; and "The Treaty of Detroit," *Fortune* 42, no. 1 (July 1950): 53. COLA and AIF were included in GM's contracts with the IEU (the anti-Communist successor to the UE) and in the UAW's contracts with Allis-Chalmers. Longer contract terms, pensions, and COLA formulas rapidly spread in the early 1950s in the major unionized industries. COLAs covered 3.5 million workers by 1953, and 15.2 million workers had pensions, Lloyd Ulman, "Unionism and Collective Bargaining in the Modern

Period" in *American Economic History*, ed. Seymour Harris (New York: McGraw-Hill, 1961), 437–444.

144. Steiber, *Steel Industry*; and Edwin Witte, "Industrial Relations in Meatpacking" in *Labor in Postwar*, ed. Warne; and Wayne Morse, "Brookings Institution 'Fixes Up' Facts to Anti-Labor Ends," *Labor and Nation* (May–June 1947): 14f.

145. William O. Douglas dissent in *NLRB v. Packard Motor Car Co.*, 330 U.S. 485 (1947).

146. Joseph Goulden, *Meany* (New York: Atheneum, 1972), 145.

147. E.g., the Steelworkers-Kaiser Long-Range Planning Committee was said to be an application of the industrial council plan idea, *Steel Labor*, May 1960, column by USW president David McDonald.

148. IEB minutes, June 6–10, 1949, 49–53f, and October 24–28, 1949, 126f; and Gerald Pomper, "Labor and Congress: The Repeal of Taft-Hartley," *Labor History* 2, no.3 (Fall 1961).

149. CIO Convention Proceedings, 1949, cited by Emspak, "Breakup of the Congress," 317–318. Truman sent a letter to the 1949 CIO convention supporting the breakup of the UE, Louis Keonig ed., *The Truman Administration: Its Principles and Practices* (New York: New York University Press, 1956), 248.

150. Hamby, *Beyond the New Deal*, 320f; American Political Science Association, "Toward a More Responsible Two Party System," *American Political Science Review* Supp. 44, no. 3, part 2 (September 1950), copy in Murphy papers, box 8, HST.

CHAPTER 5

1. Commission on the Skills of the American Workforce, *America's Choice: High Skills or Low Wages!* (Rochester: National Center on Education and the Economy, 1990); and Paul Hirst and Jonathan Zeitlin, eds., *Reversing Industrial Decline?* (Oxford, Eng.: Berg Publishers, 1989).

2. Michael Piore and Charles Sabel, *The Second Industrial Divide* (New York: Basic Books, 1984); and Michael Best, *The New Competition: Institutions of Industrial Restructuring* (Cambridge, Mass.: Harvard University Press, 1990).

3. William Abernathy, Kim Clark, and Alan Kantrow, *Industrial Renaissance* (New York: Basic Books, 1983) chapters 4–7; Harry C. Katz, *Shifting Gears: Changing Labor Relations in the U.S. Automobile Industry* (Cambridge: MIT Press, 1985), 82; and James P. Womack, Daniel T. Jones, and Daniel Roos, *The Machine That Changed the World* (New York: Rawson, 1990).

4. Mike Parker, *Inside the Circle: A Union Guide to QWL* (Boston: South End Press, 1985), 28–30, 107–11; Andy Banks and Jack Metzger, "Participating in Management: Organizing on a New Terrain," *Labor Research Review* 14 (Fall 1989): 1–55; and AFL-CIO, "Joint Labor-Management Training Boosts High-Skill, High-Wage Workplace," *Reviews of the Issues* 61 (1992).

5. Stanley Aronowitz, *False Promises: The Shaping of American Working Class Consciousness* (New York: McGraw-Hill, 1973), 148, 156f; Richard Edwards, *Contested Terrain: The Transformation of the Workplace in the Twentieth Century* (New York: Basic Books, 1979); and cf. Stephen Woods ed., *The Degradation of Work? Skill, Deskilling and the Labour Process* (London: Hutchinson, 1982).

6. Aronowitz, *False Promises*, 156–157.

7. Ibid., 176; also, Mike Davis, *Prisoners of the American Dream* (London: Verso, 1986), 94–95.

8. Aronowitz, *False Promises*, 176.

9. "Education and Training in the United States," *The Working Papers of the MIT Commission of Industrial Productivity*, vol. 2 (Cambridge: MIT Press, 1989).

10. Bennett Berger, *Working Class Suburb: A Study of Autoworkers in Suburbia* (Berkeley: University of California Press, 1960); and Gavin Makenzie, *The Aristocracy of Labor* (New York: Cambridge University Press, 1973).

11. Orrin Peppler Oral History, March 16, 1961, ALHUA; Author interviews with Walter Dorosh, October 14, 1982 and March 18, 1989, and Tom Pollard, August 3, 1983.

12. Emma Rothschild, *Paradise Lost: The Fall of the Auto Industrial Age* (New York: Random House, 1973).

13. Walter Franke and Irvin Sobel, *The Shortage of Skilled and Technical Workers* (Lexington, Mass.: Heath/Lexington Books, 1970) table 2–10.

14. William Patterson, "Wanted: Broader Training," *American Machinist*, October 9, 1935, 749. Patterson had been in charge of Milwaukee's trade education program.

15. Harry A. Millis and Royal E. Montgomery, *Organized Labor* (New York: McGraw Hill, 1945), 440–441; and "Apprentice Training: Detroit's Problem and Opportunity" (Detroit: Detroit Manufacturers' Committee on Apprentice Training, February 27, 1935), EAD.

16. Committee on Labor, "To Safeguard the Welfare of Apprentices," U.S. House of Representatives, 75th Cong., 1st sess., 1937.

17. Ibid., 77f.

18. Christopher Tomlins, *The State and the Unions* (New York: Cambridge University Press, 1985).

19. "Region 1, Local 155," UAW STD, box 1, and Harry Dahlheimer, *A History of the Mechanics Educational Society of America in Detroit from the Inception in 1933 through 1937* (Detroit: Wayne State University Press, 1951).

20. The War Manpower Commission created the Training Within Industry (TWI) service which managed upgrading. *First Annual Progress Report*, September 1941, claims that the program did not intend to "dilute" the trades; nonetheless, unions and employers competed to given either a labor or a management cast to the training, *Second Annual Report*, September 1942, box 2067; with General Motors starting its own company-run program and UAW Ford Local 600 refusing to cooperate with TWI, box 2114, War Manpower Commission Coll., series 261, National Archives, Washington, D.C.

21. "Minutes of the Meeting of Skilled Trades Council Officers," October 11, 1949, Ray Kay Coll., box 5, ALHUA.

22. Ibid.; and *TDE* (October 1949): 1, IR.

23. *TDE* (April 1948), 2; UAW STD, box 1; James Couser Oral History, November 19, 1960, ALHUA; Harless Wagoner, *The U.S. Machine Tool Industry from 1900 to 1950* (Cambridge: MIT Press, 1968), 319; and CEA, *Midyear Report*, 1948), part 3.

24. "Journeyman-Upgrader Program," March 30, 1948, Norman Matthews Coll., box 4, ALHUA; and *TDE*, July 1950 and February 1951.

25. "The Mobility of Tool and Die Makers, 1940–1951," (Branch of Indus-

try Studies, Division of Manpower and Employment Statistics, U.S. Bureau of Labor Statistics, 1951), quoted in UAW–CIO Appeal Brief to the Wage Stabilization Board, Region VI-B, Detroit, re: Superior Tool and Die Company, "Region 1, Local 155," UAW STD Coll., box 1.

26. In joining the UAW the tool and die workers had preserved their independent council in Detroit and later won recognition for it in the UAW constitution at the 1939 convention. The 1942 convention sanctioned "wage and hour" councils for other occupational groups.

27. At the 1949 UAW convention, article 19, section 3 was added to the union's constitution to require the Skilled Trades Department to signoff on skilled trades local agreements. *TDE* (October 1949).

28. UAW Convention Proceedings, July 10–15, 1949; see John Blaich Coll., Couser Oral History, Russell Leach Oral History, (July 27, 1961), ALHUA.

29. *TDE* (February 1951).

30. *Common Sense* (newspaper of Local 155), March 1947, ALHUA; and Roger Keeran, *The Communist Party and the Auto Worker Unions*, (Bloomington: Indiana University Press, 1980), 285.

31. Quarterly Skilled Trades Council conference minutes, Matthews Coll., ALHUA; and UAW STD, box 1.

32. "Journeyman-Upgrader Program," March 30, 1948, Matthews Coll., box 4, ALHUA.

33. *TDE* (December 1949); second skilled trades conference minutes, January 17–18, 1949, 2, Matthews Coll.,

34. UAW STD, box 6; Cf. Sumner Slichter, James Healy, and E. Robert Livernash, *The Impact of Collective Bargaining on Management* (Washington, D.C.: The Brookings Institution, 1960), 89–90. Subcontracting was not among the demands in the skilled trades program because the UAW and Ford, the major offender, had concluded a special agreement on the issue in January 1949, included in the contract as article IV, section 8. The contract provision appeared to commit the company to employ UAW workers on such work, but the private letter of understanding did no such thing. See Umpire Opinion B-23 (February 14, 1964). "UAW Local 600, 1960–," Art Fox papers, Michigan State University Library Special Collections, East Lansing, Mich.

35. *TDE* (July, 1950):1.

36. *TDE* (February 1951); cf. Jack Steiber, *Governing the UAW* (Baltimore: Wiley, 1962), 141.

37. Jerry Sanders, *Peddlers of Crisis: The Committee on the Present Danger and the Politics of Containment* (Boston: South End Press, 1983).

38. Quarterly Skilled Trades Council conference minutes, November 10–11, 1950, Matthews Coll., box 4, ALHUA; and first international skilled trades conference minutes, March 3–4, 1951, Matthews Coll., box 5, ALHUA. Delegates condemned GM for ignoring trade lines in assigning workers, disrupting pay scales, refusing recognition of local apprenticeship committees, and wholesale upgrading of production workers into single-purpose jobs, UAW Administrative Letter no. 11, March 21, 1951, ALHUA.

39. Grant McConnell, *Private Power and American Democracy* (New York: Knopf, 1966), 313; and Philip Taft, *The AFL From the Death of Gompers to the Merger* (New York: Harper, 1954), 334.

40. *BW*, December 12, 1950, 62–63 and February 24, 1951, 19–20.

41.   Taft, *AFL from the Death of Gompers,* 335–338; Art Preis, *Labor's Giant Step: Twenty Years of the CIO* (New York: Pioneer Press, 1964), 428f; *BW* April 7, 1951, 35–36 and March 17, 1951. Auto managements were using the defense mobilization to cut the labor force and reorganize work, according to *BW,* July 21, 1951, 34. "Over 2500" dispute cases from the auto industry were certified to the regional Wage Stabilization Board in 18 months, "Report of the President," UAW Convention Proceedings, 1953, 37, ALHUA.

42.   "UAW Tool and Die Study Committee," Kay Coll., box 7, ALHUA; Preis, *Labor's Giant Step,* 442–451; Seth Wigderson, "The Rise of Service Unionism" (unpublished paper, Wayne State University, 1985); Robert MacDonald, *Collective Bargaining in the Automobile Industry* (New Haven: Yale University Press, 1963), 175; and Sidney Lens, "Wage Stabilization From Labor's Viewpoint," *Harvard Business Review* 30, no. 2 (March 1952).

43.   IEB minutes, February 2–4, 1952, 60f.

44.   GM agreed to a modified changeover agreement effective only in October 1952, minutes of the Second Skilled Trades Conference, January 17–18, 1953, Matthews Coll., box 5, ALHUA.

45.   *TDE* (February 1951): 3, discusses the "intelligent isolationism" of Robert Hutchins of the Ford Foundation: a "third course from both meddlesome intervention and armed isolation"; and *TDE* (July 1950): 3, reminded readers of their cooperative goal, but noted that "monopolists oppose cooperation in favor of doing business at their old monopolistic stands. Economic and social cooperation is accomplished almost exclusively by organized labor and other progressive forces."

46.   IEB minutes March 12–14, 1952, 316; Richard Gosser Coll., box 13, ALHUA; International Skilled Trades Conference minutes, November 2–3, 1951, 2, Matthews Coll., box 4, ALHUA.

47.   "Report of the President," UAW Convention Proceedings, 1953, 110. Eighteen of twenty-one UAW administrative regions had skilled trades councils in 1953. Report of the Skilled Trades Committee to the Second Skilled Trades Conference, 31, 73, Matthews Coll., ALHUA. The president of the Detroit Maintenance Council was hired on International staff.

48.   Third Skilled Trades Conference minutes, December 10–12, 1953, 8, 18–19, 34, 42, Matthews Coll., box 5, ALHUA.

49.   Lawrence White, *The Auto Industry since 1945* (Cambridge: Harvard University Press, 1971), 203–216; *American Machinist,* October 12, 1953, 121f; "Auto Industry Equipment Expenditures 1947–1966," UAW RD, box 65, ALHUA; and "Price Policy and Public Responsibility," Walter Reuther testimony before the U.S. Senate Judiciary Committee, Subcommittee on Anti-Trust and Monopoly, January 28, 1958, 47. Employment increased at the Big Three; most of the decline was in the independents.

50.   *Automation* (Washington, D.C.: CIO Committee on Economic Policy, 1955), 5–6; Harold Shepard and James Stern, "Impact of Automation on Workers in Supplier Plants," *Labor Law Journal* (October 1957), 715.

51.   Kenneth Bannon Coll., box 7, ALHUA.

52.   Author interview with Nat Weinberg, former UAW Research Department director, November 10, 1982; "Guaranteed Annual Wages," UAW RD, box 70.

53.   *Automation: A Report to the UAW-CIO Economic and Collective Bargaining Conference,* November 12–13, 1954, IR; "The Impact of Changing Technology and

other Problems of Contract Administration," *Proceedings of the Third Annual Industrial Relations Conference on Making the Labor Agreement Work*, May 3–4, 1957, (Ann Arbor, Mich.: Institute for Labor and Industrial Relations, University of Michigan and Wayne State University), 45f; Ken Bannon and Nelson Samp, "The Impact of Automation on Wages and Working Conditions in Ford-UAW Relationships," (paper delivered at the Conference on Automation and Major Technological Change), April 22, 1958, 19, IUD; MacDonald, *Collective Bargaining*, 99f. A letter to Bannon from Region 9 (Buffalo) International Representative Frank Telakowicz, February 14, 1958, reported that the new classification "controls all the basic classifications" Ford was laying off workers in traditional trades but keeping workers in the "automation" classification. Bannon Coll., box 7, ALHUA.

54. Bannon and Samp reported that solidarity worked in the traditional source of union strength in Dearborn (Local 600), but less well elsewhere, "Impact of Automation," 10, 14–16, 19–20.

55. Third International Skilled Trades Conference minutes, 51–53, 64–65, Matthews Coll., ALHUA.

56. Author interview with Walter Dorosh, March 18, 1989.

57. Alex Henderson report to Ken Bannon, August 17, 1956. Bannon Coll., box 7, ALHUA.

58. "1958 Skilled Trades," Bannon Coll., box 7, ALHUA.

59. Third International Skilled Trades Conference minutes, 52f, Matthews Coll., ALHUA.

60. *TDE* (June 1955).

61. IEB minutes, October 5, 1955, 240; and Report of the Skilled Trades Committee to the Fourth International Skilled Trades Conference, January 20–22, 1955, Matthews Coll., box 5, ALHUA.

62. IEB minutes, October 5, 1955, 269; *TDE* (August 1955); *News and Letters* (July 22, 1955), 3, IR. ISST organizers had the examples of the AFL Pattern Makers League and the independent International Die Sinkers Conference, both of which recently had won petitions to hold elections in UAW-organized plants. Some autoworkers already were represented by them. In the 1955 contracts, these unions took increased hourly wages in lieu of the 5c SUB contribution.

63. *Maverick Gazette* (c. December 1955), Kay Coll., box 3, ALHUA.

64. There were about 250,000 skilled workers in the UAW. Report of the Skilled Trades Department, UAW Convention Proceedings, 1955), 59D; and ISST membership figures from the *Detroit Free Press*, November 7, 1955 and the *Detroit News*, November 3, 1955; *The American Craftsman* (c. Winter 1957): 3–4. Toolmakers were the most prevalent of the trades involved. Workers came from all major companies and both captive and job shops. Transmission plants seemed very well represented. Kay Coll., box 5, ALHUA.

65. "Skilled Trades Questions". Kay Coll., box 5, ALHUA, *Maverick Gazette*, Kay Coll, box 3, ALHUA. Good trade unionists readily signed up, including recent British immigrant Al Gardner, Carol Isen, "Solidarity Forever? The United Auto Workers and Its Skilled Trades Members" (Unpublished paper, June 1982), part 1, p. 53. Gardner, twenty years later, was instrumental in left-wing skilled trades agitation as chair of the Tool and Die Unit at Local 600. Also, in the late 1960s and 1970s, remnants of the ISST often cooperated with left wingers, author interview with Pete Kelly, August 3, 1983.

66.   Kay Coll., boxes 3 and 5, ALHUA; Muriel Beach, "The Problems of the Skilled Worker in an Industrial Union: The UAW Case" (M.S. thesis, Cornell University: 1959), 128, asserts that the Detroit Tool and Die Council actually led the anti-ISST fight.

67.   IEB minutes, October 5, 1955, 230, 245, 255–256.

68.   Letter from Joe Shaner, president of the Detroit Tool and Die Council, to Ray Kay, February 27, 1956, Reuther Coll., box 74, ALHUA.

69.   Kay Coll., box 5, ALHUA.

70.   *Globe Machine and Stamping Co.* 3 NLRB 294.

71.   *National Tube Co.* 76 NLRB 1199; and *American Can Co.* 13 NLRB 1952.

72.   *American Potash and Chemical Corporation* 107 NLRB 1418 at p. 1423.

73.   The *Detroit News*, December 11, 1956; and MacDonald, *Collective Bargaining*, 184.

74.   An example was made of the ongoing organizing drive among engineers at Honeywell in Minneapolis. The new organization was necessary to retain and prevent decertification of these workers. Later, the Honeywell engineers chose "no union" in an NLRB election; Carl Snyder, *White Collar Workers and the UAW* (Urbana: University of Illinois Press, 1973), 60–63.

75.   UAW Convention Proceedings, 1957, 57, 272–275, 280.

76.   *Fort Die Casting Corp.* 115 NLRB 1749.

77.   *GM Corporation and Federated Tool Crafts* 120 NLRB 1215. Some ISST activists became more ideologically right wing and, according to its most prominent member, Joe Dunnebeck, he himself became a Republican as a result. *The American Craftsman* (1966), Reuther Coll., box 160, ALHUA.

78.   *Iron Age*, June 7, 1956, 88f; James L. Sundquist, *Politics and Policy: The Eisenhower, Kennedy and Johnson Years* (Washington, D.C.: The Brookings Institution, 1968), 31f.

79.   Kay Coll., box 7, ALHUA; Special Collective Bargaining Convention Proceedings, January 22–24, 1958, ALHUA; conference minutes—Joint UAW GM, Ford and Chrysler councils, May 1958, Reuther Coll., box 57, ALHUA; B. J. Widick, *Labor Today: The Triumphs and Failures of Unionism in the United States* (Boston: Houghton Mifflin, 1964), 194f; and "Proposed Skilled Trades Demands," February 1958, Bannon Coll., box 7, ALHUA.

80.   Telegram from Joe Shaner and Ray Kay, Bannon Coll., box 7, ALHUA.

81.   "Contract Ratification, Ford Motor Company," Reuther Coll., box 158, ALHUA.

82.   "Defend Your Rights," Kay Coll., box 5, Reuther Coll., boxes 74 and 158, ALHUA; "Unemployed Committees," Fox papers, Michigan State University Library Special Collections, East Lansing, Mich.; IEB minutes, February 5, 1959; *UAW Administrative Letter* 11, no. 3, February 13, 1959; and author interview with Leonard Woodcock, December 10, 1982. Walter Dorosh was hired onto Reuther's staff and later was elected president of Local 600, Interview with Walter Dorosh, October 14, 1982.

83.   Harold Arnett and Donald Smith, *The Tool and Die Industry: Problems and Prospects* (Ann Arbor: Graduate School of Business Administration, University of Michigan, 1975), 38–39.

84.   Senate Committee on Labor and Public Welfare, Subcommittee on Employment and Manpower, "Nation's Manpower Revolution," 88th Congress,

1st sess., October 16–18, 1963; and House Select Committee on Small Business, Subcommittee on Special Investigations, "Problems of the Tool and Die Industry and Associated Problems of Manufacturers and Distributors of Machine Tools," 89th Congress, 2nd sess., December 29, 1966.

85. Fox Papers, Michigan State University Library Special Collections, East Lansing, Mich.; United National Caucus leaflet, March 18, 1969; and Timothy Foley memo to Walter Reuther re: Skilled Trades Advisory Committee, April 3, 1966. Reuther Coll., box 159, ALHUA.

86. William Gould, *Black Workers in White Unions* (Ithaca: Cornell University Press, 1977), 371–395; and author interview with Robert Deuweke (coordinator of the Center for Human Resource Development, Macomb Community College), March 1989.

87. Author interview with Richard Karas (International representative, UAW Skilled Trades Department and former president of Local 155), July 1988.

88. Umpire Ruling J-66, September 11, 1961, UAW RD, box 56; and Opinion B-25 (January 7, 1966). Reuther Coll., box 159, ALHUA.

89. Author interview with Edward Allard (director of Trade and Apprentice Education at Henry Ford Community College), March 1989. In 1969, the UAW called a conference on new technology and then urged all locals to negotiate contracts that included training in computer programming for CNC machines, *Common Sense*, May 21, 1969, p. 7; and see Fox Papers, Michigan State University Library Special Collections, East Lansing, Mich.

90. Stephen L. Stuart, "An Exploratory Study to Analyze New Skills Content in Selected Occupations" (Cleveland: U.S. Manpower Administration/Battelle Institute, May 31, 1972), G-1; "Final Report on Michigan Manpower Study: An Analysis of Characteristics of the Michigan Labor Force in the Next 15 Years" (Cleveland: Battelle Institute, 1966); and Gardner Ackley speech to the U.S. Chamber of Commerce, May 2, 1966, Reuther Coll., box 390, ALHUA.

91. William Gould, *Black Workers in White Unions*, 379, 382; and Dan Georgakas and Marvin Surkin, *Detroit: I Do Mind Dying* (New York: St. Martin's Press, 1975).

92. Stephen Amberg, "The Origins of Affirmative Action in Massachusetts: Labor Market Segmentation in Construction" (Boston: The Boston Jobs Coalition, 1981); and Paul Hartman and Walter Franke, "The Changing Bargaining Structure in Construction," *Industrial and Labor Relations Review* 33, no. 2, (January 1980).

93. Bannon Coll., box 64, ALHUA.

94. Michigan Department of Public Instruction, "Statement of Principles" (press release, July 1952) quoted in Douglas R. Sherman, *The Emerging Role of Vocational Terminal Education in the Public Community Colleges of Michigan* (Ph.D. diss., Wayne State University, 1956), 11–12; cf. Steven Brint and Jerome Karabel, *The Diverted Dream: Community Colleges and the Promise of Educational Opportunity in America, 1900–1985* (New York: Oxford University Press, 1989).

95. The Trade School had prospered. An internal investigation of the school in 1947 by Ford's Industrial Relations staff noted that it made money (except during wartime price controls), "Analysis of Henry Ford Trade School Operations," Henry Ford Trade School, Office of the Secretary, box 1. HFM.

96. Report of the Dearborn board of education, pp. 3, 15. Henry Ford Trade School, Office of the Secretary, box 2, HFM.

97. "Registered Apprentices in Training, New Registrations, Completions

and Cancellations" (data supplied by the Bureau of Apprenticeship and Training, U.S. Department of Labor); cf. "Apprentice Registration Actions" (Washington, D.C.: BAT/U.S. Department of Labor, various years), UAW STD and the General Motors Labor Relations Department, unpublished data; and Kirsten Wever, Thomas Kochan, and Peter Berg, "Worker Representation and Further Training: Comparative Evidence and Policy Lessons" (Washington, D.C.: Economic Policy Institute, 1992).

98.   *NYT,* November 13, 1973, p. 89; November 14, 1973, p. 1, Bannon Coll., box 63, ALHUA; and Independent Skilled Trades Council, "Why Beg Japan For Jobs?" (1982), in author's possession.

99.   Arnett and Smith, *Tool and Die Industry,* 15; cf. Robert Averitt, *The Dual Economy* (New York: Norton, 1968), 95f; and cf. Max Holland, *When the Machine Stopped: A Cautionary Tale from Industrial America* (Boston: Harvard Business School Press, 1989).

100.   Arnett and Smith, *Tool and Die Industry,* 15–17.

101.   Author interview with Richard Steinhelper (Detroit Tooling Association), July 1988; *Common Sense,* March 24, 1971 and September 22, 1971, ALHUA.

102.   *Metalworking News,* September 25, 1989, p. 18. The National Tooling and Machining Association has launched a nation-wide preapprenticeship program that starts with teenagers still in the public schools.

103.   *The Employment and Training Report of the President* (Washington, D.C.: U.S. Department of Labor, 1977), 97; *The Employment and Training Report of the President* (Washington, D.C.: U.S. Department of Labor, 1979), table F-14; U.S. Bureau of Apprenticeship and Training, unpublished data; and U.S. Immigration and Naturalization Service, unpublished data.

CHAPTER 6

1.   Michael Piore and Charles Sabel, *The Second Industrial Divide* (New York: Basic Books, 1984), 258–277; and cf. William Abernathy, Kim Clark, and Alan Kantrow, *Industrial Renaissance* (New York: Basic Books, 1983).

2.   Charles Edwards, *Dynamics of the United States Automobile Industry* (Columbia: University of South Carolina Press, 1965), 24 chart 2, and 112 table 9.

3.   Ibid., 74 table 6.

4.   "Independent's Day," *Forbes* 69, no. 12 (June 15, 1952): 18–26; "Last Stand of the Auto Independents," *Fortune* 50, no. 6 (December 1954); Peter Drucker, *The Practice of Management* (New York: Harper, 1954), 113–114; and Frederick Harbison and Robert Dubin, *Patterns of Union-Management Relations* (Chicago: Social Science Associates, 1947), 108.

5.   Edwards, *Dynamics,* 18, 106, 146–147; *South Bend Tribune* (hereafter, *SBT*) September 3, 1948 and January 25, 1953; *Wards Automotive Yearbook 1955,* 119; and R. A. Hutchinson Papers (vice-president for exports at Studebaker), box 1, Studebaker Archival Coll., DHM.

6.   Harbison and Dubin, *Patterns,* 105.

7.   *SBT* November 6, 1952; cf. Harbison and Dubin, *Patterns,* 121 note 11; and Albert Erskine, *History of the Studebaker Corporation* (South Bend: Studebaker Corporation, 1924), 105–133.

8.   Alan Raucher, *Paul G. Hoffman: Architect of Foreign Aid* (Lexington: University of Kentucky Press, 1985). Studebaker's bankers, Glore, Forgan and Co., Kuhn Loeb and Co., Lehman Brothers, Chase Bank, First National City Bank, and Metropolitan Life Insurance Co., also were internationalist businesses.

9.   Harbison and Dubin, *Patterns*, 114, 134, 138; Robert MacDonald, *Collective Bargaining in the Automobile Industry: A Study of Wage Structure and Competitive Relations* (New Haven: Yale University Press, 1963), 365; and appendix K-9: Effects of the N.W.L.B.'s Actions in the South Bend Labor Market Area, in *The Termination Report of the National War Labor Board* (Washington, D.C.: U.S. Government Printing Office, n.d.), 1146.

10.   Harbison and Dubin, *Patterns*, 108–116, 147, 157, 164–166, 202; John Sembower, "What's Behind Studebaker's No-Strike Record," *Industrial Relations* (October 1946); and Glenn Griswold, "Humanized Employee Relations: Studebaker an Example," *Public Opinion Quarterly* (September 1940).

11.   James D. Hill, *U.A.W.'s Frontier* (UAW region 3 Auto Council, 1971); and Janet Weaver interview with Carl Shipley, December 31, 1982, DHM.

12.   "The New Studebaker is Nice, But Have You Seen the Local? Rochdale Cooperation in South Bend Has Led to Farmer-Labor Unity" (UAW Education Department Publication no. 126 c.1948), IR.

13.   Harbison and Dubin, *Patterns*, 121–125, 156, 177, 160.

14.   Loren Pennington interview with George Hupp, May 19, 1972, 17–20, ALHUA. Hupp started work at Studebaker in 1929. He was president of Local 5 from 1946–1947 and after 1948 worked for Studebaker management.

15.   Loren Pennington interview with Lester Fox, June 21, 1971, 24, ALHUA. Fox was a second generation union official at Local 5. He was first elected a steward in 1949 and held office until 1964.

16.   "GM Wage Case Research 1945–7," UAW RD, box 13. The wage structure at Studebaker was high and also compressed, as actual production worker wages were higher and skilled wages were lower than at GM and Ford; and cf. MacDonald, *Collective Bargaining*, 271.

17.   Harbison and Dubin, *Patterns*, 173; Hupp interview, 50; and Fox interview, June 21, 1971, 24.

18.   Harbison and Dubin, *Patterns*, 170–172; and MacDonald, *Collective Bargaining*, 267.

19.   Ibid., 358–359, 367.

20.   Edwards, *Dynamics*, 70–73; and *Minute Book* of the Meetings of the Board of Directors, Studebaker Corporation, September 25, 1953, November 22 and December 17, 1954, and January 20, 1956, Studebaker Archival Coll, DHM.

21.   *Automotive Industries*, March 15, 1953–1956.

22.   *Forbes* 69, no. 12 (June 1, 1952): 22.

23.   Raymond Loewy, "More Compact Power Plant Key to Better Automotive Design," *Ward's Automotive Yearbook 1955*, 11.

24.   Edwards, *Dynamics*, 76–77, tables 6-8, 112 table 9, 157 note 14, 166, and 169. Foreign sales doubled from 1954 to 1955 and almost doubled again in 1956. By 1958 they had almost quadrupled the 1956 mark and stood at 8% of the market, Lawrence White, *The Automobile Industry since 1945* (Cambridge: Harvard University Press, 1971), 50, 292–293; cf. Brock Yates, *The Decline and Fall of the American*

Automobile Industry (New York: Empire Books, 1983), 127–128; and MacDonald, *Collective Bargaining*, 268–269.

25. Edwards, *Dynamics*, 42, 87–88; Hupp interview, p. 76; and *Minute Book*, October 4, 1954.

26. *Minute Book*, February, March, and May 1956; and Raucher, *Paul G. Hoffman*, 116–119.

27. *Minute Book*, December 18, 1953; "Anna Rosenberg—She Sells Intuitions," *Fortune* 50, no. 5 (November 1954); Jerry Sanders, *Peddlers of Crisis: The Committee on the Present Danger and the Politics of Containment* (Boston: South End Press, 1983); and Bowles, *Promises to Keep*, 229.

28. "Operation '55," A. J. Porta, Vice-President Papers, box 3, Studebaker Corporation Coll., DHM; "Contracts 1937-55," UAW Local 5 Coll., box 18, ALHUA; and *SBT*, August 2 and 10, 1954.

29. Memorandum from Anna Rosenberg to Paul Hoffman, May 18, 1954, Paul Hoffman Coll., box 152, HST.

30. Hupp interview, 21.

31. Executive board and membership meetings minutes, January 19 and October 14, 1954, Local 5 Coll., box 10, ALHUA.

32. *Minute Book*, December 18, 1953 and January 14, 1955.

33. Testimony before the Joint Committee on the Economic Report, Subcommittee on Economic Stabilization, October 17, 1955, p. 20.

34. Fox interview, 11–16; and Loren Pennington interview with J. D. Hill, May 12, 1972, 40–45, ALHUA. Hill was one of the early union organizers, president 1949–1950, and then on the staff of the UAW Studebaker Department in Detroit.

35. Hupp interview, 64–65; and Janet Weaver interview with Raymond Berndt, April 1, 1980, 40–55, DHM. Berndt became the single most influential person in the Indiana CIO council, author interview with Harlen (H.J.) Noel (South Bend CIO-PAC director, 1948), June 27, 1984.

36. Melvin A. Kahn, *The Politics of American Labor: The Indiana Microcosm* (Carbondale: Southern Illinois University Labor Institute, 1970 edition).

37. Hupp interview, 9; Harbison and Dubin, *Patterns*, 142, 161–163; and Berndt interview, 47–48.

38. Pennington interview with Fox, 4.

39. Loren Pennington interview with William Ogden, May 15, 1972, 9–10, 78, ALHUA. Ogden was the principal oppositionist. As a young man he had been a coal miner, like his father, and then became an organizer of the local. He was its president 1944–1945, 1951–1952, and 1955–1957.

40. Hupp interview, 23–24.

41. MacDonald, *Collective Bargaining*, 262–266; "Minutes of Meeting Concerning Skilled Trades Policy," September 12 and 24, 1952, Local 5 Coll., box 12, ALHUA; and Hupp interview, 27–28.

42. Fox interview, 17: "why should the workers bite the bullet?" asked Fox.

43. Total Studebaker employment in South Bend was:

21,868 on September 11, 1950
15,638 on September 8, 1952

23,247 on April 6, 1953
16,417 on October 12, 1953.

"Employment by Sex," Automobile Manufacturers Association survey, Industrial Relations Department, box 1, selected weeks. Studebaker Corporation Coll., DHM.

44.   *SBT,* August 2, 6, 9, 10, and 13, 1954; and Fox interview, 12 and 21.

45.   *SBT,* August 6 and 11, 1954.

46.   Fox interview, 12–13.

47.   Executive board and membership meetings minutes, September 23, 1954, Local 5 Coll., box 10, ALHUA.

48.   *Minute Book,* March 18 and May 20, 1955; "Grievance Memoranda," January 6 and January 13, 1955, Industrial Relations Department, box 1. Studebaker Corporation Coll., DHM.

49.   *SBT,* January 17, 1955.

50.   *SBT,* January 20 and 21 and February 9, 1955; *BW,* January 29, 1955, p. 126; "Local 5 Official Bulletins, 1953-55," Local 5 Coll., box 1, ALHUA; and *Minute Book,* March 18, 1955.

51.   *Minute Book,* May 20, 1955.

52.   "Local 5 Official Bulletins, 1953-55," May 23 and June 1, 1955, Local 5 Coll., box 1, ALHUA.

53.   Ibid., July 9, 1955.

54.   *Minute Book,* May 20, July 15, 1955; and *SBT,* July 8 and 21, and 29 and August 2 and 4, 1955.

55.   *SBT,* June 11, 1955; and Janet Weaver interview with Fox, March 5, 1979, 16, DHM.

56.   "Studebaker Workers Endorse a `Get Tough' Policy," *BW,* July 16, 1955, 132.

57.   "Strike and Strategy," Official Bulletin, August 15, 1955, Local 5 Coll., box 15, ALHUA. There were 31 wildcats counted by the local press from July 1 to September 30, *SBT,* November 23, 1955.

58.   Executive board and membership meeting minutes, September 22 and October 10, 1955, Local 5 Coll., box 10, ALHUA; *Studebaker Weekly News* (Local 5) December 16, 1955, 1–4, Local 5 Coll., box 15, ALHUA; AND *SBT,* December 13, 1955.

59.   *SBT,* September 6, November 10, and December 2, 1955, "1956 Working Agreement Ratification Vote," Local 5 Coll., box 19, ALHUA; and *SBT,* January 8, 1956.

60.   *Minute Book,* January 20, 1956; and cf. *Minute Book,* January 14 and December 16, 1955.

61.   Ibid., November 18, 1955. Industrial Relations Department, boxes 1 and 4, DHM. The company was still fighting over this issue in 1962.

62.   Pennington interview with Fox, June 21, 1971, 8–9; Weaver interview with Fox, 15–16; and Pennington interview with Fox, May 19, 1972, 1.

63.   Ogden interview, 18, 27, 30–32; and Pennington interview with Fox, June 21, 1971, 10–18, 25–26, 33, 48.

64.   *SBT,* August 29, 1958; Pennington interview with Stanley Ladd, July 17, 1972, 58–59, DHM; and MacDonald, *Collective Bargaining,* 283.

65.   Cf. Steve Jeffreys, *Management and Managed: Fifty Years of Crisis at Chrysler* (New York: Cambridge University Press, 1986).

66.   William Batt, Jr., "How Your Town Can Avoid a Recession," *Colliers* (April 30, 1954); *CIO Economic Outlook* (July-August 1955), "Douglas Bill 1955" and "Area Unemployment Expansion Committee, 1956," William Batt, Jr. papers, box 2, JFK; *Area Redevelopment Hearings*, Senate Committee on Banking and Currency, 85th Congress 1st sess. March 6–May 15, 1957, 281–285; and AFL–CIO Convention Proceedings, 1955, 1957, p. 308, and 1959, pp. 225–227.

67.   Solomon Barkin, "The Promotion of Area Redevelopment in the United States," speech to the American Society for Public Administration, April 4, 1961; and cf. Sar Levitan, *Federal Aid to Depressed Areas* (Baltimore: Johns Hopkins University Press, 1964).

68.   After the Democrats swept into office in 1955, seven local leaders joined city and county government, including former president Louis Horvath. Executive board and membership meetings minutes, December 29, 1955, Local 5 Coll., box 10, ALHUA.

69.   *Redevelopment Hearings*, 646–650, 668, 698f; John Bibby and Roger Davidson, *On Capital Hill: Studies in the Legislative Process* (New York: Holt, Rinehart and Winston, 1967); and "Committee for a National Trade Policy," Hoffman papers, box 72, HST. William Batt was the committee's secretary and had been research director of the Democratic National Committee in the Truman years. After the Congress again passed the Distressed areas Bill in 1961, and President Kennedy signed it, he became an administrator of the Area Redevelopment Administration. The ARA, however, failed because it never could coordinate the disparate agencies of American government that administered education and training, economic development funds, and industrial relations; LMAC minutes, U.S. Department of Labor Coll., reel 72. JFK; and Reuther Coll., box 37, ALHUA.

70.   William Harris, "The Breakdown of Studebaker-Packard," *Fortune* (October 1956): 139; and "Studebaker Corporation 1956," Donald Montgomery Coll., box 79, ALHUA.

71.   Pennington quotes from an entry in Eisenhower's diary following a meeting between Hoffman and the president:

> All day long I have been receiving advice to the effect that all of us must do our best to keep the Packard-Studebaker combine from liquidating, which it seems to be on the point of doing. For more than a year I have been working on this particular matter, especially urging the Defense Department to give this firm some defense contracts, in the items in which it has already established a fine production record.

Loren Pennington, "Prelude to Chrysler: The Eisenhower Administration Bails Out Studebaker-Packard" (unpublished paper, DHM). Hoffman's efforts are discussed in the *Minute Book*, April 18, July 15, and November 18, 1955 and January 20, March 23, and May 2, 1956.

72.   *Detroit Times*, May 16, 1956; UAW Studebaker Dept. Coll., box 1, ALHUA; and Seymour Harris, *The Economics of the Political Parties* (New York: MacMillan, 1962).

73.   *Minute Book*, February 27 and March 23, 1956; Pennington, "Prelude," 11; "Independent's Day," *Forbes* (June 15, 1952); and cf. Charles Craypo, "The Deindustrialization of a Factory Town: Plant Closings and Phasedowns in South Bend, Indiana, 1954–1983," in Donald Kennedy, ed., *Labor and Reindustrialization: Workers and Corporate Change* (Pennsylvania State University: Department of Labor Studies, 1984).

74. Edwards, *Dynamics*, 73f.

75. Pennington, "Prelude," 15; Edwards, *Dynamics*, 98–103. Also its top managers availed themselves of their stock options and reportedly made $1 million, B. J. Widick, "The Tragedy at Studebaker," *The Nation*, February 17, 1962. After 1953, stockholder equity had been further reduced by over one-third during the years 1954–1959, Edwards, *Dynamics*, 77, table 8.

76. Theresa Schindler interviews with John Duncan (former Truck and Fleet Sales Manager of Studebaker) and Arnold Altman (former Packard dealer and later president of Avanti), March 29 and April 4, 1983, DHM. Note that the Avanti car was a Studebaker luxury design successfully developed, produced and marketed by Altman after Studebaker left the business.

77. Pennington interview with Fox, 22–23; Federal Records: CEA, reel 45, Task Force on Studebaker, LBJ; "South Bend—Studebaker Shutdown 1964," Batt papers, box 3, JFK; and B. J. Widick, "Studebaker: End of a Dream," *The Nation*, January 6, 1954, 29. About 500 employees moved, mostly skilled and management. Project ABLE, a joint venture of the U.S. Labor Department and the National Council on Aging, enrolled 1,300 of 3,500 workers over 50 years of age in a training program. 70% finished the program and 70% of these found jobs, *NYT*, November 14, 1966, 64. Studebaker bought annuities for those 60 and older, for those 40–60 it paid them 15 cents for every dollar accrued pension credit, and nothing for the rest, *NYT*, November 28, 1966, 63.

CHAPTER 7

1. Adam Przeworski, *Capitalism and Social Democracy* (New York: Cambridge University Press, 1985); Joshua Cohen and Joel Rogers, *On Democracy* (New York: Penguin Books, 1983); and cf. J. David Greenstone, *Labor in American Politics* (New York: Knopf, 1969), 361–362.

2. Clark Kerr et al., *Industrialism and Industrial Man: The Problems of Labor and Management in Economic Growth* (Cambridge, Mass.: Harvard University Press, 1960); and John Dunlop, *Industrial Relations Systems* (Carbondale: Southern Illinois University Press, 1971; originally 1958).

3. Arthur Wolfe, "Trends in Labor Union Voting Behavior, 1948–1968," *Industrial Relations* 9 (October 1969).

4. Herbert Parmet, *The Democrats: The Years After FDR* (New York: MacMillan, 1976) chapter 9.

5. James L. Sundquist, *The Decline and Resurgence of Congress* (Washington, D.C.: The Brookings Institution, 1981), 211; and John Kenneth Galbraith, *The Affluent Society* (Boston: Houghton Mifflin, 1958).

6. William Batt Papers, box 1, JFK; and William Batt Oral History, JFK.

7. Barry Goldwater speech to the 1958 U.S. Chamber of Commerce convention; *Nation's Business* (April 1958); and *U.S. News and World Report*, July 27, 1964, 76–77. William Domhoff, *Fat Cats and Democrats* (Englewood Cliffs: Prentice-Hall, 1972), 161–162, reports that the CED, in 1962, explicitly repudiated a benign view of cost-push inflation after the NAM vigorously protested a CED staff report to

that effect. The AFL–CIO obtained a transcript of a private NAM program that was sharply critical of "labor monopoly". "November 1962 Executive Council," Walter Reuther Coll., box 306, ALHUA.

8. Fred L. Block, *The Origins of International Economic Disorder* (Berkeley: University of California Press, 1977) chapter 7; and David P. Calleo, *The Imperious Economy* (Cambridge, Mass.: Harvard University Press, 1982) chapter 1.

9. E.g., Rockefeller Brothers Fund, *The Challenge to America: Its Economic and Social Aspects* (Garden City: Doubleday, 1958) and "Employment, Growth and Price Levels," Hearings before the Joint Economic Committee, 86th Congress, 1st sess. (Washington, D.C.: US GPO, 1959-60); Arthur M. Schlesinger, Jr., *A Thousand Days* (Boston: Houghton Mifflin, 1965), 622.

10. Jim Heath, *John F. Kennedy and the Business Community* (Chicago: University of Chicago Press, 1969); Seymour Harris Oral History, JFK; cf. Seymour Harris, *Economics of the Political Parties*; Robert Collins, *The Business Response to Keynes* (New York: Columbia University Press, 1981); and Harry Johnson, "Balance of Payments Controls and Guidelines for Trade and Investment," in *Guidelines, Informal Controls and the Market Place: Policy Choices in a Full Employment Economy*, ed. George Shultz and Robert Aliber (Chicago: University of Chicago Press, 1966).

11. Thomas Watson Oral History, JFK; William Moye, "Presidential Labor-Management Committees: Productive Failures," *Industrial and Labor Relations Review* 34, no 1 (October 1980); and "Labor Management Committee," Reuther Coll., box 387, ALHUA.

12. James T. Reynolds, who was assistant secretary of labor and a management appointee of Goldberg's, said that the LMAC was an example of Goldberg's "expansive vision" of the Department of Labor and notes that Kennedy frequently came to the LMAC meetings for advice to contrast with the CEA and the interest group-oriented Business Council, Reynolds Oral History, JFK.

13. LMAC minutes, March 21, 1961, May 1, 1961, and January 11–12, 1962, Department of Labor Coll., microfilm reel 72, JFK.

14. LMAC minutes, June 5, 1961, and April 3–4, 1962.

15. Robert Solow, "The Case against the Case against the Guideposts," Shultz and Aliber, *Guidelines*; and cf. Frank Pierson, *Unions in Postwar America: An Economic Assessment* (New York: Random House, 1967).

16. LMAC minutes, June 5, 1961.

17. William Barber, "The Kennedy Years: Purposeful Pedagogy," in *Exhortation and Controls: The Search for a Wage-Price Policy, 1945–1971*, ed. Craufurd Goodwin (Washington, D.C.: The Brookings Institution, 1975), 175.

18. LMAC minutes, July 10, 1961.

19. William Gomberg, "The Future of Collective Bargaining," *The Nation*, January 20, 1962, 56–61; and B. J. Widick, *Labor Today* (Boston: Houghton Mifflin, 1964), 201.

20. Barber, "Kennedy Years," 156. The UAW contract with American Motors contained profit-sharing and a career employment planning program to help workers prepare for nonauto jobs.

21. Grant McConnell, *Steel and the Presidency* (New York: Norton, 1963).

22. *NYT*, February 2, 1964, 71; Reuther testimony on "The 1964 Economic Report of the President," Joint Economic Committee, 88th Congress, 2nd session,

pt. 2, 17–31; "Briefing Paper for WP-3 Delegation," September 9, 1964, LBJ. The CEA urged the Fed to keep the money supply responsive to the settlements, Walter Heller memo to LBJ, September 15, 1964, Federal Records: CEA, reel 2, LBJ.

23. LMAC minutes, April 3–4, 1962 and September 10, 1962; Willard Wirtz (deputy secretary of labor) memo to Goldberg, December 22, 1961, says that Ford and Arthur Burns' dissents were threatening the comity of the LMAC, Department of Labor coll., Willard Wirtz papers, box 24, JFK.

24. AFL–CIO platform proposals to the Republican and Democratic conventions, 1964, quoted in Theodore Kheel, "The Changing Patterns of Collective Bargaining in the United States," in *Employment Problems of Automation and Advanced Technology*, ed. Jack Steiber (New York: St. Martin's Press, 1966), 374.

25. Hawe and Widick, *UAW and Walter Reuther*, 201–202.

26. LMAC minutes, February 5–6, 1963.

27. LMAC minutes, October 29–30, 1963.

28. LMAC minutes, October 2–3, 1962, December 10, 1962, and March 25, 1963.

29. John P. Lewis to Walter Heller, January 23, 1964, Federal Records: CEA, microfilm reel 7, LBJ.

30. Garth Mangum, *The Emergence of Manpower Policy* (New York: Holt, Rinehart and Winston, 1969), 38.

31. Robert H. Zieger, *American Workers, American Unions, 1920-1985* (Baltimore: Johns Hopkins University Press, 1986), 175–176.

32. Reuther Coll., box 434, ALHUA; and Todd Gitlin, *The Sixties: Years of Hope, Days of Rage* (New York: Bantam Books, 1987), 151–162.

33. Greenstone, *Labor*, 332–333.

34. Louise Lander ed., *War on Poverty* (New York: Facts on File, 1967), 7; and George Meany letter to Luther Hodges, secretary of commerce, December 14, 1964, Reuther Coll., box 397, ALHUA.

35. "Hearings on Toward Full Employment," U.S. Senate Committee on Education and Public Welfare, 88th 2nd (1964).

36. Walter Heller, *New Dimensions of Political Economy* (New York: Norton, 1967); Stanley Ruttenberg Oral History, 9, JFK; and Mangum, *Emergence of Manpower*, 50.

37. Margaret Weir, *Politics and Jobs: The Boundaries of Employment Policy in the United States* (Princeton: Princeton University Press, 1992), 69–75.

38. Henry Aaron, *Politics and the Professors: The Great Society in Perspective* (Washington, D.C.: The Brookings Institution, 1978); Nick Kotz and Mary Lynn Kotz, *Passion for Equality: George A. Wiley and the Movement* (New York: Norton, 1977), 164; and Robert Haveman ed., *A Decade of Federal Anti-Poverty Programs* (New York: Academic Press, 1977).

39. Myron Joseph memo to the CEA, May 11, 1964, Federal Records: CEA microfilm, LBJ.

40. "Ideas for New ARA Act 1965". Batt papers, box 4, JFK.

41. The commission members were Reuther, Joe Beirne (Communications Workers of America), A. J. Hayes (past president of the Machinists), Pat Haggerty (Texas Instruments), Edwin Land (Polaroid), Thomas Watson (IBM), Daniel Bell (Harvard sociologist), Robert Solow (MIT economist), and Whitney Young, Jr.

42. Reuther letter to all unions, March 22, 1966, Reuther Coll., box 435, ALHUA.

43. James L. Cochrane, "The Johnson Administration: Moral Suasion Goes to War," in *Exhortation*, ed. Goodwin, 199–200, 203–205, 240.

44. Ibid., 241–244, 254, Reuther Coll., box 390, ALHUA.

45. John P. Lewis to Walter Heller, January 23, 1964, Federal Records: CEA microfilm, LBJ. LMAC data show various calculations of the same relationships and all agree. James Reynolds to Reuther, March 11, 1966; cf. *Historical Statistics of the United States, Colonial Times to 1970*, pt. 1 (Washington, D.C.: U.S. Bureau of the Census, 1975) series F 163-185. Major collective bargaining settlements (affecting 10,000 workers or more) averaged 2.3% in 1963, 3.0% in 1964, and 3.3% in 1965.

46. Gardner Ackley memo to Vice-President Hubert Humphrey, May 10, 1967, EX BE 4/automobiles, LBJ; *Ward's Automotive Reports* (1978); *Fortune*, June 15, 1968, 188; and *Fortune*, May 15, 1969, 168. The Textile Workers Union (TWI) president, William Pollock, called Ackley a "reactionary" in a letter to Reuther, April 20, 1966. The TWU won a settlement of about 5.5%. Reuther Coll., box 390, ALHUA.

47. Federal Records: CEA, reel 2, LBJ.

48. Walter Reuther letter to LBJ, March 22, 1966, Federal Records: CEA reel 38, LBJ; and Reuther Coll., box 377, ALHUA.

49. Walter Reuther letter to George Meany, November 18, 1966, Reuther Coll., box 40, ALHUA; and Joseph Goulden, *Meany*, 349.

50. John Herling, *Right to Challenge: People and Power in the Steel Workers Union* (New York: Harper, 1972), 101.

51. John Dunlop, "The Task of Contemporary Wage Theory," in *New Concepts in Wage Determination*, ed. George Taylor and Frank Pierson (New York: McGraw-Hill, 1957), especially 131–134.

52. Richard Herding, *Job Control and Union Structure* (Rotterdam: Rotterdam University Press, 1972), 287–289.

53. Nat Goldfinger (AFL–CIO Research Department director) memo to Reuther, May 3, 1966, Reuther Coll., box 390, ALHUA. "AFL-CIO/UAW Relations; Wage-Price Control Controversy," Reuther Coll., box 40, ALHUA; and *John Herling's Labor Letter*, December 10, 1966.

54. Reuther memo to the LMAC, November 28, 1966, Reuther Coll., box 377, ALHUA; and Nat Weinberg memo to Walter Reuther, April 30, 1966, Reuther Coll., box 390, ALHUA.

55. IUD executive board meeting minutes, July 7, 1966 and December 15, 1966, Reuther Coll., box 324, ALHUA; and Reuther speech to the IUD convention, November 18, 1965, Reuther Coll., box 588, ALHUA.

56. Ken Bannon Coll., box 20, ALHUA. By 1967 the difference between the wages of non-auto building trades in Detroit and construction workers employed by the Big Three was as much as 25% in some crafts.

57. Bannon Coll., box 26, ALHUA.

58. Reuther speech to I.G. Metall automation conference, March 17, 1965, Reuther Coll., box 397, ALHUA; *AFL–CIO News*, March 20, 1965; "UAW Ponders Pay Hike Impasse," *Detroit Free Press*, August 26, 1966; "Wait Till '67, Reuther Tells Skilled Trades," *Detroit Free Press*, August 29, 1966; "Skilled Trades Department 1966," Reuther Coll., box 159, ALHUA. The AFL–CIO executive council considered the guideposts broken by its August 24 meeting, as did the CEA; Cochrane, "Johnson Administration," 259–263.

59. Goulden, *Meany*.

60.   The subcommittee on guideposts did not include Reuther. Its members were George Taylor, George Meany, Joe Keenan, and Thomas Murphy.

61.   Nat Weinberg to Reuther, December 13, 1966, Reuther Coll., box 392, ALHUA; and Weinberg to Reuther, March 28, 1967 and June 9, 1967, Reuther Coll., box 391, ALHUA.

62.   The UAW's choices for the economists' panel were Lloyd Ulman, Alvin Hansen, Gerhard Colm and Neil Chamberlain.

63.   Willard Wirtz memo to the president, January 25, 1967, and Joseph Califano and Larry Levinson memo to the president, January 11, 1967, EX LA, LBJ; and John T. Connor memo to the president, December 20, 1966, FG 730, LBJ.

64.   Weinberg memo to Reuther, April 26, 1967; LMAC minutes, May 2, 1967 and May 23, 1967, Reuther Coll., box 392, ALHUA; Secretary of Commerce Trowbridge letter to Reuther, June 26, 1967, Reuther Coll., box 392, ALHUA.

65.   Cochrane, "Johnson Administration," 276–278.

66.   Reuther Coll., box 434, ALHUA.

67.   Reuther to Willy Brandt, lord mayor of Berlin, June 18, 1965, Reuther Coll., box 463, ALHUA.

68.   Reuther Coll., boxes 377, 378, 477, ALHUA. Reuther told the CCAP convention, in April 1966, to "mobilize a counterthrust" to "stiffen the political backbones in Washington," Lander, *War on Poverty*, 141; and "UAW Plans Own Urban Renewal Program," *Detroit Free Press*, February 8, 1967.

69.   *John Herling's Labor Letter*, December 12, 1966. Reuther testimony before the Senate Government Operations Subcommittee, reported in the *Detroit Free Press*, December 6, 1966; *News from the AFL–CIO*, December 26, 1966, ALHUA; and David Broder, "Johnson Tactics Widen Party Rift," *Washington Post*, November 29, 1966.

70.   Reuther Coll., box 390, ALHUA.

71.   Meany strongly criticized Reuther (although without naming him) for his support of Model Cities' preapprenticeship training in a speech to the twelfth National Legislative Conference of the Building and Construction Trades Department, Reuther Coll., box 324, ALHUA.

72.   Leonard Woodcock Coll., box 197, ALHUA.

73.   *Ford Facts*, February 16, 1963, May 11, 1963, and March 14, 1964, IR; The *Detroit Free Press*, December 8, 1966; B. J. Widick, *Detroit: City of Race and Class Violence* (Chicago: Quadrangle Books, 1972), 148. The NAACP had launched a national campaign to integrate the Big Three. The *New York Times*, June 11, 1964, 22, "Local 600, 1960–," Art Fox papers, Michigan State University Library Special Collections, East Lansing, Mich.; Reuther Coll., box 324, ALHUA; and author interviews with Pete Kelly (UNC leader and president of GM Local 160), August 3, 1983 and June 21, 1984; author interview with John Snow (chair of Ford Local 600, Maintenance and Construction Unit), May 9, 1984. Some of the radical skilled trades leaders were reelected in the mid-1970s; cf. James Geschwender, *Class, Race and Worker Insurgency* (New York: Cambridge University, 1977); Dan Georgakas and Marvin Surkin, *Detroit: I Do Mind Dying* (New York: St. Martin's Press, 1975); and Steve Jefferys, *Management and Managed: Fifty Years of Crisis at Chrysler* (New York: Cambridge University Press, 1986), 168–187.

74.   Meany quoted in The *Detroit Free Press*, March 22, 1966 p. 8A, citing the guideposts, repeal of section 14b of the Taft-Hartley Act, and legalization of

common situs picketing at construction sites. John Herling wrote, in 1966, that "never before—with the exception of the Eisenhower administration—has the White House staff been so alien, in knowledge and attitude, to organized labor," quoted in Goulden, *Meany,* 339.

75. Reuther Coll., box 324, ALHUA.

76. IUD executive board meeting minutes, December 15, 1966, 120, Reuther Coll., box 324, ALHUA.

77. Reuther letter to Meany, November 18, 1966; and Reuther Coll., box 40, ALHUA; Goulden, *Meany,* 349. The UAW had done work for the CIA, too. Meany said dissent was harmful to democracy, *NYT,* November 16, 1966. The AFL–CIO endorsed guns and butter, see Meany's New Year statement, *Washington Post,* January 1, 1967.

78. *UAW Administrative Letter* 18, no. 16, December 28, 1966 and *UAW Administrative Letter* 19, no. 1, February 8, 1967, ALHUA.

79. The IUD executive board voted 30 to 8 to support the UAW's call for a special convention, minutes, March 11, 1968, Reuther Coll., box 324, ALHUA.

80. Nelson Lichtenstein, "UAW Bargaining Strategy and Shop-Floor Conflict: 1946–1970," *Industrial Relations* (Fall 1985): 377; *Ford Facts,* April 18, 1964, IR; and Walter Heller to LBJ, May 21, 1964, Federal Records: CEA reel 2, LBJ.

81. Eli Chinoy, *Automobile Workers and the American Dream* (Boston: Beacon Press, 1955); and William Form, *Blue Collar Stratification: Autoworkers in Four Countries* (Princeton: Princeton University Press, 1976), 125.

82. UAW president's report, pt. 1, 10–11, ALHUA.

83. Cray, *Chrome Colossus,* 448f.

84. Kimbal Kehoe, "Strategy in a Labor Union: A Study of the UAW" (M.B.A. thesis, Harvard University, 1975), 88, 108; Babson, *Working Detroit* (New York: Adama Books, 1984), 183; Cray, *Chrome Colossus,* 461; Lichtenstein, "UAW Bargaining"; and "1967 Production Standards," Bannon Coll., box 26, ALHUA.

85. Nelson Lichtenstein, "Walter Reuther and the Rise of Labor-Liberalism," in *Labor Leaders in America,* ed. Melvyn Dubofsky and Warren Van Tine (Urbana: University of Illinois Press, 1987), 299.

86. *Wage Chronology: Ford Motor Company, June 1941–September 1973,* Bulletin 1787 (Washington, D.C.: U.S. Department of Labor BLS, 1973); "News From the UAW" (October 22, 1967), Bannon Coll., box 26, ALHUA; and *NYT,* October 25, 1967, p. 43 and November 28, 1967, p. 35.

87. Lyndon B. Johnson, *Vantage Point* (New York: Holt, Rinehart and Winston, 1971), 445; Block, *Origins of International Disorder,* 191; Economic Report of the President (1966), 165–168; Calleo, *Imperious Economy,* 52–53, 60; and Cochrane, "Johnson Administration," 215.

88. Johnson, *Vantage Point,* 451. From November 1966, when the decision was made to expand the money supply, until November 1968, the money supply increased from $169.2 billion to $193.6 billion. *Federal Reserve Bulletin* (July 1967, July 1968, November 1968, November 1969).

89. Reuther Coll., box 435, ALHUA.

90. Parmet, *Democrats,* 262, 283; Reuther Coll., box 472, ALHUA; Barefoot Sanders memo to the president, February 8, 1968, EX LA: Labor Management Relations, LBJ; and Johnson, *Vantage Point,* 456–459.

91. Reuther Coll., box 338, ALHUA.

92. Kevin Phillips, *The Emerging Republican Majority* (New York: Arlington House, 1969); and Everett Carl Ladd and Charles Hadley, *Transformations of the American Party System* (New York: Norton, 1975).

93. Herbert Stein, *Presidential Economics* (New York: Simon and Schuster, 1984), 145–158, 172–173.

94. IEB minutes, March 23, 1972, 13; Woodcock Coll., box 37, ALHUA; and Arnold Weber, *The Pay Board's Progress* (Washington, D.C.: The Brookings Institution, 1978).

95. Between 1970 and 1979 the proportion of union workers covered by COLA clauses increased from 25% to 60%. Richard Freeman and James Medoff, *What Do Unions Do?* (New York: Basic Books, 1984), 54.

96. UAW RD, Harry Chester papers, box 89; AFL–CIO, "A Program to Build America's Jobs and Trade in the Seventies," Woodcock testimony before the House Ways and Means Committee, May 15, 1972; and Pat Greathouse speech to the North American-Japan International Metalworkers' Federation, Tokyo, July 11, 1977, Bannon Coll., box 61, ALHUA. Woodcock became president of the UAW in spring 1970, after Reuther was killed in a plane crash. He had been an associate of Reuther since the late 1930s, was elected to the IEB in 1947, and was the director of the union's General Motors department in 1970.

97. Weir, *Politics and Jobs*, 119–121.

98. Katherine Van Wezel Stone, "The Post-War Paradigm in American Labor Law," *Yale Law Journal* 90, no. 7 (June 1981): 1509 at pp. 1541–1552; and James B. Atleson, *Values and Assumptions in American Labor Law* (Amherst: University of Massachusetts Press, 1983), 124–130, 160f.

99. General Motors Corp. v. NLRB, 191 NLRB 951-52 (1971), quoted in Atleson, *Values and Assumptions*, 130.

100. Bannon Coll., boxes 30, 63, ALHUA. The 1973 GM contract passed easily—workers were financially exhausted from striking in 1970; UAW RD.

101. Harry Katz, *Shifting Gears: Changing Labor Relations in the U.S. Automobile Industry* (Cambridge, Mass.: MIT Press, 1985), 43.

102. Cf. Thomas A. Kochan, Harry C. Katz, and Robert B. McKersie, *The Transformation of American Industrial Relations* (New York: Basic Books, 1986), 148–177.

103. Sar Levitan and Martha Cooper, *Business Lobbies: The Public Good and the Bottom Line* (Baltimore: Johns Hopkins University Press, 1984), 119–120; Paul Hartman and Walter Franke, "The Changing Bargaining Structure in Construction," *Industrial and Labor Relations Review* 33, no. 2 (January 1980); Irving Siegel and Edgar Weinberg, *Labor-Management Cooperation: The American Experience* (Kalamazoo, Mich.: The Upjohn Institute for Employment Research, 1982), 47–48; and cf. Thomas Byrne Edsall, *The New Politics of Inequality* (New York: Norton, 1984).

104. William J. Crotty, *Political Reform and the American Experiment* (New York: Thomas Y. Crowell, 1977), 238–245; and Denise L. Baer and David A. Bositis, *Elite Cadres and Party Coalitions* (Westport, Conn.: Greenwood Press, 1988). table 3.1.

105. Ibid., 65; Crotty, *Political Reform*, 248; and cf. Ben Wattenberg and Richard Scammon, *The Real Majority* (New York: Coward, McCann, 1972).

106. Crotty, *Political Reform*, 262; Christopher Lydon, "Divided Democrats Face Major Fight at Charter Convention in Kansas City," *NYT*, October 16, 1974, p. 31; and Baer and Bositis, *Elite Cadres*, 65–66.

107. Mildred Jeffrey to Leonard Woodcock, August 26, 1974, Woodcock Coll., box 197, ALHUA.

108. Ibid.; Austin Scott, "23 Black Democrats Protest Compromises in Party Reforms," *The Washington Post*, September 29, 1974; and Crotty, *Political Reform*, 250.

109. Lydon, "Divided Democrats."

110. Steve Schlossberg to Leonard Woodcock, October 22, 1974, Democratic Planning Group press release, October 1, 1974, and Robert Strauss to Leonard Woodcock, November 25, 1974, Woodcock Coll., box 197, ALHUA; Jules Witcover, "Democratic Reformers Pledge Fight Funds," The *Washington Post*, October 2, 1974); and R. W. Apple, "Democrats Draft a Charter for Party," *NYT*, December 6, 1974, p. 26.

111. Christopher Lydon, "Labor's Power Broker Frustrated by Democrats," *NYT*, December 6, 1974, p. 26.

112. Apple, "Democrats Draft Charters."

113. Crotty, *Political Reform*, 252.

114. Woodcock Coll., boxes 197, 243, ALHUA.

115. Woodcock Coll., box 243, ALHUA; and Initiative Committee for National Economic Planning, "For A National Economic Planning System," *Challenge* 18 (March–April 1975).

116. Woodcock Coll., box 219, ALHUA; Bannon Coll., box 61, ALHUA.

117. Weir, *Politics and Jobs*, 138; Samuel Huntington, "The United States," in *The Crisis of Democracy*, ed. Michel Crozier, Samuel Huntington and Joji Watanuki (New York: New York University Press, 1975), 59–118; and Thomas Ferguson and Joel Rogers, *Right Turn* (New York: Hill and Wang, 1986), chapter 1.

118. Weir, *Politics and Jobs*, 126, 147.

119. Douglas Fraser Coll., box 2, ALHUA. Fraser became president of the UAW after Woodcock retired in 1977 (and became representative and then ambassador to China). Fraser's home base was Chrysler. Levitan and Cooper, *Business Lobbies*, 122.

120. Fraser Coll., box 2, ALHUA; Levitan and Cooper, *Business Lobbies*, 122–135; and Edsall, *New Politics*, 125f.

121. Levitan and Cooper, *Business Lobbies*.

122. Fraser letter of resignation, July 19, 1978, Fraser Coll., box 2, ALHUA.

123. Siegel and Weinberg, *Labor-Management Cooperation*; and Ferguson and Rogers, *Right Turn*, 109–110.

124. Walter Dean Burnham, "The 1980 Earthquake: Realignment, Reaction or What?," in *The Hidden Election: Politics and Economics in the 1980 Presidential Election*, ed. Thomas Ferguson and Joel Rogers (New York: Pantheon, 1981), table 1 and appendix table A.

CHAPTER 8

1. Michael L. Dertouzos, Richard K. Lester, Robert M. Solow, and the MIT Commission on Industrial Productivity, *Made in America: Regaining the Productive Edge* (Cambridge, Mass.: MIT Press, 1989); and Jeffrey Allen Hunker, *Structural Change in the U.S. Automobile Industry* (Lexington: Lexington Books, 1983), 33–43.

2. Alain Lipietz, "An Alternative Design for the Twenty-First Century," in

Options in Economic Design, ed. S. G. Pendse (Westport, Conn.: Greenwood Press, 1987); James P. Womack, Daniel T. Jones, and Daniel Roos, *The Machine that Changed the World* (New York: Macmillan, 1990); Thomas Kochan, Harry Katz, and Robert McKersie, *The Transformation of American Industrial Relations* (New York: Basic Books, 1986); and Edward E. Lawler III, Gerald E. Ledford, Jr., and Susan Albers Mohrman, *Employee Involvement in America* (Houston: American Productivity and Quality Center, 1989).

3. Mike Parker and Jane Slaughter, *Choosing Sides* (Boston: South End Press, 1988); Knuth Dohse, Ulrich Jurgens, and Tomas Malsch, "From Fordism to Toyotism? The Social Organization of the Labor Process in the Japanese Automobile Industry," *Politics and Society* 14, no. 2: 115–146; and Ruth Milkman, *Japan's California Factories: Labor Relations and Economic Globalization* (Los Angeles: Institute of Industrial Relations, UCLA, 1991).

4. Sally Klingel and Ann Martin eds., *A Fighting Chance: New Strategies to Save Jobs and Reduce Costs* (Ithaca: ILR Press, 1988). One of the exceptions is GM's Saturn discussed below.

5. Kochan, Katz, and McKersie, *Transformation*; Mike Parker, *Inside the Circle* (Boston: South End Press, 1985); and Harley Shaiken, Stephen Herzenberg, and Sarah Kuhn, "The Work Process under More Flexible Production," *Industrial Relations* 23, no. 2 (1986).

6. Andy Banks and Jack Metzger, "Participating in Management: Union Organizing on a New Terrain," *Labor Research Review* 14 (Fall 1989): 1–55; AFL–CIO Committee on the Evolution of Work, *The Future of Work*, (August 1983) and *The Changing Situation of Workers and Their Unions*, (February 1985); cf. George Strauss, Daniel G. Gallagher, and Jack Fiorito, eds., *The State of the Unions* (Madison: Industrial Relations Research Association, 1991).

7. Michael Piore and Charles Sabel, *The Second Industrial Divide: The Possibilities of Prosperity* (New York: Basic Books, 1984). Michael Best, *The New Competition: Institutions of Industrial Restructuring* (Cambridge, Mass.: Harvard University Press, 1990); and cf. Paul Hirst and Jonathan Zeitlin eds., *Reversing Industrial Decline? Industrial Structure and Policy in Britain and Her Competitors* (Oxford, Eng.: Berg, 1989).

8. Barry Bluestone and Irving Bluestone, *Negotiating the Future: A Labor Perspective on American Business* (New York: Basic Books, 1992), 191–201.

9. Labor-Management Council, *Project Agenda* (Detroit: IPS Labor-Management Project, 1990); Michael Schippani, "Labor and Industrial Relations Strategies in the State of Michigan," in *Economic Restructuring and Emerging Patterns of Industrial Relations*, ed. Stephen R. Sleigh (Kalamazoo, Mich.: W. E. Upjohn Institute for Employment Research, 1993), 109–120; Joel Rogers, Wolfgang Streeck, and Eric Parker, "The Wisconsin Training Effort," in *Dollars and Sense: Policy Choices and the Wisconsin Budget*, vol. 2, ed. James Conant, Robert Haveman, and Jack Huddleston (Madison: Robert LaFollette Institute of Public Affairs, 1991); and Eric Parker, "Work Reorganization, Industrial Relations and Vocational Training: The Wisconsin Regional Training Partnership," (paper presented at the American Sociological Association meeting, August 1993).

10. Paul Weiler, *Governing the Workplace: The Future of Labor and Employment Law* (Cambridge, Mass.: Harvard University Press, 1990). Lawrence Mishel and Paula Voos, eds., *Unions and Economic Competitiveness* (Armonk, N.Y.: M.E. Sharpe, 1992); and Howard Wial, "The Emerging Organizational Structure of Unionism in Low-Wage Services," in *Rutgers Law Review*, 45 (Spring 1993): 671–738.

11. Cf. Alan Fox, *Beyond Contract* (London: Faber and Faber, 1974); and Karl Polanyi, *The Great Transformation* (New York: Farrar and Rinehart, 1944).

12. Charles Noble, *Liberalism at Work: The Rise and Fall of OSHA* (Philadelphia: Temple University Press, 1986).

13. Sar Levitan and Frank Gallo, *A Second Chance: Training for Jobs* (Kalamazoo, Mich.: The Upjohn Institute for Employment Research, 1988); Paul Osterman, *Employment Futures: Reorganization, Dislocation and Public Policy* (New York: Oxford University Press, 1988); and Richard Belous, *The Contingent Economy: The Growth of the Temporary, Part-Time and Subcontract Workforce* (Washington, D.C.: The National Planning Association, 1989).

Index

Abel, I. W., 246, 248, 253
Abernathy, William J., 298n.2, 312n.3, 319n.1
Ackley, Gardner, 200, 246, 254
Addes, George, 133, 148
Administered pricing, 98, 197, 235
Affirmative action, 201
AFL (American Federation of Labor): and apprenticeship, 70–71, 178; in Chicago, 54–55, 56, 57, 58–61; conflict with CIO, 95, 96, 117; in Detroit, 50–51, 52, 53, 87; and electoral politics, before the New Deal, 51, 53, 55, 56, 59, 60, 63, 70, 74; and electoral politics, in New Deal era, 102, 103, 154; favors unrestricted scope for collective bargaining, 124; and industrial unionism, 14, 52, 61, 63, 74, 84, 88, 89, 95; Korean War mobilization dispute, 185–186; in Milwaukee, 63–64; in modern society, 14; and NLRB, 96–97; opposition to national wage-price negotiations, 124; reconversion policy, 118–119, 120; republicanism, 40, 59, 71; and Roosevelt administration, 87–88, 96–97; southern organizing drive, 138, 145; and Taft-Hartley Act, 150–151; and trade agreements, 41; and vocational education, 50, 58–59, 70–71; and Wilson administration, 61, 74. *See also* AFL–CIO
AFL–CIO (American Federation of Labor–Congress of Industrial Organizations): AFL and CIO in, 230; COPE, 230, 266; coordination with Democrats, 233, 236, 238; Democratic party reform opposition, 266–268; electoral organizer for Democratic party, 230–231, 260, 268; and equal employment opportunity, 201, 254; failure to repeal right-to-work provision, 243; automation, 239–240; Industrial Union Department, 230, 249, 253, 255, 329n.79; labor law reform, 271; Labor Management Advisory Committee, 236; Labor-Management Committee, 264–265, 271; nonrepresentative Executive Council, 233, 250, 256; proposed merger of Commerce and Labor departments, 252; public sector, 231, 240; race and gender, 231, 242, 253–255, 267; reaction to incomes policy, 236, 238, 246, 247–248, 251, 272; sectionalism of, 231; shorter hours proposal, 197, 240; trade, 232, 262; UAW critical of, 256; union autonomy in, 233, 250; and Vietnam war, 256, 260; and War on Poverty, 243. *See also* AFL; CIO
Allis-Chalmers, 38, 69, 144, 149
Amalgamated Clothing Workers Union (ACW), 57, 75, 89, 270, 271
American Liberty League, 91
American Motors, 222, 225

Ford Motor Company (*cont.*)
achieved, 167; Sociology De-
partment, 53; speed-up, 101, 165;
Trade School, 52, 202–203;
unionization, 85, 95, 107,
309n.104. *See also* automobile
industry; UAW
Ford Trade School, 52, 202–203
Fordism, 26
Foremen, 145, 147, 169
Form, William, 329n.81
Foster, James, 302n.61, 308n.69
Fox, Alan, 292n.2, 333n.11
Fragnoli, Raymond R., 293n.8,
294nn.20, 27, 295nn.34, 38
Franke, Walter, 313n.13, 318n.92,
330n.103
Frankel, David M., 290n.17
Fraser, Douglas, 249, 271, 272
Fraser, Steven, 290n.11, 296n.49,
297n.82, 301n.51
Freeman, Richard, 330n.95
Friedlander, Peter, 290n.16

Gaer, Joseph, 302n.61
Galambos, Louis, 289n.8
Galbraith, John K., 141, 232, 260,
324n.5
Galenson, Walter, 299n.20
Gallagher, Daniel G., 332n.6
Gallo, Frank, 333n.13
General Motors Corporation: absenteeism in 1960s, 257; business
strategy, 82, 97–98, 176,
208–209; Cadillac, 49, 52; collective bargaining with UAW, 94,
126–129, 156–159, 167, 184, 187,
189, 198, 238, 258, 261, 264, 279,
281; grievance system, 135, 159,
257; internal opposition to COLA
and AIF, 309n.109; Labor-Management group, 271–272; opposes craft separatism, 196, 198;
pattern contract in 1950, 167;
performance in 1960s, 247;
postwar labor policy of, 114–115,
121; quality of work life program, 264; quits, 258; Saturn,

281; Sloanism, 82; southern
strategy, 264; training, 52, 185,
193, 199; unionization by UAW,
87, 88, 92, 94, 95–96, 309n.104;
wildcat strikes, 258. *See also* auto
industry; UAW
Georgakas, Dan, 318n.91, 328n.73
Geschwender, James, 328n.73
Gintis, Herbert, 26, 291n.32
Gitlin, Todd, 326n.32
Goldberg, Arthur, 236, 238, 239
Golden, Clinton, 99, 183, 301n.38,
306n.47, 308n.68, 309n.90
Goldfield, Michael, 291nn.23, 36
Goodwin, Craufurd, 304n.10,
305n.25, 309nn.93, 106,
310nn.119, 120
Gordon, David, 291n.32, 292n.4
Gould, William, 318nn.86, 91
Goulden, Joseph, 312n.146,
327nn.49, 59, 329nn.74, 77
Government structure, 27–28,
42–43
Green, Paul M., 295n.45
Greenstone, J. David, 289n.5,
324n.1, 326n.33
Griswold, Glenn, 320n.10
Gross, Bertram, 163, 269, 311n.132
Guaranteed annual wages, 100,
189

Hadley, Charles, 290n.18, 330n.92
Hall, Peter, 290n.13, 291n.34
Halpern, Martin, 300n.30, 305n.33,
306n.39
Hamby, Alonzo, 306nn.48, 51,
307n.60, 310n.126, 312n.150
Hansen, Alvin, 122, 142, 303n.2,
307n.55, 328n.62
Harbison, Frederick, 240, 289n.1,
302n.63, 303n.71, 309n.104,
310n.112, 311n.143, 319nn.4, 6, 7,
320nn.9, 10, 13, 17, 18, 321n.37
Harris, Howell John, 134, 295n.35,
296n.56, 303nn.69, 70, 304n.6,
305nn.18, 34, 307n.61, 308n.71
Harris, Seymour, 303n.2, 310n.122,
323n.72, 325n.10

Studebaker Corporation (*cont.*)
support for, 224–225; flexible
labor management, 210–211;
new managerialism, 214–216,
221; specialist product strategy,
209; teams, 210; inability to gain
new credit, 225; uaw attitude
toward company's problems,
216–217, 223. *See also* uaw Local 5
Sundquist, James, 306n.43, 317n.78,
324n.5
Supplier sector, 41, 204–205, 281
Surkin, Marvin, 318n.91, 328n.73
Sweeney, Vincent, 311n.139

Tabb, William, 291n.33
Taft, Philip, 314nn.39, 41
Taft-Hartley Act, 144–145, 147–148,
195
Taylor, George, 110, 119, 135, 168,
246, 302n.54, 304n.17
Taylor Society, 15
Taylorism, 26, 175, 204
Teamsters Union, 137, 147, 249,
260, 261
Thomas, R. J., 95, 119, 129, 133
Tomlins, Christopher L., 293n.10,
296n.56, 297n.82, 299nn.17, 18,
300n.34, 313n.18
Trade: 3–4, 17, 27; before the New
Deal, 34–35, 41, 47, 74; Burke-
Hartke bill, 262; and collective
bargaining, 262–263; impact on
the automobile industry in the
1980s, 274–275, 279; ITO treaty,
163; Kennedy Round, 259; in
1900, 41; problems of, 171, 203,
207, 224, 231–232, 240; trade
adjustment assistance, 240, 262;
Trade Expansion Act, 240.
Training: 171; Comprehensive
Employment and Training Act,
262; Fitzgerald Apprenticeship
Act, 177–178; Manpower Development and Training Act,
240–241; National Commission
on Technology, Automation and
Economic Progress, 245; Smith-

Hughes Act, 50. *See also* industrial relations
Tripartism, 108, 161
Truman, David, 290n.14
Truman administration: alienates
organized labor, 131–132; cold
war policy and labor, 153, 160;
coordination with cio's legislative agenda, 143, 162; fact finding boards, 126, 127, 166; Fair
Deal program, 163; implicit
Keynesianism, 121, 162, 164;
intervention in collective bargaining in 1946, 129, 131; Korean War mobilization and
organized labor, 185–186; calls
labor-management conference,
124; moves to establish New
Deal credentials, 143, 155, 162;
multiclass program, 164; military Keynesianism 164, opposes
Employment Act development,
164; price controls, 132; and
sectoral health and pension
plans, 131, 166; supports cio
purge, 312n.149; wage-price
policy, 125, 129–130, 160
Tyson, Laura, 290n.15

Uaw (United Auto Workers Union),
89–90; annual improvement
factor, 158; Catholics in, 107,
149, 308n.82; collective bargaining in 1945–1946, 125, 127–128;
in 1947, 146, 147–149; in 1948,
156–159; in 1950, 166–167; in
1955, 189, 192; in 1958, 197,
222–223; in the 1960s, 199,
257–258; in the 1970s, 264; in
the 1980s, 279, 281; Communists
in, 94, 95, 105, 134, 149, 154,
157, 182–183; contract ratification votes, 264; cost of living
allowance, 157, 158, 159, 258,
261; critical of liberal economic
policy, 122–123, 165, 238, 239,
243, 249, 251, 253; dispute with
AFL–CIO, 247, 249–250, 256, 260;